Margaret Atwood: Works and Impact

Margaret Atwood

Works and Impact

Edited by
Reingard M. Nischik

ANANSI

First published in hardcover in 2000 by Camden House

This edition published in 2002 by
House of Anansi Press Inc.
110 Spadina Ave., Suite 801
Toronto, ON, M5V 1K4
Tel. 416-363-4343
Fax 416-363-1017
www.anansi.ca

Distributed in Canada by
Publishers Group Canada
250A Carlton Street
Toronto, ON, M5A 2L1
Tel. 416-934-9900
Toll free order numbers:
Tel. 800-663-5714
Fax 800-565-3770

06 05 04 03 02   1 2 3 4 5

National Library of Canada Cataloguing in Publication Data

Margaret Atwood : works and impact / edited by Reingard M. Nischik.

Includes bibliographical references and index.
ISBN 0-88784-682-3

1. Atwood, Margaret, 1939– — Criticism and interpretation.
I. Nischik, Reingard M.

PS8501.T86Z762 2002   C813'.54   C2002-903858-8
PR9199.3.A8Z765 2002

 **Canada Council   Conseil des Arts
for the Arts   du Canada**

*We acknowledge for their financial support of our publishing program
the Canada Council for the Arts, the Ontario Arts Council, and the Government of Canada
through the Book Publishing Industry Development Program (BPIDP).*

November is the month of entrance,
month of descent.

— Margaret Atwood, "Doorway," from *Interlunar*

To be sixty years young is far more cheerful
than to be thirty years old.

— anonymous American author

A word after a word
after a word is power.

— Margaret Atwood,
"Spelling," from *True Stories*

Contents

Preface and Acknowledgments

WITH AN UNDERTAKING such as this one, the planning and preparation of which bridged two continents and two years, considerable acknowledgments are in order. First of all, I would like to thank the usually overworked contributors to this volume for meeting my rather stringent deadlines for handing in their articles, and for promptly dealing with queries and suggestions for change. I particularly want to thank the contributors to the "transmitters" section of this book (editors, publishers, translators, literary agents, and assistants) for eventually letting themselves be convinced to supplement their often non-public support work for Margaret Atwood with a short statement about it for this volume. Susanne Becker, Nathalie Cooke, Alice Palumbo, and Ellen Seligman supplied useful information in addition to their own contributions to this volume. Lothar Hönnighausen, after having written his article for this book, organized a fruitful Margaret Atwood Symposium at the University of Bonn in June 1999, at which some of us were given the opportunity to present our contributions to an interested audience before publication.[1]

Secondly, I want to thank my efficient "AmCanTeam" at the University of Constance, who proved their stamina when, due to the belatedness of some contributions for another volume, they were suddenly faced with the preparation and production of two (almost) camera-ready book manuscripts. Claudia Becker spent late hours at the computer keying in the corrections and producing the first clean versions. Lisa Roebuck, our Canadian student, took care of language and formal matters for most of the contributions before "Giving Birth" kept her from further contributing to the birth of this book. Stefan Ferguson reliably saw to language and computer problems, helped with the proofreading, produced the index. Mirjam Berle and Lesley Adams

---

[1] Sadly, Walter Pache's article, written at the beginning of 1999, was one of the last by this great scholar before his unexpected death from heart failure in January 2000 at the age of 59. Three weeks later, an academic ceremony in his honor was to have been held in Augsburg on the occasion of his sixtieth birthday. Professor Walter Pache contributed a tremendous amount to the development of Canadian Literature Studies in Germany, and was a staunch Atwood supporter from the 1970s onwards. He will be sorely missed.

grappled with the *Chicago Manual of Style* and the Works Cited lists. Mirjam Berle also helped with the proofreading, and, together with Stefan Ferguson, acted as troubleshooter. Annette Zerpner spent hours in the library checking quotations. Caroline Rosenthal not only handled and elaborated upon masses of information to produce a fine article for this volume; she also, while staying in Toronto in the summer of 1999, solved some final bibliographical riddles and selected on the spot the Atwood cartoons reprinted here. Margret Jäger-Junge, after having produced one camera-ready book manuscript on the computer, conscientiously surfaced to add the finishing touches to the manuscript for the present volume.

Thirdly, I am grateful to Professor James Hardin, my general editor at Camden House, and to Jim Walker of Camden House's Rochester, New York office for promptly responding to any queries which cropped up during the preparation of this book; to Shelly Rafferty Withers for her careful reading of the final print-out; to Edna Hajnal in Toronto for her helpfulness and advice in guiding us through the Thomas Fisher Rare Book Library; to Charles Altman and Isaac Bickerstaff for permission to reproduce the images of Atwood; to the Association for Canadian Studies in German-speaking Countries and the Canadian Government for a grant towards the printing costs; and to the *Zeitschrift für Kanada-Studien* for permission to reprint a shortened version of an interview with Margaret Atwood first published in the *ZKS*.

Fourthly, I am grateful to Margaret Atwood's fellow writers who spontaneously put pen to paper when I asked them what Margaret Atwood means to them.

Last but not least, I thank Margaret Atwood (and her assistant Sarah Cooper) for filling in gaps, for providing private photographs, and for permission to reproduce some of Atwood's hilarious cartoons in this volume.

This book deals with Atwood's works published up to May 2000. *The Blind Assassin*, her latest novel, is included in the bibliography at the end of the book, but, since it will not be published until autumn 2000, is outside the range of the articles contained in this study.

R.N.

Constance, Germany

May 2000

"Flagpoles and Entrance Doors": Introduction

Reingard M. Nischik (University of Constance)

THIS VOLUME WAS prepared for the occasion of Margaret Atwood's sixtieth birthday in November 1999. With Atwood at the height of her creative powers, its first aim is to take stock of the full breadth of her works and international impact. Secondly, the book has been conceived to serve as a wide-ranging introduction to the writer and her works. Last but not least, it should be seen as a tribute to a writer who, for more than thirty years now, has enthralled a steadily growing international audience with her remarkable creative wizardry and productivity.

A writer of fiction and poetry, as well as literary and cultural criticism, Margaret Atwood is one of the most fascinating, versatile, and prolific authors of our time, a superb writer in every genre she has chosen to tackle. Her extraordinary intellectual and imaginative powers and gift of language, the uncanny topicality of her themes, her never-failing humor, as well as her exceptional talent for combining intellectually challenging writing with a high readability, have made her a favorite with readers, critics, and scholars alike. A spokeswoman for human rights — of which her acute awareness of gender differences forms an integral part — a Canadian nationalist, a brilliant observer of contemporary Western culture who in her works questions conventional modes of perception and evaluation, Atwood is one of the most important literary chroniclers of our time.

Not surprisingly, in the year the author turns sixty, the Atwood industry is booming. Since publication of *The Handmaid's Tale*, her books, translated into some thirty languages, have become international bestsellers. In a work published in 1997 by two Canadian historians, Rawlinson's and Granatstein's *The Canadian 100: The 100 Most Influential Canadians of the Twentieth Century*, Margaret Atwood is ranked in fifth place, a gratifyingly high position for someone who is neither a politician nor an industrial magnate, but a writer by profession. She ranks above Pierre Elliott Trudeau or René Lévesque, and is well ahead of the next writer on the list, Robertson Davies. Although the authors

of *The Canadian 100* are as aware as everyone else of the problems involved in such a variegated ranking, their high placing of Margaret Atwood certainly seems convincing:

> Atwood has been *the* public voice of Canadian letters for the past
> quarter century. No living, critically acclaimed woman author [and I
> would add: male author, RN] can claim such consistent attention.
> Few Canadians have had such impact. (32)[1]

There is a flourishing "Margaret Atwood Society," an Allied Organization of the MLA, which publishes the biannual *Newsletter of the Margaret Atwood Society* and has established the Atwood-Discussion-List,
an Internet bulletin board. 1998 saw the publication of *two* biographical books on Margaret Atwood, one by Nathalie Cooke and one by
Rosemary Sullivan, which attracted a surprising amount of general and
critical attention (cf. Cooke). In academic quarters, Atwood is the most
frequently studied Canadian writer at the university level (cf. Rosenthal). The production of critical studies of Atwood's works — mono-
graphs and essay collections on her writing — has increased steadily in
recent years (cf. "Bibliography: Books on Margaret Atwood"), demonstrating the high status Atwood has attained in the world of literary
studies.

By 1999, the year Margaret Atwood turned sixty, it seemed time to
take stock. This volume, then, sets out to provide a survey of Atwood's
achievements thus far and to assess her national and international impact. The following fifteen articles were written specifically for this
book by international contributors from Germany, Canada, the USA,
Britain, and France. The articles try to present as wide-ranging a treatment of their respective topics as is possible within the confines of some
fifteen pages each. The contributions also pay attention, where appropriate, to the developments concerning their topic over the years. In
accordance with the title of this volume and our intention to study the
writer, her works, and their reception, the book is divided into four
main sections: "Life and Status," "Works," "Approaches," and "Creativity — Transmission — Reception." A concluding two-part bibliography lists Atwood's book publications according to genre and critical
studies of Atwood in book form published so far.[2]

---

[1] For a similar survey, cf. the beginning of the Rosenthal article in the present
volume. In the following, references to names in brackets without further
qualifications refer to the respective articles in this volume.

[2] A lot of the important research on Atwood, of course, is documented in
critical articles; for this, check the *MLA Bibliography* and, even more compre-

In the first section, Nathalie Cooke, Susanne Becker, and Caroline Rosenthal deal with the — as these articles demonstrate — tricky question of Margaret Atwood's life and status, corroborating Atwood's own, penetratingly simple formulation in *Cat's Eye*, "There is never only one, of anyone." In the opening article, Nathalie Cooke, author of the acclaimed *Margaret Atwood: A Biography* (1998), cunningly starts off her biographical treatment of Atwood by noting various kinds of biographical approaches to Canada's literary superstar. Resorting to feline imagery (there's an Atwood scholar for you!), she bases her study on the images of the "stuffed cat," "lion," "tiger," and "pussycat," each of which has a particular bearing on important aspects of Atwood's life, status, and personality. At first, Cooke supports a reconstruction of Atwood's identity along the lines of the "tiger" *and* "pussycat" models, but finally opts for the more dynamic biographical metaphor implied in a portrait of Atwood painted by her friend, Toronto artist Charlie Pachter. It is entitled "It Was Fascination I Know" and evokes "the endless possibility of transformation."

Susanne Becker, who has worked for German TV since her student days, devoted parts of her Ph.D. thesis to Atwood, and has interviewed her on several occasions. Appropriately, she writes about Atwood, the media star. Becker, while documenting Atwood's extraordinary talent for public appearances (and anyone who has seen Atwood perform will agree), traces in her article the productive tension between the opportunities and the costs of Atwood's celebrity, between her using the media and being used. This tension has proved fruitful for Atwood's writing, in which she approaches the subject from the wider perspective of her preoccupation with the formation, representation, and reconstruction of identity (see also Müller, Hill Rigney, Irvine). Becker demonstrates how Atwood puts her experience with the printed and electronic media to good use, referring in particular to *Lady Oracle*, *Cat's Eye*, and *Alias Grace*.

Caroline Rosenthal rounds off the explicit treatment of Atwood's status in the first section by addressing the question of "Canonizing Atwood: Her Impact on Teaching in the US, Canada, and Europe." After presenting the telling results of her international survey, which further substantiate Atwood's exceptional standing, Rosenthal focuses on "academic imperialism" in the United States, which seeks to appropriate Atwood as an international American author, while neglecting her Canadian identity. At the same time, Rosenthal demonstrates that

---

hensive, the yearly "Current Atwood Checklist" in the *Newsletter of the Margaret Atwood Society*.

Atwood has nowhere been more controversial than in her own country (cf. Canadian Brian Fawcett's term, "Atwood bashing"). This North American discrepancy in her survey results leads Rosenthal to comment on fundamental differences in American and Canadian culture, with Canada, ironically, ritualizing the deflation of national icons (as Atwood puts it: "Americans worship success; Canadians find it in slightly bad taste," in Atwood 1982, 372). An author who, at the beginning of her writing career, set out as a critic in *Survival: A Thematic Guide to Canadian Literature* (1972) to conceptualize a Canadian literature, is now, some thirty years later, a canonized writer herself and, whether praised or challenged, has become "a mark for new departures."

The first and second sections of this book are linked by photographs of Margaret Atwood. These photographs offer glimpses of Atwood's development from a budding writer (cf. Cooke's biography) to a celebrity: Atwood at age thirteen at Niagara Falls, Ontario (i.e. the Canadian side, yet proving that she has always encompassed the US!); Atwood as family woman, private life being publicized (cf. Becker); Atwood accompanied by other prominent Canadians, from Leonard Cohen to Michael Ondaatje; Atwood in her frequent role as a sought-out interviewee, here in the backyard of her house in Toronto; Atwood dressed up flashily (see the Atwood/Metzler interview) as "covergirl" (Becker) of *Saturday Night* to draw attention to their first printing of the wonderful Atwood short story "Death by Landscape"; and, last but not least, Atwood (before, during, after) reading from her works — at an annual Canadian Studies conference in Europe (Grainau, Germany), or at an annual Writers' Festival in Canada (Eden Mills, near Guelph, Canada, in September 1998).

The second section of the book, "Works," features survey articles on Atwood's writing in the most important genres she has excelled in (cf. "Bibliography: Margaret Atwood's Book Publications"): her novels, her short fiction (and prose poetry), her poetry, and her literary and cultural criticism. These articles, by Alice Palumbo, Charlotte Sturgess, Lothar Hönnighausen, and Walter Pache, deal with all of Atwood's books in these genres published up to 1999. The articles on Atwood's creative writing convey her remarkable thematic and formal variety and discuss the developments in her fiction and poetry. Yet they also demonstrate how these works, spanning almost four decades (1961–1999), share interconnected concerns and techniques, so that a distinct Atwoodian voice is discernible in every genre. In these contributions, as also in those of the next section, "Approaches," Atwood's thematic preoccupations and some of her literary techniques emerge: her nationalistic focus on Canada and her insistence on Canadian cultural autonomy in relation to Canada's overpowering southern neighbor; her interest in power structures, gender difference, and gender politics; human rights questions; the formation, reconstruction, and representation of identity; problems of individual subjectivity; her probing of the dimension of time, the relevance of the past, and the functions of memory; her often playful subversion of clichés, conventions, and any fixed categories; her rewriting/revision of received stories such as fairy tales and her revisionist mythmaking; her intertextuality, generic pluralism and hybridity; the multiplicity of perspectives in her works; the constructionist problems of writing and the crucial function of language; and, last but not least, Atwood's stylistic precision and elegance, her flexible diction, her deadpan irony, unfailing humor, and deflationary wit.

Walter Pache, rounding off the "Works" section with a rare article on Atwood's literary criticism, describes Atwood as "an academic, a *poeta doctus*, if ever there was one" (cf. also her many honorary degrees). Atwood, known for the unconventional generic plurality of her fiction and poetry, successfully creates a concept of criticism as a creative art, while pointing out that "a writer has to write something before a critic can criticize it" (*Second Words*, 11). Pache deals with Atwood's three books of criticism, *Survival*, *Second Words*, and *Strange Things: The Malevolent North in Canadian Literature*. He sees Atwood as a critic who is playfully at odds with "the obscure ritualized games" professional critics play with each other "instead of applying themselves to the more practical task of elucidating textual and cultural difficulties for the benefit of the public." As Atwood practices it, literary criticism is a "practical, text-centered, and value-oriented craft," helping readers enter into the text through their own imagination.

The third section of the book, "Approaches," is by definition incomplete; with a writer of Atwood's breadth and stature, this subject would require a book of its own. We had to make do without separate articles on such important topics as Margaret Atwood's linguistic and narrative style (see Grace and Weir 1983, Nischik 1991, Staels 1995), Atwood and multiculturalism, Atwood and historiography (see Kuester 1992), and without a summary article on critical/theoretical approaches to Atwood (see McCombs 1988, 1–21; Mycak 1996, 9–29) — reconciling ourselves to necessities with the consolation that these aspects are touched upon in the present articles.

Coral Ann Howells's splendid article on generic hybridity in Margaret Atwood's novels, which opens the "Approaches" section, is a case in point. Howells deals with one of Atwood's hallmarks, her "continuous experimentation across genre boundaries, and the political and ideological significance of such revisions." In her treatment of *The Hand-maid's Tale*, *Cat's Eye*, *The Robber Bride*, and *Alias Grace*, Howells demonstrates Atwood's expressive, "slightly postmodern" (Atwood) re-creation of genres such as the dystopia, the fictional autobiography, the kunstlerroman, the Gothic romance, and the historical novel. Along the way, this article — by one of the most distinguished Atwood schol-ars — deals with issues such as the specific role of historiography in At-wood's writing, the self-consciously postmodern aesthetic inherent in her duplicitous narrators and narrative constructions, and her chal-lenging engagement with questions of femininity, identity, and gender.

The latter issues are taken up in Barbara Hill Rigney's article on At-wood's "Narrative Games and Gender Politics," which, after surveying the construction of female characters in Atwood's novels, sets out to tackle this problem: "How, then, given such negative portrayals of women, can we construct a feminist ethic for Atwood, how infer a woman-centered poetic?" Hill Rigney shows how complex Atwood's dealings in gender politics are, how she takes her characters as well as her readers "above and beyond the gendered stereotypes," and how gender structures are dependent on language and the construction of stories. While Atwood makes us acutely aware of gender issues, "she refuses to be canonized in any area but the literary."

Paul Goetsch's article puts Margaret Atwood's nationalism into the context of Canadian nationalism since the 1950s. Goetsch refers to early influences on her thinking and to the virulent ideas of Canadian nationalism of the 1960s and 1970s (next to Atwood, W. L. Morton, George Grant, Dennis Lee, Northrop Frye). Goetsch, who published his Ph.D. thesis on Hugh MacLennan in 1961, compares Atwood's nationalism to that of MacLennan, the leading literary nationalist of the 1950s and early 1960s in Canada. Goetsch describes both writers as "typical representatives of the postcolonial drive to project an autono-mous national identity by constructing a coherent culture or litera-ture." One of their differences lies in "their identification of the imperial center," with Atwood having been in the vanguard of Cana-dian anti-Americanism of the 1960s and 1970s. Goetsch then concen-trates on the impact of *Survival* (cf. also Pache's assessment of this key work on Canadian literature and culture), and on the development of Atwood's nationalism "from a sense of crisis to a feeling of self-confidence."

Ronald B. Hatch also begins his article, "Margaret Atwood, the Land, and Ecology," with a reference to *Survival*, specifically to At-wood's thesis that "Canadians are survivalists in the midst of a vast, un-knowable land." Hatch offers a close reading of relevant poems, novels, and short stories by Atwood, assessing the significance of the land, nature, and ecology in her writing, as well as her frequent environmental activities. The environment in general — be it the land- or urbanscape — plays a crucial role in the texts of a writer who once called her writing "autogeographical rather than autobiographical," and who, before choosing her base in Toronto, had spent long periods of her life in the country and, indeed, the wilderness (see Cooke). Hatch shows how Atwood uses the land in her writing, especially in her poetry, less in a referential than in a metaphorical mode, or as a medium for dealing with problems of representation in general. He points, for instance, to the plight of the modern individual who, when confronted with the land, distances himself/herself from it, rather than becoming part of it.

Lorna Irvine's article analyzes the ingenious ways in which Atwood deals with contemporary popular cultural trends, evaluating the workings of "kitsch," "camp," and "trash" in her fiction. Irvine describes Atwood as a "theoretician of culture," investigating and finally dismissing the traditional distinction between elite and popular culture. Atwood's interest in collective and individual identity, the significance of the past for the present, and the dynamics of memory and forgetting, finds a correlative in kitsch, which has been described by Susan Stewart as "souvenirs of an era and not of a self." While kitsch has historical, exotic, and melancholic connotations, "camp" refers to recycled culture which stresses "an imaginative, excessive, and witty playfulness." Irvine sees the Royal Porcupine of *Lady Oracle* and his grotesque parodies of contemporary cultural excesses as the perfect example of "camp." "Trash" in Atwood's writing pinpoints "the dissociation between popular objects of consumption and their consumers," as well as the class issues involved in the conventional hierarchical view of "high" and "popular" culture. Irvine concludes that Atwood, in her use of elements of popular culture, is "persistently searching for ways to reinvest the past with meaning and the present with desire."

Sharon R. Wilson deals with a more time-honored kind of "cultural recycling," a specific aspect of the pronounced intertextuality of Atwood's writing: the mythic intertexts in her works. Once again, Atwood's erudition (see Pache), and her concern for linking past and present, become apparent in the way she bases contemporary themes on ancient myths and the rewriting of them. Wilson presents an impressive array of mythic intertexts for Atwood's works of visual art (see the illustrations and cover designs for many of her books), poetry, and fiction, and states that "Atwood's treatment of particular myths and myth types remains fairly consistent from early to recent texts." Wilson comments on the mythological substructures at work in *The Robber Bride* and *Alias Grace*, and distinguishes five vital functions of the mythic intertexts in Atwood's writing. These intertexts "highlight national, political, postcolonial, and gender themes," and, in revising patriarchal myths, create a "feminist mythology, but it is always one as unafraid to laugh at itself as at literary tradition, institutions, history, and patriarchy."

Rounding off the "Approaches" section, Klaus Peter Müller's article probes the implications of a constructionist approach to Atwood's work, taking a new look at a number of aspects treated in other articles (by Cooke, Howells, Hill Rigney, Hatch, Wilson), but also including sections on language and postcolonialism. Constructionism, which is practiced both in the humanities and the sciences, "underlines the importance of the human mind for any understanding of reality, and claims that reality is not only obviously there, but is also constructed by human beings, who give value and meaning to it." This approach indeed penetrates to the core of Atwood's thematic preoccupations and methodology: her probing of the destabilized relation between fact and fiction, her fascination with dual and multiple perspectives, variable identities, and "true lies," with "the inherent ambiguity of the nature of truth" (Hill Rigney). Commenting on a wide range of Atwood texts, from some of her interview statements to her poetry and fiction, and inviting interesting comparisons with the other contributions just mentioned, Müller demonstrates how in Atwood's writing "reality is not the truth, but a construct people believe in." This also implies a strong emphasis in her work on the responsibility of human beings for their natural, social, and personal environments. Müller explains how her texts, a far cry from the arbitrariness of radical postmodernism, seek to ensure "that the seeing becomes authentic" (Atwood).

The final section, "Creativity — Transmission — Reception," presents a variety of perspectives on Atwood's creativity in contributions by a scholar, by Atwood herself (in an interview), by some of the most important transmitters of her work, and by some fellow writers. By featuring some palpable manifestations of her reception — cartoons, books — this final section also harks back to the beginning of the book ("Life and Status").

Helmut Reichenbächer opens this group of contributions with a link to the preceding "Approaches" section. He employs the methodology of genetic criticism, an approach which aims to analyze the different versions of a literary text which precede the finally fixed published version. Profiting from some of the "286 boxes or 44.5 meters of material" of Atwood manuscripts in the Thomas Fisher Rare Book Library at the University of Toronto, Reichenbächer investigates "that sequence of events which comprise the arduous process of literary creation." For his analysis of "the physical evidence of the imaginative processes," he chooses Atwood's first published novel, *The Edible Woman*, which was composed in five distinct documented stages. Reichenbächer's systematic, step-by-step analysis of Atwood's revisions reveals how she empowers the reader by gradually eliminating explanatory passages from the text. Thus, even in her first published novel, through the continuous reshaping of the text, we see Atwood striving towards a text format which she brought to perfection in her later works.

In the interview with Margaret Atwood by Gabriele Metzler, the only reprinted text in this volume, we get to know not only Atwood's own views on creativity, but also why she is one of the most frequently interviewed contemporary writers. The interview text is based on a quickly improvised, tape-recorded interview which took place in circumstances not usually considered conducive to creative thinking: a very busy dining room at eight-thirty in the morning, with people interfering and a recalcitrant, distracting tape-recorder. In spite of this, Atwood performed with the ease in the face of "the media" (cf. Becker) which has contributed to her reputation: acutely to the point, though always "looking at the other side of [the] dailiness" (Alice Munro) of the writer's profession, wittily, didactically in the best sense of the term, and, indeed, creatively transgressing borders.

The next group of texts includes rare statements written specially for this occasion by some of Atwood's publishers, editors, translators, literary agents, and assistants. These comments by some of the most important long-term mediators and transmitters of Atwood's work allow us to catch some glimpses of the publishing process through the eyes of people who have worked largely behind the scenes. Along the way, we are given further peeks into this astonishing writer's working methods.

In the section "Cartoons by and on Margaret Atwood" the four cartoons by Atwood, selected out of a total of about a dozen originals by Atwood, show the author's involvement with comparative North American culture (see the "Kanadian Kultchur Komix" series published in the 1970s under the pseudonym Bart Gerrard) and with the status of the artist in yet another creative medium. These are clever, funny, ironic, provocative comments by a multi-talented observer and critic of contemporary North American culture.

Looking at these cartoons, especially "Portrait of the Artist as a Young Cipher," and at the most recent photos of Atwood as internationally acclaimed writer and major cultural force in Canada, a few recollections and personal words may be in order. Let us just briefly remember the state of Canadian literature in the formative period of Atwood's development into a professional writer, the late fifties and early sixties, when Atwood was around twenty. As she herself states with hindsight: "In 1961, five novels by English-speaking Canadian novelists were published in Canada. There were approximately three literary magazines. You were doing well if you sold 200 copies of a book of poetry, a thousand of a novel. Many novelists had been one-book writers" (in Stanzel/Zacharasiewicz, 137). Atwood had completed the manuscript of her first novel, *The Edible Woman*, in 1965, but she did not get it published before 1969. It was only with her winning the important Governor General's Award for Poetry in 1966 for her second poetry collection, *The Circle Game*, that she became a powerful voice in what we can call the "Canadian Renaissance" of the late sixties and seventies. Atwood in this period of Canadian nationalism and anti-Americanism promoted Canadian literature and culture with the many talents at her disposal: predominantly through her creative writing, but also through her formative work for the Canadian Writers' Union and the League of Canadian Poets, by her promotion of Canadian publishing houses specializing in Canadian culture, such as the House of Anansi Press, by her much requested public appearances (readings, speeches, lectures, interviews), and last but not least by the publication of *Survival*, the debatable yet highly influential *Thematic Guide to Canadian Literature*, which put Canadian literature on the map for the public and significantly contributed to a decade of thematic, self-centered criticism of Canadian literature in the Canadian academic world.[3] In an acceptance speech in New York in 1997 (reprinted in *The New York Times Book Review*) on the occasion of her being awarded another American literary prize, Atwood retrospectively pointed out:

> There was a great advantage to being a Canadian back in 1956, the year I started writing in a manner I then considered serious; there was no heritage of intimidating geniuses looming above you as you wrote. There were a few Canadian writers then, but with their usual modesty the Canadians hid them from view, and you had to dig for them at the very back of bookstores, among the maple syrup cookbooks and the autumn scenery. All that has now changed.

---

[3] *Gaining Ground: European Critics on Canadian Literature* (ed. Robert Kroetsch and Reingard M. Nischik, Edmonton 1985), which focused on the craft rather than the themes of CanLit writing, was just one attempt to redress the balance. An influential article was Frank Davey's "Surviving the Paraphrase" (1976).

What Atwood does not mention is the extent to which she herself has been instrumental in bringing this change about through her own remarkable contribution to Canadian culture and to world literature.

I would like to conclude on a personal note. This book only saw the light of day because in late 1997 I was asked to write the article on Atwood for a lexicon of established female writers around the world. When I started to write that article in 1998, I stumbled across the year of Atwood's birth — 1939 . . . does that not mean ...? I counted and recounted and could not believe that Atwood would turn sixty in 1999! After disposing of all further doubts (i.e. after more recountings), I spread the message to colleagues around the world, and the response was always similar. Here is the first sentence of Linda Hutcheon's response to me of 26 May 1998: "I cannot believe Atwood will be 60!" Or note Atwood editor Liz Calder's expression: "She's such a spring chicken!" Although I realized at the time that we would not be able to bring out such a book in time for her sixtieth birthday, I decided that this momentous date nevertheless called for some special endeavors, and the contributors thought so, too.

I was also reminded of a lunch with Margaret Atwood a few years ago when, without having reserved a table, we entered a scenic restaurant. There were all sorts of international flagpoles adorning the entrance door, but, alas, there was no Canadian flag. "They have forgotten the Canadian flag," I said, and Atwood responded, "No, they have not forgotten it, it just fell off" (and, indeed, there was one unoccupied flagpole). We caught the last unoccupied table (call that luck) and later got talking about the Nobel Prize. After some remark of mine, Atwood immediately responded, "No. One: I belong to the wrong country. Two: I belong to the wrong sex." "Three," I added, "you are too young." In the meantime, I have checked. Of all the winners of the Nobel Prize for Literature since 1901, 92 % were male, "the other North American Literature" (Pache) has never been represented, and the four female writers who were awarded this prize since the Second World War were all over sixty. So there you are. Perhaps one day we will see that missing flag in the row of flagpoles, after all? Whether or not it would concern Canada's foremost writer, we look forward to seeing how Margaret Atwood will surprise us yet again.

Works Cited

Atwood, Margaret. "After *Survival* . . . Excerpts from a Speech Delivered at Princeton University, April 29, 1985." In Franz K. Stanzel and Waldemar Zacharasiewicz, ed. *Encounters and Explorations: Canadian Writers and European Critics.* Würzburg: Königshausen & Neumann, 1986: 132–38.

———. *Second Words: Selected Critical Prose.* Toronto: Anansi, 1982.

———. *Survival: A Thematic Guide to Canadian Literature.* Toronto: Anansi, 1972.

———. "The Writer: A New Canadian Life-Form." *New York Times Book Review*, 18 May 1997, 39.

Cooke, Nathalie. *Margaret Atwood: A Biography.* Toronto: ECW Press, 1998.

Davey, Frank. "Surviving the Paraphrase: Thematic Criticism and its Alternatives." *Canadian Literature* 70 (Autumn 1976): 5–13.

Grace, Sherrill E. and Lorraine Weir, ed. *Margaret Atwood: Language, Text, and System.* Vancouver: University of British Columbia Press, 1983.

Kroetsch, Robert and Reingard M. Nischik, ed. *Gaining Ground: European Critics on Canadian Literature.* Edmonton, Alberta: NeWest, 1985.

Kuester, Martin. *Framing Truths: Parodic Structures in Contemporary English-Canadian Historical Novels.* Toronto: University of Toronto Press, 1992.

McCombs, Judith, ed. *Critical Essays on Margaret Atwood.* Boston: Hall, 1988.

Mycak, Sonia. *In Search of the Split Subject: Psychoanalysis, Phenomenology, and the Novels of Margaret Atwood.* Toronto: ECW Press, 1996.

Newsletter of the Margaret Atwood Society.

Nischik, Reingard M. *Mentalstilistik: Ein Beitrag zu Stiltheorie und Narrativik. Dargestellt am Erzählwerk Margaret Atwoods.* Tübingen: Narr, 1991.

Rawlinson, H. Graham and J. L. Granatstein. *The Canadian 100: The 100 Most Influential Canadians of the 20th Century.* Toronto: McArthur & Company, 1997.

Staels, Hilde. *Margaret Atwood's Novels: A Study of Narrative Discourse.* Tübingen/Basel: Francke, 1995.

Sullivan, Rosemary. *The Red Shoes: Margaret Atwood Starting Out.* Toronto: Harper Flamingo, 1998.

I. Life and Status

Lions, Tigers, and Pussycats:
Margaret Atwood (Auto-) Biographically

Nathalie Cooke (McGill University, Montreal)

THERE ARE FOUR kinds of biographies: ones that describe ordinary people as just that, ones that claim extraordinary people are truly extraordinary, ones that make ordinary people seem extraordinary, and ones that cut extraordinary people down to ordinary size.[1] In Atwood's case, the sheer volume of critical attention (prompting collections such as the present one) suggests that the first category — double ordinary — does not apply. Oddly enough, however, it was the first and is the most persistent response to Atwood and her work. It is the one that reads the ordinary and credible circumstances in Atwood's fiction and poetry as directly related to the circumstances of Atwood's own life. It is the one that reads Atwood's protagonists as Atwood herself. It is implicit in the personal questions Atwood gets after her readings. Were you overweight as a child (like Joan Foster of *Lady Oracle*)? Did you live near a ravine (like Elaine of *Cat's Eye*)? It is also implicit in the unspoken questions and furtive glances: "Uh . . . that uncomfortable young woman in *Surfacing* — the one who never tells her name — were you, you know, a bit like her? As . . . hmmm . . . bad as that awful Zenia?" (For the sake of biographical accuracy: No to the overweight question. Yes to the ravines — everyone who grows up in Toronto lives near one. No. And No.) It's the kind of biographical approach Atwood hates, by the way, one she vehemently denies by saying that she does not (with a marked emphasis on the "not") write true confessions. "I believe in artistry," she explains. She believes that "there's a difference between true confessions and writing a novel" (Peri, 31).

In terms of my title's feline theme, this would be a *stuffed cat* approach to biography (since the biographical fallacy allows no room for creative inspiration on the part of the artist, and levels of irony in the work itself; no room for craft and craftiness). This biography is a quick patched-together ragtag kind of affair; a collage, with individual char-

[1] This list is loosely derived from a statement in Alain de Botton's wonderful send-up of biographical convention in *Kiss and Tell*.

acteristics of the various protagonists in Atwood's fiction pinned on the figure of Atwood herself. Rather like paper clothes on a paper doll, the shape of the person emerges from behind the paper and becomes no more than a two-dimensional paper construct herself. In Atwood's case, this involves lots of talk about dark ravines and deep holes, social discomfort in childhood and awkward communication in early romantic relationships. It fails precisely because it is unable to account for one of the greatest strengths of Atwood the person, and the most engaging aspect of her writing: endless transformation.

Atwood as Literary Lion

Strangely, the other popular biographical approach lies at the opposite extreme to the stuffed cat one, and takes the biographical subject out of the ordinary domestic sphere and places her in the great mythic and wild beyond, as *literary lion*. Lionized both within Canada and abroad, Margaret Atwood is one of the most prolific, best-enjoyed and respected writers of our age, perceived to be extraordinary. She is author of over 35 books translated into more than 30 languages; recipient of more than ten honorary degrees, most recently a Doctorate of Letters from Oxford University in England (1998); twice winner of Canada's Governor General's Award; Companion of the Order of Canada (1982); recipient of such honors as the *Los Angeles Times* Fiction Award (1986), Government of France's Chevalier dans l'ordre des Arts et des Lettres (1994), twice Regional Winner of the Commonwealth Literary Prize (1987, 1994), and recipient of the *Sunday Times* Award for Literary Excellence (1994) and National Arts Club Award (New York, 1997). Atwood's name, her face, is known the world over.

The *lion* biography goes something like this: Born the second child of well-educated middle-class parents, Atwood quickly learned to keep pace with her clever older brother, Harold (today a star in his own field, neurophysiology). Spending her early summers in the bush as a result of her father's work as an entomologist, and benefiting from the close companionship of her mother (herself a very interesting independent thinker), Atwood gained an intellectual and practical resourcefulness that would serve her in later years. One other gift from her close-knit extended family (most of whom were in the Maritimes) was a healthy sense of humor, perhaps the source of the engaging wit of her writing, and certainly the source of her sanity during the hectic years of a demanding writer's schedule. Atwood completed her undergraduate degree in English at the University of Toronto (where she met Canadian poet Jay Macpherson and the well-respected critic

Northrop Frye) in 1961 and went on to graduate work at Harvard (under Professor Jerome Buckley). In 1966, she won the Governor General's Award for her second book of poetry, and her literary star has continued to rise. (This could be followed by a long annotated list of publications and awards, and a quote from her literary agent, Phoebe Larmore, who tells us that representing Atwood is like representing a "dynasty" of writers, that Atwood is "larger than life," a "genius," "magnificent in what she creates and the expanded and exquisite way she lives her life."[2])

Being lionized is also something that Atwood hates. After all, the practical implications of such intensive media scrutiny include an invasion of one's privacy and, perhaps even worse, a commitment on the part of the media to the creation of an icon. Atwood discusses the process of "stellification" in a 1978 interview with writer Joyce Carol Oates, explaining that the danger of such rapid lionization is that the writer might become nothing but a "vaporous ball of gas" (81). But, she continues, this can only happen if the writer gets a swelled head, becomes too "captivated" by her own image. And, in Canada, where we are fed and nurtured on the pap of self-consciousness and ironic self-appraisal, this is not very likely. Atwood phrases it bluntly: "We," in Canada, "cut tall poppies" ("Diary," 305; cf. also Rosenthal in the present volume).

The Tiger

This Canadian reticence is precisely why I was so surprised with all the hoopla surrounding Atwood's emerging biography in the Fall of 1998; it made one think that nobody had written a biography about a living Canadian writer ever before. Of course, that's nonsense. We have biographies of Leonard Cohen, Timothy Findley, Irving Layton, Carol Shields, and even of the very private Alice Munro and Michael Ondaatje. So what made Margaret Atwood any different? Well, it was the *lion factor*, for one thing. For another, it was the absence of any extensive biographical commentary on this seemingly (even though Atwood would deny it to the last ditch, angrily, defensively, articulately) autobiographical writer. But then there was something else as well — something about her fearsome reputation. And this is where the *tiger* comes into the discussion, as the third kind of biographical approach,

---

[2] Interview with the author (25 April 1996).

one that perceives an ordinary person as rather daunting, frightening, extraordinary.

Two phrases dogged me during the research for my own Atwood biography. The first was a compliment paid to Atwood by an old and close friend of hers. "Peggy's cheeks," the friend mused, "were the colour of warm rose petals." Do you recognize it? It took me a while, but I knew it sounded familiar. That's what people used to say about the Queen Mother. There's a hint of awe there, of being in the presence of — yes — royalty.

The other phrase came as a warning from one of Atwood's colleagues. "Be very, very careful," he said. "You have a tiger by the tail." That I had the tail at all was a function of Atwood's having given me a list of people to contact, together with addresses and phone numbers and a letter of introduction. "You see how irritatingly candid I am being?" (26 August 1995), she teased me early on in the process, knowing full well that I, and many of her other readers, expected precisely the opposite of a forthcoming biographical subject.

We knew that there was a tiger at the other end of the tail, that is, because we had heard from those who had found one there. After all, biographical accounts of Atwood did emerge well before 1998. They weren't full-length biographies. Instead, they were biographical glances, snippets, sketches; it's worth taking you on a whirlwind tour through the biographer's boneyard.

There's a very interesting film made by Australian filmmaker Michael Rubbo in 1984. It is filmed at the Atwood family cabin, the rustic setting for Atwood's novel *Surfacing*. (Atwood often explains, by the way, that her work is autogeographical, by which she means that she works hard to capture a setting as precisely as possible.) Rubbo camped near the Atwood cabin, in a tent, with his assistant and a collection of Atwood's books — lined up neatly, like little soldiers, on a small bookshelf in said tent. It rained a lot that week, so we see interviews taking place under overturned canoes, and Rubbo himself looks progressively more miserable. I gather that he threw his back out and sprained an ankle, which might partially explain it (Atwood, 28 November 1995).

Rubbo's plan was to expose the autobiographical underpinnings of the novel *Surfacing*, thereby accounting for Atwood's tendency towards Gothic themes and ghostly presences (something I don't do awfully well in my own biography, assuming, as I do, that they spring from Atwood's creative imagination. Remember that element of artistry . . .). Among other things, Atwood's mother, whose eyes twinkle as she talks warmly and proudly about her daughter and puts the finishing touches on a homemade apple pie, undermines Rubbo's plan. No dysfunctional family this.

Best of all is the evening when the Atwood family takes control of the camera and stages a send-up of the whole project. "Who is this woman?" they ask, sitting at the table around Atwood, who is wearing a paper bag on her head. They're all laughing. That we witness this mutiny is to Rubbo's credit (he must have swallowed his pride hard when he decided to put that clip in his film); that the mutiny happened at all has something to do with the family's mischievousness (see the note on healthy sense of humor in the *lion* biography above) and the *tiger factor*.

Atwood's public rebuttal of Rubbo was milder. In the US version of *Bluebeard's Egg* she includes a few autobiographical stories which serve as "an answer to people who mistakenly thought the heroine's parents in *Surfacing* were pictures of [her] own parents" (Lyons, 225). But Atwood's rebuttals can be pretty fierce. She practices, as one writer put it to me, the "pre-emptive thrust." "So it's really a biographical question," she once snapped at Montreal writer Mark Abley, who interviewed her just after she had published *Morning in the Burned House*, which included an elegiac sequence written soon after the death of her beloved father. "Do you want to wring some feeling from me? Do you want to get me to express emotion? Is that what you have in mind?" (3).

Sometimes the rebuttals appear in fictional works. Think of Robert Fulford. I like what he says about Atwood — it's intelligent and gutsy. Atwood doesn't like it, though, because Fulford sees her as a "politician" (187) and pragmatist as well as, and perhaps even ahead of being, a writer. Fulford exposes some of Atwood's fiction as autobiographical (193) and posits that, contrary to what she says, she loves and thrives on celebrity (193). This may not seem like provocation, but it is — especially coming from one Canadian to another. Self-promotion is, after all, very unCanadian. Not done in Canada, at least not openly. Fulford's take on Atwood, in other words, is challenging rather than chummy. Atwood's response was to write him into a story called "Uncles," assigning him the role of Percy Marrow, who mentors a young woman named Susannah. Percy Marrow is, in Fulford's own words, "a disreputable" and "disloyal" journalist whose secret nickname is "Vedge," for vegetable marrow, because he's shaped like one. Atwood would not comment on the connection between Fulford and Marrow to me; she was careful nonetheless to point out that she is not Susan-nah.[3]

When attacks seem vicious and personal Atwood doesn't say any-thing at all — herself. One involves a writer named William Wigle, who included a character called Margaret Atwood in one of his stories. The Canadian Writers' Union spoke up against him, as well as against Fraser Sutherland, the editor of the journal in which the story was published. In Atwood's subsequent novel, *Lady Oracle*, there is a journalist by the name of — yes, you've got it — Fraser. Mischievously, one of Atwood's writer pals suggested that she call him "Will Fraser" — a reference to his role in the novel, and a direct reference to the whole Will Wigle epi-sode.

The *tiger* approach to an Atwood biography would go something like this, and it would refer to her as "Margaret" or "Atwood" — never as "Peggy": Born in 1939, and raised during a time when girls were taught that they should only speak if and when they were spoken to, or, alternatively, if they had nice things to say, Atwood's honest and forth-right way of speaking her mind is striking. Atwood does not suffer fools lightly (a collage of first paragraphs of journalistic interviews with At-wood which outline her fearsome reputation might follow). Atwood is known as an outspoken defender of humanitarian values, an able and active advocate for women's rights and for freedom of speech. She also voices her support of Canadian cultural autonomy and ecological awareness. (An annotated list of her leadership and administrative posi-tions in Amnesty International and PEN Canada, as well as various humanitarian awards and relevant publications might follow here.) At-wood's feminism can be traced either: (i) to the strong female role models within her family (her own mother, who set up camp in the bush during many summers while Atwood's father was doing research on insects, is only one example of the remarkable strength of the women in Atwood's mother's family); (ii) to the strong atmosphere of female empowerment at Victoria College in the University of Toronto (where Atwood encountered formidable female instructors, including Jay Macpherson and, together with a group of intelligent young women, studied in an atmosphere where their ideas rather than their gender determined the response); (iii) to a growing sense of resentment about the double standards which she encountered during her first year of study at the soon-to-be-affiliated-with-Harvard Radcliffe College (where women's access to the Widener library was restricted, for exam-ple, or they were expected to serve tea and cookies in the class breaks);

[3] Handwritten marginal notes (Fall 1996).

(iv) or, and this is something that has not been discussed at all in Atwood criticism to date, to a group of very strong-minded and interesting women with whom she worked at Canadian Facts Marketing Company the year before she went to UBC, or, to put it another way, the year prior to the one in which she completed her first published book of poetry, her first published novel, and early draft sketches for much of her subsequent fiction.

Directly relevant to Atwood's growing interest in human rights were her travels to Saint Vincent (which inspired *Bodily Harm*) and her 1980 discussion with Carolyn Forché about the situation in El Salvador (which gave rise to some poems in *True Stories*). Atwood's comfort in speaking out can be traced to a supportive family that encouraged Atwood and her brother to take responsibility in and for their community.

Atwood says that one of her favorite ancestors is Mary Webster, who survived hanging as a witch. The biography of Atwood as *tiger* might be organized around this image and focus on this female ancestor's strength and her strong instinct for survival, not to mention the disadvantages (for Mary Webster, accused witch) of being ahead of her time and its advantages (for Margaret Atwood, writer).

By way of an aside, a version of the *tiger* biography was one of the best and most frequent responses to my question — why is Atwood so successful? Because she was perceptive enough to recognize the important social issues of her time and was not afraid to be the first one to speak up. British Columbia friend and writer Brian Brett talked of Atwood's uncanny knack for anticipating trends, for recognizing what he called "paradigm shifts." After all, she wrote *The Edible Woman* before we had really come to identify or understand *anorexia nervosa*; she wrote *Alias Grace* before the O. J. Simpson and Paul Bernardo trials, so that its publication was simultaneous with media discussion of those issues.

Pussycat

A tiger — perhaps. But Atwood presents herself as far less magisterial, more endearing: as pussycat, in fact, an image she solidifies in a poem which refers to her collaborations with her friend from Camp White Pine (they were counsellors together in younger days), the Canadian artist Charles Pachter (perhaps best known for his series of paintings of Canadian icons, his moose series, and for his Canadian flag, which adorned Canadian postage stamps for a time). Atwood sent a copy of this poem, "Owl and Pussycat: Some Years Later" to Pachter before its publication; he is, after all, the owl in the poem — with the bifocals, minus some hair now. Atwood is the pussycat.

In this poem, ostensibly a sequel to Lear's "The Owl and the Pussy-cat," the speaker muses about the artistic success of these two creatures several decades after their first meeting, measuring their hard-won achievements ("prizes," "trophies") against their earlier ambitions (to "change the world"), questioning the size and value of their artistic talent (perhaps theirs is only "small talent," "rubbed" and polished like "silver spoons"), gauging their audience and their impact. Has the world been changed for the better by their singing? Their art? Perhaps. And that, of course, is why the poem urges "moulting" owl and "arthritic" pussycat to "sing on" by the light of the moon — just in case they can do more.

As Atwood depicts herself here, as elsewhere, she is not a tiger at all. Rather, Atwood presents Atwood as short and soft-spoken, buried under a mass of curls, as one who, like everyone else in the contemporary world, often feels rather small, perhaps even bumbling, as she is "blown" by the winds of chance.[4]

In her comic strips (cf. the cartoon section in this book) she is a diminutive little figure, often overwhelmed by the situations she finds herself in. She very kindly let me reprint a wonderful comic strip about her time at Victoria College in my biography, and one can see her transformation from high school student to bohemian in her own self-caricatures. In the 1970s, under the pseudonym Bart Gerrard, Atwood sketched a little series about "Survivalwoman," a tiny and soft-spoken little kilt-clad superheroine who looked a lot like Atwood. My favorite episode occurs when she does battle with the American superhero, "Superham," using the Canadian tools of her trade, mainly deflationary wit.

If you look closely at Atwood's self-portraits, she usually puts a curl of hair bang smack in the middle of her forehead (cf. the image by Charles Altman in the cartoon section). You know the old saying, *there was a little girl who had a little curl right in the middle of her forehead, and when she was good she was very very good, and when she was bad she was horrid.* These cartoon or stick-figure self-portraits are self-deprecating and funny, proof that Atwood takes her work seriously, but does not take herself too seriously. Paradoxically, they also invite us to recognize that size has little to do with impact — something "Survivalwoman" knows well.

---

[4] Atwood. Letter to the author (26 August 1995).

Tiger or pussycat? In Atwood's case, you can't be one without being the other. The appeal of the pussycat is precisely the power of the tiger. There's something very engaging about the very down-to-earth Atwoodian figure with the streak of humor and a curl in the middle of her forehead — the one who doesn't take herself too seriously and who, in the process, is wickedly funny and deadly serious.

It's no tiger, for example, who roars with laughter remembering the indignities of her first book signing. It was in the Men's Sock and Underwear department of Edmonton's Hudson's Bay store. The book was her first novel, *The Edible Woman*. She sold two copies and, not surprisingly given the book title and the location of the book signing, frightened a lot of men. "There they were," Atwood remembered, "furtively wishing to purchase their Y-front jockeys, and there was I with a book called *The Edible Woman*. Too terrifying" (28 November 1995).

It's no tiger who remembers her first waitressing job in what is now the Venture Inn at Avenue and Bloor in Toronto. Caught in "the Lunchtime from Hell," Atwood describes herself "frazzling" around "like a trapped Junebug, shedding hairpins, dripping cloth or filthy plate in hand" while her boss walked by with regular customers showing her off as his employee with an M.A. (Atwood, "Case," 47). This is the oh-so-very-human-and-down-to-earth Peggy (haven't we all felt like a trapped Junebug at one point or another?) whose appeal and sense of humor makes for the writerly magic of Margaret Atwood when experience is transformed into fiction. After all, this young, Erma Bombeck-like protagonist shows up in *Lady Oracle*. Remember Joan Foster, working as a waitress, trapped by a marriage proposal?

And the color of her cheeks through this whole episode? Nothing so delicate as warm rose petals, one may be sure. At least not as Atwood describes it. Mind you, that friend who described Peggy as having cheeks the color of warm rose petals was talking about her at just about this time in her life. Queen or commoner? It's all in the eye of the beholder. If Peggy has cheeks the color of warm rose petals, then Margaret understands the power and peril of the regal metaphor. (As she tells Joyce Carol Oates, being associated with a queen means that one will be stung to death later on when one can't lay eggs any more. [80]) Atwood also knows that Crazed Cashiers and cats have a place in the Canadian landscape, whereas tigers are rather more conspicuous and nowhere near as endearing.

So what would the *pussycat* biography look like? First, it would be told in the voice of Peggy — down-to-earth, middle-class, full-of-a-sense-of-fun, friendly. Peggy is *not* Margaret (the capable, hard-working, professional writer), a point Atwood made by sending me a copy of Lois Gould's wonderful article on the world's various Margarets. "To be larger than life," writes Gould, "they have to call themselves Peggy. (*Not* Maggie: that's just Margaret trying vainly to lighten up. As in Thatcher.)" Peggy, for starters, is flawed: she can't spell (never could), isn't particularly athletic, and so on.

Next, Peggy would describe the moment at which she began writing as a kind of revelation, a descent of the muse's thumb. (It could not, after all, be the direct result of the child's early resolution to become a writer, of subsequently focused ambition and hard work. That would sound too serious, might even hint of high ambitions and a too serious sense of self. Very unCanadian. Not very likeable.) There might also be some detail about growing up — favorite clothes, a school dance, the odd embarrassing moment (though not *too* embarrassing or revealing), anecdotes about summer camp (people and pranks mostly), early jobs (waitressing, for instance, or a brief stint at the Sportsman's Show).

Finally, Peggy would tell us what it *feels like*, from the inside looking out, to be a well-known writer. She would explain that, as she surveyed the literary scene in her early years, the outlook for her was pretty bleak. The biographies of her literary forebears predicted a hard life — the cost of creative genius being eccentricity, at the very least, and madness leading to suicide, at the worst. Those same biographies suggested that, for a woman writer, the middle-class dream of a house with a picket fence and 2.6 children was a real long shot. More likely were a lonely turret and a crust of bread. Then, when success did come in the early 1970s, it came at a high price: some rather vicious, and occasionally personal attacks. She would describe how it felt to become a "thing," what it was like to "dodge the flak." The older Peggy would then look back on her life — the first marriage to fellow Harvard student and writer James (Jim) Polk, which ended amicably; subsequent partnership with writer Graeme Gibson and the birth of their daughter, Jess Atwood Gibson — with a warm, genuine, and endearing sense of appreciation.

All these Peggy stories have been told, of course. As a start, one should look at "Where is How" (*Publishers Weekly* 8 Aug. 1991), "Why I Write Poetry" (*This Magazine* Mar.-Apr. 1996), and read through the interviews collected by Earl Ingersoll in *Margaret Atwood: Conversations*. My own favorite stories about the flawed Peggy (the flaws are pretty trivial and the telling hilarious) are Atwood's own "Margaret in Marketland" (about the marketing research firm which serves as the real-life source of Seymour Surveys in *The Edible Woman*; box 90; file

37 Atwood Papers) and "A Flying Start" (from *That Reminds Me: Canada's Authors Relive Their Most Embarrassing Moments*, ed. Marta Kurc). By the time you get to one of her most recent statements, you would swear that she seems positively ordinary. For example, in "The Writer: A New Canadian Life-Form" (*New York Times Book Review* 18 May 1997), her confessions of being the "girliest" in her tastes, the "shortest" and "the most sluggish and the feeblest of character" of those in her family, despite her later admission that her family was like a "quartet of 20-foot-tall hyperactive giants" (39), make her seem far more approachable than Margaret Atwood's fearsome reputation (or her reputation for being fearsome) might otherwise suggest.

So which is it, tiger or pussycat? For me, the answer is both. Further, this discrepancy between *tiger* and *pussycat*, Margaret and Peggy, has never struck me as inconsistent or problematic. I see that, at some level, all writers are double. Atwood seems to see this as well. Think, for example, of her profiles of fellow writers Marie-Claire Blais, George Bowering, Dennis Lee, Anne Sexton. Always, but always, she examines at least two sides of the writer — the one revealed and the one concealed. There is a similar doubling in Atwood's writing (think of the sophisticated play of doubles and foils in *Alias Grace* and *The Robber Bride*, not to mention the interplay between speaker and reader in much of her poetry as one interpretation is overturned to reveal another). And there is a similar doubling in Atwood's own persona, as Peggy and Margaret, happily settled in Toronto with Graeme Gibson, as well as traveler, internationally celebrated writer, and spokesperson for human rights. Peggy is the stay-at-home-and-read or enjoy-some-time-with-friends type, the one who wants to hear from her mother every morning; Margaret, as writer, is the moral adventurer. Were I to have written a psychobiography, this pervasive and sophisticated layering of doubles behind and through Atwood's work would have been the focus of it.

This sense of doubleness figures in Charlie Pachter's 1968 portrait of Atwood, where he depicts her sprouting wings behind her as she offers a caterpillar on a twig to the viewer's gaze. The painting, entitled "It Was Fascination I Know," speaks of growth and transformation, of energy, even magic. The image of a developing pupa, Margaret with wings spread out behind her, depicts her poised on the cusp of transformation. In 1968 Atwood was 29, and Pachter's portrait revealed her emergence onto the literary scene, foretold the triumphant trajectory that her career would follow, was already beginning to follow. In 1999, as Atwood turns 60, this portrait can be read differently, not only as an early comment on Atwood's creative energies, but also as a comment on the form and subject of her writing — the endless possibility of transformation. As such, it offers a more dynamic biographical metaphor than the feline ones — multi- rather than uni-dimensional, fascinating rather than forced (like the fallacy of the stuffed cat), formidable (like the lion), or frightening (like the tiger). And, it seems like a more appropriate metaphor for the daughter of a forest entomologist; "pussycat" seems overly domestic, inappropriately impotent, something hidden away in a house somewhere, rather than out in our world, watching and changing it.[5]

Works Cited

Abley, Mark. "Dire Things: An Interview with Margaret Atwood." *Poetry Canada Review* 15.2 (1995): 1–3, 28–29.

Atwood, Margaret. "Case of the Crazed Cashier." *Toronto Life*, March 1990, 46–47.

———. "Diary Down Under." *Second Words: Selected Critical Prose*. Toronto: Anansi, 1982: 296–306.

———. "A Flying Start." In *That Reminds Me: Canada's Authors Relive Their Most Embarrassing Moments*. Ed. Marta Kurc. Toronto: Stoddart, 1990: 11–13.

———. Letters to the author, 26 August 1995, 28 November 1995.

———. "Margaret in Marketland." Atwood Papers. Thomas Fisher Rare Book Library, University of Toronto. Box 90, file 37.

———. "Owl and Pussycat, Some Years Later." *Paper Guitar: 25 Writers Celebrate 25 Years of Descant Magazine*. Toronto: Harper Collins, 1995: 15–21.

———. "Where is How." *Publishers Weekly*, 8 August 1991.

———. "Why I Write Poetry." *This Magazine*, March-April 1996.

———. "The Writer: A New Canadian Life-Form." *New York Times Book Review*, 18 May 1997, 39.

Botton, Alain de. *Kiss and Tell*. New York: Picador, 1995.

Cooke, Nathalie. Interview with Phoebe Larmore, 25 April 1996.

———. *Margaret Atwood: A Biography*. Toronto: ECW Press, 1998.

---

[5] A version of this paper was presented at Marianopolis College in Montreal, Quebec (11 March 1999).

Fulford, Robert. *Best Seat in the House: Memoirs of a Lucky Man.* Toronto: Collins, 1988.

Gould, Lois. "The Margaret Factor." *New York Times Sunday Magazine,* 24 November 1996.

Ingersoll, Earl G., ed. *Margaret Atwood: Conversations.* Willowdale, Ontario: Firefly, 1990.

Lyons, Bonnie. "Using Other People's Dreadful Childhoods." In Ingersoll 1990: 221–33.

Oates, Joyce Carol. "Dancing on the Edge of the Precipice." In Ingersoll 1990: 74–85.

Peri, Camille. "Witch Craft." *Mother Jones* 14.3 (1989): 28–45.

Rubbo, Michael, dir. *Once in August.* Canadian Writers Series. National Film Board of Canada, 1984.

Celebrity, or a Disneyland of the Soul: Margaret Atwood and the Media

Susanne Becker (Mainz)

"YOU HAVE THE BODY of a goddess," her lover, the Polish count, tells the young heroine of Margaret Atwood's third novel, *Lady Oracle* (1976, 158). The shapely Joan Foster, however, is haunted by her obesity as a young girl. "I was fifteen, and I'd reached my maximum growth: I was five feet eight and I weighed two hundred and forty-five, give or take a few pounds" (*LO*, 78). A year later she has lost a hundred pounds and leaves her mother's house for adventure and romance, and for Gothic visitations from a "Fat Lady," which persist even after Joan becomes a famous writer. When *Lady Oracle* first appeared, public meetings with Margaret Atwood were dominated by one single question: "How did you manage to lose all that weight?!"

It was the mid-seventies, and Margaret Atwood had become "Canada's most gossipped-about writer," as the Canadian news magazine *Maclean's* introduced its interview with Atwood and its review of *Lady Oracle* (6 September 1976). Atwood responds: "It's probably because I do think some things are private" (*Maclean's*, 6). However, the three-page *Maclean's* interview is a prototype of Atwood's media appearances at the time. It starts with a whole page of questions and answers about Jess, Atwood's daughter with Graeme Gibson, about motherhood, and relationships. Interspersed are three photographs taken by Graeme Gibson showing (1) a dreamy, (2) a smiling, and (3) a skeptical Margaret Atwood in an embroidered blouse. All of this amounts to the recognition that, "at the ripe young age of 36," Atwood had turned into a "national monument" (*Maclean's*, 7) who can be "really frightening." But then, of course, the last word is Atwood's:

> I'm probably as frightening as everybody else, and most people are quite frightening under the right circumstances, when you get them in a situation with their backs to the wall. I think it's probably harder to get me in that situation, because I'm always looking behind, over my shoulder; I know where the wall is. You'll notice that it's you who's sitting in the corner. (7)

Margaret Atwood, it is clear, always puts interviewers in their place. A media star in the firmament of world literature, a powerful communicator of Canadian culture as well as human rights issues on a global scale, she encounters — and uses — the publicity machine and the media business with superiority, dignity, and generosity. I have been asked to contribute this essay on the Atwood-media connection because I have interviewed her myself on several occasions, mostly for German television. Our first such meeting was a real-time five-minute on-camera interview about *The Handmaid's Tale* coming out in German at the Frankfurt Book Fair in 1987. Atwood was placed impressively in front of her books, and I sat with my back to the crowd of fans, who were gradually pressing into the camera set, books clutched to their bosoms and pens in hand, hunting for autographs. I found this quite frightening, but Atwood, accustomed to such attention, calmly talked about the new novel before doing the celebrity round of the fair. Fame, she said that day, made her life both more crowded — with the manifold demands on her time and support — and more independent — with the freedom to write without having to teach at university. In this essay, I would like to look at Atwood's media celebrity in three interwoven ways: its development since the seventies, her own ironic voice about it in her essays and fiction, and my own experience with it over the last twelve years.[1]

In that first interview, Atwood told me why she had dedicated *The Handmaid's Tale* to her ancestor Mary Webster. Webster had been persecuted as a witch, but she survived being hanged from a tree, spending a whole night dangling from the rope, waiting for morning. Atwood summarized the scene with a dramatic voice: "I thought that if I came out to the public with this book, I should have a strong neck!" Indeed, this novel about a young woman forced to bear children under a totalitarian regime after a fundamentalist take-over in the US sparked great controversy and media attention, and managed to become both an international bestseller and an important movie. *The Handmaid's Tale* is also, in some ways, Atwood's strongest manifesto for freedom of the press — its abolition in the novel signifies an end to individual freedom and human rights. Atwood belongs to those writers of contemporary world literature who always address, both within and beyond their work, pressing global issues. Whether she takes on Canadian politics, for example the current question of a Torontonian mega-city, or the

---

[1] I do so with some reservation because it means stepping into that dangerous space between art and life that makes Atwood sarcastic and her publicists cringe and that I have always avoided. But it has also fascinated me.

larger ecological and human rights issues that she has made her cause, her voice has an impact. As she said in 1980: "If we cease to judge this world, we may find ourselves, very quickly, in one which is infinitely worse" (1980; 1982, 333). This act of judging is something, according to Atwood, "that writers can do" (personal interview, 1991) — and she has always taken on the challenge to voice her views, with skeptical distance and critical clairvoyance, about the world around her and us; meanwhile her ease with public appearances has cemented her fame. Margaret Atwood and the media is thus a story of the tension between the possibility and the curse of such celebrity; between using the media and being used.

To start with the possibilities: her public influence is great. As is well known, one of her chief targets is Canadian-American relations: "The history of Canada, and therefore of Canadian literature, has been profoundly influenced — and not always for the better — by the almost nine thousand kilometer border that we share with the most powerful country in the world" (Atwood and Gibson 1996). Due to her international high profile, her voice on this issue has been heard on both sides of the border. When the debate about North American Free Trade threatened to split the Canadian nation in 1987, Margaret Atwood took on this important issue of North American politics, and her decidedly anti-Free-Trade ideas have been discussed in the international media over and over again. Recently, an important discussion on "America the Brazen" and the resentment its domineering gestures create abroad (by James Walsh, *TIME*, 4 August 1997) focused on one of her most ironic and memorable images of Canadian-American relations:

> About the only position they have adopted towards us, country to country, has been the missionary position, and we were not on top. I guess that is why the national wisdom vis-a-vis Them has so often taken the form of lying still, keeping your mouth shut and pretending you like it. ("Speech Presented to the Parliamentary Committee on Free Trade," 3 November 1987, Atwood Papers).

Atwood's provocative metaphors and her wry humor have also been her best weapons against the curse of celebrity: the curiosity and sensationalism inextricably linked to public figures. Since she became a highly outspoken protagonist of the emerging Canadian literary scene in the late sixties, there has been a fascination with Atwood's personality and with her personal life. Looking back on that time of hand-publishing one's own poetry, and of publicizing "CanLit," Atwood usually attributes the related national gossip to the new experience for a reading public caught between the colonialisms of British tradition and American expansion of having "writers of their own." She wrote (and hand-published) her first collections of poetry to great national acclaim; wrote her first novels, which won her important national prizes — and brought her early international fame; and wrote the first thematic guide to Canadian literature and her own ironic manifesto against cultural victimization, *Survival* (1972), to great national controversy. She supported the small Canadian publisher, House of Anansi Press (founded in 1966), joined Amnesty International in 1972, co-founded the "Writers' Union of Canada" with Graeme Gibson and others, and, later, the Canadian PEN: enough politics and public activity to be in demand for articles, reviews, lectures, speeches — and, of course, for revelations about herself. Her personality, her family, and her circle have remained a national public issue, as the checklists on scholarly and popular writing about Atwood, published annually by the Margaret Atwood Society, amply reflect.

Another public issue is the whole uncanny parade of public Atwood-mystifications, some created in awe, some in rage, some in confusion. In the eighties, Margaret Atwood became one of the most sought-after "covergirls" of the Canadian magazine landscape.[2] Styled as "Woman of the Year," Atwood smiled from the cover of *Chatelaine* in January 1981, with the celebratory and highly personal article, "The Magnificent Margaret Atwood," that starts in no uncertain terms:

> There are so many reasons to celebrate the mysterious multifaceted Margaret Atwood. She's a novelist, poet and critic of international stature. She's a devoted mother, a strong feminist and a champion of the writing community. Her enigmatic face is a part of the fabric of our lives, and her achievements make us rejoice that she's a woman and a Canadian. (Timson, 1981)

Styled as the prototype of "The Modern Woman in Canadian Fiction," a thoughtful Atwood graced the cover of *City Woman* one year later (Spring 1982) with an article that, typically, connects her to her urban, creative, articulate heroines. Similarly, *Saturday Night* styled her in August 1988 as a Gothic heroine within a romantic landscape to introduce the publication of her Neo-Gothic short story "Death by Landscape" (cf. photograph section). As these covers and the related Atwood cult suggest, even in the eighties, the decade of postmodern skepticism and intellectualizing, the conflation of Atwood the writer

---

[2] Many thanks to Linda Hutcheon for sharing her own Atwood press collection with me.

with her fictitious heroines prevails, a conflation that bridges the con-
sciousness-raising seventies and the confessional nineties.

Of course, Atwood herself has reviewed the resulting images and
myths — which are, naturally, not always as flattering as my examples
above — with characteristic irony. It seems that her approach does exhibit a certain development, starting with "talking back." Her early essays, collected in *Second Words* (1982), often address "mis-
representations" as she announces in the introduction:

> From 1972 (or publication of *Survival*) to 1976 . . . I was being at-
> tacked a lot; much of what I wrote then was in response to some of
> these attacks, the more intellectually serious ones, I think. (People
> who attack me for having curly hair, breast feeding and making public
> appearances I can't do much about.) . . . The third period . . . runs
> from 1976, in which I published *Lady Oracle* and had a baby, thus be-
> coming instantly warm and maternal and temporarily less attacked, to
> the present. (1982, 14)

It is Atwood's strategy to address, summarize, and thus control much
of the media imagery about her.

In my first media encounter with Margaret Atwood, she walks
through the snow, purposefully, dreamily, with her hands in the pock-
ets of a dark coat, along high, snow-covered pines, while a disembodied
dark female voice recites, in German, the famous last paragraph from
Surfacing: "This above all, to refuse to be a victim." Then — cut —
Margaret Atwood is joined by writer-husband Graeme Gibson, and
now they walk through the snow together, while a male commentator
explains that she is the representative of a small but important literature, from Canada, that the German readership tends to forget because
of US cultural imperialism. An interview about nationalism, nature, and
feminism follows, during which Atwood sits with her back to a brooding winter landscape: "I think feminists adopted me ..." she says. This
was the way German television introduced Margaret Atwood to German viewers ("aspekte," ZDF; 16 March 1979). Years later, I spoke to
Graeme Gibson about that scene. He smiled: "We filmed that in Bonn,
you know. But they thought it might look Canadian enough, because
of all the snow." They had played the game and it worked: to her German readers, it established Margaret Atwood firmly as a Canadian figure — never to be confused with American writers.

Atwood's media personalities: the Canadian icon, the modern
heroine, and maybe even sometimes, the visionary. When *The Handmaid's Tale* was made into a movie directed by Volker Schlöndorff (it
appeared at the International Film Festival in Berlin in 1990), Margaret
Atwood was so well known and so popular in Germany that her arrival

in Berlin for the premiere was a cultishly celebrated media event. Her appearance on stage in a silver dress after the screening triggered standing ovations. Moreover, her presence at the *Berlinale* meant popular support for the film, attention that Schlöndorff sadly needed. Atwood was among the most sought-after interview stars of an international film festival that usually only stalks Hollywood stars with that intensity. After she had stated numerous times that the story of the film was a fiction, but that it was based on her research about things that had already happened, or that could easily happen, or that we already have the technology for, the international film press transformed her from a writer into a prophetic figure. She really needed that strong neck there!

She also needed, as always in her public encounters, her ironic voice. Linda Hutcheon has shown irony to be one of the major forms of the Canadian postmodern and she has shown Margaret Atwood to be one of the purveyors of such a Canadian attitude (1988, 17–18). In Hutcheon's definition, irony — like parody — presupposes a certain complicity with that which it contests, and that paradox remains unresolved. In this sense, Atwood's ironic voice seems to derive its power from her ability to anticipate public demands and to counter rather than deny them.

But then, Margaret Atwood's characteristic wit and irony exhibit their power most effectively when tackling issues of celebrity in her fiction. As a writer, her parodic play with the media world has long opened up another dimension to the Atwood-media relationship. What the realms of literature and the media, or rather, literary and media stories share are — with differing emphasis — the structures of representation and communication. Thus, approaching Atwood and the media also means approaching the important and rapidly changing relationship of these different worlds of communication in the late twentieth century.

The issue of representation has always played an important role in Atwood's work. As early as *Surfacing* (1972), it is clear to the nameless narrator that representation is an essential means of expressing power relations (see Strobel 1992, 36). All Atwood heroines are somehow on the run from its possible violence; yet, at the same time, they are also complicit in its perpetuation. In *Surfacing*, David urges his wife to pose nude for his movie "Random Samples." Anna, albeit hesitantly, does take off her bikini; and although she gives him the finger and jumps into the lake, her belly-flop is actually filmed. In this scene, the video camera becomes the technical sign for the male gaze that also demands — and gets! — Anna's pathetic daily make-up sessions. As often happens in Atwood's work, the violence of representation implies reducing an imaginative and creative female figure to some kind of feminine ideal — a pin-up, a "goddess," etc. Of course, these ideals are also created and distributed by the media machinery, with a potential for seduction of its own. Atwood's narratives highlight "the pornography of representation" (to use Susanne Kappeler's phrase); they focus on ways of resisting and of refusing representation without forgetting the seductiveness of media images to women. In *The Edible Woman* (1969), Marian MacAlpin fears her fiancé's camera but puts on the red dress he likes; and her escape from being not only photographed by, but also married to, the man who wants her to be different is a narrow one. In *Bodily Harm* (1982) — the novel that was both anticipated and criticized as Atwood's most direct response to the often vicious media hype around her at the time (see e.g. *Chatelaine*, January 1981) — the heroine is herself a journalist and she is just as much the fabricator of magazine sensationalism as she is the victim of its related excesses. Atwood's parody of the powers of representation explores their paradoxes with complex and sometimes surprising endings.

A striking example of Atwood's complex turn on violence and the seduction of feminine ideals is her Gothic parody *Lady Oracle* (1976). Of course, the Gothic's own emotional trajectory between love and horror is largely a play with feminine desire on the border between romance or melodrama on the one hand and the expectations of everyday life on the other. Atwood's heroine Joan Foster refuses the separation between the two worlds. She desperately adopts a new self, and correspondingly, a new name for every role dreamt up by her or demanded of her. She is Joan Delacourt, the fat child and teenager; Joan Foster, famous poet and wife of Arthur Foster; Louisa Delacourt, secret writer of best-selling costume Gothics, to name only the most consistent ones. "I always tried to keep my various two names and identities as separate as possible," Joan muses, responding to the question about why she does not tell her husband about her childhood or her publishing career. "It was fear, mostly. When I first met him, he talked a lot about wanting a woman whose mind he could respect and I knew that if he found out I'd written *The Secret of Morgrave Manor*, he wouldn't respect mine" (33). While her obesity as a child goes against the ideal little girl that her mother would like her to be, as an adult she tries to play the part of housewife and political activist that pleases her husband. This one role, however, proves much too small for her as it leaves no space for her fantasies and romantic yearnings, which have been shaped by the Hollywood movies and romance plots of her teenage years. She thus adopts additional "selves" — and these fantasy personalities as well as their related plots multiply throughout her story. When expectations from outside clash with her own desires, she enacts a Gothic romance on the sly: her affair with animal artist "The Royal Porcupine." And when she becomes a famous writer by publishing the prose poem "Lady Oracle," she learns that all her varied selves are still not enough. "Do you play the guitar?" her publishers ask at the first marketing meeting. "No," Joan replies surprised; the response: "I thought we could do you as a sort of female Leonard Cohen" (*Lady Oracle*, 251).

In *Lady Oracle*, such hilarious scenes about a woman vis-à-vis conflicting ideals and about a writer vis-à-vis constructed public personalities abound. Ironically and revealingly, it is when Joan leaves behind all desire to adapt that she really stuns her surroundings. In a radio interview, she frankly admits that she had written her famous poem in an automatic writing experiment. Her interviewer, a loud young macho, who had opened the encounter with the provocative question "'Would you say that you are a happily married woman?'" (264) flees: she does not fit his image of the intellectual "bitch." What ultimately saves Joan Foster in this novel is her refusal to let herself be reduced to one or another ideal, and her ability to try to live out her fantasies. This results, more often than not, in chaos, but it also keeps her from the frustrations of living only half a life, a fate sadly exemplified by her mother. Moreover, it enables her to use her celebrity and the related public expectations to escape.

As a famous writer, Joan encounters different implications of artistic fame. There is, for example, one of Atwood's most quoted attacks on the double-standard in judgments about successful women that she calls "*sexual compliment-put-down*" (1982, 199). Joan experiences this in the form of compliments on her looks and put-downs of her writing that culminate in her meeting with The Royal Porcupine:

> "I guess you're a publishing success," he said. "What's it like to be a successful bad writer?"
> I was beginning to feel angry. "Why don't you publish and find out?" I said.
> "Hey," he said, grinning, "temper. You've got fantastic hair, anyway. Don't ever cut it off." (*Lady Oracle*, 266)

But another, more Gothic image of the female writer is presented to Joan, which Atwood has elsewhere called "*Ophelia* . . . a female version of Doomed Dylan, with more than a little hope on the part of the interviewer that you'll turn into Suicidal Sylvia and give them something to really write about" (1982, 184). The classic image of the doomed

artist modeled after the tragic death of Sylvia Plath is parodically enacted by Joan, who escapes from the complications of her life in Toronto by means of a staged suicide in Lake Ontario.

While *Lady Oracle* brings together much of Atwood's sometimes vicious, sometimes hilarious mockery, her later novel *Cat's Eye* (1988)
explores notions of artistic celebrity on a more serious note — but with
the same ironic edge. Artist Elaine Risley, returning to Toronto for a
retrospective of her work, wanders through the city and, amidst childhood memories, encounters a poster promoting her exhibition. She realizes that her face has been adorned with a mustache!

> I suppose I should be worried about this mustache. Is it just doodling,
> or is it political commentary, an act of aggression? . . . As it is, I study
> the mustache and think: *That looks sort of good.* The mustache is like a
> costume. . . . Then, suddenly, I feel wonder. I have achieved, finally, a
> face that a mustache can be drawn on, a face that attracts mustaches. A
> public face, a face worth defacing. This is an accomplishment. I have
> made something of myself, something or other, after all. (20)

The mustache becomes a sign of her celebrity, but it also comes to
signify the possibility of change. In the ensuing dynamics of marketing
her art in the gallery and in the papers, the attractions and horrors of
fame are again being played out with much Atwoodian emphasis on the
importance of fighting against idealization and fixation. The interview
with the young feminist journalist, for example, in which Elaine avoids
being reduced to another role model for women artists, opens thus:

> "I thought you would be different," says Andrea as we settle.
> "Different how?" I ask.
> "Bigger," she says.
> I smile at her. "I am bigger." (92)

Besides putting her finger on presuppositions that might determine a
whole media image, this passage also superbly parodies Atwood's own
experience at first encounters or in accounts of personal meetings. One
quotation, from the article "Margaret Atwood in Australia," should
suffice here:

> "I had an idea that Margaret Atwood would be large, big-framed,
> erudite and fierce," a journalist admitted in a September issue of the
> *Canberra Times.* She was not the only Australian who had misappre-
> hensions of a towering, fist-pounding man-hater. The Canadian
> author and poet surprised the audience at a literary luncheon in the
> Australian capital by being neither burly nor defiantly unattached; her
> husband and daughter were with her. (Stanton 1983, 13)

Most impressively, the issues of representation, media construction, and the ensuing power play all become the focus of Atwood's latest novel, *Alias Grace* (1996). It has been read mostly as a historical novel, set in the nineteenth century, and telling the story of Grace Marks, an infamous Canadian suspected of murdering her master and his housekeeper, and sentenced to life in jail in a spectacular trial in Toronto in 1843. However, Atwood's exploration of the construction of celebrity — told in a mixture of historical documents, newspaper reports, romanticized accounts, and fictional plots — pointedly mirror the workings of celebrity, sensationalism, and media hype in the late twentieth century.

Significantly, Grace Marks was a servant girl of fifteen when she became a "famous murderess," and her youth and beauty as well as the erotic potential of her story — or rather the combination of sex, murder, and rebellion — contributed greatly to her ambiguous career as an infamous figure in nineteenth-century Canada. Was she sexually involved with her partner in crime, who was hanged following their trial on 21 November 1843? Was she involved with her master? Was he involved with the housekeeper? Why were master and housekeeper murdered? The irresolvability of these and further speculations are epitomized in the wildly differing public views which her fictionalized voice summarizes effectively:

> Sometimes when I am dusting the mirror with the grapes I look at myself in it. . . . I think of all the things that have been written about me — that I am an inhuman female demon, that I am an innocent victim of a blackguard forced against my will and in danger of my own life, that I was too ignorant to know how to act and that to hang me would be judicial murder, that I am fond of animals, that I am very handsome with a brilliant complexion . . . that I am a good girl with a pliable nature and no harm is told of me, that I am cunning and devious, that I am soft in the head and little better than an idiot. And I wonder, how can I be all of these different things at once? (*Alias Grace*, 23)

What better discarding could there be of the constructions of celebrity? Moreover, playing out Grace's narrative of desires, assumptions, and lies in a most commonsensical voice, Atwood balances accounts of everyday life with glimpses of horror and sensational drama. Significantly, those in Grace's surroundings — especially the fictitious nerve specialist Simon Jordan who researches her subconscious and rather melodramatically falls in love with her — distrust anything normal in her life and believe all the salacious details. However, in her last letter to Simon, Grace muses:

> You were . . . eager . . . to hear about my sufferings and my hardships in life . . . I could tell when your interest was slacking . . . but it gave me joy every time I managed to come up with something that would interest you. (*Alias Grace*, 457)

Atwood's Grace points to the workings of private voyeurism and public constructions, and to ways of subverting them.[3] Atwood's voice points in the same direction throughout this novel as well as in recent interviews. And it seems that, at the same time, her own approach to such curiosity has also changed. Her ironic response to attacks and projections has turned into ironic anticipation — and it also takes place in a new medium, the Internet. The Margaret Atwood homepage (www.web.net/owtoad) offers a whole set of answers to questions that could be or frequently are asked, starting with the promisingly personal link to "Life and Times," followed by the suggestive one to "Graeme Gibson." It signals Atwood's awareness and partly ironic, partly serious response to a very nineties public interest in the private lives of the famous. For the decade of the spreading Internet is also the decade of Diana and the paparazzi, of Oprah Winfrey and public confession TV, and of Bill Clinton and the Starr Report. Celebrity in the global village precludes privacy. And Atwood, with the wink of an eye, interacts with that state of the world.

"Question Three. Now for something a little different. Are your novels autobiographical?" Thus opens an unpublished 20-page exploration that Atwood herself wrote in 1982 about often-heard interview questions. (You can find it in the Atwood Papers, at the Thomas Fisher Rare Book Library in Toronto.) She raises issues that have become even more pertinent in the nineties, from the "People magazine nosiness that we've come to associate with personality cults" to the "belief that women are more subjective, that the only stories they can tell are their own" (3, 4). It helps to recall that she has repeatedly and patiently insisted that writing is a craft. And that novels are not a "Disneyland of the soul,"

> ... containing Romanceland, Spyland, Pornoland, and all the other Escapelands which are so much more agreeable than the complex truth. When we take an author seriously, we prefer to believe that her vision derives from her individual and subjective and neurotic tortured soul — we like artists to have tortured souls — not from the world she is looking at. (1981; 1982, 393–94)

---

[3] For more extended readings of Atwood's novels see my *Gothic Forms of Feminine Fictions* (Manchester 1999).

The public desire for such Disneylands — today's media parks — prevails. And so does, after all, the desire for the author's soul. One year ago, a literary journalist met Margaret Atwood for an interview about *Alias Grace*. Sitting in the back garden of her house in Toronto "beneath a brooding sky," he "feels a hint of wildness, a sense of something dark, melodramatic, Gothic" (Bone 1996, n.p.). Atwood herself, he reports, has a terrible headache as they start to discuss Grace's life and fame as murderess who claims she acted under influence and has forgotten the grisly details. Later, he reflects that he has spent the afternoon in Atwood's back garden "discussing a set of fictional characters who might as well be spirits" and wonders "whether Grace might not be the author's alter ego. Perhaps Atwood is possessed in the same way that Grace claimed to be at the time of her crime."

As if that were not enough, the story continues in the form of a fax from Atwood, "apologising for the fact that, because of her throbbing head, she cannot remember a word she said the day before." His conclusion is clear: "Far-fetched, yes, but uncanny nonetheless." Margaret Atwood and the media: a story in the uncanny space between life and art, or, between the world and the watchful writer.

Works Cited

Atwood, Margaret. *Alias Grace*. Toronto: McClelland & Stewart, 1996.

———. *Cat's Eye*. Toronto: McClelland & Stewart, 1988.

———. *The Edible Woman*. Toronto: McClelland & Stewart, 1988.

———. *The Handmaid's Tale*. Toronto: McClelland & Stewart, 1985.

———. *Lady Oracle*. Toronto: McClelland & Stewart, 1976.

———. "On Being a 'Woman Writer': Paradoxes and Dilemmas." In *Second Words: Selected Critical Prose*. Toronto: Anansi, 1982: 190–204.

———. *Second Words: Selected Critical Prose*. Toronto: Anansi, 1982.

———. "Speech Presented to the Parliamentary Committee on Free Trade." Atwood Papers, 3 November 1987. Thomas Fisher Rare Book Library, University of Toronto, Toronto.

———. *Surfacing*. Toronto: McClelland & Stewart, 1972.

Atwood web site: http://www.web.net/owtoad/.

Atwood, Margaret and Graeme Gibson. "Desde el Invierno." 1996. Atwood web site: http://www.web.net/owtoad/desde.html.

Becker, Susanne. *Gothic Forms of Feminine Fictions*. Manchester: Manchester University Press, 1999.

————. Margaret Atwood, interview by S. Becker. Frankfurt, October 1987. Toronto, January 1989. Toronto, October 1989. Toronto, February 1991.

Bone, James. "A Woman Possessed." *Times* (London), 14 September 1996.

Dewar, Elaine. "Thoroughly Modern Orphans." *City Woman* (Spring 1982): 23–32.

Hutcheon, Linda. *The Canadian Postmodern: A Study of English-Canadian Fiction.* Toronto/New York/Oxford: Oxford University Press, 1988.

————. "Margaret Atwood." In *Canadian Writers Since 1960.* 1st ser., ed. W. H. New. Detroit: Book Tower, 1986: 17–34.

Kappeler, Susanne. *The Pornography of Representation.* Oxford: Polity Press/Basil Blackwell, 1988.

Slinger, Helen. Margaret Atwood, interview by H. Slinger. *Maclean's,* 6 September 1976, 4–7.

Stanton, Susan. "Margaret Atwood in Australia." *Cross-Canadian Writers' Quarterly* 5.2/3 (1983): 13–14.

Strobel, Christina. "On the Representation of Representation in Margaret Atwood's *Surfacing.*" *Zeitschrift für Anglistik und Amerikanistik* 40.1 (1992): 35–43.

Sullivan, Rosemary. *The Red Shoes: Margaret Atwood Starting Out.* Toronto: Harper Flamingo, 1998.

Timson, Judith. "The Magnificent Margaret Atwood." *Chatelaine,* January 1981, 41–70.

Walsh, James. "America the Brazen." *TIME Magazine,* 4 August 1997, 4–9.

Canonizing Atwood: Her Impact on Teaching in the US, Canada, and Europe

Caroline Rosenthal (University of Constance)

> When I began to teach Canadian literature in 1985, one of my most surprising classroom discoveries was the violently polarized responses toward Canada's most widely recognized writer, Margaret Atwood. No writer on the Canadian curriculum, in my experience, excites as much reverence — and its reverse emotion, hostility — as Atwood. (York in Wilson et al. 1996, 43)

> Margaret Atwood is one of the most brilliant, controversial, versatile, abrasive, and enigmatic figures in our literature — possibly in any contemporary literature. (Keith 1982, 95)

Introduction: Research Project

IN A 1997 *GLOBE & MAIL* SURVEY titled "The Takeout Window of Canadian Nationalism," Atwood is listed among the ten most famous and internationally known Canadians (Christie 1997). Although Wayne Gretzky leads the inventory and Atwood ranks only after Céline Dion and Anne Murray, she is significantly the only English-Canadian author who is listed at all. Even though her prominence in the countries under consideration varies — Atwood is listed second last in Canada while in the US she ranks sixth, the UK seventh, and in Germany she is the fourth best known Canadian — these statistics confirm what I had guessed at before I started research for this article, namely, that internationally Margaret Atwood is better known than any other English-Canadian author.[1]

While her fame as a writer was easily proven, gathering material on her impact on teaching proved to be more difficult. I set out to collect

---

[1] The percentage figures show that Atwood is still better known in Canada (where she is recognized by 66%) than in Germany (45%). However, on a list of 10 Canadians, 9 other personalities from sports and entertainment rank before her in Canada. In the UK she is known by 37% and in the US by 40%.

solid data on how often and in which contexts Atwood's work has been taught in Germany, the US, the UK, and Canada over the last two decades. However, whereas the Association for Canadian Studies in German-speaking Countries publishes a listing of all Canadian Studies courses taught in Germany in their newsletter, there are no such listings for the other countries. I thus had to rely on information from selected universities, Canadian Studies Associations, and those university teachers who kindly responded to my questions. A questionnaire I placed on the Atwood discussion list on the Internet yielded many intriguing replies from Atwood scholars as far afield as South Africa, China, and Argentina. The questionnaire inquired whether Atwood had been taught in departments other than the humanities, which of her works — novels, critical essays, short stories, or poetry — had been taught most often, which genre the respondents thought Atwood was best at, and whether Atwood's fame has promoted the study of other Canadian authors in the respective country.

The following conclusions are based on the results of about 100 questionnaires as well as on various publications concerned with teaching Atwood or the teaching of Canadian literature in general. The most comprehensive guide to teaching Atwood's work is *Approaches to Teaching Atwood's* The Handmaid's Tale *and Other Works* edited by Sharon R. Wilson, Thomas B. Friedman, and Shannon Hengen (New York: MLA, 1996). As a newsletter of the Margaret Atwood Society (No. 20, Spring/Summer 1998, 1) informs us, the book has become one of the MLA best sellers, which not only indicates the book's excellence but shows that the interest in teaching Atwood is ever increasing. In their introduction to the volume, the editors summarize the results of their research, which correlate with my own findings:

> Margaret Atwood's works are widely taught in world literature, comparative literature, humanities, women's studies, Canadian Studies, emerging English literatures (formerly Commonwealth literature), American literature, English literature, science-fiction, and communications courses in universities, colleges, junior colleges, and secondary schools not only in the United States and Canada but throughout the world. In addition, *The Handmaid's Tale*, currently the most widely taught Atwood text in the United States, is used in economics, political science, sociology, film, business, and other disciplines outside the humanities, and it has been adopted by several universities ... as a required text for all undergraduates. (Wilson et al. 1996, 1)

The aspects of Atwood's work that are most likely to be treated in the classroom parallel those addressed in Atwood criticism, discussed below: gender politics and women's roles, women's attitudes to the body, narrative voice and design, language, subversion of traditional literary forms (e.g., dystopian/utopian, Gothic), revisionist myth-making, history, satire, irony, Canadian nationalism, spirituality, and the environment. (10)

For the reasons mentioned above, rather than coming up with water-tight statistics, I unearthed different tendencies in how Atwood's work is being taught, which led me to further speculation. Issues such as the duality of the national as well as international reputation of an author came to the forefront. Is it significant that Atwood is successful in the US, often without being identified as a Canadian author? Another interest was whether the further establishment of Atwood's work in academic curricula has altered teaching approaches to her work. Did course descriptions and syllabi change with the progressive canonization of Atwood's work? What I became most curious about in the course of my research is Canada's specific relationship to its most renowned author, who is proudly referred to as a superstar, on the one hand, and who is rejected for being one on the other. In Canada, Atwood's fame apparently triggered countermovements which challenge her now canonical status in Canadian literature. This observation led to assumptions about general forces at work in the formation of Canadian culture. While this paper neither seeks to be a teaching guide nor to analyze any of Atwood's works, it attempts to elucidate Atwood's status in, and her impact on, teaching in selected countries.

Survey Results

1: Germany

A survey of Canadian Studies classes in Germany from 1981 to 1999 reveals that Atwood has been taught more often than any other Canadian writer. In frequency, Atwood is followed by Margaret Laurence, but whereas Laurence has been taught 17 times during that period, Atwood, in comparison, has been taught 51 times.[2] Her impact on university teaching has steadily increased. Although I could only include those courses which explicitly mention Atwood in the title or course description, I am positive she has been taught in numerous other courses all over Germany, as I know holds true for my own university. For instance, at the University of Constance, although Atwood's name

[2] Figures were taken from the newsletter of the Gesellschaft für Kanada-Studien which is published twice a year. *Mitteilungshefte* 1981–1998.

never appeared in the course's title, I have included *The Handmaid's Tale* in a class on Historiographic Metafiction, some of her short stories in a class on "20th Century North American Short Stories," her poems and essays in an "Introduction to Canadian Studies" class, her lectures and essays in a course which dealt with early Canadian exploration texts and their postmodern rewritings. Atwood has also been taught in a class on "Female Utopias." And now that Professor Nischik is teaching her second class exclusively on Atwood's work — with a tremendous student response — Atwood is finally visible in the curriculum. She has been there before, however, which shows that whether teaching classes on contemporary feminist, Canadianist, or science fiction issues, it is hard to get around her.

The contexts in which Atwood has been taught in literature courses in Germany since 1981 have changed significantly due to the further establishment of both Canadian literature in general, and Atwood's work in particular, at German universities. Whereas in the beginning she was included in courses along with other authors under thematic aspects, today her status is so unchallenged that there are courses exclusively on Atwood as a feminist or a Canadian writer. Moreover, she is often simply taught as a well-established author without even mentioning her Canadian identity. More recent publications in Germany indicate that besides being taught at university level, Atwood is being taught increasingly in high schools. Selected short stories by Margaret Atwood have been edited and annotated by Reingard M. Nischik and have been published by the renowned German publishing house Reclam (Nischik 1994). Barbara Korte has published an article on how to teach Atwood's *The Handmaid's Tale* to senior high school students (Korte 1990).

As far as genre is concerned, the survey showed that Atwood's novels have received most attention in teaching, followed by her short stories which have been widely anthologized. Even her critical pieces have received more attention than her poetry. Although recent publications indicate that more attention is being paid to Atwood's poetry today, this has not yet taken effect in teaching. A surprising result which holds true for all countries I surveyed is that although Atwood's novels are taught most, many scholars think Atwood is at her best when writing poetry.

2: USA

As a first step, I contacted the Association for Canadian Studies in the US (ACSUS) for information on teaching Atwood. Although they could not provide me with the desired listing of Canadian Studies courses, in his kind reply to my inquiry, the executive director gave a foreboding statement on teaching Atwood in the US:

> A problem you may run into is that very often Atwood is not taught as a "Canadian" author, but as an accomplished author who happens to be Canadian (in fact, I would wager that many students who read Atwood are unaware that she is Canadian). Thus Atwood would appear in syllabi at schools, colleges, and universities that have never even heard of "Canadian Studies."[3]

Other responses from teachers across the US confirm that Atwood is rarely taught explicitly as a Canadian author. She is often included in American Literature courses which simply interpret "American" as "North American" (whatever that means)[4] and efface Canada. Her short stories are, for instance, extensively taught in introductory literature courses, freshman composition courses, or Women's Studies courses, yet even the anthologies which include her stories may or may not acknowledge her Canadian identity. One US scholar related that at an MLA meeting in Toronto a few years ago a Canadian stood up at an Atwood session and complained bitterly that Atwood is included on syllabi of "American" writers without further comment.

When in my questionnaire I asked scholars whether Atwood was taught as a Canadian or, rather, an international author, some respondents were irritated because surely every (renowned) writer has a dual status as both a national and an international author. We think of James Joyce as Irish as well as international, acknowledge Thomas Mann as a German and an international writer, and so forth. International seems to indicate that an author has made it beyond national canons and that his or her fame is proven and acknowledged beyond the academic circles of his or her country. The two criteria are by no means exclusive, and I am far from emphasizing the national background of authors as an essential criterion for an understanding of their writing. However, it seems to me that in the context of US-American and Canadian relations, this issue develops a slightly different dynamic. In contrast to the United States, Canada has never elevated and revered its cultural heroes within Canada and has never marketed its culture as aggressively

---

[3] I would like to thank scholars around the world who have kindly replied to my questionnaires and inquiries, making this study possible.

[4] John Gray in his book *Lost in North America: The Imaginary Canadian in the American Dream* (1994) questions the term "North American" in various ways. In Gray's opinion, it often simply disguises the meaning "US-American."

abroad. As a consequence, famous Canadians do not become *international* in the US but *American*; they become "lost in North America" (Gray 1994). Their dual status does not read Canadian/international but American=international. I would like to illustrate this point with a recent teaching experience.

In my "Introduction to Canadian Studies" class a few terms ago, I did a warm-up quiz with my students. Besides answering questions like "do moose lose their antlers?," "when did confederation occur?," etc., students were supposed to name the five Canadians on a list of ten people. The amazing thing was not that they could not spot the Canadians, but that they assumed everybody famous — like Glenn Gould or Pamela Anderson — naturally must be US-American. This incident shows that "US-American" seems to be the unmarked, the standard, whereas "Canadian" is always marked, always the deviation from standard very similar to the binary opposition of male and female. Donna Bennett and Nathalie Cooke comment on the correlation of gender and national issues in a Canadian context as follows:

> To an international audience, much of Atwood's writing — both poetry and prose — appears primarily feminist in its emphasis: but to a Canadian audience it is distinctly Canadian, even nationalist. One of the reasons that the same elements of the text signal one thing for feminists and another for Canadianists is that Canadians, like feminists, have had to construct themselves out of a larger culture in which they felt invisible. In the late 60s each group began a journey into an unknown region that lacked maps and even names for what the groups would discover. (Bennett and Cooke in Wilson et al. 1996, 33)

Many US scholars responded that they have taught a variety of Atwood's works, including her essays, but did not identify her as a Canadian. Given that Atwood explicitly deals with Canadian national and cultural identities and that a lot of her fiction wittily draws on and plays with US and Canadian national stereotypes, I find it puzzling how anyone can overlook the Canadian content. Coral Ann Howells offers the following explanation:

> Margaret Atwood is a Canadian writer whose work is so well known internationally that readers tend to forget that she is Canadian. Atwood herself never forgets this, and her writing is grounded in a strong sense of her cultural identity as a Canadian and a woman. These are not, however, limiting categories, for her writing challenges boundaries of nationality and gender in its explorations of what it means to be a human being. (Howells 1993, 5)

Although I think Howells is right that Atwood addresses universal issues which transgress the category of nation, I find it telling that apparently she cannot be recognized as a universal *and* a Canadian writer at
the same time and to the same degree that other authors can retain this
dual status. The point is not that her status becomes international, but
that it changes to being American in certain contexts.

Atwood is a case in point of what one respondent called "academic
imperialism" in the US-Canadian literary relationship. A Canadian
Ph.D. candidate who had responded to my original questionnaire for-
warded a recent American Internet dispute to me. The debate started
with the request of an American professor who was "looking for read-
able, teachable, and lovable American novels of literary merit" and who
cited Margaret Atwood's *The Handmaid's Tale* as "the most obvious
model." While she praises Atwood's elegant writing and her unmatched
"level of aesthetics," she clearly claims her as an American writer. In the
ensuing debate on the Net, Canadian scholars suggest other novels to
her but also point out that Atwood is a Canadian writer, and they give
reasons why they think her national background is important for the
understanding of her work. One scholar remarks that not reading Atwood as Canadian leaves out a fundamental aspect of her work, namely
how it satirizes US-American culture. Reading Atwood from a Canadian perspective, he claims, taught him a lot about American culture. In
response, the American professor who had originally started the debate
wrote that she designated Atwood's *The Handmaid's Tale* as an American text because "the book was mainly if not totally written while she
resided in Massachusetts; and the setting and thematics of the novel are
clearly American." She adds that in her view teaching authors by nation
is simply outdated. I find that claim dangerous in general; after all, de-
claring nationalism an obsolete category is a privilege of those who
have defined a national literature for themselves and who are internationally recognized as having a distinct literature of their own. In the
Canadian-US literary relationship nation does gain importance, as one
Canadian scholar points out in his e-mail reply. He first of all states that
while *The Handmaid's Tale* refers to American topics and was written
during one of Atwood's many stays in the US, the perspective and
textual construction remains Canadian. He goes on to say that no
CanLit professor would teach an American novel as a Canadian text
simply because the setting is Canadian. Secondly, he points out that
teaching the text as an American novel not only effaces Atwood's Canadian identity but it "renders the entire scene of Canadian literature
and literary studies invisible to American students." I traced this debate
because it once again shows that especially in the US Atwood is not

simply identified as an international author but is made into an international *American* author by overwriting her Canadian identity.

Overall, Atwood is taught enthusiastically in the US. Respondents praised her satiric take on everything around her, her wit, humor, her mix of "the traditional and skewed," her "cold eye," her political courage, and said that she was among the best contemporary writers. One scholar reported that she has been an Atwood fan for eons but that in 1979, when she wanted to write her doctoral thesis on Atwood, she was turned down because her supervisor felt Atwood lacked literary merit. Whether scholars appreciate Atwood or find her work disturbing, this certainly would be an impossible answer today as the institutionalization of Atwood's work is very well on its way.

Another indication of Atwood's establishment in teaching is the appearance of her work on high school curricula. Curiously, more than one US teacher reported that they do teach Atwood in high school but have had some difficulties with parents and school boards. One teacher said that he had to deal with opposition from school board members and parents who felt that Atwood was too "pornographic," and another wrote that several parents opposed the teaching of Atwood's work and that their children were exempted from those classes. This, of course, says as much about the US and its school system as about how Atwood is being received there. Nonetheless, Atwood is taught increasingly in high school in the US. One teacher responded that her juniors are reading nothing but Margaret Atwood this term as a model for how to study an author thoroughly. They are looking at the novels, essays, poems, and short stories without, however, looking at any Canadian issues.

Naturally, many teachers in the US are aware of and do teach Atwood in her Canadian context. Yet, as she is not often read as a Canadian author, almost all scholars responded that Atwood's fame has not encouraged the study of other Canadian authors in US academic institutions.

Responses from the US say a lot about the status of Canadian literature in the US in general, and I would like to wrap up this section with another teaching experience. An exchange student from the US who had attended both my Canadian literature classes at the University of Constance sent a book review to me after she had returned to Oregon to prove that US Americans *do* pay attention to Canadian literature. The article, a review of Alice Munro's *The Love of a Good Woman*, is introduced by the following back-handed compliment:

> Before reading Munro for the first time, it was necessary for one skeptical critic to shed a long-held prejudice. . . . The prejudice was that

"revered Canadian writer" is somehow synonymous with "boring beyond belief." . . . Canadians, even those who win the Governor General's Award or whatever other postcolonial literary prizes they hand
out up there, aren't necessarily boring. (Baker 1998)

3: United Kingdom and Other Countries

An obvious difference to the reception of Atwood's work in the US is
that in the UK she generally is identified as a Canadian author, especially when included in postcolonial class contexts. Her celebrity thus
does promote the study of other Canadian authors and *does* encourage
publishers to be more adventurous with other Canadian writers. In
England, Atwood is also very well established outside academia and
easily fills the National Theater in London when reading from her
works. An indication of Atwood's canonization is not only that she is
being taught more and more in high school, but that *The Handmaid's
Tale* has been an A-Level set text for many years and has figured on the
GCSE exams in Britain. In France, the novel is on the list of texts for
the 1999 Agrégation and CAPES competitive exams. These qualifying
exams are held nationally once a year for French students who wish to
become high-school teachers of English as a foreign language. In Ireland, *Cat's Eye* is on the Leaving Certificate English syllabus, as one of
the optional texts students can choose to study. The Leaving Certificate
in the Republic of Ireland is the second level termination examination
and results determine admission to university.

Although I did not address countries other than the US, UK, Germany, and Canada, various e-mail responses to the questionnaire from,
for instance, Sweden, Argentina, or South Africa prove Atwood's international standing. A scholar from the University of Stellenbosch, Western Cape, South Africa replied that in 1997, 1998, and 1999 Atwood's
Cat's Eye has been taught in a first-year lecture series which at peak
times was attended by as many as 500 students, *Wilderness Tips* was
used in a third-year essay writing seminar, and "Gertrude Talks Back"
from *Good Bones* was used as an unusual introduction to *Hamlet*.

4: Canada

As hinted at earlier, responses from Canada were the most controversial
and intriguing in this survey. Very few Canadian scholars praised Atwood's work but rather felt that they had to put her achievements and
success into perspective. Most of them seemed to be annoyed that Canadian literature is often identified with Atwood internationally, and
that in most countries her fame has not promoted the study of other

Canadian authors. Some academics thought that Atwood's texts are distorted outside of Canada, especially in the US, because academics there tend to focus on the Atwood work set in the US. One reason for negative responses to Atwood by Canadian scholars thus stems from the concern that Atwood's fame might eclipse other important, worthy-to-be-known Canadian authors. Yet, this does not explain the replies I received from Canadian scholars who claimed, for instance, that Atwood is grossly overrated or that she is at best a second-rate short story writer. Others said that Atwood's writing lacked depth because she had not done enough research on her earlier novels, others that she was only famous because she had been cleverly marketed and as a result, her texts were readily available. One Canadian respondent summed up replies she got from colleagues concerning Atwood's work: "'Oh, I don't like Atwood's writing.' They mean her novels; few know her poetry. I think that for some she is 'too famous,' for others she writes in a 'popular' style which doesn't interest them; for others she is 'a feminist' ..., for others she is 'boring' (i.e. mainstream)." These responses startled me, not because I am surprised that among all the enthusiastic responses there are also critical remarks about Atwood, but because all these replies came from Canada. My immediate outsider's guess was that this might reveal something about Canadian culture and the making of literary canons.

I believe the discussions about Canada's national and cultural identity over the last decades have not shown that Canadians have a weaker sense of who they are than Americans, but that the willingness to question your own national identity is a vital part of what it means to be Canadian. Much in contrast to the US, Canadians have always treated national icons with irony and self-deprecating humor. Whereas the US ritualize nationalism in their rhetoric of political speeches as well as in their treatment of national symbols and heroes, Canada ritualizes the nonreverence of national icons and the absence of a coherent national mythology. There has not been a "Canadian Dream" or a Canadian equivalent to the US-American idea of a manifest destiny (Nischik in Vahrson). Earle Birney ironically pinpointed the US/Canadian contrast in his 1947 poem "Can.Lit.": "No Whitman wanted / it's only by our lack of ghosts we're haunted." Against this background the often critical replies to Atwood's work from Canadian academics might be easier to place. Atwood is "haunting" the canon today because she has become a literary monument, and as questioning cultural icons seems to be part of the understanding of Canadian culture, Atwood is praised as well as challenged.

In an attempt to further investigate Atwood's status in Canada I sent out more questionnaires to Canadian scholars asking them what they thought was at the root of negative responses to Atwood's work. Bill New confirmed my own suppositions by replying: "Canadians are (congenitally?) suspicious of heroes; we like people with flaws ... because 'heroes' (those perfect beings) are what Americans like." New elaborates this aspect in his latest book *Borderlands: How We Talk about Canada*: "Canadian culture debunks heroes, or at least acknowledges 'heroes' to be human sized, ordinary, and therefore flawed — any claim to superstar status ... is over time viewed with suspicion and dismissed as arrogance" (New 1998, 53). This might explain why scholars seem to feel they have to take Atwood down a peg or two. Brian Fawcett describes what he calls the "let's bash Atwood" phenomenon in a reaction to the derisive comments he received for writing a positive review of Atwood's *Wilderness Tips* in 1990:

> In a way, I was responding not just to the new book, but to the outbreak of "let's bash Atwood" rancour that seems to be in the air these days. Predictably, *Wilderness Tips* has since received a surprising number of unkind reviews across the country. ... It is worth noticing that the rancour seems to be spreading beyond literary circles. This morning on the radio, I heard a recording by a Vancouver group called the Sarcastic Mannequins that suggested Atwood has a Canadian flag tattooed on her posterior, and that the Mannequins . . . wanted to commit certain indignities upon the flag or Atwood. It's a scary, bewildering phenomenon. (Fawcett 1990, 8)

Some critics apparently thought at the time that Atwood had been overexposed and that it was about time to cut her down to normal size. On the other hand, the act of the Mannequin group probably cannot only be interpreted as a "let's bash Atwood" action but as a way to handle Canadian nationalism with humor and irony by exposing and ridiculing two national symbols at once: the flag and Atwood. As New has pointed out, "irony becomes a way of disempowering whatever appears to be a larger or more dominant force. Irony, that is, is a public, seemingly self-deprecating technique of private preservation, and at the same time (though outsiders will not always recognize it) a collective technique" (New 1998, 47–48).

Another aspect which possibly explains the "bashing" of Atwood is related to the inevitable and necessary reshaping of the literary canon. It is ironic, however, that Atwood made the questioning of the canon possible as one of the first writers to promote Canadian literature, and has now become a canonized author herself whom some want to debunk. Bennett and Cooke point out that Atwood and her generation of

writers helped shape the Canadian literary canon as we know it and by
rewriting earlier texts helped to establish a Canadian literary tradition:

> But in Canadian literature a tradition, even a recently created one, is
> not to be trusted. The generation that has followed Atwood's has
> learned from hers a deep-set resistance. ... Ironically, today Atwood in
> particular, and the writers of her generation in general, are seen as
> embodying the authority that they saw as external and inauthentic to
> their experience. ... Today as a new generation seeks its own space,
> Atwood becomes a central figure from which new departures will be
> measured, not only in literary but also in popular circles. She has be-
> come a sort of icon. ... The rejection of Atwood (which tends to ap-
> pear in the book chats of critics and the parodies and lampoons of
> writers) comes at a time when Canada's national identity, won pain-
> fully and well in the late 1960s and 1970s, is endangered. The nation-
> alism of Atwood's generation seems to speak neither to the
> multiethnic reality of Canada's cities nor to the current split between
> Canada's traditional English-French solitudes. (Bennett/Cooke 1996,
> 41)

Atwood has become a cultural landmark, this time a mark for new departures. Contrary to the above statement, however, there are voices
which claim that Atwood has got a lot to say about issues of multiculturalism. Kathryn VanSpanckeren professes that Atwood's texts are very
often used in classes which examine point-of-view and subject positions: "Through assignments in guided self-discovery, creative writing
students learn from Atwood's examples to enter new viewpoints and to
grasp the inadequacy of essentializing, monocentric views and uncritical
'realism'" (VanSpanckeren in Wilson et al. 1996, 82). She goes on to
say that the study of Atwood's works enables students to "experience
how viewpoint determines meaning. The assignments can also be used
to sensitize an increasingly multicultural student population to the crucial importance of subject position" (83).

Atwood herself comments on the critical reception of *Survival: A
Thematic Guide to Canadian Literature*, which was one of the first attempts to grasp Canadian literature, and whether praised or condemned served as a departure point for the teaching of CanLit:
"'Survival was fun to attack. In fact still is; most self-respecting professors of CanLit begin their courses, I'm told, with a ritual sneer at it'"
(Atwood quoted in Nicholson 1994, 3). This shows, of course, that
praise or sneer, *Survival* is a canonical Canadian text, for any comment
on the canonical status of a work further enhances its establishment in
the canon.

Conclusion

As the survey has shown, Atwood's impact on teaching is profound as both writer and critic. Not only is her work taught in a variety of different contexts within the humanities as well as other departments, but it raises and intersects many different issues: Canadian, feminist, anthropological, and cultural studies concerns as well as postcolonialist issues. The enthusiasm for her work, as well as the criticism of it, both show that she is still a yardstick for measuring new departures. Various recent incidences give proof of Atwood's cultlike status. On the Internet, besides the numerous more or less official Margaret Atwood pages (some of which are listed in the bibliography), you can consult the "unofficial shrine" of Margaret Atwood, a homepage with scarce information on Atwood but with a photograph displaying her with a Western hat and raucous smile. This spring on the Atwood discussion list there ensued an ironic competition over the right title with which Atwood scholars should address one another. One scholar opened the discussion with "greetings fellow Atwoodites" while others preferred the exalted title "Atwoodies," or the term "Atwoodians." The title is reminiscent of ingroups such as staunch fans of *Star Trek* who address each other as "Trekkers." Apparently, Atwood is not only being canonized in the holy institutions of academia but in pop culture as well. Last but not least, I learned from the Internet that there is a music band which calls itself "Alias Grace" in honor of Margaret Atwood. We will see what else there is to come.

Works Cited

Baker, Jeff. "Oh, Canada." *The Sunday Oregonian*, 6 December 1998, E5.

Bennett, Donna. "Conflicted Vision: A Consideration of Canon and Genre in English Canadian Literature." In *Canadian Canons: Essays in Literary Value*. Ed. Robert Lecker. Toronto/Buffalo/London: University of Toronto Press, 1991: 131–49.

Bennett, Donna and Nathalie Cooke. "A Feminist by Another Name: Atwood and the Canadian Canon." In *Approaches to Teaching Atwood's* The Handmaid's Tale *and Other Works*. Ed. Sharon R. Wilson, Thomas B. Friedman, and Shannon Hengen. New York: MLA, 1996: 33–42.

Birney, Earle. "Can.Lit.: or them able leave her ever." Repr. in *An Anthology of Canadian Literature in English*. Ed. Russell Brown, Donna Bennett, and Nathalie Cooke. Toronto: Oxford University Press, rev. and abr. 1990: 296.

Christie, James. "The Takeout Window of Canadian Nationalism." *Globe & Mail*, 9 August 1997, D 3.

Davey, Frank. "Critical Response." *Critical Inquiry* (Spring 1990): 673–81.

Fawcett, Brian. "Field Notes: Me and My Gang." *Books in Canada* 20.9 (1990): 8–9.

Fee, Margery. "Canadian Literature and English Studies in the Canadian University." *Essays on Canadian Writing* 48 (1993): 20–40.

Gray, John. *Lost in North America: The Imaginary Canadian in the American Dream.* Vancouver: Talonbooks, 1994.

Henighan, Tom. *Ideas of North: A Guide to Canadian Arts & Culture.* Vancouver: Raincoast Books, 1997.

Howells, Coral Ann. "Teaching Canadian Literature Outside Canada." *The Dolphin* 27 (n.d.): 109–14.

———. *York Notes on Margaret Atwood's* The Handmaid's Tale. London: Longman York, 1993.

Hunter, Lynette. *Outsider Notes: Feminist Approaches to Nation State Ideology, Writer/Readers and Publishing.* Vancouver: Talonbooks, 1996.

Irvine, Lorna and Paula Gilbert Lewis. "Altering the Principles of Mapping: Teaching Canadian and Québec Literature Outside Canada." In *Studies on Canadian Literature: Introductory and Critical Essays.* Ed. Arnold E. Davidson. New York: MLA, 1990: 323–37.

Keith, W. J. "Approaches to Atwood: Taste, Technique, Synthesis." *Essays on Canadian Writing* 23 (Spring 1982): 88–96.

Korte, Barbara. "Margaret Atwood's Roman *The Handmaid's Tale*: Interpretationshinweise für eine Verwendung im Englischunterricht der Sekundarstufe II." *Die Neueren Sprachen* 89.3 (1990): 224–42.

Lecker, Robert. "The Canonization of Canadian Literature: An Inquiry into Value." *Critical Inquiry* (Spring 1990): 656–81.

———. "Introduction." In *Canadian Canons: Essays in Literary Value.* Ed. Robert Lecker. Toronto/Buffalo/London: University of Toronto Press, 1991: 3-16.

MacPherson, Heidi, Danielle Fuller, and Susan Billingham, ed. *CanText: The Newsletter of the BACS Literature Group* 1.1 (September 1998).

Murray, Heather. "From Canon to Curriculum." *University of Toronto Quarterly* 60.2 (Winter 1990/1): 229–43.

———. *Working in English: History, Institution, Resources.* Toronto/Buffalo/London: Toronto University Press, 1996.

New, W. H. *Borderlands: How We Talk About Canada.* Vancouver: University of British Columbia Press, 1998.

Newsletter of the Margaret Atwood Society, Spring/Summer 1998.

Nicholson, Colin. "Introduction." In *Margaret Atwood: Writing and Subjectivity: New Critical Essays*. New York: St. Martin's Press, 1994: 1–11.

Nischik, Reingard M., ed. *Margaret Atwood: Polarities: Selected Stories*. Stuttgart: Reclam, 1994.

Nischik, Reingard M. and Robert Kroetsch, ed. *Gaining Ground: European Critics on Canadian Literature*. Western Canadian Literary Documents Series VI. Edmonton: NeWest, 1985.

Timpson, Annis May and J. G. Baggini. *Canadian Studies in the UK: A Directory of Canadianists, Courses and Research*. British Association for Canadian Studies, 1995.

Vahrson, Jutta. "Es gibt keinen kanadischen Traum." Interview with Reingard M. Nischik. *Südkurier*, 27 April 1995, 18.

Wilson, Sharon R., Thomas B. Friedman, and Shannon Hengen, ed. *Approaches to Teaching Atwood's* The Handmaid's Tale *and Other Works*. New York: MLA, 1996.

Websites and Addresses

ACCUTE:
Association of Canadian College and University Teachers of English
Department of English
Laurentian University
Sudbury, Ontario
Canada P3E 2G6
e-mail: accute@mun.ca
http://www.mun.ca/accute

Association for Canadian Studies (ACS)
P.O. Box 8888 Station Centre-Ville
Montréal, Québec
Canada H3C 3P8
e-mail: acs-aec@uqam.ca

Association for Canadian Studies in the U.S. (ACSUS)
David Biette, Executive Director
Suite 920, 1317 F Street NW, Washington DC 20004–1105 USA
http://canada-acsus.plattsburgh.edu

British Association for Canadian Studies (BACS)
Jodie Robson, Administrative Secretary
21 George Square, Edinburgh EH8 9LD Scotland
e-mail: jodie.robson@ed.ac.uk

Gesellschaft für Kanada-Studien in deutschsprachigen Ländern
http://staff-www.uni-marburg.de/~ahorn/

The Margaret Atwood Society
http://www.cariboo.bc.ca/atwood/
Treasurer: Mary Kirtz
Department of English
University of Akron
Akron, Ohio 44325–1906
USA

Atwood Discussion Group
atwood-l@cariboo.bc.ca
http://www.cariboo.bc.ca/atwood/internet.htm

International Council for Canadian Studies
http://www.iccs-ciec.ca/

http://www.culturenet.ucalgary.ca/
http://www.moorhead.msus.edu/~chenault/atwood.htm
http://www.nwpassages.com/nwplink.htm
http://www.web.net/owtoad/

Photographs of Margaret Atwood

Margaret Atwood at age thirteen, 1953, Niagara Falls, Ontario. (Courtesy of Margaret Atwood.)

Margaret Atwood and her daughter Jess in 1980.
(Photograph by Thomas Victor, courtesy of Harriet Spurlin.)

Margaret Atwood and Graeme Gibson around 1988.
(Photograph by Brian Willer, courtesy of Maclean's.)

Margaret Atwood and Michael Ondaatje, mid 1980s.
(Courtesy of Harbourfront Reading Series.)

Margaret Atwood with (from left to right) Pierre Berton, Jack McClelland, Leonard Cohen, and W. O. Mitchell, mid to late 1980s. (Photograph by Brian Willer, courtesy of Maclean's.)

Margaret Atwood being interviewed by Susanne Becker
in Atwood's backyard in Toronto in October 1989.
(Photograph by Christoph Klaucke.)

THE JOE CLARK REPORT CARD: IMAGE UP, POLITICAL CLOUT DOWN
SATURDAY NIGHT
MIDWIFE CONTROVERSY • WEST BANK DIARY • BANFF BELOW STAIRS
JULY 1989
GREAT SUMMER READING
MARGARET ATWOOD
DEATH BY LANDSCAPE
A new, suspenseful tale you won't want to read around the campfire
PLUS
Wake up, Canada, the old nationalism is dead: a timely provocation for a revived and redefined Canada Day by Andrew Coyne • The Ottawa boy behind Spy, New York's bitchiest magazine • M. T. Kelly's canoe trip through the eye of time • John Fraser livens up the Confederation story with an unexpected coup d'état • And a challenging holiday puzzle
PRICE: $2.95

Atwood on the cover of Saturday Night *magazine, 1989.*
Photo © Deb Samuel, courtesy of Deb Samuel
and Saturday Night.

Margaret Atwood at Grainau, Germany, February 1992.
(Photograph by Peter O. Stummer.)

Margaret Atwood and Reingard M. Nischik at Grainau,
February 1992. (Photographer unknown.)

Margaret Atwood and Arnulf Conradi in Germany, 1995.
(Photographer unknown.)

Margaret Atwood around 1996.
(Photograph by Andrew MacNaughton.)

Margaret Atwood at the Eden Mills Writers' Festival,
September 1998. (Photographs © Danielle Schaub.)

II. Works

On the Border: Margaret Atwood's Novels

Alice M. Palumbo (University of Toronto)

IN THE POETRY COLLECTION *The Journals of Susanna Moodie*, first published in 1970, Margaret Atwood develops the idea of the double voice. Susanna Moodie, in the poem "The Double Voice," acknowledges that "two voices / took turns using my eyes" (42). These voices act in antithesis to each other, and present a synthesized point of view only after death. As Atwood writes in the "Afterword" to the collection, Moodie is "divided down the middle" (62), an example of the "violent duality" the Canadian landscape provokes in its inhabitants.

In her novels, Atwood has made constant use of the double voice, depicting characters at war with themselves and their environments. Through intertextual allusions, alterations in narrative point of view, and the use of the unconscious, Atwood shows the way in which the self is constructed from contradictory impulses, some more societally acceptable than others. The emphasis in each of her novels, as Linda Hutcheon has argued, is the movement from product to process, or the realization of her protagonists that they are not merely objects to be acted upon, but dynamic subjects (17). Her use of intertexts derived from, for example, the Gothic novel and fairy tales, places her novels on a continuum while critiquing the tradition; *Lady Oracle*, which parodies the Gothic and exists as a Gothic novel in its own right, is a good example of this.

Thematically, Atwood's novels share linked concerns. *The Edible Woman* (1969), *Surfacing* (1972), and *Lady Oracle* (1976) all examine, to some degree, consumption and consumer culture. *Life Before Man* (1979), *Bodily Harm* (1981), and *The Handmaid's Tale* (1985) analyze power relationships, both personal and societal. Finally, *Cat's Eye* (1988), *The Robber Bride* (1993), and *Alias Grace* (1996) focus on the relations between the present, the past, and the functions of memory. In all of these works Atwood examines boundaries, the ease with which they can be crossed, blurred, or eliminated, and the anxiety this produces in her protagonists.

The boundary between commodity and commodifier is deconstructed by Atwood in her first three novels. In the course of *The Edible*

Woman, Marian MacAlpin, a middle-level worker in a consumer surveys company in Toronto, finds herself gradually moving from being a
consumer to feeling consumed. Marian is just the most obvious case,
though, in a world where the lines between consumer and consumed
have blurred. Peter, Marian's fiancé, is a well-turned-out lawyer on the
rise who, Marian realizes, may be merely the sum of the lifestyle tips he
gathers from men's magazines.

Atwood problematizes the idea of authenticity and unitary identity
in the novel through Marian's dilemma. In attempting to avoid being a
consumer, Marian instead falls into a ritualistic form of progressive anorexia which makes her unable to consume anything. Marian's increasing
identification with the object consumed (her over-identification as a
victim) leads to her becoming a victim of her own body. She finds that
her attempt to remove herself from a consumer/consumed dyad is un-
tenable, as Atwood shows consumerism as permeating every aspect of
life. Ainsley, Marian's roommate, becomes pregnant as a result of media
prompting:

> "But why do you want a baby, Ainsley? What are you going to *do*
> with it?"
> She gave me a disgusted look. "Every woman should have at least
> one baby." She sounded like a voice on the radio saying that every
> woman should have at least one electric hair-dryer. (40–41)

The discourse of consumption affects even academe, as demonstrated
by Duncan, the graduate student with whom Marian becomes involved. Graduate study in English is merely the act of devouring one
text and regurgitating it in another form. The narrative enacts this itself, by devouring a number of intertexts (fairy tales, Gothic romance,
children's fiction) to produce the text itself. By literalizing her feelings
of consumption in the act of baking the "edible woman" of the title,
Marian hopes to fend off her metaphorical consumption by Peter, and
resolve her own ambivalence to marriage. However, Atwood shows
that even this symbol is ambiguous. While Peter flees the cake (and presumably his engagement to Marian), Duncan cheerfully eats it, trou-
bling Marian's simple resolution to her problems:

> "But the real truth is that it wasn't Peter at all. It was me. I was
> trying to destroy you."
> I gave a nervous laugh. "Don't say that."
> "Okay," he said, "ever eager to please. Maybe Peter was trying to
> destroy me, or maybe I was trying to destroy him, or we were both
> trying to destroy each other, how's that? What does it matter, you're
> back to so-called reality, you're a consumer." (281)

In contrast to the devouring narrative of *The Edible Woman*, *Surfacing* presents an archeology of both a time and a person on the point of serious rupture. Early 1970s anglophone Canada and its relationships with the United States and francophone Canada are presented in parallel to the story of the nameless narrator, a woman on the verge of complete breakdown due to an unvoiced, but real, grief. The manners in which this novel has been analyzed by critics (as ghost story, family story, anatomy of a breakdown) all highlight the layering of histories and cultures in the novel. In *Surfacing*, the narrator drives north from Toronto with her partner and another couple to the isolated lake in Quebec where she was brought up by stubbornly rationalist, yet idealistically innocent, parents. The narrator's father has disappeared, which prompts her first visit north in nine years. During the trip, the narrator is discomfited by the way in which everything has changed, yet not changed, as time seems to her to have congealed; meanwhile, the reader is discomfited by the narrator's mysterious evasions and absences. The narrator simultaneously affirms her doubled existence, "now we're on my home ground, foreign territory" (11), and denies it, describing a childhood split between the city and the wilderness, and an affectless present. The truth of the narrator's memories is hidden beneath feverish polarities. Her more ambiguously happy childhood is hidden behind the preternaturally idyllic one she describes, while a failed affair and an abortion lie beneath her disturbingly violent descriptions of marriage and childbirth. An unvoiced, but lurking, anxiety is the source of the narrator's need to order things in neat binaries; for her, leeches are "good" or "bad," humans are bad, animals good, and the mind and the body are two separate things. The narrator's breakdown comes in her attempt to throw off all influences of the "human" and "American," and become "natural"; since this flight from the human depends on there being rigid separations between the natural and human (giving the human increased importance even in the process of evading it), it is doomed to failure. The authentic, as Atwood shows, is found in a synthesis of the two, and not at either pole exclusively. The narrator's realization that the victim/victor binary must be transcended is the key to her integrating all aspects of her fragmented history:

> This above all, to refuse to be a victim. Unless I can do that I can do nothing. I have to recant, give up the old belief that I am powerless and because of it nothing I can do will ever hurt anyone. A lie which was always more disastrous than the truth would have been. (191)

As the narrator acts out, and resolves, her own emotional rupture, the narrative depicts Quebec and Canada shifting into a more clearly self-defined identity. Behind the characters' apocalyptic rhetoric describing the landscape and Canadian culture is a very real sense of Canada's growing unease with American hegemony, and a corresponding sense of nationalism that itself is working away from victim/victor games.

Lady Oracle takes the notion of existence on borders to a near-parodic extreme. The novel is narrated from a limbo between life in Toronto and "death" in Italy by Joan Foster, a self-confessed "escape artist" on the run from her serial identities (as former fat girl in suburban Toronto, author of supermarket costume Gothic romances, and renowned pop poet) and her blackmailer. *Lady Oracle* revisits the comedy of *The Edible Woman*; like the earlier novel, it is an "anti-comedy," to use Atwood's description, where there is no marriage and no real re-ordering of society at the close of the narrative (Ingersoll, 12). Aspects of *Surfacing* are also held up for parody. While the landscape of the north is depicted as sublime in the earlier novel, as a place where "you can see only a small part of it, the part you're in" (*Surfacing*, 31), the whole of *Lady Oracle* itself is narrated from a state Edmund Burke considered the source of the sublime experience: the contemplation of death itself (Heiland, 116). But the death is a sham, a feigned drowning in a prosaically polluted Lake Ontario. The novel is full of such ironic deflatings, the primary narrative deconstructing the assumptions of the Gothic romances Joan writes for a living while simultaneously constructing a new model of female Gothic terror based on more mundane, contemporary dangers.

Lady Oracle unfolds as a series of doubled, contradictory narratives, first as confession beyond the grave of a living woman, a purveyor of "romance" primarily concerned with the commodities of her fictional lovers. The novel presents a social archeology of life in suburban North America in the 1950s, narrated by a woman obsessed with cultural minutiae. Joan Foster, compared to Atwood's earlier protagonists, is relatively adept at negotiating media-driven consumer culture, illustrated by Atwood's use of a series of intertextual allusions, most notably 1940s women's films, 1960s art films, Victorian sensation fiction, and mass-market Gothic romance. Joan turns her childhood interest in reading the social meanings of furniture, housing, and film (itself inculcated by her social-climbing mother) into the key of her success as a pseudonymous Gothic romance writer. Part of the romantic fantasy she sells comes, she knows, from the material wealth surrounding her heroines, her "goddess[es] of quick money" (*Lady Oracle*, 132). Joan's Gothics mirror her own concerns, while the intertextual references mirror Joan's narrative. The Gothics increasingly relate her fear of disclosure and rejection, while her constant use of cinematic references (most notably to the films of Fellini) and discourse illustrates the detached manner in which she views her life. In the Gothics she speaks through the heroines (and rejected wives), while in her Fellini-fuelled fantasies she, significantly, speaks as the director. Her cinematic references also refract outward, offering unspoken alternatives for interpreting her life; her musings over why her mother named her after Joan Crawford prompt reader comparisons to *Mildred Pierce*, and awaken her fear of understanding her mother's rage at her entrapment in suburban Toronto with a silent husband and a hostile daughter.[1]

The line separating Joan's conscious self from her own rage and frustration is elided once she starts using automatic writing (a spiritualist aid to advice and prophecy) to write poetry. The themes and imagery of the poetry disturb her as something alien:

> The words I collected in this way became increasingly bizarre and even threatening: "iron," "throat," "knife," "heart." At first the sentences centered around the same figure, the same woman. After a while I could almost see her: she lived under the earth somewhere, or inside something, a cave or a huge building . . . She was enormously powerful, almost like a goddess, but it was an unhappy power. This woman puzzled me. She wasn't like anyone I'd ever imagined, and certainly she had nothing to do with me. I wasn't like that, I was happy. Happy and inept. (224)

Joan's "death" forces her to confront her many "lives," and accept the possibility of synthesis.

Symbolically, she visualizes her various selves (Joan Foster, "Lady Oracle" the famous poet, Louisa K. Delacourt the Gothic novelist, and the "Fat Lady," the embodiment of her fat past) as a group of women in the center of a maze, the plot of the Gothic she is writing blurring into her own life. The inset Gothic narrative integrates Joan's multiple selves, while the framing narrative leaves the question open. "I keep

---

[1] As Joan notes early on in *Lady Oracle*, "my mother named me after Joan Crawford . . . Joan Crawford worked hard, she had willpower, she built herself up from nothing, according to my mother" (38). This echoes the plotline of Crawford's 1945 film *Mildred Pierce*, about a woman who built herself up from nothing to become a successful entrepreneur. Crawford's character in *Mildred Pierce*, interestingly, has an ungrateful daughter for whom she has sacrificed everything. It is striking that Joan Foster, the juvenile film buff, stresses her childhood enjoyment of Susan Hayward films but barely mentions this, or any, Joan Crawford film. Joan's mother's liking for Joan Crawford films provides a hint of her (possible) interpretation of her life with her daughter.

thinking I should learn some lesson from all of this," Joan confesses, while planning to exchange one form of fantasy writing for another:

> I won't write any more Costume Gothics, though; I think they were bad for me. But maybe I'll try some science fiction. The future doesn't appeal to me as much as the past, but I'm sure it's better for you. (*Lady Oracle*, 345)

Atwood here shows the possibility of the unconscious (represented by Joan's writing, both Gothic and poetic) synthesizing identity more clearly than the conscious.

A large part of Atwood's construction of the double voice is the implied contrast, in her work, between the literary effects and devices used in the narratives, and received ideas on the inherent dullness of Canada. A certain amount of the comedy in *The Edible Woman* and *Lady Oracle* comes from the disjunction between the use of the Gothic and its placement in contemporary Toronto, while the unease in *Surfacing* comes from the unsettling realization that Canada is just as vulnerable to haunting and violence as any other place. The contrast between a fossilized, conservative English Ontario and the events taking place in it is increasingly important in Atwood's novels.

The works that follow exhibit a shift in emphasis from the first three. Where the primary problem there was to synthesize warring identities, *Life Before Man*, *Bodily Harm*, and *The Handmaid's Tale* concern themselves with the necessity for the individual to reject individual retreats from the external world and to become involved in resistance to power. This entails a rejection of the idea of powerlessness, as stated back in *Surfacing*: the protagonists of Atwood's later works all have to work hard to renounce the idea of the sheltered position of powerlessness, whether as women, or Canadians. Atwood expands on her earlier themes of the collapse between the social and personal, depicting worlds in which the boundary between the two has been completely erased. This is seen, for example, in *Life Before Man*, as the depiction of Nate's and Elizabeth's impending divorce is compared to the threat of national separation in Canada. The actual divorce, like the actual referendum on sovereignty, falls beyond the span of the narrative.

Life Before Man differs from Atwood's previous novels in its narrative structure; the novel is presented through the viewpoints of three characters. Toronto's natural history museum, the Royal Ontario Museum, serves as a focal point for the three protagonists, two of whom, Elizabeth and Lesje, are employed there. Nate, the third protagonist, is married to Elizabeth at the start of the novel and becomes involved with Lesje as the novel progresses. Displacement and absence are the organizing motifs of the novel. Events in the outside world are shown in microcosm, or indirectly; the election of the Parti Quebecois as the government of Quebec in 1976 is shown obliquely, on television screens in bars Nate haunts, and the impending separation of Quebec and Canada is related to Nate's and Elizabeth's disintegrating marriage. Similarly, the Holocaust and Canadian multiculturalism are particularized in the family history of Lesje, who is a second generation Canadian of eastern European and Jewish descent. Canada, and the lives of the protagonists, are seen at points of rupture; Atwood's novel works as a problem novel (as Coral Ann Howells has noted, comparing it to George Eliot's *Middlemarch*), but one in which larger societal changes and eruptions are tracked in small, indirect ways (87). The small-scale domestic drama of *Life Before Man*, often considered overwhelmingly depressing and dreary by critics, works as a microcosm of global change and disruption. All three characters find they must confront the "life before man" by ceasing to hide in elaborate fantasy worlds (as Nate and Lesje do) or in obsessive blaming of the past (as Elizabeth does). The double voice can be seen in the narrative itself, as Atwood contrasts the pessimism of the plot with the optimism of the act of writing it.

"We tell ourselves stories in order to live," Joan Didion wrote in the essay "The White Album" (11), and Atwood works with this idea of the recuperative power of storytelling in *Bodily Harm* and *The Handmaid's Tale*. Rennie Wilford, the protagonist of *Bodily Harm*, resembles Didion's journalist persona in "The White Album," a reporter who has begun "to doubt the premises of all the stories [she] ever told [herself]" (11). Offred, the eponymous narrator of *The Handmaid's Tale*, tells and retells her own story in order to live in the oppressive future world of Gilead, a theocratic dystopia set in a future United States. Atwood has described *Bodily Harm* as an "anti-thriller"; the intertextual use of murder mysteries, spy thrillers, and children's detective board games highlights the primary narrative of the novel, which concerns the gradual awakening to political awareness of a detached "lifestyles" journalist, appropriately described by Sharon Rose Wilson as a "life-tourist" (136).

> Most of the people she knew thought Rennie was way out ahead of it, but she saw herself as off to the side. She preferred it there. (26)

After a series of events in Toronto that illustrate varieties of "bodily harm," namely a bout with breast cancer and a narrowly-averted assault in her home, Rennie goes on a working vacation in the Caribbean in order to write a travel piece on less-visited islands and take stock of her

life. Rennie's series of close calls with death has made her doubt her
ability to write successfully about surfaces, the principal theme of her
journalism (and thus the basis of her entire career). Rennie's loss of
faith in what she regards as her primary ability leads her to mistake the
external signs on the islands of St. Antoine and Ste. Agathe. In her
continual misreading of the landscape and objects on the islands, Rennie illustrates Atwood's concern with the duplicity of surfaces. As
Eleanora Rao has noted, Rennie mistakes many things on the islands.
She thinks the gallows in Fort Industry is a child's playhouse, and that
the police who solicit in the airport for the policemen's ball are soldiers
(103–4). Later, however, the police do indeed become soldiers; in a
related scene of mistaken meaning, Rennie is surprised at the drug store
on St. Antoine:

> A couple of doors down there's a drugstore, also new-looking, and
> she goes into it and asks for some suntan lotion.
> "We have Quaaludes," the man says as she's paying for the lotion.
> "Pardon?" says Rennie. . . .
> Well, it's a drugstore, Rennie thinks. It sells drugs. Why be sur-
> prised? (69)

Rennie's inability to read signs and events correctly on the islands leads
her into what she loathes, "massive involvement" (34). By taking
things at face value, she manages to transport illegal weapons into the
hands of a political candidate; by insisting on "reading" the events
around her as mere kitsch, or pulp novel plotlines (see Irvine in this
volume), she places herself in real danger by refusing to acknowledge
the truth in what she thinks of as cultural clichés. By focusing on the
banality of the surfaces, as she does by regarding the near-assault on her
in Toronto as a solution in a game of Clue ("Miss Wilford, in the bedroom, with a rope," 14), she misses the network of intrigues, conspira-
cies, and threats on St. Antoine, a newly-independent former colony of
Britain having its first elections. Arrested for "suspicion," she is thrown
into Fort Industry (transformed from heritage site to prison), another
demonstration of Atwood's literalization of literary clichés as Gothic
imprisonment becomes real. Rennie and her fellow Canadian prisoner
Lora trade stories, and after Lora's savage beating by prison guards,
Rennie works up the courage to touch her battered body, thereby con-
cretizing her realization that "she is not exempt" (301). She resolves to
report what she has seen on the islands (an attempted coup against the
government, and its violent repression), recuperating with her report-
age the lives of those like Dr. Minnow, an assassinated candidate, and
Lora, as well as the actuality of political violence. The ending is am-

biguous, however, as its relation in future tense makes it unclear whether Rennie is in fact released from prison.

The Handmaid's Tale, Atwood's best-known novel, continues this examination of violence, and the importance of bearing witness. "I would like to believe this is a story I'm telling," Offred the narrator says, echoing Didion's words on the importance of storytelling as a survival tool, "I need to believe it. I must believe it" (49).

> If it's a story I'm telling, then I have control over the ending. Then there will be an ending, to the story, and real life will come after it. (49)

Offred's tale, in which she constructs, by necessity, a listener, takes place in the Republic of Gilead, the government devised by fundamentalist Christians at some unspecified date in the future in the United States. In a continuation of the theme first seen in *Life Before Man* of the gradual blurring of the boundary between the personal and the social, the Republic of Gilead is shown to have completely conflated the two. Women's reproductive capacity is the basis of the state in Gilead; society is constructed to maximize the possibility of reproduction, while making it obvious that women are merely extensions of their reproductive organs. All of society is run on the lines of the patriarchal family, and Offred's name is derived from the man to whom she belongs. "Handmaids" are concubines, "two-legged wombs" (146); as Offred says of her body, "I don't want to look at something that determines me so completely" (73). The novel refers back to narratives of Puritan New England in its construction of a theocracy where all inhabitants are subsumed into their appointed roles. Marked as much by her red dress as a handmaid as Nathaniel Hawthorne's Hester Prynne is by her red "A" as an adulteress, Offred strives in her narrative for the multiplicity that Gilead denies her in body. Offred's voice is doubled in her continual re-telling and re-visioning of the past; she often tells several versions of the same story, and the "Historical Notes" section at the close of the novel makes it clear that Offred's voice is itself a construction, and not a simple unitary confession. Again, Atwood problematizes the happy ending, as Offred's ultimate fate after producing the evidence of her story is left unclear; as in *Life Before Man*, the act of storytelling itself is regarded as positive, although the contents of the story are not.

The examination of macro power relations in *Bodily Harm* and *The Handmaid's Tale* shifts, in *Cat's Eye*, *The Robber Bride*, and *Alias Grace*, into an analysis of power in women's relationships, and the conflict between the conscious and unconscious, and memory and the present. *Cat's Eye*, written in the form of a Bildungsroman, depicts the story of Elaine Risley, a noted artist returning to her hometown of Toronto after years away in Vancouver. While in Toronto, Elaine is the subject of a retrospective show, and finds herself dealing with the painful memories of her childhood in suburban Toronto. Atwood contrasts Elaine's detached, ironic narrative with her paintings, which articulate all that Elaine cannot bring herself to utter. Elaine's dreams, as well as her paintings, recuperate her past, and present her anger at her treatment by her friends as a child. The pre-adolescent psychodrama, in which Elaine is progressively tormented and emotionally abused by her three best friends (and nearly killed as a result of a prank one of them, Cordelia, pulls), is played out in a precisely depicted Canadian suburb in the 1940s; the horrible events are grounded by their placement in mundane life. The differences in the girls' socio-economic backgrounds contribute to their ferocity in legislating acceptable feminine behavior. Elaine and Cordelia are marked out by the other girls for their different families, and in the course of the novel they exchange positions of power, each acting as the abject twin of the other. Atwood utilizes the discourse of science, here theoretical physics, to present the properties and actions of memory (as series of transparencies, as series of strings, as dimensions that can leak into each other), and how it influences the present. Elaine's own memories are finally integrated, and recuperated, in a series of events that accentuate the double voice of the narrative; first her paintings tell her story, then she speaks to exorcise Cordelia (and by implication her childhood guilt).

The Robber Bride can be described as one long act of exorcism, as Tony, Charis, and Roz, the three protagonists, strive to rid themselves of the influence of Zenia, the "robber bride" of the title. In this novel, Atwood uses intertextual allusions and genres as organizing motifs for each character: Tony sees her life, and her interactions with Zenia, using the rhetoric of history, while Charis sees her own relationship with Zenia through New Age prophecy, and Roz through the language of mystery novels and fairy tales. Zenia wreaks havoc with the lives of each of the women after insinuating herself as their missing, all-understanding best friend. In assessing the damage, each of the women uses various narrative strategies to understand what happened, as exemplified in Roz's discussions with her therapist:

> Together the two of them labour over Roz's life as if it's a jigsaw puzzle, a mystery story with a solution at the end. They arrange and rearrange the pieces, trying to get them to come out better. They are hopeful: if Roz can figure out what story she's in, then they will be

able to spot the erroneous turns she took, they can retrace her steps, they can change the ending. (382–83)

Atwood utilizes almost incessant duplication in *The Robber Bride*. The novel is cast as both Gothic novel and fairy tale, each of the women has a hidden twin (Tony has a "secret identity" of her unborn twin; Roz has two names, each reflecting half of her ethnic and religious background; and Charis is doubled with Karen, her birth name and repository of the memories of her childhood sexual abuse), and each of the women is paired with Zenia. Roz even has twin daughters. The stories of each woman's encounter with Zenia resemble each other, as Zenia convinces them that they are both unique and not alone. Zenia is a confidence trickster, having faked her own death (and thus is a "ghost" in her return to Toronto on the eve of the Gulf War), lured the husbands or boyfriends of the three women away, and relieved them of various sums of money. In fact, Zenia is one sustained fiction, and Atwood indicates that what is more important than the facts of her life is the impact she has on others. As the lost twin of Tony, Charis, and Roz, Zenia enacts the return of the repressed, and is the repository of their submerged aggression and anger. Coming to terms with Zenia means accepting their own potential for hostility, anger, and rage, and integrating it into themselves. Cut yourself off from these conventionally nonfeminine emotions, and they will return to you in distorted form; Atwood uses the rhetoric of the Gothic in describing Zenia as a ghost, a vampire, or a patched-together monster. The story of Zenia, recounted once more after her death at the close of the novel, may have a moral, or not, as Tony reflects:

> Still, there was supposed to be a message. *Let that be a lesson to you*, adults used to say to children, and historians to their readers. But do the stories of history really teach anything at all? In a general sense, thinks Tony, possibly not. (462)

History is shown in *The Robber Bride* to be both "patched together from worthless leftovers" and "flags, hoisted with a certain jaunty insolence . . . glimpsed here and there through the trees . . . on the long march into chaos" (462).

The psychic damage caused by the wholesale repression of ranges of emotion is explored again in *Alias Grace*. While *The Robber Bride* played out this theme with the interactions of the four major characters, *Alias Grace* follows this conflict into the individual psyche. The historical base of the narrative is the nineteenth-century murder mystery surrounding Grace Marks, an Irishwoman accused of murdering her employer, Thomas Kinnear, and his housekeeper, Nancy Montgomery, in a village north of Toronto in 1843. Sixteen years later, a group of social reformers in Kingston (the site of the provincial prison) engage an American alienist, Simon Jordan, to examine Grace and determine her guilt or innocence. Grace has claimed to have no memory of the murders, and the testimony of her trial lawyer and the warden of the provincial insane asylum in Toronto is so contradictory that only a doctor, it is felt, can get to the bottom of the mystery. Grace, like Zenia, is the vehicle for whatever others want to see in her. At one point she enumerates the opinions of her as published in the provincial newspapers:

> I think of all the things that have been written about me — that I am an inhuman female demon, that I am an innocent victim of a blackguard forced against my will and in danger of my own life, that I was too ignorant to know how to act and that to hang me would be judicial murder, that I am fond of animals . . . that I am a good girl with a pliable nature and no harm is told of me, that I am cunning and devious, that I am soft in the head and little better than an idiot. (23)

The prison governor's daughters think of her in terms of romantic literary heroines, and Grace tends to use the language and discourse of Romantic narratives (Sir Walter Scott in particular) when thinking to herself. The figure of Grace Marks herself is, in a way, "alias" Grace, since all who see her project their own needs, and narratives, upon her. Simon Jordan grows to think of himself as her "rescuer" from prison, and of Grace herself as the object of all his desires. Provincial asylum visitor Susanna Moodie writes of Grace in metaphors right out of Charles Dickens's *Oliver Twist*, much to the disgust of the asylum warden, who views Grace as an object lesson in human evil. Finding the authentic Grace is difficult, if not impossible; the mesmerism session designed by Grace's clerical supporters in order to divine the truth of the murders of Kinnear and Montgomery brings out the voice of Mary Whitney, Grace's fellow servant in her first posting in Toronto. Mary Whitney herself may or may not exist; Atwood presents evidence to prove both that Mary was real, and died of a botched abortion, and that Mary is the projection of all of Grace's own feelings of rage and hostility. The murders themselves are shown to have some degree of ambiguity about them. Grace was tried for only one, the murder of Kinnear, as an accessory, and as such was sentenced to death (her fellow accused James McDermot was found guilty and hanged). She was never, therefore, tried for the murder of Nancy Montgomery, the murder which she may or may not have actually committed. Grace is obviously haunted by something, whether repressed memories or guilt, and Atwood leaves this, and Grace's ultimate fate, open. The conclusion to

Alias Grace recalls the final paragraphs of Charlotte Brontë's *Villette* in its ambiguousness regarding Grace's future, while it recapitulates Atwood's concern with the acceptance of one's potential for aggression and rage.

"Don't ever / ask for the true story," Atwood warned in the title poem to the 1981 collection *True Stories*. In her novels she reminds us that it is nearly impossible to expect one single "true story" to emerge from the wealth of alternatives: changes in perspective and context alter interpretations of facts and narratives. The novels depict society, and characters, in a state of flux, or on the cusp of change. Offred refers to herself and her friends in her former life as those who "lived in the gaps between the stories" (67). The Reverend Verringer, in *Alias Grace*, explains that the difficulty in interpreting Grace's behavior under hypnosis may be the result of being between times:

> "Two hundred years ago, they would not have been at a loss . . . It would have been a clear case of possession. Mary Whitney would have been found to have been inhabiting the body of Grace Marks, and thus to be responsible for inciting the crime, and for helping to strangle Nancy Montgomery. An exorcism would have been in order."
> (405)

The continual process Atwood characters are involved with in developing viable senses of identity is shown in the manner in which they negotiate these thresholds in time. The "violent duality" Atwood wrote of in *The Journals of Susanna Moodie* is an active strategy for engaging with a contingent world. The double voice in the novels vividly shows this, and the dangers inherent in suppressing parts of the self. "I live / on all the edges there are," the early poem "Evening Trainstation, Before Departure" ends (*Circle Game*, 16), and this state, analogous to that of Canada itself as one long border culture, is depicted in Atwood's novels. From Marian MacAlpin's perception of the permeability of the boundary between eater and eaten, to Grace Marks's embodiment of the fragility of the line between the self and others, Atwood has shown characters learning to negotiate "all the edges there are."

Works Cited

Atwood, Margaret. *Alias Grace.* Toronto: McClelland & Stewart, 1996.

———. *Bodily Harm.* Toronto: McClelland & Stewart, 1981.

———. *Cat's Eye.* Toronto: McClelland & Stewart, 1988.

———. *The Circle Game.* Toronto: Anansi, 1966.

———. *The Edible Woman.* Toronto: McClelland & Stewart, 1972.

———. *The Handmaid's Tale.* Toronto: McClelland & Stewart, 1985.

———. *The Journals of Susanna Moodie.* Toronto: Oxford University Press, 1970.

———. *Lady Oracle.* Toronto: McClelland & Stewart/Seal, 1977.

———. *Life Before Man.* Toronto: McClelland & Stewart, 1979.

———. *The Robber Bride.* London: Bloomsbury, 1993.

———. *Surfacing.* Toronto: McClelland & Stewart, 1972.

———. *True Stories.* Toronto: Oxford University Press, 1981.

Bouson, J. Brooks. *Brutal Choreographies: Oppositional Strategies and Narrative Design in the Novels of Margaret Atwood.* Amherst: University of Massachusetts Press, 1993.

Didion, Joan. *The White Album.* New York: Farrar, Strauss, Giroux-Noonday, 1990.

Heiland, Donna. "Postmodern Gothic: *Lady Oracle* and its Eighteenth-Century Antecedents." *Recherches Sémiotiques/Semiotic Inquiry* 12.1/2 (1992): 115–36.

Howells, Coral Ann. *Margaret Atwood.* London: Macmillan, 1996.

Hutcheon, Linda. "From Poetic to Narrative Structures: The Novels of Margaret Atwood." In *Margaret Atwood: Language, Text and System.* Ed. Sherrill E. Grace and Lorraine Weir. Vancouver: University of British Columbia Press, 1983: 17–32.

Ingersoll, Earl G., ed. *Margaret Atwood: Conversations.* Willowdale, Ontario: Firefly, 1990.

Rao, Eleonora. *Strategies for Identity: The Fiction of Margaret Atwood.* New York: Lang, 1993.

Wilson, Sharon Rose. "Turning Life into Popular Art: *Bodily Harm*'s Life-Tourist." *Studies in Canadian Literature* 10.1/2 (1985): 136–45.

Margaret Atwood's Short Fiction

Charlotte Sturgess (University of Strasbourg)

THREADING THROUGH ALL OF Margaret Atwood's short fictions are the themes and concerns which are present in different shapes in her longer works, and which have now come to be recognized as the distinctive Atwood signature. She has published six collections of short fiction to date; three are collections of short stories, and three comprise fiction and prose poetry. (The last of these "hybrid" volumes consists almost entirely of pieces already published in the other two.)

Therefore, although critics have concentrated principally on the power structures, the play of subjectivities, and the nationalist ethos underpinning Atwood's novels, these preoccupations are also present in her short fiction. The object of this study will be to examine the development of those themes and issues which characterize all of Atwood's work, within the particular limits of her stories and prose poems.

From *Surfacing* and *Survival* onwards, Atwood has constantly drawn attention to Canada's status as a victim of American domination, just as she has repeatedly examined power relations between men and women, and women's marginalization in culture and society. This, however, is not a defeatist stance on her part, but a concern with "the pointlessness of splitting the world into discriminatory categories and opposites" (Rao, 8). Yet her artistic vision and committed political position lead her to inscribe those oppositions into her work, just as they seek to revise, modify, and transform them in the name of other possibilities. The early stories in the collection *Dancing Girls* present female characters who, whatever their social and professional status, do not manage to escape problems of identity. The conflict between the self and representation is, in fact, even more radical for such characters in search of independence, and often the only solution in the end seems to be one of radical alienation. As the narrator of "A Travel Piece" states of the main character: "Her job was to be pleased, and she did this well . . . was good at asking interested, polite questions and coping with minor emergencies" (*DG*, 140). Similarly, the female character in "Polarities" is "a small model of . . . efficiency," unlike the male character/focalizer "whose mind shambled from one thing to another"

(38). This story epitomizes Atwood's rendering of post-sixties consciousness and the deepening divide between the sexes as women's increasing emancipation brought a fresh set of conflicts to the fore, and a
constant challenging of former roles. The very problem of roles and
self-definition is taken up in the title: "Polarities" does not buy into the
old myth of complementarity, of man and woman finding completion
in each other's image, but is a critique of that dream. For "polarity"
cannot but bring to mind cold, isolated Arctic outposts on the margins
of white, urban civilization. (This is significant since the action is concerned with urban space, which paradoxically is implicitly qualified as
no-man's land.) Furthermore, "polarities" imply an extreme and re-
lentless positionality, resulting in its own form of emotional isolation
and marginalization. There is a "sense of the pervasiveness of regressive
narcissism in the cultural situations that [Atwood's] texts mirror and
critique" (Hengen, 45), for Morrison and Louise are worlds apart from
the start; a feminist consciousness that "didn't take favours" is opposed
to an unreconstructed chauvinism that reveals itself in Morrison's
teaching practices: "He liked the old way: you taught the subject and
forgot about them as people" (DG, 39). In this story, as in others of
the collection where the problems of domination and the relation to
the other are foremost, the failure of 1960s culture to resolve women's
place in society despite increasing emancipation predominates. "Polarities" presents an obsessive working and revising of notions of territory
(both as personal identity and urban cityscape), and the metaphor of
space, which organizes the plot and embodies the seemingly impossible
resolution of opposites. Louise's apartment is described as "less like a
room than like several rooms, pieces of which had been cut out and
pasted onto one another" (41), thus mirroring the gradual coming-
apart of her mental equilibrium. If Louise's identity is shown as a com-
posite of multiple borrowings, Morrison's is one of polar iciness, a
"chill interior, embryonic and blighted" with "nothing for her to take"
(59). At the heart of the story is the need to match the self to place and
to (Canadian) history, for Louise's madness comes from her inability to
answer the question "where is here?" which is presented as coterminous
with "who am I?" This is Atwood the literary and cultural cartographer
speaking as she seeks to map out a Canadian identity. As she states in
Survival: "For members of a country or a culture, shared knowledge of
their place, their here, is not a luxury but a necessity" (19). The story
seems to endorse a rather negative vision of relationships, for Morrison
realizes that it is the "hopeless, mad Louise" (62) he secretly craves; yet
there is a promise of revision at the end of the story, and one, significantly, which links the scripting of a primitive consciousness in the

"blue, glacial" eyes of an old woman and the "yellowish grey" eyes of the timber wolves to Morrison's gaze on a feminine landscape opening up before him as he listens to "something . . . being told, something that had nothing to do with him" (64). Boundaries of the self collapse into an otherness that is both land and feminine space, which transcends the chaos of history and modern urban culture.

Nonetheless, despite the destabilizing of fixed positions, this story, like others in *Dancing Girls*, has clear victims. In "The Man from Mars" the victim is not female, but the immigrant as "other." A nameless Asian upsets the comfortable middle-class life of female character Christine. Although we are told the story from a woman's perspective this time, Atwood shows us that discrimination is not only a matter of gender, but of class and ethnicity as well. Just as the man "from Mars," an alien to Christine's lifestyle and cultural references, fits no category she can recognize, she herself fits no identifiable feminine criteria: "She was an exception, she fitted none of the categories they commonly used when talking about girls . . . she was an honorary person" (29). Paradoxically, whereas there seems to be no such thing as a feminine subject here, for such a concept is presented as a contradiction in terms, it is the immigrant as the ethnic "other" who reinstates Christine as feminine in the eyes of the males around her. His obsessive tracking of her on the university campus "rendered her equally mysterious" (28). The story presents a narrative of misconceptions, since not only does Christine have no idea why the immigrant has chosen her as the focus of his obsession, but the immigrant's identity, his nationality, is also an open question. First the Asian immigrant is mistaken for a Frenchman, then for a "foreign potentate" by Christine's hopeful mother. Only at the end of the story, when the mysterious immigrant is deported back to his home country of Vietnam, is the question of his nationality answered. The story undergoes an ironic turnaround in the end, for it is then Christine who obsessively questions his motives and mentally explores his homeland from newscasts on the war.

The impression we are left with is that cultural constructions of ethnicity and gender have at least been challenged, if not radically displaced. Christine herself has escaped, if only temporarily, from the codes which relegate her to the laws and limits of feminine desirability in a Western culture where "womanliness tends to be portrayed . . . as a mask, a disguise that stubbornly resists interpretation; . . . merely a simulation to please a masculine scopic economy of pleasure" (Rao, 132). The Asian victim does at least provoke a measure of interest in his plight. It seems, however, that subject/object tensions result in painful

loss for the characters, and solutions, when there are such, remain fragile and unresolved.

Although these same tensions are present in the later collection of
short fictions and prose poems *Murder in the Dark*, which appeared in
1983, the focus for the dismantling of crippling oppositions between
the sexes is centered in language itself. In "Iconography," for example,
the male gaze and the female reflection of that gaze become a play on
subject and verb as Atwood shifts linguistic borders in order to under-
line, and undermine, a politics of domination. Internalizing the codes
that make her merely a represented object, and not a representing subject, the nameless woman in the poem (who could stand for "every-
woman") gradually succumbs to total estrangement from her own
individual desires and needs. For although the poem begins with masculine desire: "He wants her arranged . . . He wants her, arranged. He
arranges to want her," it develops through strategies of linguistic ma-
nipulation and appropriation until finally, like a circus clown, the
woman mimes her own absence, since "It can never be known whether
she likes it or not. By this time she doesn't know herself" (*MID*, 52).
This and other prose poems expose the hierarchies of gender and
power, often in comic or ironical fashion as in "Women's Novels": "I
like to read novels in which the heroine has a costume rustling dis-
creetly over her breasts, or discreet breasts rustling under her costume;
in any case there must be a costume, some breasts, some rustling, and,
over all, discretion" (34).

Here, the stereotypical formula of Gothic romance is manipulated in
order to show how much the model fits expectations of femininity in
general. Other pieces like "Murder in the Dark" expose language as a
game, a maze where interpretation is always deferred, a play of text and
reader in which the premises of fiction as "true lies" are foregrounded.
What is striking in much of this volume is Atwood's focus on the
communicational quality inherent in direct address in order to fore-
ground silence or subjective erasure:

> Whether to speak or not: the question that comes up again when you
> think you've said too much, again. ("Mute," 49)

> You aren't really a god but despite that you are silent. When you're
> being worshipped there isn't much to say. ("Worship," 51)

While questions of female subjecthood and the grounding of the subject in language itself trace the development of Atwood's work and reveal themselves here in a mobile poetic/prose form, the companion
volume *Good Bones*, which mixes all types of genres, from fairy tale to
prose poetry to biography and more, continues a playful subverting of

clichés and representations. "Making a Man" overturns the myth of creation as well as the cultural/sexual practice of "making" women. Here, it is women who are exercising control of body borders on their male creations, who are stitching and "giving that tummy a good tuck" (*GB*, 56), turning the saying around that has little girls made of "sugar and spice and all things nice" in order to fabricate candy bridegrooms to "pop one of these dapper devils into your mouth" (57). In "The Female Body" a whole panoply of stereotypes is subverted: woman as Barbie doll, as product, as the lost other half that man is constantly seeking, as the focus of fairy-tale encodings where enclosure in "a pumpkin, in a high tower, in a compound, in a chamber, in a house, in a room" are all designations of passive containment (46). If Luce Irigaray has questioned the very plurality of women's desires, which express "a passage in/through the other" (Irigaray, 105) rather than domination of the other, it has distinct echoes in all these multiple fictional genres juxtaposed, reflecting and deflecting, playing with repetition and metonymy, and transgressing boundaries of meaning.

Atwood also plays with gender and genre limits and with forms of popular culture in her later short story collections. "Loulou; or, The Domestic Life of the Language" from the collection *Bluebeard's Egg*, explicitly takes up the challenge of women's place in discourse. Loulou, a maternal figure to a group of poets whom she both literally and metaphorically nurtures, seems firmly situated on the side of nature within the nature/culture dyad, while the poets, professional manipulators of words, are positioned on the side of culture. Their favorite sport, while eating her meals, is defining and redefining her in terms she cannot understand: "*Mamoreal*, one of them said . . . causing Loulou to make one of her frequent sorties into the dictionary to find out whether or not she'd been insulted" (*BE*, 61). Just as she is mother to them all, she is also their Muse, their sexual fantasy, their sexual object (for the group around her kitchen table includes "her first husband for sure, and the man she lived with after that for three years . . . and her second husband . . . and two ex-lovers" (64). Yet, although Loulou is a stereotypical representation of woman as mother earth (even her profession as a potter points to this), the originality of the story lies in the fact that, as the focalizer, Loulou has singular definition and contours for the reader, whereas the poets are designated collectively and are seemingly interchangeable. What is more, the poets never find a fitting definition for Loulou; their poems are about her, but addressed to "'my lady,' 'my friend's lady,' 'my woman,' 'my wife,' 'my friend's wife'" (63), and so Loulou is not only enclosed in the poets' versions of ideal womanhood, but such versions mean she escapes definition altogether. It could then be claimed that her very silencing is the point of departure for a challenging of cliché categories. Indeed, all seems to point to this, for the poets' major preoccupation is precisely the part of Loulou that escapes their definitions. They claim the name does not fit the personality; Loulou the woman refuses to embody completely the linguistic sign "Loulou": "Loulou, as a name, conjured up images of French girls in can-can outfits ... But then there was the real Loulou — dark, straight-haired ... The thing was, Phil said, what existed in the space between Loulou and her name?" (66).

Meanings and modes of representation are also challenged through the rewritings and revisions of fairy tales and myths that permeate many of these stories. Sometimes they are present as random motifs, at other times we have a complex interweaving and embedding of narratives. Such is the case in "Bluebeard's Egg," which, as the title suggests, meshes story and folktale to the extent that their plots merge, and the main characters Sally and Ed take on traits from the tale itself. So "Bluebeard's Egg" is intertextual in as many ways as its fairy-tale encodings are multiple. Sharon Wilson has pointed out that it is closer to the Grimms' "Fitcher's Bird" than Perrault's "La barbe bleu" [Bluebeard] which, to cite Atwood herself, makes "the woman dependent upon brothers coming to her rescue after she has entered the forbidden room" (Wilson, 265–70). Moreover, Sally has touches of the Snow Queen, and "as the wives of Bluebeard/Fitcher/The Robber Bridegroom, she is in danger, like false brides in the Grimms' Tales, of being replaced with other interchangeable women" (Wilson, 268). Sometimes reminiscent of an ugly stepmother, sometimes of Bluebeard himself, Sally, like Ed (whose name and inscrutable character cannot but remind us of the pristine egg in the magician's tale) partakes in a radical destabilizing of gender categories. In such stories which blur genre limits, the cultural constructions of identity are not only represented as oppositional ones, but these oppositions themselves are collapsed. Ed is multiple; as a surgeon/magician in his "cramped, darkened room" (143) which is "a dangerous place ... a massage parlour, only for women" (145) he is not the same Ed who is framed "in terms of the calendar art from the service-station washrooms of [Sally's] childhood" (133). Similarly, Sally the ironical manipulator of cultural constructs, who "knows for a fact that dumb blondes were loved, not because they were blondes, but because they were dumb" (132), is other than Sally the purveyor of received wisdom, lacking in self-awareness: "Sometimes Sally worries that she's a nothing, the way Marylynn was before she got a divorce and a job" (138). For much of the story Ed is in the garden, encoded in fairy-tale imagery, in "a wilderness ... of bushes and branches" where he "manages to make it through the forest with all its witches and traps and pitfalls" (131, 133). By contrast, Sally, as the controlling gaze, is at the window, although this in itself is ambivalent, for are not princesses destined to watch and wait at windows? It is she, not he, who is given the Bluebeardesque means to "hack her way through the brambles" (133) to rescue him. So, as Atwood constantly shifts the goal-posts of our readerly expectations, and notions of "inside/outside, active/passive, safe space/wilderness" are subverted, it is the egg which retains the potential to generate storytelling in the end (Sarbadhikary, 88). Whether Sally, like Ed's former wives, "gets the axe," or whether she manages to save the marriage, is left unresolved.

Not only are genre limits collapsed in many of these later stories, but popular culture, Gothic, and romance scenarios are reworked in subversive ways. "True Trash" from *Wilderness Tips*, Atwood's most recent collection of stories, interweaves *True Romance* dramas and the "real life" story of Ronette, a waitress at an expensive boys' summer camp, who transgresses all the taboos of romance narratives when she sleeps with the well-off students and gets pregnant. As one narrative folds into another, it is once again the frame story of Ronette and the boys at the camp that seems to merge with that of the romance magazine, and in this way the values and repressions of an era are held up to scrutiny. The title itself questions notions of value by putting them in uneasy juxtaposition, for how can "trash" be "true"? Moreover, the names of characters are coded; "Ronette" is reminiscent of a 1960s pop group, "Darce" has undertones of Austen's aloof and arrogant hero Darcy. As in Austen's plots, the gaining of property and the maintaining of propriety are the subtexts of the magazine the waitresses are reading during their breaks. The message is that poor girls are inevitably at risk from male predators and the result is a life of regrets. Sexuality, in the "ruminating mouths glistening and deep red like mushed-up raspberries" (*WT*, 10) of girls like Ronette, classes them as both "cheap" and "enticing." In the world of the rich boy, sexuality, or lack of propriety, is synonymous with "cheap," or lack of property, and Atwood shows the world of the early sixties as obeying much the same laws as the formulaic romance magazines. But "trash," meaning both "rubbish" and "slut," is made problematical by the story. For as Donny realizes early on, "most of the things in his life [were] expensive, and not very interesting" (10). He questions the essential bond made in capitalist society between market value and "interest" (itself an ambivalent term), for although one usually follows the other, the link breaks down here. Furthermore, it is Ronette, the "trash" of the story, who will be Donny's sexual initiation, and her "cheap" act gains high personal value for him. His mother's words, "only Italians and cheap girls have pierced ears," overlap with other, more personal versions: "It would hurt to have a hole put through your ear. It would take bravery" (16). Likewise, the "moan-a-drama" narratives constantly interrupt the main one until they seem to share the same frame of reference. When the waitresses are sun-bathing with the boys, the description merges one narrative into the other:

> They're on one of the pink granite islands, the four of them: Joanne and Ronette, Perry and Darce. . . . The western sky is still peach-toned and luminous, the soft ripe juicy moon is rising . . . It's the Summer Issue, thinks Joanne. *Lazy Daze. Tanning Tips. Shipboard Romance.* (24)

Although the story shares many of the characteristics attributed to such romance dramas, which traditionally figure a heroine's fragile social identity, an inscrutable male, unequal power relations, and a final interpretation as "true love" (see Radway), it subverts others. There is no final romantic resolution to the story, and we realize that the pregnancy is attributable to a teenage boy and not a romance hero.

However, although undoubtedly concerned with contemporary crises of identity and their gender constructions, Atwood has equally, in her later work, given space to those myths of wilderness and colonization, of national territory and appropriation, which make up her nationalist ethos, revised and revisited. As Coral Ann Howells has stated, "wilderness is the major figure in Canadian iconography of landscape," and this takes us "from *Surfacing* and *Survival* in the early 1970s where wilderness features as the sign of a distinctive national heritage, up to *Wilderness Tips* which signals a point of crisis and collapse of the Wilderness myth" (Howells, 2, 3). The collection is indeed the encounter between different representations and narratives of the Canadian wilderness. "Death by Landscape," as Simone Vauthier has pointed out, is both a rewriting of Atwood's own postulate in the 1970s that "Death by nature . . . is an event of startling frequency in Canadian literature," and also a narrative mediated through the pictorial landscapes of the Canadian "Group of Seven" painters who identified Canadian identity as inextricably linked to its particular landscape (Vauthier, 32). But this story does not present the healing, regenerated self of the female character of *Surfacing*. Instead, the resolution of an accident in the midst of the Canadian bush at a summer camp in the 1940s leaves the adult Lois "so traumatized by that disappearance of her friend Lucy that she has refused to go anywhere near the wilderness ever since" (Howells, 7). Loss and a fragile equilibrium characterize this story as they do "The Age of Lead," which takes up a historical narrative of exploration, the failed Franklin expedition to the Arctic in the nineteenth century, and ends with a final vision of global pollution where "wilderness" has become an outmoded concept in a postmodern world. The title story "Wilderness Tips" radically questions Canada's contemporary self-image and its link to a white colonial settlement myth. The disruptive effect of an immigrant from Eastern Europe, George, on a middle-class Canadian family he has married into, works to subvert their comfortable prejudices and complacency. Set in a lakeside cottage called Wacousta Lodge after a nineteenth-century novel about a white man passing as an Indian, the narrative thus "exposes the Wilderness as a fabrication of nineteenth and early twentieth century white male anglophone colonialists of heroic imagination, fascinated by the Otherness of the wild" (Howells, 6). This is the legacy of an autocratic great-grandfather, whose colonial appropriative vision the great-grandson is unable to share, for he knows he is "not a success, not by his great-grandfather's standards" (*WT*, 211). Enmeshed in a conflictual past and present, prey to George's mercenary ambitions, the family is shown to be at odds with its heritage and unable to renew the myth of colonial tradition in order to adjust to a modern multicultural Canadian reality. At the end of the story, the landscape threatens literally to collapse and disappear "as if the trees, the granite outcrops, Wacousta Lodge, the peninsula, the whole mainland were sliding gradually down, submerging" (221).

If these revisions of national self-perception are a way of "suggesting that this romantic myth of endless wilderness has made possible the careless destruction of wilderness as place" (Howells, 6), then Atwood's short fictions have increasingly been the site of the destabilizing and questioning of such myths. Just as clichés of femininity and masculinity are constantly foregrounded, so the very concentrated "self"-centered (rather than plot-centered) forms of short fiction allow for condensations, plurality of genre, multiplicity of perspective. They favor the collapsing of fixed categories that are a central issue in all of Atwood's work. Since her first collection of short stories, *Dancing Girls*, she has increasingly sought to undermine and revise the cultural myths and oppositions that make up the historical Canadian narratives of identity.

Works Cited

Atwood, Margaret. *Bluebeard's Egg*. London: Virago, 1988.

————. *Bones and Murder*. London: Virago, 1995.

————. *Dancing Girls*. London: Virago, 1984.

————. *Good Bones*. Toronto: Coach House Press, 1992.

————. *Murder in the Dark*. Toronto: Coach House Press, 1983.

————. *Surfacing*. London: Virago, 1979.

————. *Survival: A Thematic Guide to Canadian Literature*. Toronto: Anansi, 1972.

————. *Wilderness Tips*. London: Virago, 1992.

Hengen, Shannon. *Margaret Atwood's Power: Mirrors, Reflections and Images in Select Fiction and Poetry*. Toronto: Second Story Press, 1993.

Howells, Coral Ann. MS of Lecture on "Questions of Survival in *The Handmaid's Tale*" given at the University of Strasbourg, France (29 January 1999).

Irigaray, Luce. "This Sex Which is Not One." In *New French Feminisms*. Ed. Elaine Marks and Isabelle de Courtivron. Hemel Hempstead: Harvester, 1981: 99–106.

Radway, Janice. *Reading the Romance: Women, Patriarchy, and Popular Literature*. London: Verso, 1987.

Rao, Eleonora. *Strategies for Identity: The Fiction of Margaret Atwood*. New York: Lang, 1993.

Sarbadhikary, Krishna. "Signifying Authority: The Short Stories of Margaret Atwood and Audrey Thomas." In *Margaret Atwood: The Shape-Shifter*. Ed. Coomi S. Vevaina and Coral Ann Howells. New Delhi: Creative Books, 1998: 81–98.

Vauthier, Simone. "Paysages/visages: 'Death by Landscape.'" *Image et Récit* (1993): 31–49.

Wilson, Sharon Rose. *Margaret Atwood's Fairy-Tale Sexual Politics*. Jackson: University of Mississippi Press, 1993.

Margaret Atwood's Poetry 1966–1995

Lothar Hönnighausen (University of Bonn)

O N THE OCCASION OF THIS ESSAY on Margaret Atwood's poetry, I take my cue both from her painter Elaine Risley, favoring "a chronological approach" for this retrospective exhibition, and from her gallerist Charna, who "wants things to go together tonally and resonate" (*Cat's Eye*, 91). Atwood's work has been categorized and subdivided into so many styles and phases, in which she supposedly was a Canadian nationalist, literary lobbyist, liberal parodist, Amnesty International activist, or changed back and forth from poet to prose writer, from aggressive feminist harpy to soft-souled wife and mother, from progressive young woman to stone-faced sibyl, that the use of any traditional evolutionary scheme in approaching it is out of the question. Along the same lines, Atwood's poetic stance, which has been over-simplistically described as either *autobiographical* or *mythopoeic*, is probably neither or both, resulting, as with other writers, from the stylization, in changing forms, of a changing stream of experience.[1] In any case, her sixtieth birthday seems to call not so much for yet more scholarly theorizing than for intense rereading, particularly of her poetry, which is not as well known as her fiction.

Although there are many affinities between Atwood's poetry and her fiction, her poems, in contrast to her novels, stories, or essays, seem to occur like entries into a kind of artistic logbook. Writing poetry for Atwood appears to be an irresistible, ongoing process of perception, reflection, and aesthetic organization. What makes this process of poetic exploration relevant to her readers is the radicality with which she puts things to the test, and the inventive craftsmanship with which she

---

[1] On Atwood and her work as the subject of diverse categorizations, of canonization as well as of witch hunts, and particularly on her own role-play ("meta-iconization") in deconstructing the clichés ("iconizations") of consumerism, see York, 229–70. See Mallinson for a competent overview of Atwood's volumes of poetry from *The Circle Game* to *True Stories*. See also Wagner-Martin, "The Making of *Selected Poems*, the Process of Surfacing," and "'Giving Way to Bedrock': Atwood's Later Poems."

organizes her experiences as poems: "As for the ego — I wonder if it really exists? . . . One is simply a location where certain things occur, leaving trails & debris . . . something in one that organizes the random bits though" (Sullivan, 220).

Furthermore, there are some other continuous traits which endear Atwood the poet to her readers: her nimble intelligence and her comic sense, her precision and scientific curiosity, her inexhaustible productivity, and her insistence on shaping rather than shouting. If her literary personae hardly ever appear in a tragic predicament, they are often plagued by doubt and revulsion, but fortunately many convey a wry sense of humor. The fascinating experience for Atwood's readers is to share with her the wide range of her artistic moods and modes of expression, as the overview of the following volumes of poetry will show: *The Circle Game* (1966), *The Animals in That Country* (1968), *The Journals of Susanna Moodie* (1970), *Procedures for Underground* (1970), *Power Politics* (1971), *You Are Happy* (1974), *Two-Headed Poems* (1978), *True Stories* (1981), *Interlunar* (1984), *Morning in the Burned House* (1995).

In a retrospective of Atwood's poetry, the title poems of her various volumes obviously constitute nodes which can serve as points of departure and foci for the proposed rereadings. Atwood's debut as a fully fledged poet, *The Circle Game*, for which she received the Governor General's Award for 1966, was as convincing as her first novel, *The Edible Woman*, dating from 1965 and published in 1969.[2] Both the volume of poetry and the novel fuse the narcissism of an antagonistic love affair with wider thematic concerns, such as the doubtful realities of the contemporary consumer and media culture, and both these apprentice works display the same amazing assurance of tone and performance. In fact, the basic poetic techniques that Atwood adopts in her first book of poetry undergo no substantial changes, notwithstanding many subtle modifications, from her first through her most recent volume. There are no fixed stanza forms, no rhyme, no regular meter, but a sure and continuous voice informs the poem through its remotest ramifications, and through the varying lengths of stanzas and lines.[3] This medium proves flexible enough to accommodate widely

[2] Margaret Atwood's first published book was *Double Persephone* (1961), but she regarded this group of mythopoeic poems, inspired as much by T. S. Eliot's *Waste Land* as by Northrop Frye, apparently as apprentice work and opened *Selected Poems* (1976) with thirteen poems from *The Circle Game*.

[3] On the prose poem as a new genre of Atwood's, see Merivale. For Atwood's distinction between prose poem and short story, her commentaries on the in-

varying topics, presenting, to somebody with the artistic ingenuity and shaping power of Atwood, every opportunity for formal precision.

The title poem, "Circle Game," is one of Atwood's many poetic cycles, a genre of which she seems so fond because the cycle form contains additional potential for variation and for structuring, for openness and formal firmness. Furthermore, the motif of the children's "Circle Game" allows metaphoric development and lends coherence not only to the seven parts of the poem, but also to the whole volume, in which, from the black humor of the opening hide-and-seek in "This is a Photograph of Me" to the metamorphoses of "Eventual Proteus," various games are played, for instance, "An Attempted Solution for Chess Games," and "Playing Cards"; also, several time-honored North American roles are parodically reenacted in "The Explorers" and "The Settlers." In "The Circle Game," Atwood realizes this potential for structuring by juxtaposing the circular movement of the children in part *i* and the frustrations of the narcissistic lovers in part *ii*. In both cases, the traditional romantic implications are inverted: the children's eyes are not cheerful or happy, but "fixed on the empty / moving spaces just in / front of them," and the lovers are equally "fixed" on their own reflections, "... groping through a mirror / whose glass has melted / to the consistency / of gelatin," and on the "people in the next room" (44–46). Both the motif of children's games and the motif of the narcissistic and voyeuristic lovers are developed like musical reprises. In part *iii* and part *v* it becomes clear that the children have obviously understood more of the "legends / ... of monstrous battles" (47) than the adults had realized, and in parts *iv* and *vi*, the voyeuristic power game of the lovers, "I watch you / watching my face / indifferently / ... a wart perhaps," takes a new turn through the use of geographic imagery, "So now you trace me / like a country's boundary / ... and I am fixed, stuck / down on the outspread map" (49), and through the parodic introduction of Victorian sentimentalisms, like "orphan game" and "Victorian Christmas-card" (51–52). The various motifs of this somewhat schematic and lengthy work are tied together in part *vii*, culminating in a final outburst characteristic of the frustrations and emancipations of the sixties: "I want the circle / broken" (55). What made critics and readers in 1966 so sure that with *The Circle Game* a major new poetic voice had emerged in Canada, was that the young poet had authentically captured a new kind of sensibility, manifesting itself, for instance, in her ironic treatment of the reality-

---

ception of her poems, and the role of voice and syllable, see Hammond, particularly 77–79.

photography theme. The opening poem, "This is a Photograph of Me," starts harmlessly enough with a description of the quality of the photo, "a smeared / print: blurred lines," and of what looks like a fairly ordinary scenery, "like a branch, a small frame house, a lake, some low hills," but then takes a turn that is at once dramatic and absurd, uncanny and ironic: "The photograph was taken / the day after I drowned // I am in the lake, in the center / of the picture, just under the surface" (17). Part of Atwood's accomplishment lies in her transformations of space. In "My Ravines" she personalizes a recognizable Toronto scenery — the ravines also figure prominently in her novel *Cat's Eye* — and makes it the location of new and far-reaching experiences, "while the young boys / climbed and swung . . . bursting purple / as ancient rage, in // old men's / dreams of slaughter" ("My Ravines," 28). In "On the Streets, Love," the background of consumerist popular culture, "The billboard lady / with her white enamel / teeth and red / enamel claws, is after // the men / when they pass her" (38), metonymically suggests the dehumanized quality of a contemporary love affair, and in "Pre-Amphibian" an erotic dream fulfills itself in a symbolistic underwater seascape (76).

The love-theme also informs some poems in the next volume, *The Animals in That Country*, but the thrust here is clearly ecological, announcing itself in the title poem "The Animals in that Country." "Provisions" makes fun of city dwellers, whose list of "provisions" for survival in a harsh natural environment culminates in "four toronto streetcar tickets // and . . . a bundle / of . . . filing-cards / printed with important facts" (1). "The Animals in that Country" and its companion poem "The Festival" relate environmental issues to more comprehensive philosophical concerns, focusing on the cultural contextualizations of animals (Gingell; Vogt). In contrast to the sophisticated ritual patterning of fox hunting in British or bull-fighting in Spanish culture, the deaths of animals in Canada are not culturally or aesthetically integrated, occurring as banal road accidents. Subtle artist that she is, Atwood conveys this cultural difference through the contrast between the parodic use of stylizing language for the European examples, "the fox run / politely to earth, the huntsmen / standing around him, fixed / in their tapestry of manners" (2), and the direct statement of the short stanzas encapsulating the Canadian predicament, "In this country the animals / have the faces of / animals. // Their eyes / flash once in the car headlights / and are gone" (3).

A close reading of the whole volume reveals the wide range and subtlety of Atwood's poetic investigation of environmental concerns. The tortoises in "Elegy for the Giant Tortoises," as a result of the parodic insistence on regular three-line stanzas, appear as "sadder than tanks and history" (23), and the animals in "The Totems" withdraw, leaving only their hollow masks behind. "Sundew" is marked by an uncanny symbolistic conflation of human figure and landscape, and "The Green Giant Murder" paints a scene, reminiscent of Gulliver's travels to the island of Lilliput, in which the green giant (Nature) is swarmed over by hypothesizing detectives: "Some say he did it / himself" (33). Finally, the ten "Speeches for Dr Frankenstein" re-embody Mary Shelley's famous Romantic critique of Enlightenment progressivism, "Now I wince / before this plateful of results" (44), and have a particular appeal in an age worried about gene technology and nuclear holocaust.

The last example illustrates Atwood's subtle awareness of the political dimension of environmentalism. In "It Is Dangerous to Read Newspapers," the protagonist contrasts her sheltered student life with the horrors of the Vietnam war, "and the jungles are flaming, the under-/ brush is charged with soldiers," insisting on her responsibility for the consequences of consumerist imperialism: "I am the cause, I am a stockpile of chemical / toys, my body / is a deadly gadget" (30). However, Atwood is not carried away by her thematic concerns, remaining the conscientiously crafting artist even when taking up far-reaching political and sociocultural issues. In "At the Tourist Centre in Boston," she devises a new satirical language to explode the clichés of the tourist industry, "and the mother is cooking something / in immaculate slacks by a smokeless fire, / her teeth white as detergent" (18), and, in view of this "manufactured / hallucination," she confronts the "Unsuspecting / window lady" (19) with the kind of disturbing revelation that later the heroine of *The Journals of Susanna Moodie* will experience in the wilderness: "Do you see nothing / watching you from under the water?" (19)[4]

In "Notes from Various Pasts," as in her novel *Surfacing*, the challenge is to penetrate "far under even the memory / of sun and tidal moon" (10), and to accept the losses involved when the unconscious rises to the level of poetic discourse. Fortunately, Atwood's powers of concretization are such that she is able to articulate the inarticulate and to verbalize deep sea wisdom, "messages / from a harsher level" (10):

---

[4] On the shamanistic implication of the descent to the subaquatic realm in Atwood's poetry and in the novels *Surfacing* and *Lady Oracle*, see Van-Spanckeren, particularly 197.

> The words lie washed ashore
> on the margin, mangled
> by the journey upwards to bluegrey
> surface, the transition. (11)

Given the comprehensiveness and insight of Atwood's environmental views, it is not surprising to find her, in several poems of *The Animals in That Country*, inverting traditional North American values and drawing caricatures of such cherished icons as the trapper, the pioneer, and the cowboy. "The trappers" are "trapped / between the steel jaws of their answerless / dilemma," and suffer from "the guilt they feel because / they are not animals" (34–35). The pioneer is not the heroic icon of Hollywood Westerns but rather the kind of figure adumbrated in Crèvecoeur's *Letters of an American Farmer* XII, "Distress of a Frontier Man," and in Atwood's own Susanna Moodie poems. In a similar vein, she poetically critiques surveying and map-making, which play such an important role in the history and mythology of North American culture. The cowboy in "Backdrop Addresses Cowboy" has become the subject of a witty farce, breathing the parodic spirit of postmodernism: "Starspangled cowboy / sauntering out of the almost- / silly West" (50).

The Journals of Susanna Moodie (1970) is a seminal text in the history of our understanding of frontier women and, for understandable reasons, easily Atwood's most popular volume of poetry.[5] The nineteenth-century intertext of the Moodie journals presented Atwood with a congenial female persona for embodying the anxieties and longings of a late twentieth-century woman. Furthermore, the wilderness, of which Atwood herself had firsthand knowledge, constituted an imaginary world with which she could identify. Most importantly, this remote and yet familiar material provided scope for both distance and empathy, helping her to a new kind of objectivity which constituted a countervailing force to the subjectivism of her lyrical gift. Content and graphic shape of the tripartite epigraph to this mixed media work suggest the

---

[5] On the conflict between European aesthetics and the experience of the wilderness in Susanna Moodie, see Johnston. On *The Journals of Susanna Moodie* as depicting a struggle between female and male space, see Davey, 23. On the Gothic element in *The Circle Game*, *The Journals of Susanna Moodie*, and *Power Politics*, see McCombs, "Atwood's Haunted Sequences." On the poems and the collages in *The Journals of Susanna Moodie*, see Weir.

artist's resolute if painful effort to shape a noncolonial self and to perceive a new world:

> I take this picture of myself
> and with my sewing scissors
> cut out the face.
>
> Now it is more accurate:
>
> where my eyes were,
> every-
> thing appears (7)

Although the cycle has none of the optimism often associated with the frontier, there is nevertheless a kind of moral progress (Walker, 159). In the first poem, "Disembarking at Quebec," Moodie's "own lack / of conviction . . . makes / these vistas of desolation," and an original metaphor of alienation transforms her into "a word / in a foreign language" (11). In the last poem, "A Bus Along St Clair: December," Susanna Moodie has risen from the dead ("Resurrection," 58), and re-emerges, "Though they buried me in monuments / of concrete slabs, of cables" (60), as a disconcerting but inspiring mythic presence in the Toronto of Atwood's own time. Through the radical exposure of her heroine to nature and her shamanistic view of animals — linking *The Journals of Susanna Moodie* to the preceding volume, *The Animals in That Country* — Atwood has opened up a new imaginative territory (VanSpanckeren, 183–204). What enabled her to do so was her creation of a new language of perception and reflection. The heroine's language in "The Wereman" indicates that she is not out — as the popular cliché of feminism would have it — to portray the husband as a sinister force and herself as victim, but to express the difficulty of redefining, in the disconcerting strangeness of the wilderness, their identities and their relationship:

> My husband walks in the frosted fields
> an X, a concept
> defined against a blank;
> ...
>
> Unheld by my sight
> what does he change into (19)

Moodie's traumatic quest for identity and her preoccupation with problems of perception and cognition are also the deeper reason for her insistence, in view of the elemental chaos of "The Two Fires," on form: "Concentrate on / form, geometry, the human / architecture of the house" (22). In "Paths and Thingscape," where the substitution of the new metaphor *thing*-scape for the common term *land*-scape encapsulates Moodie's cognitive and psychological difficulties, the problem is the absence of the familiar European cultural and aesthetic codes (Johnston 29–32). Instead of being confirmed in her identity by the *ensemble* of a familiar landscape, Moodie and the other settlers are forced to construct a new world from the perception of isolated "things" and signs, "the sky's codes" (20). Her fear, "I am watched like an invader / who knows hostility but / not where," and her hope that "each / thing . . . will without moving move / around me / into its place" (21), reflect basic anthropological needs for which Atwood is the first to find a poetic language.

She continues this quest for a language of archetypal as well as subconscious experience in *Procedures for Underground* (1970). "Underground" is not, as Atwood humorously puts it, a "sewage manual or a handbook on revolution" (in Sullivan, 220). It is rather, as Sullivan explains, "the territory of the psyche, laced with collective mythologies and personal obsessions" (220). But to Atwood, who has an unorthodox belief in the supernatural, regarding it as a "valued and necessary part of the human mentality" (224), *underground* also means the sphere in which epiphanies and metamorphoses take place. How she envisions the linkage of the psychoanalytic and the spiritual can be seen from "Dream: Bluejay or Archeopteryx," depicting, in the first part, an encounter with "that other / self of mine" (8), and revealing, in the second, the numinous in the kind of underwater scenario also evoked in her novel *Surfacing*:

> in the water
> under my shadow
> there was an outline, man
> surfacing, his body sheathed
> in feathers, his teeth
> glinting like nails, fierce god
> head crested with blue flame. (*PU*, 9)

In "Buffalo in Compound: Alberta," the epiphany of the "zeus-faced god" emerges unexpectedly from a banal touristic description, "glad our car is / near" (70), of a herd of buffalo:

but we thought we saw
in the field near them the god
of this place: brutal,
zeus-faced, his horned
head man-bearded. (71)

In the aftermath of this epiphany, the impression of the disappearing buffalo retains a strange dignity, enhancing the otherworldly quality of the event: "Then they were going / in profile, one by one, their / firelit outlines fixed as carvings // backs to us now / they enter / the shade of the gold-edged trees" (71). In view of this visionary dimension, it is hardly surprising that, in *Procedures for Underground*, animals play not only an important environmentalist role but, as in *The Journals of Susanna Moodie*, also assume a shamanistic function. In "Fishing for Eel Totems," a poem subtly deploying leitmotifs of communication, "listening to signals," "no words," "alphabet," "grey tongue hanged silent" (68–69), the protagonist learns that the "earliest language / was not our syntax of chained pebbles // but liquid, made / by the first tribes, the fish / people" (69).

The rich imaginary scenery of the title poem, "Procedures for Underground," invokes the Homeric Hades as much as the Indian myths of the Canadian Northwest (Davey, 109). Its continuous and insistent voice, addressing the artist as a shamanistic figure, has a haunting solemnity: "You will walk wrapped in an invisible / cloak. Few will seek your help / with love, none without fear" (25). The procedures explored in *Procedures for Underground* are astonishingly varied, ranging from the psychoanalytic conservation of grotesque parental figures in the pop art vision of "Eden is a Zoo" to the collapse of the icons of popular culture, "the / red and silver / heroes had collapsed inside / their rubber suits," and the protagonist's search "for the actual, collect lost / bones, burnt logs / of campfires, pieces of fur" (49) in "Comic Books vs. History (1949, 1969)."

Power Politics (1971) is the volume that brought Atwood the reputation of being aggressively feminist and a "man-hater" (Ostriker, 487), because the times were still guided by codes that the sixties and books like *Power Politics* exploded. Readers who recognize that poetry is not a direct expression of personal feelings, and who take it for granted that women reflect upon love relations as critically as men, will have no difficulties with these witty poems. Moreover, Atwood's commentary on the title, stressing the interconnectedness of private and public spheres (Sullivan, 248), suggests that we read these poems in the context of the cultural revolution of the sixties that brought the post-Second World

War era to a close. If we approach these poems as inheriting the zeit-geist of change and inversion, of William S. Burroughs, Allen Ginsberg, Robert Rauschenberg and Claes Oldenburg, of Beat, Pop Art, the civil rights movement, and women's lib, we will not be shocked by the "cruelty" of Atwood's epigraph, "you fit into me / like a hook into an eye // a fish hook / an open eye" (1), but will rather intuit and enjoy its black humor.

Atwood's parodic inventiveness is superbly exemplified by the ironic regularity of the six four-line stanzas of "My Beautiful Wooden Leader," in which the pompous male partner is heralded as a *wooden* equestrian statue ("My beautiful wooden leader / with your heartful of medals / made of wood") and bidden an equally ludicrous farewell:

> Magnificent on your wooden horse
> you point with your fringed hand;
> the sun sets, and the people all
> ride off in the other direction. (7)

No less amusing is "They Eat Out," where, after the farcical argument "over which of us will pay for your funeral // though the real question is / whether or not I will make you immortal," the female protagonist in comic bravado — the realistic description enhancing the comedy — raises "the magic fork / over the plate of beef fried rice // and plunge[s] it into [... his] heart" (5). Following this murderous deed is a funny pop art resurrection, parodically foregrounded by couplets and ludicrous enjambments:

> There is a faint pop, a sizzle
>
> and through your own split head
> you rise up glowing;
> the ceiling opens
> a voice sings Love Is A Many
> Splendoured Thing
> you hang suspended above the city
>
> in blue tights and a red cape,
> your eyes flashing in unison. (5)

The protagonist's deadpan commentary on the self-aggrandizement of her superman is: "As for me, I continue eating; / I liked you better the way you were, / but you were always ambitious" (5).

This spirit of witty mannerism, "You are widespread and bad for the garden, / hard to eradicate" ("He Is a Strange Biological Phenomenon," 8), carries on into parts two and three of the volume, although there are also poems inspired by reconciliatory feelings, "They are Hostile Nations" (38), and, on an agonizingly personal note, "Your Back Is Rough" (34). What seems most original in *Power Politics* is a new breathtaking irony and brutality in the rendition of love, where previous generations of poets had felt obliged to offer slush:

> yes at first you
> go down smooth as
> pills, all of me
> breathes you in and then it's
>
> a kick in the head, orange
> and brutal, sharp jewels
> hit and my
> hair splinters.
>   ("Yes at first You," 22)

You Are Happy (1974), marking a transitional stage between the early and the late poetry, is rather a mixed bag, with significantly only a handful of poems doing full justice to the title. However, poems such as "Digging" and "Spring Poem" clearly reflect aspects of Atwood's new life with Graeme Gibson on their farm in Mulmur Township, Ontario. Both the plodding work and the emotions in "Digging," "I dig with anger / I dig because I am hungry, the dungpile scintillates with flies" (19), and "Spring Poem," "we are burning / last year's weeds . . . I dream of reconciliations / with those I have hurt / unbearably" (22–23), are a far cry from the malicious wit and the grotesque pop art of many poems in *The Circle Game* and *Power Politics*. The happiness of "You Are Happy" emerges only, after many natural details have been registered with indifference, at the end of a walk with the partner, during which the cold had seemed the overwhelming experience:

> When you are this
> cold you can think about
> nothing but the cold, the images
>
> hitting into your eyes
> like needles, crystals, you are happy. (28)

The songs of Circe's transformed lovers ("Pig Song," "Bull Song," etc.) in section two of *You Are Happy* are solid rather than great poetry, contrasting with the intensity of the Circe/Mud poems in section three. Circe, whose persona here dominates the perspective, is not only the *femme fatale* of the Romanticists and the no-nonsense woman of Atwood's own *Power Politics*, but, thanks to the clever contrariness of the metaphors "rubber" and "steel," a dazzling wearer of many masks and a reflector of the desires of the beholder:

> My face, my other faces
> stretching over it like
> rubber, like flowers opening
> and closing, like rubber,
> like liquid steel,
> like steel. Face of steel.
>
> Look at me and see your reflection. (56)

What makes this resurrection of Homer's Circe distinctive is her brutal victimization, "Holding my arms down / holding my head down by the hair // mouth gouging my face" (55), and the melodramatic messiness surrounding her, "my front porch is waist deep in hands, bringing their blood hoarded in pickle jars" (49). The poems are artistically important because they chart, in a new language, the trajectory of a new kind of sensibility. It is characterized by an affection for anti-heroes, "the ones left over" (47), and an inversion of the heroic expansionism of Tennyson's Ulysses, "Don't you get tired of saying Onward?" (51). Hardly less remarkable is the parody, in one of the interspersed prose poems, of the male tradition of constructing an *ideal beloved*: "When he was young he and another boy constructed a woman out of mud . . . and make love to her" (61).

Of the reflective poems in the fourth part, "There Is Only One of Everything," the eponymous poem is easily the most important in the volume, focusing on the thisness — Gerard Manley Hopkins's *inscape* — of objects and events, such as "The cat / with the divided face, half black half orange," the softly glowing "table / and freak plates," and, as the culminating point, the narrator's casual and unique perception of her partner:

but the way you dance by yourself
on the tile floor to a worn song, flat and mournful,
so delighted, spoon waved in one hand, wisps of roughened hair

sticking up from your head, it's your surprised
body, pleasure I like. I can even say it,
though only once and it won't

last: I want this. I want
this. (92)

As the poem encapsulates in the final stanza, through growing intensity
and regressive articulation, this moment of his naive delight and her
love, it becomes epiphanic and makes clear why the volume is entitled:
You Are Happy.

In my view, *Two-Headed Poems* is neither a document of "despair"
nor a "positive statement about culture" (cf. Wagner-Martin, 87).
Rather, it is a mature, unflinching assessment of the human condition,
marking the poet's staying power and her increased thematic range.
The "two-headedness" suggested by the metaphor of the Siamese twins
in the epigraphs of the title poem, "*The heads speak sometimes singly,
sometimes together, sometimes alternately within a poem. Like all Siamese
twins, they dream of separation*" (59), extends far beyond the doubleness of "writer and woman," and encapsulates the conflictual themes of
most of the poems in the book, as well as the dialogical structure of the
particular imagination at work. In that sense, the impressive poems
which open the volume, "Burned Space" and "Foretelling the Future,"
are two-headed, or variations of the mask motif, "A Paper Bag" and
"Five Poems for Dolls." The heart in "The Woman Who Could Not
Live / With Her Faulty Heart" and "The Woman Makes Peace / With
Her Faulty Heart" — not the "candy shape . . . symbol," but the dissected organ — is "duplicitous" (15) and shares "an uneasy truce / and
honour between criminals" (87).

How carefully the volume is crafted can be seen from its symmetries
as well as from its contrasts. The title poem in the middle of the book is
flanked by the two poems of the "Woman with the Faulty Heart" and
the two parts of the "Daybooks I" and "Daybooks II." The "Five Poems for Grandmothers" are neither idyllic nor snug and are followed by
the surrealistic "The Man With A Hole In His Throat" and by the dis-
tortive pop art of "Note from an Italian Postcard Factory." These two
poems, in disturbingly juxtaposing heterogeneous details, remind one
of René Magritte and provide a fitting transition to the "Footnote to

the Amnesty Report on Torture," which, in approaching its theme from the perspective of the man "who works here" (45), creates a particularly haunting effect. The sinister theme is continued in the black humor of "Marrying the Hangman" and the "Four Small Elegies."

The following eleven sections of rather involved poetry under the title "Two-Headed Poems" (59–75) seek to explore poetically the two-headedness of, or contradictions in, contemporary Canadian politics and communication: the achievements of the Trudeau era and the threats of the nuclear age, the emancipation from Great Britain and the increasing dependence on the US, the worry about national unity, the conflict between Canada's anglophone and francophone cultures, and about the inferiority of a language as a consequence of the lack of cultural independence (McCombs 1988, 151–60): "That is a language for ordering / the slaughter and gutting of hogs" (74). However, the theme of two-headedness is more impressively embodied in such richly concrete poems as "Marsh, Hawk," where the view, gliding from the waste dump, "burst truck / tires, abandoned, bottles and cans hit / with rocks or bullets" (88), becomes entangled in the claustrophobic "Expanse of green / reeds," finally achieving the resolution of physical tension and the freedom of fulfillment in the imagery of the opening marsh rushes and the rising hawk:

> we want it to open, the marsh rushes
> to bend aside, the water
> to accept us, it is only
> revelation, simple as the hawk
> which lifts up now against
> the sun and into
> our eyes, wingspread and sharp call
> filling the head/sky, this,
>
> to immerse, to have it slide
> through us, disappearance
> of the skin, this is what we are looking for,
> the way in. (89)

True Stories (1981) takes over where *Two-Headed Poems* left off, the title being parodic in the double sense that there are no true but only "two-headed stories," "The true story is vicious / and multiple and untrue" (11), and that the texts in the book are not really stories, but *poems* dealing with cases of abuse and torture, particularly of women (Hollis, 117–45). Atwood had learned about those cases in the course of her Amnesty International work and from such friends as the poet Carolyn Forché, to whom the title poem of the section "Notes Towards a Poem That Can Never Be Written" is dedicated (Sullivan, 326). The black humor of the cycle of burlesque prose poems entitled "True Romances," "he cut her up and left her in four garbage cans around the city, or maybe not in cans, do they have cans there?" (40) makes for a smooth transition to "A Conversation," the first poem of the cycle, "Notes Towards A Poem That Can Never Be Written," in which the "maker of machines / for pulling out toenails, / sending electric shocks / through brains or genitals" (46) is the subject of small talk between two society ladies, "Why was he at that party?" (46). "Christmas Carols" *tells the truth* by bitterly satirizing anti-abortionists, "A Women's Issue" by presenting cases such as the ritual circumcision of women in the parodic form of a museum guide:

> Exhibit C is the young girl
> dragged into the bush by the midwives
> and made to sing while they scrape the flesh
> from between her legs, then tie her thighs
> till she scabs over and is called healed.
> Now she can be married. (*TS*, 54)

The first of the five sections of "Trainride, Vienna-Bonn" starts off from the contrast between the narrator's anti-German cliché, "It's those helmets and the faces... ruthless and uniform" (58) and the disconcerting friendliness of Germans on the train. The second section ingeniously relates the landscape seen from the train to that of Pieter Breughel the Elder's *Hunters in the Snow* (1564), which Atwood probably had just seen in the Kunsthistorische Museum in Vienna. Transforming, in section iii, the Breughel-scene into a Nazi-like persecution-scene, "a man / running, and three others, chasing, / their brown coats / flapping" (60), the narrator asks herself, in section iv, the decisive moral question about the Hitler and Stalin era that hardly anybody who is not a German ever asks herself:

> This is the old fear:
> not what can be done to you
> but what you might do
> yourself, or fail to.
>
> This is the old torture. (*TS*, 61)

There are, in addition to these "Amnesty International" poems, "true stories" in the sense of "Landcrab I" and "Landcrab II" in the first part of the book, and "Vultures" and "Mushrooms" in the second, in which sardonic meditations arise from scientific observation: "Attack, voracious / eating, and flight: / it's a sound routine / for staying alive on the edges" (12). But there are also the "true stories" of the love poems "Sunset I," "Variations on the Word *Love*," "Sunset II," particularly, and "Rain," which, in depicting an impressionistic landscape, "It rains & rains & the trees / light up like stones underwater: / a haze of dull orange, / a yellow mist, / on the ground a purple kelp / of shed leaves" (88), presents "truth" as revelation:

> This is not a season
> but a pause
> between one future & another,
> a day after a day,
> a breathing space before death,
> a breathing, the rain
> throwing itself down out of the
> bluegrey sky, clear joy. (89)

In contrast to the sinister darkness of the political scenery in *True Stories*, the darkness of *Interlunar* (1984), although feared by the uninitiated, is of a spiritual and potentially promising kind: "The darkness / that you can walk so long in / it becomes light," and "This darkness / is a place you can enter and be / as safe in as you are anywhere" (103). From the opening poem "Doorway" (29), defining November, the month of the author's birth, as "the month of entrance" (29), to the concluding title poem "Interlunar" (102), the concern is with transitions and dialectical reversals of the kind suggested by the central image of the interlunar, the concomitant of the moon's reappearance.

The "Snake Poems," combining scientific description with the traditional mythic or religious connotations of snakes, provide a fitting prelude to the emergence of the archaic in ordinary life, "A Holiday": "My child . . . playing at barbarism" (34), and to the unorthodox religion of "The Healer," "Precognition," "Hidden," and "The Saints": "Prayers peel off them / like burned skin healing" (41). The exploration of the tension between love and death in the Orpheus and Eurydice cycle presents a new dimension of this time-honored motif by including, between "Orpheus (1)" and "Orpheus (2)," a series of poems on sexually disturbed, "deadly" lovers, from "Genghis Khan" and

"The Robber Bridegroom," "He would like not to kill. He would like / what he imagines other men have, / instead of this red compulsion" (62), to the frustrated males burning a woman as a witch in "Harvest." The title poem, "Interlunar," is the last of a series of strong meditative poems that one might figuratively call "still lives," because they turn the objects mentioned in the titles ("The White Cup," 89; "A Stone," 94; "Sumacs," 95) into foci of existential vision. Remembering the dazzling wit of Atwood's early poetry, one realizes what a long way she had to travel to achieve the stillness of "Interlunar":

> The lake, vast and dimensionless,
> doubles everything, the stars,
> the boulders, itself, even the darkness
> that you can walk so long in
> it becomes light. (103)

A striking example of Atwood's variety and capacity for change is her development, in "New Poems" in *Poems Selected and New 1976–1986*, of a new kind of short prose, hovering between sketch, prose poem, and short short story, and which in *Murder in the Dark* (1983) and *Good Bones* (1992) becomes the dominant genre. "An Angel," "I know what the angel of suicide looks like" (*PSN*, 157), may historically hark back to Oscar Wilde, Ernest Dowson, and the prose poems of the *fin de siècle* but, by also employing farcical elements and pop art effects, "You wouldn't believe a thing she said if it weren't for the wings" (*PSN*, 158), moves considerably beyond late Victorianism. "Men at Sea," in replacing the vitriolic irony of *Power Politics* with humor, and the poignancy of verse with the greater graphic homogeneity of prose, provides the reader with a new version of her feminist commitments. Along the same lines, "Adventure Story," parodying female as well as male pioneers, leaves no doubt that, despite its title, the text itself is not an adventure story at all but a verbally suggestive prose poem: "The victorious one reaches the immense perimeter and is engulfed in the soft pink atmosphere of paradise, sinks, enters, casts the imprisoning skin of the self, merges, disappears" (*PSN*, 163). Nevertheless, there is no doubt that the emergence of narrative impulses and the ease of diction — both in the volume *Poems Selected and New 1976–1986* (1986) and in *Morning in the Burned House* (1995) — is undoubtedly prepared for by the short prose pieces in *Murder in the Dark* (1983) and *Good Bones* (1992).

The grimly humorous voice of the "Aging Female Poet" group of verse poems in the "New Poems" in *Poems Selected and New*, exploding

the different foibles of young and old men, is very different from, but
no less impressive than, the dramatic swagger of the young woman in
the early volumes of poetry. Of particular interest in connection with
the modulations of Atwood's lyrical voice is the language of poems
such as "Another Elegy," which, in evoking its theme, the burning of a
witch, becomes self-conscious and the subject of parodic play:

> When I say *body*, what
> is that a word for?
> Why should the word *you*
> remain attached to that suffering?
> ...
>
> I think of your hair burning
> first, a scant minute
> of halo; later, an afterglow
> of bone, red slash of sunset.
> The body a cinder or luminescent
> saint, or Turner seascape.
> Fine words, but why do I want
> to tart up death?
>
> ("Another Elegy," *PSN*, 168)

An attitude of commonsensical toughness and humor informs the
first section of *Morning in the Burned House* (1995). It contains such
delightful poems as "February," with its comic mixture of Canadian
spring yearning and catlore, "jumps up on the bed and tries / to get
onto my head. It's his / way of telling whether or not I'm dead" (11),
and "A Sad Child," in which a parent — the syntax indicates her irrita-
tion — takes up the reproaches of a sentimental child, "*I am not the fa-
vourite child*" (4), bringing her comic scenario of melodramatic
endgames to an unsentimental close:

> My darling, when it comes
> right down to it
> and the light fails and the fog rolls in
> and you're trapped in your overturned body
> under a blanket or burning car,
>
> and the red flame is seeping out of you
> and igniting the tarmac beside your head
> or else the floor, or else the pillow,
> none of us is;
> or else we all are. (*MBH*, 5)

In section two, a portrait gallery of famous women, the comic toughness of section one turns into parody ("Ava Gardner Reincarnated as a
Magnolia"), often taking on a tinge of black humor ("Manet's Olympia"). In reconceiving Manet's 1863 repainting of Titian's 1538 Venus
of Urbino, a chatty guide proves helpful: "She reclines, more or less. /
Try that posture, it's hardly languor"; "Above the head of the (clothed)
maid / is an invisible voice balloon: *Slut*" (24). The most important
feature of Atwood's postmodernist all-over painting is the fine red
threadline under Olympia's black ribbon, "where the head / was taken
off and glued back on" (24). This "glued on" head has the final word,
addressing its feminist critique to the hypocritical "Monsieur Voyeur":
"*I, the head, am the only subject / of this picture. / You, Sir, are furniture. / Get stuffed*" (25).

This banter spills over into "Romantic," the opening poem of section three, which admirably captures male pretentiousness, "Men and
their mournful romanticisms / that can't get the dishes done" (45),
but does not leave women unscathed either, "Still, who's taken in? /
Every time? / Us, and our empty hands, the hands / of starving
nurses" (45). However, in the poem with the laconic title "Cell," the
irony of the narrative voice takes a more sinister turn:

> Now look objectively. You have to
> admit the cancer cell is beautiful.
> If it were a flower, you'd say, *How pretty*,
> with its mauve centre and pink petals. (47)

The turning point of the volume is the last poem in section three, "A
Pink Hotel in California," linking a childhood episode, "My father
chops with his axe / and the leaves fall off the trees. / It is nineteen
forty-three" (76), with the present of 1994, and preparing for the memorial poems of section four, written on the occasion of the death of
Atwood's father. Among these rather personal poems, "Bored" is particularly noteworthy as capturing, in the remembered minutiae of her
childish boredom, "Holding the log / while he sawed it. Holding /
the string while he measured . . ." (91), and in banal details, "I would
look / at the whorled texture of his square finger, earth under the nail"
(92), the poignancy of Atwood's grief:

> Now I wouldn't be bored.
> Now I would know too much.
> Now I would know. (*MBH*, 92)

A similar contrast between a realistic account of childhood memories and the more intense stylization of the last stanza produces the stunning effect of "Morning in the Burned House," concluding section five and the volume. Atwood's growing autobiographical urge,[6] like Goethe's in *Dichtung und Wahrheit*, does not spring from nostalgia. Rather, the polarity of the title, "Morning" — "Burned House," encapsulates the poet's equal acceptance of past and present. In turning the biographical fact of "the burned house" into a literary motif, the poet stresses both the pastness of the past and its phoenix-like re-emergence as a work of the imagination. In that sense her burned "thin green shorts // and grubby yellow T-shirt" do indeed hold her "cindery, non-existent, radiant flesh" (126). In the careful balance between the rich reality of its minutiae, "every detail clear, / tin cup and rippled mirror" (126), and its formal control (in this instance the unusual regularity of three line stanzas), the poem is characteristic of Atwood, and the last stanza particularly illustrates her aesthetic achievement. Through its contrast with the grubby yellow T-shirt and through its isolated and final position, the word "incandescent" regains its full force and emerges as an icon of the poetic work:

> and grubby yellow T-shirt
> holding my cindery, non-existent,
> radiant flesh. Incandescent. (127)

---

[6] See also her fictionalized memoir, *The Labrador Fiasco* (1996).

Works Cited

Atwood, Margaret. *The Animals in That Country.* Toronto: Oxford University Press, 1968.

———. *Cat's Eye.* London: Bloomsbury, 1989.

———. *The Circle Game.* Toronto: Anansi, 1966.

———. *Double Persephone.* Toronto: Hawkshead, 1961.

———. *Good Bones.* Toronto: Coach House Press, 1992.

———. *Interlunar.* Toronto: Oxford University Press, 1984.

———. *The Journals of Susanna Moodie.* Toronto: Oxford University Press, 1970.

———. *The Labrador Fiasco.* London: Bloomsbury, 1996.

———. *Morning in the Burned House.* Toronto: McClelland & Stewart, 1995.

———. *Poems Selected and New 1976–1986.* Toronto: Oxford University Press, 1986.

———. *Power Politics.* Toronto: Anansi, 1971.

———. *Procedures for Underground.* Toronto: Oxford University Press, 1970.

———. *Selected Poems.* New York: Simon & Schuster, 1976.

———. *True Stories.* Toronto: Oxford University Press, 1981.

———. *Two-Headed Poems.* Toronto: Oxford University Press, 1978.

———. *You Are Happy.* Toronto: Oxford University Press, 1974.

Buchbinder, David. "Weaving Her Version: The Homeric Model and Gender Politics in Selected Poems." In VanSpanckeren and Castro 1988: 122–41.

Davey, Frank. *Margaret Atwood: A Feminist Poetics.* Vancouver: Talonbooks, 1984.

Davidson, Arnold E. and Cathy N. Davidson, ed. *The Art of Margaret Atwood: Essays in Criticism.* Toronto: Anansi, 1981.

Djwa, Sandra. "Back to the Primal: The Apprenticeship of Margaret Atwood." In York 1995: 13–46.

Gingell, Susan. "The Animals in Atwood's Country." *The Literary Criterion* 19 (1984): 125–37.

Grace, Sherrill E. "Margaret Atwood and the Poetics of Duplicity." In Davidson and Davidson 1981: 55–68.

Grace, Sherrill E. and Lorraine Weir, ed. *Margaret Atwood: Language, Text and System.* Vancouver: University of British Columbia Press, 1983.

Hammond, Karla. "A Margaret Atwood Interview." *Concerning Poetry* 12 (1979): 73–81.

Hollis, Hilda. "Between the Scylla of Essentialism and the Charybdis of Deconstruction: Margaret Atwood's *True Stories.*" In York 1995: 117–45.

Johnston, Susan. "Reconstructing the Wilderness: Margaret Atwood's Reading of Susanna Moodie." *Canadian Poetry* 31 (1992): 28–54.

Kadar, Marlene. "*The Journals of Susanna Moodie* as Life Writing." In *Approaches to Teaching Atwood's* The Handmaid's Tale *and Other Works.* Ed. Sharon R. Wilson, Thomas B. Friedman, and Shannon Hengen. New York: MLA, 1996: 146–52.

Lauter, Estella. *Women as Mythmakers: Poetry and Visual Art by Twentieth Century Women.* Bloomington: Indiana University Press, 1984.

Mallinson, Jean. "Margaret Atwood." In *Canadian Writers and Their Works.* Ed. Robert Lecker, Jack David, and Ellen Quigley. Toronto: ECW Press, 1985: 17–81.

Mandel, Eli. "Atwood's Politics." In Grace and Weir 1983: 53–66.

McCombs, Judith. "Atwood's Haunted Sequences: *The Circle Game, The Journals of Susanna Moodie,* and *Power Politics.*" In Davidson and Davidson 1981: 35–54.

———. "From 'Places, Migrations' to *The Circle Game*: Atwood's Canadian and Female Metamorphoses." In *Margaret Atwood: Writing and Subjectivity. New Critical Essays.* Ed. Colin Nicholson. New York: St. Martin's Press, 1994: 51–67.

———. "Politics, Structure, and Poetic Development in Atwood's Canadian-American Sequences: From an Apprentice Pair to *The Circle Game* to *Two-Headed Poems.*" In VanSpanckeren and Castro 1988: 142–62.

Mendez-Egle, Beatrice, ed. *Margaret Atwood: Reflection and Reality.* Edinburg, Tex.: Pan American University, 1987.

Merivale, Patricia. "From 'Bad News' to 'Good Bones': Margaret Atwood's Gendering of Art and Elegy." In York 1995: 253–70.

Ostriker, Alicia. "'What Are Patterns For': Anger and Polarization in Women's Poetry." *Feminist Studies* 10.3 (Fall 1984): 485–503.

Simmons, Jes. "'Crept in upon by green': Susanna Moodie and the Process of Individuation." In Mendez-Egle 1987: 139–53.

Sullivan, Rosemary. *The Red Shoes: Margaret Atwood Starting Out.* Toronto: Harper Flamingo, 1998.

VanSpanckeren, Kathryn. "Shamanism in the Works of Margaret Atwood." In VanSpanckeren and Castro 1988: 183–204.

VanSpanckeren, Kathryn and Jan Garden Castro, ed. *Margaret Atwood: Vision and Forms.* Carbondale: Southern Illinois Press, 1988.

Vogt, Kathleen. "Real and Imaginary Animals in the Poetry of Margaret Atwood." In VanSpanckeren and Castro 1988: 163–82.

Wagner, Linda W. "The Making of *Selected Poems*, the Process of Surfacing." In Davidson and Davidson 1981: 81–94.

Wagner-Martin, Linda. "'Giving Way to Bedrock': Atwood's Later Poems." In York 1995: 71–88.

Walker, Cheryl. "Turning to Margaret Atwood: From Anguish to Language." In Mendez-Egle 1987: 154–71.

Weir, Lorraine. "Meridians of Perceptions: A Rereading of *The Journals of Susanna Moodie.*" In Davidson and Davidson 1981: 69–79.

Wilson, Sharon R. "Sexual Politics in Margaret Atwood's Visual Art." In VanSpanckeren and Castro 1988: 205–14.

Woodcock, George. "Metamorphosis and Survival: Notes on the Recent Poetry of Margaret Atwood." In Grace and Weir 1983: 125–42.

York, Lorraine M., ed. *Various Atwoods: Essays on the Later Poems, Short Fiction, and Novels.* Toronto: Anansi, 1995.

"A Certain Frivolity":
Margaret Atwood's Literary Criticism

Walter Pache (University of Augsburg)

'Tis Not Quite Thirty Years Since

BACK IN THE EARLY 1970s not many European scholars crossed the Atlantic to study that dimly perceived phenomenon, the Other North American Literature. The few who did, however, soon noticed that Canada was in the midst of a fascinating period of transition and innovation. Not only was there a palpable awareness that literature and literary criticism were central to the national project, but authors themselves became visible, taking on new roles as mediators and communicators.

In those far-away days, Margaret Atwood, the novelist and poet, had already established her reputation as one of the leading figures on the literary scene. Her novel *The Edible Woman* had appeared in 1969, followed by the poetry collections *The Journals of Susanna Moodie* a year later and *Power Politics* in 1971. Atwood emerged as a literary critic a little later. Although she had published quite a number of book reviews, essays on various writers, and other critical pieces (beginning in her *Acta Victoriana* days in the early sixties), it was the publication of *Survival: A Thematic Guide to Canadian Literature* in 1972 that really put her on the literary map — first in Canada, but soon enough abroad. Almost instantaneously, public interest focused on the young writer and turned her, for better or for worse, into a public figure. In the last thirty years, Margaret Atwood has come to be identified with the struggle for Canadian literature to such an extent that a recent reviewer, Ray Robertson, could write with some justification: "Any author whose work . . . can be found in both airport newspaper shops *and* on graduate school syllabi all over the world must be doing something right."

Atwood's amazing ubiquity as a role model makes it rather difficult to assess her achievement as a critic. In a particular way, Atwood seems to personify the merger of divergent critical traditions. She has, at the same time, stimulated controversial reactions ranging from almost iconic veneration to fierce resentment. Nevertheless, I shall attempt to explore some of Atwood's theoretical premises and views of the critic's craft, to survey the main areas of her critical oeuvre and place it within the broader context of contemporary Canadian criticism, to refine its impact, and to speculate a little about what may lie ahead for her as a critic, as well as for us as readers.

Survival and After

It is a truism to state that Margaret Atwood, in more than one way, represents the vigorous expansion — the "renaissance," as it used to be called — of Canadian literature since the early 1960s. Her career, both as a creative writer and critic, has accompanied, and indeed stimulated, the process of literary emancipation and diversification that character-izes the Canadian situation. Since it is the remarkable continuity as well as the range of her critical oeuvre on which her unusual reputation rests, I would like to briefly consider three publications which seem to encapsulate her progress as a critic: first, obviously, *Survival* (1972), then the essays and articles of her middle period, gathered in the vol-ume *Second Words: Selected Critical Prose* (1982), and finally the more recent collection of interconnected papers published under the title *Strange Things: The Malevolent North in Canadian Literature* (1995).

Survival, without any doubt, is a seminal text, not only because it constructs an extremely powerful formula for a literature which epito-mizes the fundamental and anachronistic clash of the modern mind with a pre-modern natural environment, but also because it sets out all the elements of Atwood's critical method, which was modified and differentiated but not radically altered in the years to follow. At the same time, it was a controversial book from the very date of its publica-tion. Although it has been pointed out that *Survival* was originally conceived as a "money-maker to help out the house of Anansi"[1] by a writer who deliberately refused to be a professional critic, the book was read and reviewed in a different and much more comprehensive con-text. It offered a starkly generalizing hypothesis — the famous *victim theory* — formulated by an outsider, who felt free to blend elements of academic and journalistic style. It was also the book of a young author, who didn't much care whether she made staid academics frown. In the

[1] Linda Hutcheon in *Dictionary of Literary Biography.* Ed. W. H. New.

meantime, of course, Atwood's debut work has become a classic. But it has retained a good deal of its initial power to irritate. Looking back a decade, its author once wrote: "*Survival* was fun to attack. In fact, it still is; most self-respecting professors of CanLit begin their courses, I'm told, with a short ritual sneer at it" (*Second Words*, 105).

The general reader tends to react differently. Re-reading the text more than a quarter century after it first came out, one is not quite sure what to admire most: the boldness of its reductive approach, or the evocative, even provocative analysis from which this approach takes its cue. Moreover, some of the basic concepts that delighted or angered early readers have since become conventional wisdom. Whether we like it or not, our critical perception is shaped by the notorious pattern of the four *victim positions* (*"deny the fact that you are a victim"* / *"acknowledge the fact that you are a victim, but to explain this as an act of Fate [... etc.]"* / *"refuse to accept the assumption that the role is inevitable"* / *"be a creative non-victim,"* Survival, 36–38), and by the comparative thematology of Canadian literature that Atwood derives from it. Her analysis of the pessimistic, even fatalistic mood that manifests itself in archetypal configurations, such as the experience of empty space, man's alienation from nature, or artists and immigrants as prototypes of individual failure, has become firmly entrenched in critical discourse.

Survival reflects Atwood's strong fascination with literary archetypes. There are several references to Robert Graves's influential study *The White Goddess: A Historical Grammar of Poetic Myth* (1948). But (as she would be the first to admit) her critical approach is largely based on Northrop Frye's concept of Canadian *garrison mentality*, initially expressed in his famous "Conclusion" to Carl F. Klinck's *Literary History of Canada* (1965). Atwood's early work is strongly permeated by Frye's ideas on the fundamental paradoxes confronting Canadian identity: "It is less perplexed by the question 'Who am I?' than by some such riddle as 'Where is here?'" (Frye 1976, 338) — to quote just one famous key sentence. And yet, without ever denying this huge debt, the Atwood of *Survival* quite confidently ventures into new territory. Frye's abstract theory is shrewdly instrumentalized so that it becomes a critical tool that has since proved extremely effective — not only by providing clear-cut and usable categories for literary interpretation, but also by stimulating ongoing controversies. Some of these general questions are central to the Canadian condition, for instance the question as to how the literary imagination responds, not only to the geographic situation, but also to the spiritual climate in which it finds itself.

For all its juvenile shortcomings (like occasional oversimplification for the sake of argument), *Survival* was a remarkable milestone in Canadian criticism, not least because it resolutely insisted on the importance of a "national" and archetypal point of view instead of measuring Canadian literature solely with the normative yardstick of international modernism. By placing the emphasis on its achievements rather than on its shortcomings, it conceptualized Canadian literature and defined the Canadian canon. Moreover, it inaugurated a fresh synthesis of textual analysis, literary history, and political assessment. In combining a scholarly approach with journalistic elements, *Survival* seems to experiment with a multilayered text, catering to the specialist without losing sight of the general reader. This dual perspective has since become the hallmark of Atwood's critical prose, together with her stylistic precision, a flexible and elegant diction that shifts effortlessly from the academic to the informal level, more often than not spiced with deadpan irony, and a keen, frequently mordant wit.

Survival set the pace for Atwood's extremely successful career as a critic. Many of her subsequent pieces are occasional criticism in the best sense of the word: short essays that respond to topical problems, addressing, beyond their communicative public aspects, their more general, contextual implications. What this means in practice becomes particularly evident when we look at *Second Words* (1982). Although this volume contains a number of texts published prior to *Survival*, it focuses on the following period during which Atwood became the public personality she is today. The new demands made on her — notably by the mass media — are reflected in an astonishing formal variety: book reviews and introductions to books appear next to longer critical texts and public speeches held on various occasions. Even more surprising is the wide choice of subject matter, both Canadian and international, testifying to Atwood's catholic taste as well as to her profound erudition. There are references to William Shakespeare and Robert Service, to Herman Melville and Gwendolyn MacEwen, to Edgar Allan Poe and Al Purdy, to the Brontë sisters and to George Bowering. Despite this impressive array of names, Atwood's essays concentrate on issues, movements, ideas, rather than on individual authors.

Taken as a whole, *Second Words* displays a distinctly political bias, even providing a kind of running commentary on the chief issues of the 1970s and 1980s: the Canadianness of Canadian literature ("Canadian Monsters: Some Aspects of the Supernatural in Canadian Fiction," 1977), women and writing ("The Curse of Eve — Or, What I Learned in School," 1978), the politics of literature ("An End to Audience?" 1980), the difficult dialogue with the southern neighbor ("Canadian-American Relations: Surviving the Eighties," 1981), and, increasingly, human rights questions ("Amnesty International: An Address," 1981). Atwood also never hesitates to raise her critical voice in support of younger writers if she feels they are in danger of being overlooked or unfairly treated by mainstream critics.

What holds this heterogeneous bunch together? For all its eclectic diversity in subject matter and methodology, Atwood's oeuvre reflects a genuine concern for the social responsibility of the writer, and also a deep commitment to criticism as a vital human activity, which is nevertheless of secondary importance to the creative writer. As the title of the volume suggests (and as the author herself points out in her preface), most of the critical texts can be read as companion pieces to Atwood's fictional and poetical work, exploring, expanding, and explaining its central aspects. But under all circumstances, Atwood insists, the writer's prime obligation is to his or her creative potential, which must be used delicately. As she states in an early interview:

> I'm always interested to see what they [other people] have to say . . . they come up with things I hadn't thought of. So that's fun. But if you start doing that too much with your own work, it's like thinking about the technique of skiing when you're halfway down a hill.[2]

Thematically, Atwood's more recent criticism appears to be firmly embedded in the groundwork first laid out in *Survival*. Literature and culture in Canada are viewed as a productive response to the challenge posed by its precarious existence on the fringe of an alien, even hostile space, understood in a geographical as well as in a political sense. Yet this does not mean that her criticism has remained sterile and static. On the contrary, it has changed continually, though not radically, producing an ongoing critical discourse which, to a certain extent, owes its very existence to the writer herself. In the course of this process, the archetypal pattern has shed some of its gloomy pessimism, and, though the argument has lost some of its abrasiveness, it has gained in subtlety while retaining the familiar flavor of relaxed irony.

A remarkable result of that mellowing process is *Strange Things* (1995). As the subtitle *The Malevolent North in Canadian Fiction* indicates, it is a more closely organized volume than *Second Words*. Thematically interrelated, the four essays on the North explore and dissect literary myths as projections that are based on certain collective assumptions — an essentially deconstructive approach. The arctic and subarctic North, defined by writers like Rudyard Kipling and Robert Service as the unalterable essence of Canadian identity, is re-interpreted

---

[2] Interview with Mary Ellis Gibson in Ingersoll 1990: 39.

as a cultural construct. In Atwood's view, the myth-building force of "North" is not so much a malevolent force, but perceived rather as an emblem of the utterly alien and extra-human. The complex imaginative process that converts authentic events into cultural myths is demonstrated in a series of four case studies that analyze literary texts in their intertextual connections.

In the opening essay, the disastrous failure of Sir John Franklin's search for the Northwest Passage is shown, in a series of literary transformations, to change from a tale of human heroism into one of vanishing without a trace. The Franklin myth encodes Northern space as a sinister *femme fatale*, who spells doom and annihilation. The other extreme, the romantic construction of primordial Northern nature as a realm of freedom from civilization and its deformations, is exemplified in the tragi-comical figure of Archie Belaney, whose re-invention of himself as "Grey Owl" has been fictionalized as hubris or farce. Together with the other Northern myths discussed — the cannibalistic Wendigo myth, and the modification and deconstruction of male wilderness ideology in women's writing from Pauline Johnson and Susanna Moodie to Marian Engel and Margaret Laurence ("Linoleum Caves") — *Strange Things* draws a very complex yet graphic picture of an ambiguous metaphor, central to the Canadian imagination. It also demonstrates quite impressively how Atwood, reacting to postmodern urban society as well as to environmental and ecological concerns, has continued to widen her critical range. Atwood winds up arguing that Northern space is being mythologized while it is fast disappearing: "The North is not endless. It is not vast and strong, and capable of devouring and digesting all the human dirt thrown its way" (*Strange Things*, 115–16) is her sobering ecological conclusion.

Throughout Atwood's critical oeuvre the feminist factor is clearly of paramount importance. It operates on several levels. In a way, the subversive and parodistic slant of her approach corresponds to the woman's position: writing against the domination of the male master discourse. Both as a writer and a critic Margaret Atwood has time and again stood up as an advocate of women's rights, taken up current issues of emancipation, and exposed the dangerous deficits of established patriarchal hierarchies. At the same time, however, she has always resolutely avoided committing herself to a definitive mode and code of *female writing*. Whether this refusal, as Frank Davey, one of her most outspoken critics, has assumed, is rooted in what he calls "an essentialist view of female nature" (Davey 1988, 77) as pastoral and intuitive, anti-rational and anti-linear, seems questionable. Atwood refuses to endorse feminist clichés because she intensely dislikes the role of the orthodox ideological mouthpiece: "Am I a propagandist? No! Am I an observer of society? Yes! And no one who observes society can fail to make observations which are feminist. That is just based on real-life common sense."[3] Again, Atwood's stance is decidedly anti-ideological because she sees herself primarily as a writer. She is afraid that any direct and active involvement in the ideological struggle for power might seriously damage the independence of creative imagination. This point is explicitly made in contributions dealing with the woman question, e.g. "Paradoxes and Dilemmas: The Woman as Writer" (1976),[4] but occurs frequently elsewhere. Instead of applying someone else's feminist theory, Atwood prefers to look at woman's role in society, more specifically at the woman writer's role in society, from the independent point of view of the woman writer in society. She works by pinpointing inconsistencies and contradictions, keeping a keen eye on changing conventional attitudes, rather than lending her voice to an abstract critique of the system.

"A Good Amateur Plumber": Atwood's Critical Principles

Atwood's feminism is an integral part of her critical approach, just as her concept of criticism is inseparable from her creative work. This close coherence is reflected both by the intertextual and metafictional complexity of her narratives and the individual viewpoint she adopts in her critical prose. And yet there are clear priorities. While it may be an exaggeration to claim that Atwood's critical pieces are merely by-products of her writing, the critic plays second fiddle to the poet and novelist because "a writer has to write something before a critic can criticize it" (*Second Words*, 11). It is this fundamental bias that informs her critical principles.

Ever since the days of *Survival*, Atwood — an academic, a *poeta doctus*, if ever there was one — has carefully cultivated the persona of non-academic, even anti-academic, critic. She continues to claim that whatever she writes does not aspire to scholarly status nor propound any critical theory. "As a theorist, I'm a good amateur plumber," she once remarked with characteristic understatement in an interview with Geoff Hancock, "You do what you have to do to keep your sink from over-

---

[3] Interview with Sudhakar Jamkhandi in Bouson 1993: 3.

[4] Reprinted as "On Being a 'Woman Writer': Paradoxes and Dilemmas." In *Second Words*, 190–204.

flowing" (in Ingersoll, 208). Literary criticism, in other words, helps authors to get their bearings by providing landmarks of orientation. Yet it would be misleading to interpret such remarks as expressions of pure modesty. They also, and perhaps primarily, provide a subtle comment on the state of academic criticism. Atwood casts a suspicious eye on the sterile exercises of professional critics — "Canadianists and thesis-writers" (*Strange Things*, 114), for example — and the obscure ritual-ized games they play with the initiated few, instead of applying them-selves to the more practical task of elucidating textual and cultural difficulties for the benefit of the public. Critics and readers alike, she seems to suggest, are better served by a witty dilettante than by a seri-ous theorist. In a fake review of *Second Words*, Atwood, in one of her histrionic moods, has a fictitious (and confusingly spelled) "Margarets Atwood" proclaim: "Perhaps it's her lack of professional status that ac-counts for a certain frivolity and even audacity in these pieces" (in McCombs 1988, 253).

However much we may enjoy the glorious spirit of self-irony, we must not be taken in by the parodistic tone. Behind the seeming casu-alness there lurks an acute analytical mind. Atwood's literary criticism quite deliberately sets out to occupy the gaps left by the professionals. She prefers to close in on observable phenomena ("You can't have a thought about a stone without first seeing a stone," *Second Words*, 11), relying on her creative imagination and her sharp intellect alike. She stresses the communicative role of the critic whose task it is to evaluate literature not just as private entertainment and formal artifact, but as a vital part of public discourse — an aspect that is particularly relevant in a country like Canada, which many observers until not so long ago preferred to regard as a kind of critical wasteland.

Margaret Atwood is aware of this multilayered background. The dual discourse of her critical approach is calculated to integrate dispa-rate elements like the thematic and the formal. She never loses sight of the fundamental aesthetic obligation the writer is under, but incorpo-rates topical issues like nationalism, feminism, or, more recently, human rights. From the early stages of her career, she has regarded writing as "a political manifesto" (*Survival*, 13), as a forum for educated discus-sion of questions vital to the individual and society, e.g. of Canada's collective emancipation. The writer as critic, she has consistently ar-gued, must alert the Canadian public as well as readers abroad to the project of strengthening the country's distinctive national profile in an international environment. Unlike the United States, "Canada sees it-self as part of the world; a small sinking Titanic squashed between two icebergs, perhaps, but still inevitably a part" (*Second Words*, 379), to quote just one of her many aphorisms to that effect. The powerful synthesis of the "national" and the "international" discourse, it seems to me, is a key factor in Atwood's concept, as is her understanding of literature both as a medium of Canadian culture *and* as aesthetic construct.

Beyond the political level, there is clearly a moral undercurrent to Atwood's literary criticism that is somewhat reminiscent of critics like Matthew Arnold. Now that the faith in transcendental values has largely been lost, it is literature that functions as the touchstone of communal values, as "guardian of the moral and ethical sense of the community" (*Second Words*, 346). Criticism, in turn, by constantly evaluating literary works, must try to establish a viable consensus amongst the community. Thus, Rosemary Sullivan's assessment of Atwood the writer (in her Atwood article in the 1982 *Oxford Companion to Canadian Literature*) is equally true of Atwood the critic: "In a peculiarly Canadian way Atwood is a staunch moralist, essentially a writer of ideas — coldly, often brutally, insisting that modern man must reinvent himself" (31). Moreover, Atwood is optimistic enough to assume that an educated public, if spoken to in an intelligent and convincing fashion, will be accessible and willing to enter into an open dialogue. This basic trust in common sense and in the autonomous individual as *animal rationale*, or at least — as even Jonathan Swift conceded — *rationis capax*, points beyond Victorian ideas on the moral function of literary criticism to an eighteenth-century concept of enlightened rationalism and of liberal humanism.

The message is simple. Only if writers and critics have the liberty to take up whatever subject they prefer and feel free to treat it in any conceivable way, can they successfully resist totalizing ideologies that today more than ever threaten to limit or even extinguish the freedom of individual thought and action. Atwood never claims to exhaust her subject — nor, indeed, her readers — by telling it all; her approach is open-ended, and avoids generalization wherever possible: "It is usual for a critic to present some general conclusions at the end of an effusion such as this," she concludes her essay on "Canadian Monsters," "I'm not sure that I have any to offer" (*Second Words*, 251). Like Virginia Woolf — a writer whose "impressionistic" approach has a good deal in common with her own — Atwood does not conceive of the critic as the reader's antagonist or as a legislator who lays down the laws for a "correct" textual analysis, but rather sees herself as a guide helping her readers into the text, stimulating them to follow their own instinct and use their own imagination. As Virginia Woolf writes in 1925:

As for the critics whose task it is to pass judgement upon the books of the moment, whose work, let us admit, is difficult, dangerous, and often distasteful, let us ask them to be generous of encouragement, but sparing of those wreaths and coronets which are so apt to get awry, and fade, and make the wearers, in six months time, look a little ridiculous. (1994, 241)

The Writer and the "Footnote Crowd"

Faced with Margaret Atwood's high profile as a public personality and the unmistakable frankness of her views, one is tempted to regard her as a critic *sui generis*. But of course she occupies a specific position within the context of the critical debate and its changes during the past quarter century, even if it is not easy to determine exactly where to place it. Is it modernist or postmodern, feminist or nationalist, structuralist or deconstructivist? Opinions differ widely. The lack of a consensus is aggravated by the fact that, despite the heated debate that has raged about *Survival* to this day, relatively little has been written about Atwood's role as a critic. Atwood seems to elude professional pigeonholing. Most significantly, she does not fit into the pattern of "privatization" (Lecker 1994, 88), which, a couple of years ago, Robert Lecker defined as one of the chief tendencies of literary criticism. Lecker argues that literary criticism, after the enormous publicity gained during the 1960s and 1970s when literary nationalism was the order of the day, has in recent years "become a private affair, removed from public access, divorced from its communal frames" (Lecker, 88). As Lecker sees it, this development is ambiguous, since it implies that while critical discourse has lost "its monologic, nationalist, and hegemonic focus" (Lecker, 89), at the same time it has tended to become esoteric and to neglect its communal obligations. This increasingly academic bias, according to Lecker, is epitomized by Northrop Frye's famous garrison construct, which brought "Canadianness" into focus, but turned it into a self-conscious, elitist, i.e. ultimately private project, disconnected from the public debate.

In such a gloomy scenario, Margaret Atwood very much emerges as the odd woman out. As far as Frye's impact is concerned, she is both disciple and heretic. As "Peggy" Atwood, as she later remembered, she entered Victoria College in 1957[5] — the year *Anatomy of Criticism* was published — and took Frye's legendary Milton course in her third year.

---

[5] Cf. Atwood, "Northrop Frye Observed." In *Second Words*, 398–406.

There followed a lifelong association with the eminent scholar that has left its traces throughout her oeuvre. Frye's magisterial influence manifests itself not only in the wide scope of Atwood's literary learning, but also in her thorough familiarity with the traditional British canon and her skill in classifying and categorizing. Even if all that is at stake is the difference between American, British, and Canadian humor, the typological approach to literature permeates her writing, along with the basic belief in the mythological substructure of modern culture.

Atwood's critical outlook, as I have pointed out earlier, was shaped by Frye's assumption that Canadian culture rested on the sometimes violent tensions between a primitive environment and civilization's urge to survive. As a keen observer of the literary, political, and social scene, Atwood departs from such a dualistic platform. By incorporating new critical issues, she widens her scope and gains fresh methodological insights. Typically, such new questions center round the status of the text. How are texts produced? How do they function, both as reflections of the "real world" and as pieces of the intertextual mosaic? In fact, today Atwood tends to face much more squarely than before what Linda Hutcheon has termed in *The Canadian Postmodern* the "very postmodern paradox" (Hutcheon 1988, 157) of the text as process *and* product, as artifact *and* "part of life." The self-reflexive element of fiction *and* the narrative quality of critical reflection are deliberately brought into play. Although Atwood never completely abandoned the archetypal perspective, her initially quite static critical "system" has gradually developed a new dynamism. This is accompanied by the awareness that the rules of writing are conventions and can therefore be modified and parodied. If critical categories, Atwood seems to imply, are not immovable essentials but have only relative validity, their true function is catalytic, i.e. they spark off a critical dialogue which is open-ended. All criticism is merely an approximation. Final judgments and verdicts may be deferred until further notice. Consequently, in recent years Atwood has expressed much more emphatically her profound respect for the "enormous complexity not only of the relationships between Man and Woman, but also of those between those other abstract intangibles, Art and Life, Form and Content, Writer and Critic, etcetera" (*Second Words*, 190).

It is perhaps the calculated inaccuracy of this closing "etcetera" (and the bravado behind it) that has irritated academic critics — more so than the deliberate distance Margaret Atwood has always kept from what she called the "footnote crowd" (*Second Words*, 105) (as opposed to the "real" audience) ever since she first appeared on the public stage. Atwood's provocative aloofness, along with her stubborn refusal to be divided into writer and critic, has occasionally led to the accusation that she delivers public pronouncements about victimization and survival as the main subjects of her art rather than formulating any consistent critical opinion.[6] Some would put it more bluntly, claiming that what she says as a critic is of limited relevance to either writers or readers. Atwood, in turn, is undeterred by such polemical charges: "People often have difficulty handling somebody who does more than one thing. That's their problem. It's not a difficulty for me" (Twigg 1981, 226), she once laconically told her interviewer.

It is interesting to note that attacks from professional literary critics have frequently been triggered precisely by this seeming lack of a critical rationale. Notably, *Survival* has since its publication been taken to task for being Marxist or capitalist, for being reductionist or merely reflecting a fashionable zeitgeist point of view that only pandered to the mass market. It is perhaps not entirely by accident that a good deal of such polemics originated from critics whose productions have so far failed to reach a broader readership. Frank Davey's censorious verdict on *Survival* as a "layman's guide to Canadian literature" that was "of limited use to educators" (Davey 1974, 30 and 34) is a strange case in point.

There are various other charges which the so-called "educators" have leveled against Atwood's idiosyncratic approach. It has been earmarked as "ultimately irrelevant" (Banerjee 1990, 90) due to a mysterious "parodistic insincerity," as a result of a narrow, Toronto-based, United Empire Loyalist vision of Canada, as a centralist master discourse, denouncing other traditions of writing, and — last but not least — as a viewpoint that, by championing "modernism . . . as the canonical mainstream of contemporary Canadian literature" (Scobie 1991, 57–58), marginalized postmodern alternatives. It has also been suggested that *Survival* and the critical essays that followed in its wake ostensibly gave voice to an all-Canadian condition while being "clearly rooted in the nineteenth-century Establishment Anglo-Protestant sensibility that is epitomized by [Susanna] Moodie and [Catharine Parr] Traill" (New 1997, 80). The defense of pioneer space against anarchy and chaos, it is further argued, actively, even aggressively stigmatizes as the undesirable Other "wilderness, forest, moral corruption, Indians, Catholics, and French" — and by implication, one is tempted to speculate, the entire postcolonial and multi-ethnic project. Atwood's literary criticism, in short, is constructed as conservative ideology that pretends to be universal common sense.

[6] For an early example, cf. Frank Davey 1974, 34.

Objections such as these should not be shrugged off as entirely ir-relevant and off the mark, even though such critics are inclined to in-flate partial and relative perceptions into absolute truth and tend to underrate the historical factor. The very fact that Atwood's critical views have become so immensely popular at home and abroad has given them a normative quality that no one could have anticipated at the time of writing. Atwood's literary criticism has always tried to strike a delicate balance by defining a clear-cut individual position in a philo-sophically and ethnically pluralistic world. In doing so, as the author herself would be the first to admit, she foregrounds certain issues and bypasses others, subjecting the evidence to her educated yet subjective judgment. The vantage point of liberal humanism, from which Atwood surveys the contemporary scene, is no longer — as in the days of Alex-ander Pope, Matthew Arnold, or even Virginia Woolf— the uncontested consensual norm of common culture but implies a political statement. It also makes a stand against professional critical discourses which, in turn, had alienated a sizable part of the reading public. That Atwood has been able to reclaim much of this important territory is not her least achievement as a critic. It is this communicative focus that un-derlies her resistance to totalizing theories, from whatever corner, and her reluctance to be more than "slightly postmodern." In the "Marga-rets Atwood" review of *Second Words* already quoted, we find not only a reference to the intriguingly anagrammatic "Estonian-Italian post-modernist linguist and expert on metafiction, Trogwate d'Amorda" (in McCombs 1988: 251), but also the following revealing passage:

> As a book reviewer and critic, Atwood is definitely on the conservative side. Postmodernism seems to have wafted right by her, and she's not at all up to in-depth analyses of metonymy and synecdoche . . . She still seems to believe that creation is primary and that criticism of a work should bear some relation to what is actually on the page . . . But then, as a critic she is — as she's the first to point out — not a pro. (252)

Literary criticism as a practical, text-centered, and value-oriented craft — still, Atwood's method is far removed from the ivory tower of "privatization" and also vehemently opposed to what Judith Fitzgerald has recently called "the onslaught of cultureless utilitarianism" and "commodification of cultural contributions" (Fitzgerald 1998, 22), i.e. a brand of criticism that renounces cultural standards and tries to latch on to any fashionable new movement in a hectic act of "communifica-tion." In a pluralistic world of changing values, Margaret Atwood con-tinues to believe in man's capacity for rational judgment as an indispensable prerequisite for the survival of individual freedom. Criticism, if it can't make the world better, can perhaps prevent it from getting worse.

What Lies Ahead

During the 1920s, Frederick Philip Grove, the German *fin de siècle* writer turned Canadian realist, single-handedly (and rather unsuccessfully) tried to create both a new Canadian literature and a critical framework for it. Half a century later, Margaret Atwood seems to have succeeded where Grove failed. Although she is not the only writer to combine the creative and the critical mode — other notable contemporaries like George Bowering, Robertson Davies, Robert Kroetsch, or John Metcalf come to mind — it is her concept of criticism as creative art that makes her achievement unique. Atwood has shaped our literary perception to such an extent that it is difficult to imagine how we might read Canadian literature and Canadian culture without her guidance. As mediator between art and the audience, between an increasingly elusive and elitist literary theory on the one hand and a noncommittal *anything goes* on the other, between rigorous standards of sound reasoning and an awareness of the need to act as advocate of a civilization threatened by irrational forces, Atwood has become an almost emblematic figure — however strongly she would reject such a rigid role cliché that ill suits her preference for the creative anarchy of writing and reviewing in a changing world. If this is lack of professionalism, it is perhaps that very lack that has turned Margaret Atwood at sixty into the dynamic and lively institution she is today.

Looking back over the decades, we should indeed be grateful that, during the late 1960s, an up-and-coming young Canadian scholar who had just moved from Princeton to Edmonton decided to abandon her Ph.D. thesis on "Nature and Power in the English Metaphysical Romance of the Nineteenth and Twentieth Century" (Staels 1995, 4), and instead turned to reviewing contemporary books in brilliant essays that more often than not opened with concise epigrammatic statements like: "In reading Gwendolyn MacEwen's poetry it is a temptation to become preoccupied with the original and brilliant verbal surfaces she creates, at the expense of the depths beneath them" (*Second Words*, 67). This is unmistakably the confident voice Margaret Atwood has created. Apart from characterizing MacEwen's poetry, the sentence could also be applied to Atwood's own way of writing and the dual perspective it conveys. Without any question, we have all gained enormously from Atwood's critical depths and surfaces. We look forward to what lies ahead.

Works Cited

Atwood, Margaret. "Canadian-American Relations: Surviving the Eighties." In Atwood 1982: 371–92.

———. "Canadian Monsters: Some Aspects of the Supernatural in Canadian Fiction." In Atwood 1982: 229–53.

———. *The Edible Woman.* Toronto: McClelland & Stewart, 1988.

———. *The Journals of Susanna Moodie.* Toronto: Oxford University Press, 1970.

———. "On Being a 'Woman Writer': Paradoxes and Dilemmas." In Atwood 1982: 190–204.

———. *Power Politics.* Toronto: Anansi, 1971.

———. *Second Words: Selected Critical Prose.* Toronto: Anansi, 1982.

———. *Strange Things: The Malevolent North in Canadian Literature.* Oxford: Clarendon, 1995.

———. *Survival: A Thematic Guide to Canadian Literature.* Toronto: Anansi, 1972.

Banerjee, Chinmoy. "Alice in Disneyland: Criticism as Commodity in *The Handmaid's Tale.*" *Essays on Canadian Writing* 41 (1990): 74–92.

Bouson, J. Brooks. *Brutal Choreographies: Oppositional Strategies and Narrative Design in the Novels of Margaret Atwood.* Amherst: University of Massachussetts Press, 1993.

Davey, Frank. *From Here to There.* Erin, Ontario: Porcepic, 1974.

———. "Margaret Atwood: A Feminist Poetics." In *Reading Canadian Reading.* Winnipeg: Turnstone, 1988: 63–85.

Fitzgerald, Judith. "Critical Condition." *Books in Canada* 27.5 (1998): 21–23.

Frye, Northrop. *Anatomy of Criticism: Four Essays.* Princeton, N.J.: Princeton University Press, 1957.

———. "Conclusion." In *Literary History of Canada.* Vol. 2. Ed. C. F. Klinck. 2nd ed. Toronto: University of Toronto Press, 1976: 333–61.

Graves, Robert. *The White Goddess: A Historical Grammar of Poetic Myth.* London: Faber & Faber, 1959.

Hancock, Geoff. "Tightrope-Walking over Niagara Falls." In Ingersoll 1990: 191–221.

Hutcheon, Linda. *The Canadian Postmodern: A Study of Contemporary English-Canadian Fiction.* Toronto: University of Toronto Press, 1988.

Ingersoll, Earl G., ed. *Margaret Atwood: Conversations*. Princeton, N.J.; Ontario Review Press, 1990.

Lecker, Robert. "Professionalism and the Rhetoric of English-Canadian Criticism." *Zeitschrift für Kanada-Studien* 14.1 (1994): 87–117.

McCombs, Judith, ed. *Critical Essays on Margaret Atwood*. Boston, Massachusetts: Hall, 1988.

New, W. H. ed. *Canadian Writers Since 1960*, 1st ser. Dictionary of Literary Criticism, vol. 53. Detroit, Michigan: Gale Research Company, 1986.

———, *Land Sliding: Imagining Space, Presence, and Power in Canadian Writing*. Toronto: University of Toronto Press, 1997.

Robertson, Ray. Review of *The Red Shoes: Margaret Atwood Starting Out*, by Rosemary Sullivan. *Books in Canada* 27.7 (October 1998): 20, 31.

Scobie, Stephen. "Leonard Cohen, Phyllis Webb; and the End(s) of Modernism." In *Canadian Canons: Essays in Literary Value*. Ed. Robert Lecker. Toronto: University of Toronto Press, 1991: 57–70.

Staels, Hilde. *Margaret Atwood's Novels: A Study of Narrative Discourse*. Tübingen/Basel: Francke, 1995.

Sullivan, Rosemary. "Atwood, Margaret." In *The Oxford Companion to Canadian Literature*. Ed. William Toye. Toronto/Oxford/New York: Oxford University Press, 1983: 30–33.

Twigg, Alan. "What to Write." In *For Openers: Conversations with 24 Canadian Writers*. Madiera Park: Harbour, 1981: 219–30.

Woolf, Virginia. "How it Strikes a Contemporary" (1925). In *The Essays of Virginia Woolf*, vol. 4. Ed. Andrew McNeillie. London: Hogarth Press, 1994: 233–42.

III. Approaches

Transgressing Genre: A Generic Approach to Margaret Atwood's Novels

Coral Ann Howells (University of Reading, UK)

> It's the same with any form. You have to understand what the form is doing, how it works, before you say, "Now we're going to make it different ..., we're going to turn it upside down, we're going to move it so it includes something which isn't supposed to be there, we're going to surprise the reader. (Margaret Atwood in Ingersoll, 193)

HOW DO WE THINK about literary genre today? And, more pertinently, how does Margaret Atwood think about genre? Her nine novels may be read as variously alluding to popular women's romance, Gothic romance, fairy tales, wilderness survival narratives, domestic comedy, science fiction fantasy, spy thrillers, the dystopia, the kunstler-roman, the fictive autobiography, and the historical novel. To consider generic perspectives with an emphasis on pluralism would seem to be the appropriate course to take in our contemporary context of post-structuralism and postmodernist aesthetics. Atwood's position is signaled in my opening quotation, which represents a balance between respect for generic traditions and an insistent challenge to traditional limits. Indeed, it is a position close to what Linda Hutcheon describes as "that postmodern paradox of complicity and critique" and which she sees as characteristic of Atwood's fiction (Hutcheon 1988, 146). If the novel is, as Atwood suggests, "a vehicle for looking at society — an interface between language and what we choose to call reality" (in Ingersoll, 246), then it is culturally specific in other ways as well, and we are likely to find correspondences between the destabilization of genres in contemporary literary theory and the fiction which is now being produced. This essay will examine the genres which have been most influential on Atwood's novel writing since the mid-1980s: the dystopia, the kunstlerroman, the fictive autobiography, the Gothic romance, and the historical novel, with the aim of highlighting Atwood's continuous experimentation across genre boundaries, and the political and ideological significance of such revisions.

In the 1980s and 1990s genre theory has been radically transformed by the structuralists and poststructuralists, and though it is true that "nothing has happened, really, that hasn't happened before" (Atwood 1992, 221), a study like Paul Hernadi's *Beyond Genre* (1972) with its scholarly survey of genre criticism up till 1970 now looks like literary history. Influenced by critics like Jonathan Culler (*Structuralist Poetics*) and Tzvetan Todorov (*Genres in Discourse*), we have learned to see genres as literary "norm[s] or expectation[s] to guide the reader in his encounter with the text" (Culler 1975, 136), or, as "choices among discursive possibilities, choices that a given society has made conventional" (Todorov 1990, 10). These structuralist definitions were given a further spin by the poststructuralist recognition that different generic interpretations of texts are possible ("that different interpretations are different generic interpretations," Culler 1981, 59). The poststructuralist emphasis on textuality, intertextuality, reader response, and historical specificity has led to distinctions between genres becoming radically destabilized. Yet, although explicit theorizing about genre has gone out of fashion, the concept of genre does not go away, for both writers and readers are aware of the force of genre codes and conventions. As Frans de Bruyn has remarked: "The greatest challenge that the concept of genre poses to contemporary theory is its refusal to disappear, its insistence on a rapprochement rather than a rupture, between the old and the new in theoretical discourse" (in Makaryk 1993, 84). Critics now tend to view genres not as categories, but as rhetorical strategies or social institutions which are responsive to particular historical and ideological imperatives (cf. Cooke 1995, 209). Hutcheon makes this situation very clear when she spells out how postmodernist fiction (in which she includes *The Handmaid's Tale*) emphasizes pluralism and specificities of location which challenge "conventions that are presumed to be literary 'universals,' but can in fact be shown to embody the values of a very particular group of people — of a certain class, race, gender, and sexual orientation" (Hutcheon, 108). This attitude of contestation challenges systems of authority and order which include not only genre but also the literary canon and the traditional discipline of history. The critical emphasis now is on marginality and the transgression of genre boundaries, as the title of a book on the contemporary Canadian long poem by Smaro Kamboureli would seem to indicate: *On the Edge of Genre* (1991).

Indeed, the title of one of the Atwood sessions at the 1998 MLA conference was "Border Country: Genre-Discipline Crossings in Atwood's Work." In that title, where interestingly all the texts discussed belong to the mid-1980s and 1990s, we see the recognition of Atwood's generic dislocations and transformations in a context of post-modern critique: "Atwood signals the fact that conventional patterns, whether they belong to narrative, myth, or the body of implicit maxims that constitutes our ideology or vision of the world, are socially constructed, and as such, may be transformed or reconstructed" (Dvorak 1998, 81).

Dystopia

Taking Atwood's recent novels in chronological order, we turn first to her dystopian text *The Handmaid's Tale* (1985). Here it is not difficult to see that it is Atwood's choice of a female narrator which turns the traditional dystopia upside down, engaging in the debate about gender and genre which is one of Atwood's abiding concerns.[1] The dystopia is a dominantly masculine genre. When Atwood spoke in France in November 1998 about the genesis of her novel and her extensive reading of utopias/dystopias, the vast majority of the examples were by male writers: George Orwell's *1984*, Aldous Huxley's *Brave New World*, Arthur Koestler's *Darkness at Noon*, Thomas More's *Utopia*, Samuel Butler's *Erewhon*, William Morris's *News from Nowhere* — to list some of the names mentioned (Atwood 1999, 20–21). (The two feminist utopias were Charlotte Perkins Gilman's *Herland* and Marge Piercy's *Woman on the Edge of Time*, and the only feminist dystopia was *The Stepford Wives* by Ira Levin.) Atwood's analysis of the doubled genre of utopia/dystopia offers fascinating insights into her own inflections of the form, with her focus on its satiric function and on the themes of patriarchal tyranny and absolute social control: "Both utopias and dystopias have the habit of cutting off the hands and feet and even heads of those who don't fit in the scheme" (Atwood 1999, 19–20). Atwood chooses a feminine perspective: "It's the story of one woman under the [Gileadean] regime, told in a very personal way, and part of the challenge for me was the creation of her voice and viewpoint" (Atwood papers 1986, Box 96, File 11). This gender factor, which is highlighted thematically and re-emphasized by the change to a male narrator in the Historical Notes at the end, radically shifts the emphasis of the genre. To quote Virginia Woolf on the difference that gender makes:

---

[1] For an annotated bibliography of criticism of *The Handmaid's Tale*, see Thompson 1997, 84–98. I shall pay fuller attention to recent French criticism of this novel, with its strong emphasis on generic perspectives.

> It is probable, however, that both in life and in art the values of a
> woman are not the values of a man. Thus, when a woman comes to
> write a novel, she will find that she is perpetually wishing to alter the
> established values — to make serious what appears insignificant to a
> man, and trivial what is to him important. (Woolf 1929, 49)

Atwood's version focuses on what has traditionally been left out of the
dystopia. Offred, the Handmaid in Gilead, is marginalized and disem-
powered because of her sex, so that her story shifts the structural relation between the private and public worlds of the dystopia, where the
officially silenced Other becomes the central narrative voice, displacing
the grand narratives of the Bible and official Gileadean history. This is
herstory, a deconstructive view of patriarchal authority, which in turn is
challenged at an academic conference two hundred years later by the
male Cambridge historian Professor Pieixoto, who tries to discredit
Offred's version for its lack of documentary information. However, by
this stage, Offred has the author's support (in the pun "Denay,
Nunavit") and she also has the reader's sympathy, so that history does
not succeed in undermining herstory after all. Indeed, the Historical
Notes belong to the dystopian genre (cf. Orwell's appendix in *1984* on
Newspeak), but the reader's discovery that what we have been reading
is an edited reconstruction of cassette recordings seriously complicates
any simple dystopian reading by adding yet another generic layer, with
its satire on academic conferences and on objective views of history
(Greene 1998).

Depending on the reader's perspective and the criteria chosen, *The
Handmaid's Tale* might be interpreted as belonging to a whole range
of genres. Is it at all a "feminist dystopia" (Fullbrook 1990)? Given
Gilead's fundamentalist doctrine of biological essentialism, Atwood's
feminist concerns are plain, but so too are her concerns for basic human rights. Gilead is a failed utopia for everyone, with its male bodies
regularly hung on the Wall, its religious intolerance, its racial oppression, and beyond that Atwood's wider vision of environmental threat
and the potential abuses of technology (Leclaire 1999). If, on the other
hand, attention is focused on Offred as narrator and her powers of resistance through storytelling, another range of generic readings shimmers into view. The novel may be read as belonging to the genre of
women's fictive autobiography, prison narrative or survival narrative,
comparable with *Bodily Harm* and *Alias Grace* (Howells 1998), or it
may even be read as a parodic version of female romance (Sturgess
1999). According to formal criteria, it may be classified as an epistolary
novel addressed to "Dear You" and delivered two hundred years later
(Kaufman 1989).

This brief outline of the range of generic perspectives which have been taken on this novel reminds us of Atwood's comment on the text as reconstruction:

> So if you like, the tale that we have is a reconstruction of a reconstruction. . . . However, every reading of every text is always a reconstruction. The reconstructor is the reader, who reads the text and then rearranges the elements of it in his or her mind according to his or her own priorities. (Atwood 1999a, 13)

We might conclude that *The Handmaid's Tale* is a dissident dystopia, though it cannot be reduced to that generic classification. Though it shares many of the thematic features of traditional models of the genre, it subverts the masculine dystopian fascination with institutional politics or military tactics by focusing on the silenced Others in Gilead. Likewise, Offred's story with all its gaps and confessions of unreliability challenges Professor Pieixoto's deterministic view of history and the role of historiography as authentication of the past, in favor of something far more arbitrary and subjectively reconstructed. The novel's discourse mixes so many generic conventions, and Offred's language shifts so dynamically between realism, lyricism, and fantasy, that I believe it effects a revision of Atwood's own earlier views on utopias/dystopias. Back in 1976, in a review of *Woman on the Edge of Time*, Atwood had commented that utopias (and dystopias) seem to be "products, finally, of the moral rather than the literary sense" (Atwood 1982, 276). *The Handmaid's Tale* combines both: it is a moral outcry and a warning to late twentieth-century readers, while it also shows a keen awareness of the fabricated quality of storytelling. Atwood's double awareness of the moral and the literary, the politically engaged and a self-conscious postmodern aesthetic, is emblematized in Offred's narrative commentary on bodies — human bodies (not gendered) and the body of the text: "I'm sorry there is so much pain in this story. I'm sorry it's in fragments, like a body caught in crossfire or pulled apart by force. But there is nothing I can do to change it" (*THT*, 279).

Kunstlerroman, Fictive Autobiography

To turn from *The Handmaid's Tale* to *Cat's Eye* (1988) is to see the genre of fictive autobiography transformed into the kunstlerroman, for this novel is "The Portrait of the Young Artist as a Falling Woman" and a "portrait of the artist as a no-longer-young woman" (Davidson 1997, 69, 14), told in the first person by middle-aged painter Elaine Risley on the occasion of her first retrospective exhibition in Toronto.[2] Biography or autobiography, whether factual or fictional, is concerned with the construction of the identity of the biographical subject and his/her representation in the text. Through what cultural and social matrices does identity become intelligible, and is there a stable, essential self? The genre encourages us to think about the terms by which identity is constructed. Who is Elaine Risley? This fictive autobiography presents a double figuring of the female artist through Elaine's discursive memoir, accompanied by descriptions of her paintings, culminating in the retrospective exhibition at the end with its promisingly titled picture "Unified Field Theory." These two accounts, however, offer variant versions of a self and highlight nothing so much as the problematical construction of female subjectivity in fiction. The novel has been described as a fictive confession (Cooke 1995), a quest novel (Davidson 1997, 60), and a survival narrative having affinities with Atwood's wilderness survival stories, while it might also be seen as a feminist critique of science in Elaine's resistance to the master discourses of biology and theoretical physics practiced by her father and brother. Combining as it does the discourses of fiction and autobiography, painting and science, there is a case to be made for such varying generic readings, and indeed the narrator's own self-projection encourages such multiplicity:

> Even when I've got the distance adjusted, I vary. I am transitional; some days I look like a worn-out thirty-five, others like a sprightly fifty. So much depends on the light, and the way you squint. (*CE*, 5)

Such resistance to classification might be said to be a distinctive characteristic of life-writing in the feminine, for "the female autobiographical 'I' is more like a process than a product, and its discourse is more likely to be iterative, cyclical, incremental and unresolved, even a mystery" (Grace 1994, 191), or as Elaine says more economically, "There is never only one, of anyone" (*CE*, 6). The first challenge is to define "in the feminine." Traditionally, the feminine is associated with delicacy, gentleness, and domesticity, with a focus on love stories and family plots, but "in the feminine" has a more general definition in the late twentieth century — pertaining to women. If we think of the examples of womanhood in *Cat's Eye*, with Elaine's mother, Mrs. Smeath, Miss Stuart, and Elaine's contemporaries like Cordelia and Susie, plus the younger women at the Sub-Versions art gallery, we may consider that this novel revises the concept of "in the feminine" while revising the autobiographical genre. As Elaine declares in a negative attempt to de-

---

[2] For an annotated bibliography of *Cat's Eye*, see Davidson 1997, 105–10.

fine her identity: "I am not Woman, and I'm damned if I'll be shoved into it" (*CE*, 379). Yet Elaine is not Man either, and her life-writing represents the opposite of a traditional masculine construction of a centered self with its confirmation of power and authority. Instead, her memoir, reconstructed in a nonlinear fashion as a series of flashbacks and associative processes, charts a changing self which operates through disguises, a parade of doubles and different personas, always in transition and always exceeding its representations in language or painting.

In order to understand Elaine's project of constructing herself as subject, it is necessary to consider the different coordinates which she uses — time, space, and doubles — for this is a multidimensional figuring of identity: "There are, apparently, a great many more dimensions than four" (*CE*, 332). Back in her home town of Toronto for her retrospective, Elaine encounters that "specular moment" which Paul de Man identifies as the genesis of the autobiographical impulse, with its sudden alignment between past and present selves which opens up multiple possibilities for self-figuration (de Man 1979, 926). Trying to identify her present position, Elaine discovers that she is living in at least two time dimensions at once as she remembers the past, for "Time is not a line but a dimension, like the dimensions of space. . . . It was my brother Stephen who told me that" (*CE*, 3). The novel is filled with echoes of her dead brother's voice in allusions to his theories about curved space, light, black holes, and the uncertainty principle. In significant ways, Stephen's scientific theories have shaped Elaine's imagination as an artist, for his theories and her paintings occupy the same area of speculation on the mysterious laws which govern the universe. Indeed, it is his theoretical physics lecture on "The First Picoseconds and the Quest for a Unified Field Theory" which gives Elaine the title for the final painting in her exhibition. The boundaries between science and art dissolve in what might be seen as an act of gendered transgression, where a sister's paintings show one way in which a woman might both resist and incorporate the master discourse, transforming cosmological theory into private testimonial through a different mode of figuration.

It was her brother who announced, "Cordelia has a tendency to exist" (*CE*, 242). That ambiguous classification of Elaine's "best friend" from schooldays, who is also her tormentor and her own dark double, signals another dimension in Elaine's project of self-representation, that of the repressed which continues to haunt her. Her figuring of lack and loss is emblematized in her painting of Cordelia entitled "Half a Face," and is the focus of the quest theme, for Elaine searches incessantly for Cordelia on her return to Toronto. It is in this space, haunted by an absent presence, that the Gothic makes its appearance, with Elaine's memories of threatening games of death and burial instigated by Cordelia and the more sinister adolescent power games in the cemetery where Elaine takes her revenge, only to find that she is still trapped:

> There's the same flush of shame, of guilt and terror, and of cold disgust with myself. But I don't know where these feelings have come from, what I've done. (*CE*, 253)

Only at the end does Elaine manage to free herself by forgiving Cordelia as she stands on the bridge, so that she is able to let Cordelia "*go home*" (*CE*, 419) and to recognize what she has lost: "This is what I miss, Cordelia: not something that's gone, but something that will never happen. Two old women giggling over their tea" (*CE*, 421).

Problems of perception and perspective are of crucial importance for a painter like Elaine, who sees everything through the "cat's eye" of her visual imagination. The retrospective exhibition at the end might be taken as the final statement in her curiously doubled autobiography, and indeed the retrospective is the informing principle of this kunstlerroman, for it is already programmed on the Contents page at the beginning, where all the chapter titles are given the names of Elaine's paintings. (There is only one exception, "Iron Lung," which she cannot paint because she is still inside a metaphorical iron lung, "being breathed by time.") Throughout the novel these paintings offer a counter-discourse to the memoir narrative, figuring events from a different perspective, for when Elaine looks through her artistic cat's eye she sees more than she consciously registers. Her paintings are truly "sub-versions," uncovering a complex network of conflicting energies and emotions which Elaine never truly understands, any more than she understands her own vocation which comes upon her in the middle of a biology exam "like a sudden epileptic fit" (*CE*, 255). Elaine cannot explain those crucial moments which determine her career as an artist though she can paint versions of two of them — her childhood vision of the Virgin Mary on the bridge and that Proustian moment when, as an adult, she finds her cat's eye marble: "I look into it, and see my life entire" (*CE*, 398). Both these events figure in the "Unified Field Theory" painting, where the Virgin holds the cat's eye marble as she floats above the layers of Elaine's childhood traumas and buried memories. This painting is her attempt to represent her "life entire" and the forces which have shaped her as a subject. Yet, just as the retrospective exhibition offers a teasing and surprisingly provisional representation of Elaine as an artist, so this, the largest of her pictures, offers not a portrait of the artist but a multilayered figuring through which a "self" might be inferred. Once again Elaine escapes any reductive definition:

> I can no longer control these paintings, or tell them what to mean. Whatever energy they have came out of me. I'm what's left over. (*CE*, 409)

There is no unified textual identity for the female autobiographical subject here, nor does this novel itself have a unified generic identity. Instead, the text roams across borders between present and past, the self and its doubles, the living and the dead, in a manner which closely resembles Atwood's other kunstlerroman, *Lady Oracle*: "My life had a tendency to spread, to get flabby, to scroll and festoon like the frame of a baroque mirror" (*LO*, 7), where the fictive autobiography combines with the form of the female Gothic romance.

Gothic Romance

It is to the Gothic romance that I wish to turn, though not to *Lady Oracle* which is a Gothic parody ("a realistic comic novel collides with Gothic conventions — I give you *Northanger Abbey*," as Atwood advised her readers. Howells 1996, 65; Rao 1994). I shall not turn to *Surfacing* as wilderness Gothic combined with the ghost story in the manner of Henry James, but to *The Robber Bride*, which is a Gothic tale set in Toronto of the 1990s. This time Atwood surprises her readers by writing a postmodern Gothic romance which contains a network of references to other traditional genres. There are allusions to the Grimms' fairy tale of "The Robber Bridegroom" in an updated feminized version, to folktales and popular horror comics about vampires and soul stealers, to the Old Testament, as well as many references to nineteenth-century Gothic fictions like Mary Shelley's *Frankenstein*, Charlotte Brontë's *Jane Eyre*, and Bram Stoker's *Dracula*. The novel contains the key Gothic elements of the unspeakable and the buried life (Sedgwick 1986, 4–5), though it also exploits the shock effects which occur when Gothic transgresses generic borders between fantasy and realism, crossing from the female romance to the detective thriller and to documentary history. One of the protagonists, who is a female military historian, describes the effects of this cross-generic narration: "She likes using it: she likes the faint shock on the faces of her listeners. It's the mix of domestic image and mass bloodshed that does it to them" (*RB*, 3).

As Gothic romance, the novel is structured around the adventures of a demonic woman called Zenia (the Robber Bride of the title), who has tormented her three women friends in Toronto since the 1960s and comes back to haunt them in 1990. It is a story about transgressions, magic mirrors, shape changers and dark doubles, betrayals and emotional vampirism ("What was needed was a bowl of blood. A bowl of blood, a bowl of pain, some death," *RB*, 13), until Zenia's final defeat when her body is burned up and her ashes scattered over the deepest part of Lake Ontario. The tale is told through the life stories of the three women friends who have survived Zenia, and it ends with homecomings and, arguably, the restoration of family and social order. How does a traditionally Gothic villainess like Zenia survive as such a powerfully threatening force in a novel set in contemporary Toronto? Zenia is the focus of all the stories; she is necessary to these women, whether she is alive or dead. We should also note that Zenia has three different versions of her life story, which she tells to each of her friends in order to gain their trust, and then to rob them of their money and their men. (At least this is what her friends tell one another and the reader, for the novel is structured out of three fictive autobiographies, and Zenia never gets to tell her story in her own voice.) She is a transgressive figure, having multiple identities but no fixed identity. Is she real or is she imaginary? The answer is that she is both, for Zenia is a nomadic subject who migrates from one story to another, operating on borderline territory between the real and the fantastic, always outside the fold and on the loose. She is threatening because she represents the return of the repressed; for all these women she is their dark double and their object of desire:

> The Zenias of this world . . . They've slipped sideways into dreams; the dreams of women too, because women are fantasies for other women, just as they are for men. But fantasies of a different kind. (*RB*, 392)

As the Other Woman, Zenia represents the otherness which these women cannot acknowledge, but which is necessary for self-definition. Atwood uses the Gothic villainess to highlight the way that fantasy works, affecting women's concepts of themselves, just as she uses the powerfully disruptive force of Zenia's seductiveness to challenge feminist thinking about sexual politics and gender relations. Zenia is the undead, always returning and needing to be destroyed again and again. At the end of the novel, all three women reject her and she commits suicide. Or was she murdered? And will she stay dead? We do not really know, for there are, as we have seen, limits to the truth-telling of any autobiographical account, even if there are three of them.

So Zenia becomes history, or rather "She will only be history if Tony chooses to shape her into history . . . because she is dead, and all of the dead are in the hands of the living" (*RB*, 461). Atwood's female historian has a postmodern attitude to her discipline (more like Offred's than Professor Pieixoto's), recognizing the subjective element in any narrative reconstruction of the past. History is a discontinuous text with many gaps, so that different interpretations of the facts are always possible. These views recall those of American historiographer Hayden White, who has suggested that the narratives of history always reconstruct the available facts of the past for readers in the present according to ideologically congenial perspectives (White 1978). Certainly Tony's narrative of Zenia's career, while it fits her own personal agenda, also constructs Zenia as the representative twentieth-century victim. Zenia as postwar immigrant to Canada is the Jewish persecution victim of the Second World War, as she is also the victim of sexual abuse and male violence, a drug addict, and a sufferer from cancer and AIDS. Through her multiple identities she embodies the diseases, neuroses, and traumas which are buried in the foundations of Western culture, not only in Europe but in the New World as well.

This novel may also be read as contemporary Canadian social history in its chronicle of changing cultural fashions in postwar Toronto, ending with a street map of that city placed over a map of medieval Europe, while world events swirl around the narrative. Arguably, there is a new awareness here of Canada in a globalized context (Howells 1996, 163–64; Morton 1998), as well as an attempt to refigure Canada's narrative of nationhood in the multicultural 1990s. Who is a "true Canadian" anyway? Multiple versions of Canadianness are evidently in circulation in this novel, and as Atwood shows, Canada is not in any way separated from the rest of the world's wars and their casualties. *The Robber Bride* turns Gothic romance upside down by using and revising its conventions to become a worldly text which engages not only with questions of femininity and feminism, but also with national and international political issues. Once again, Atwood the shape-shifter has transformed her favorite genre, demonstrating that her writing "is both canonical and postcanonical, nationalistic and postnationalistic, realistic and postmodern" (Hengen 1995, 275).

Historical Novel

Alias Grace (1996) is a historical novel, and shortly after its publication Atwood gave a lecture in Ottawa putting it in its generic context within the Canadian literary tradition, though the very title of her lecture, *In*

Search of Alias Grace, should have alerted listeners and readers to certain enigmas, not only in the story, but also in her methodology. Atwood's attitude to writing history has much in common with that of her fictive historian in *The Robber Bride*:

> The past no longer belongs only to those who lived in it; the past belongs to those who claim it, and are willing to explore it, and to infuse it with meaning for those alive today. The past belongs to us, because we are the ones who need it. (Atwood 1997, 39)

Atwood writes a historical novel in a postmodern context, for as she says, no writer can escape being contemporary, and though she does not write "historiographic metafiction" (Hutcheon 1988, 61), her historical novel is structured on those "parodic principles" described by Martin Kuester, where traditional structures are accommodated "to a new textual, social, and national environment" (Kuester 1992, 148). Atwood's means of accommodation produce a hybridized text that combines historical documentary with genres now familiar to her readers, like women's fictive autobiography and Gothic romance, plus some nineteenth-century surprises like spiritualism, mesmerism, and women's quilt making. And in what way might this historical novel "belong" to the late twentieth century? I would suggest that like *The Handmaid's Tale* it offers a general questioning of the truthfulness of history, and more specifically, that it challenges myths of English-Canadian colonial innocence, acknowledging both the legacy of history and questioning inheritance.

As Atwood has remarked, "The lure of the Canadian past, for the writers of my generation, has been partly the lure of the unmentionable — the mysterious, the buried, the forgotten, the discarded, the taboo" (Atwood 1997, 19). In *Alias Grace* Atwood looks back to the past and finds it not at all innocent, for she chooses to tell the story of a notorious double murder. This is her version of the story of Grace Marks, the sixteen-year-old Irish servant girl who was accused with her fellow servant James MacDermott of murdering their Scottish employer, Thomas Kinnear, and his housekeeper, Nancy Montgomery, who was also his mistress, on Kinnear's farm outside Toronto on 23 July 1843. Grace was not hanged for murder though MacDermott was. Instead she was imprisoned for thirty years in the Provincial Penitentiary at Kingston (plus a period in the Toronto Lunatic Asylum). She always maintained that she had no memory of the murders, though she must have been there at the time they were committed. Finally, she was pardoned in 1872 after a long campaign to prove her innocence and went to the United States where possibly she married and changed her name. Anyway, she disappeared from the records. The crucial question remains: Was Grace innocent or was she guilty? As Atwood has remarked in the "Author's Afterword": "The true character of the historical Grace Marks remains an enigma" (*AG*, 465). This is exactly the kind of story to attract Atwood's attention.[3] Not only is it impossible to make a reliable reconstruction of the crime from the contradictory historical records available, but the story has all the classic Gothic ingredients: unspeakable secrets, murder, criminality, demonic possession, madness, and it is very much tied up with nineteenth-century anxieties about women and what they might be capable of. Are they pure and innocent, or are they devils, and which is Grace?

In Atwood's novel, Grace Marks tells her story while in prison to a young American doctor named Simon Jordan, who is interested in the fashionable new theories about nervous and mental disorders. He tries to persuade her to remember the day of the murders, with the double purpose of restoring her to psychic health, and of solving the riddle of her guilt or innocence. Needless to say he is unsuccessful, for though Grace tells him a great deal about her family and her life as an immigrant servant girl, she always manages not to tell him about her role in the murders. She seems to suffer from traumatic memory loss. Grace's oral storytelling would lead us to classify this novel as a fictive autobiography. However, hers is not the only version, for Atwood has done a great deal of historical research ("The past is made of paper," Atwood 1997, 20) and Grace's narrative is presented to us already framed by the prefatory materials and the "Author's Afterword" which condition our readerly expectations. The novel begins with a plethora of voices — from nineteenth-century poets, Susanna Moodie's account of meeting Grace Marks in *Life in the Clearings* (1853), contemporary newspaper reports, an extract from the Kingston Penitentiary Punishment Book, a newspaper sketch of the accused at the time of the trial, and even a popular ballad about the murder. Within such pre-existing discourses, Grace's own shockingly Gothic nightmare of Nancy Montgomery's murder, perhaps an attempt to insert her own story (but who knows?), goes almost unnoticed. This multivoiced representation poses awkward questions about the reliability of historical interpretation: "What does the past tell us? In and of itself, it tells us nothing. We have to be listening first, before it will say a word, and even so, listening means telling, and then retelling" (Atwood 1997, 37). To whose voice should we

---

[3] Before she wrote the novel, Atwood had already written two dramatic versions of the Grace Marks story: *The Servant Girl* (1974) for CBC Radio, and an unpublished play, *Grace* (1978–9).

listen? Atwood sets out to question the relation between fact and fiction, for there are so many stories about Grace Marks in circulation. It is as if they are all different aliases for the protagonist. Not only is she "Grace Marks alias Mary Whitney" at the trial, but she is made to represent a wide range of Victorian constructions of Woman. Grace is victim and suffering saint, she is whore, madwoman, murderess, Dr. Jordan's muse, and Scheherazade. With so many aliases, who is the true Grace Marks? Indeed, the title signals a disturbing absence of the original behind the name. Like *The Handmaid's Tale*, *Cat's Eye*, *The Robber Bride*, this novel recognizes that no written history (or oral herstory) allows either the real woman's voice or the true story of the past to be recovered.

Grace may be trapped by history just as she was imprisoned in Kingston Penitentiary, but through her storytelling she manages to elude Dr. Jordan's insistent probing for the truth: "I approach her mind as if it is a locked box, to which I must find the right key; but so far, I must admit, I have not got very far with it" (*AG*, 132). And he never does, for Grace shimmers before him as a shadowed, doubled self, where storytelling is never an unlocking but a keeping of secrets. Grace turns out to be another of Atwood's duplicitous narrators, where telling is presented as self-conscious reconstruction designed for a listener, not as a fixed text with only one meaning to be deciphered or one stable identity to be represented. In response to Reverend Verringer's opinion that "The truth shall make you free," Dr. Jordan replies: "The truth may well turn out to be stranger than we think" (*AG*, 83). Grace has a vigorous resistance to being found out, though whether that is because she is guilty or because she resents being cross-examined by men in authority is never clear. Is she a consummate actress (as Dr. Jordan suspects at the time of the neurohypnotism scene), or is she transparently innocent?

Several critics have commented on the quilting motif as a dominant component in this feminine autobiography, for Grace is shown sewing industriously in her interviews with Dr. Jordan: "Grace's skill at quilting disparate selves into aesthetic patterns is paralleled by her storytelling talents" (Vevaina 1998, 68). Even this metaphor may be double-sided however, and perhaps the first quilt pattern, "Jagged Edge," is the appropriate emblem for Grace's narrative. She is expert at following other people's patterns, though she is quietly critical of such conformity, and when she has a chance to design her own quilt at the end, she changes the pattern "to suit my own ideas" (*AG*, 459). Her quilt is a variant on the Tree of Paradise pattern, where the signs of good and evil are so closely interwoven that nobody could tell them apart:

> I intend to put a border of snakes entwined; they will look like vines or just a cable pattern to others, as I will make the eyes very small, but they will be snakes to me; as without a snake or two, the main part of the story would be missing. (*AG*, 459–60)

Only in this quilt does Grace repossess her traumatic history, as she pieces together materials from clothes belonging to herself and her two dead women friends, Mary Whitney (her own dark double) and Nancy (possibly her murder victim). This seems to be an emblem of reconciliation, though it is no public confession, and it brings these women together (like the three friends in *The Robber Bride*) in an alliance of sisterhood. Grace never says that she is innocent; she only claims not to remember, and forgetting is not the same as innocence. This is perhaps another way in which Grace's amnesia makes her nineteenth-century story belong to our own time, for Freud "taught us that we were not so much the sum of what we could remember, as the sum of what we had forgotten" (Atwood 1997, 11). The mystery of Grace remains, however. We do not know the truth any more than Atwood the novelist does, for she too is trapped in history and can be no wiser than her sources.

To conclude this discussion of generic perspectives, I refer back to the words of Northrop Frye, Atwood's former professor at the University of Toronto:

> The purpose of criticism by genres is not so much to classify as to clarify traditions and affinities, thereby bringing out a large number of literary relationships that would not be noticed as long as there were no context established for them. (Hernadi 1972, 131)

Atwood's novels cause us to add a revisionary clause to Frye's statement, for in their generic hybridity they suggest another purpose of such criticism, which is to take into account the significance of generic divergences. Insistently challenging the limits of traditional genres, Atwood draws the reader's attention to the multiple inherited scripts through which our perceptions are structured. She asks: "But meanwhile, while we still have the chance, what should we ourselves tell? Or rather, what *do* we tell?" (Atwood 1997, 38). The answer is, for Atwood, one of her "true stories":

The true story lies
among the other stories ...

after all. Why do you

need it? Don't ever
ask for the true story.
(Atwood 1982a, 11)

Works Cited

Atwood, Margaret. *Alias Grace*. London: Bloomsbury, 1996.

———. *Cat's Eye*. London: Virago, 1994.

———. "Genesis of *The Handmaid's Tale* and Role of the Historical Notes." In Lacroix, Leclaire, and Warwick 1999: 7–14. (1999a)

———. *The Handmaid's Tale*. London: Vintage, 1996.

———. "*The Handmaid's Tale*: A Feminist Dystopia?" In *Lire Margaret Atwood*: The Handmaid's Tale. Ed. M. Dvorak. Rennes: Presses Universitaires de Rennes, 1999: 17–30.

———. *In Search of Alias Grace*. Ottawa: Ottawa University Press, 1997.

———. *Lady Oracle*. London: Virago, 1993.

———. Margaret Atwood Papers, Thomas Fisher Rare Book Library, University of Toronto, Toronto.

———. *The Robber Bride*. London: Virago, 1994.

———. *Second Words: Selected Critical Prose*. Toronto: Anansi, 1982.

———. *True Stories*. New York: Simon & Schuster, 1982. (1982a)

———. *Wilderness Tips*. London: Virago, 1992.

Cooke, Nathalie. "The Politics of Ventriloquism: Margaret Atwood's Fictive Confessions." In York 1995: 207–28.

Culler, Jonathan. *The Pursuit of Signs*. London: Routledge & Kegan Paul, 1981.

———. *Structuralist Poetics: Structuralism, Linguistics and the Study of Literature*. London: Routledge & Kegan Paul, 1975.

Davidson, Arnold E. *Seeing in the Dark: Margaret Atwood's* Cat's Eye. Toronto: ECW Press, 1997.

Dvorak, Marta. "What's in a Name? Readers as Both Pawns and Partners or Margaret Atwood's Strategy of Control." In *Margaret Atwood:* The Handmaid's Tale/Le Conte de la Servante: *The Power Game.* Ed. J.-M. Lacroix and J. Leclaire. Paris: Presses de la Sorbonne Nouvelle, 1998: 79–99.

Fullbrook, Kate. *Free Women: Ethics and Aesthetics in Twentieth-Century Women's Fictions.* Hemel Hempstead: Harvester-Wheatsheaf, 1990.

Grace, Sherrill. "Gender as Genre: Atwood's Autobiographical 'I.'" In *Margaret Atwood: Writing and Subjectivity.* Ed. Colin Nicholson. London: Macmillan, 1994: 189–203.

Greene, Michael. "In Its Own Way Eloquent: Irony, History, and *The Handmaid's Tale.*" In The Handmaid's Tale: *Margaret Atwood.* Ed. M. Dvorak. Paris: Ellipses, 1998: 103–11.

Hengen, Shannon. "Zenia's Foreignness." In York 1995: 271–86.

Hernadi, Paul. *Beyond Genre: New Directions in Literary Classification.* Ithaca and London: Cornell University Press, 1972.

Hite, Molly. "An Eye for an Eye: The Disciplinary Society in *Cat's Eye.*" In York 1995: 191–206.

Howells, Coral Ann. *Margaret Atwood.* London: Macmillan, 1996.

———. "Questions of Survival in *The Handmaid's Tale.*" In *Margaret Atwood:* The Handmaid's Tale/Le Conte de la Servante: *The Power Game.* Ed. J.-M. Lacroix and J. Leclaire. Paris: Presses de la Sorbonne Nouvelle, 1998: 35–48.

Hutcheon, Linda. *The Canadian Postmodern: A Study of Contemporary English-Canadian Fiction.* Toronto: Oxford University Press, 1988.

Ingersoll, Earl G., ed. *Margaret Atwood: Conversations.* London: Virago, 1992.

Kamboureli, Smaro. *On the Edge of Genre: The Contemporary Canadian Long Poem.* Toronto: University of Toronto Press, 1991.

Kaufman, Linda. "Special Delivery: Twenty-First Century Epistolarity in *The Handmaid's Tale.*" In *Writing the Female Voice: Essays on Epistolary Literature.* Ed. E. C. Goldsmith. London: Pinter Publisher, 1989: 221–44.

Kuester, Martin. *Framing Truths: Parodic Structures in Contemporary English-Canadian Historical Novels.* Toronto: University of Toronto Press, 1992.

Lacroix, J.-M., J. Leclaire, and J. Warwick, ed. The Handmaid's Tale: *Roman Proteen.* Rouen: Université de Rouen, 1999.

Leclaire, Jacques. "*The Handmaid's Tale*: A Feminist Dystopia?" In Lacroix, Leclaire, and Warwick 1999: 85–94.

Makaryk, Irena, ed. *Encyclopaedia of Contemporary Literary Theory: Approaches, Scholars, Terms.* Toronto: University of Toronto Press, 1993.

Man, Paul de. "Autobiography as Defacement." *Modern Language Notes* 94 (1979): 931–55.

Morton, Stephen. "Postcolonial Gothic and the New World Disorder: Crossing Borders of Space and Time in Margaret Atwood's *The Robber Bride*." Panel Abstract, MLA 1998. *Newsletter of the Margaret Atwood Society* 21 (Fall/Winter 1998), 3.

Rao, Eleonora. "Margaret Atwood's *Lady Oracle*: Writing against Notions of Unity." In *Margaret Atwood: Writing and Subjectivity.* Ed. Colin Nicholson. London: Macmillan, 1994: 133–52.

Sedgwick, Eve Kosofsky. *The Coherence of Gothic Conventions.* London and New York: Methuen, 1986.

Sturgess, Charlotte. "The Handmaid as a Romance Heroine." In Lacroix, Leclaire, and Warwick 1999: 71–76.

Thompson, Lee Briscoe. *Scarlet Letters: Margaret Atwood's* The Handmaid's Tale. Toronto: ECW Press, 1997.

Todorov, T. *Genres in Discourse.* Cambridge: Cambridge University Press, 1990.

Vevaina, Coomi S. "Quilting Selves: Interpreting Margaret Atwood's *Alias Grace*." In *Margaret Atwood: The Shape-Shifter.* Ed. C. S. Vevaina and C. A. Howells. New Delhi: Creative Books, 1998: 64–74.

White, Hayden. "The Historical Text as Literary Artefact." In *Tropics of Discourse: Essays in Cultural Criticism.* Baltimore and London: Johns Hopkins University Press, 1978: 81–100.

Woolf, Virginia. "Women and Fiction" (1929). Reprinted in *Virginia Woolf: Women and Writing.* Ed. Michele Barrett. London: The Women's Press, 1979.

York, Lorraine M., ed. *Various Atwoods: Essays on the Later Poems, Short Fiction, and Novels.* Toronto: Anansi, 1995.

Alias Atwood:
Narrative Games and Gender Politics

Barbara Hill Rigney (Ohio State University, Columbus, Ohio)

PROBABLY EVERY SECONDARY SCHOOL TEACHER of English literature in the world introduces Jane Austen's *Emma* by quoting Austen herself, who claimed she had "created a heroine whom no one but myself will very much like." Margaret Atwood's heroines, if we can even designate them as such, are similarly ambiguous and morally suspect, often as "clueless" as Emma, sometimes guilty of worse crimes than Emma or Austen could have possibly imagined, and Atwood herself seldom appears to "like" any of them very much at all. What, then, about Atwood's narratives solicits her readers' sympathies for these characters and secures Atwood's place, second only to Austen's perhaps, in the canon of feminist rhetoric? Surely we readers, as much as her characters, are victims of Atwood's trickery and pawns in her narrative games which become more complex and less predictable with the publication of each poem and every novel.

But Atwood has warned us for years that her intentions are dishonorable and that she plays for keeps: "That's me in the dark. I have designs on you, I'm plotting my sinister crime, my hands are reaching for your neck . . . Just remember this, when the scream at last has ended and you've turned on the lights: by the rules of the game, I must always lie" (*Murder in the Dark*, 30). But does Austen's Emma "lie" because she is a fabricator of fictions about herself as well as about others; does Henry James's governess in *The Turn of the Screw* "lie" to us, to herself, or maybe even to Henry James; do any or even all of Atwood's heroines actually "lie," or are they simply unreliable narrators because they are mad, evil, or simply guilty?

The most duplicitous of all of Atwood's female protagonists, Grace Marks in *Alias Grace*, has been convicted by everyone but Atwood and her readers of murder in the first degree. Grace (amazing and otherwise) begins her first explanation not with the words, "This is what happened," but "This is what I told Dr. Jordan," to whom she has every practical reason to lie, for he is among the few who can argue for her sanity, her innocence, her freedom. It is the perverse aspect of this novel that neither Dr. Jordan, the reader (and maybe not even Grace, given the possibility that she is truly insane and therefore does not recognize her own reality), nor Atwood herself ever learns the "truth" from Grace, who tells her story only to keep from being returned to the Kingston Penitentiary or to the Provincial Lunatic Asylum in Toronto. As she daily, chapter by chapter, "spins out her yarn," she stitches, expertly and artistically, on the intricate patterns of quilts for which she provides such telling names as "Jagged Edge" and, later and more sinister (since Grace has been convicted of bludgeoning with an ax handle and then dismembering the body of her former employer's mistress), "Hearts and Gizzards." So, as in all literatures, particularly those written by women and particularly those written by Atwood, the image of the woman as fabricator, seamstress, weaver, spider, becomes one with the image of tale-teller, writer.

Equally pervasive in Atwood's fictions and poetry is the dangerous and seductive Siren, to whom all singers-writers are also related. Circe, in Atwood's "Circe/Mud Poems," can turn men into pigs, and so can Grace in *Alias Grace*. As an older, but not necessarily wiser physician warns Dr. Jordan: "Many older and wiser heads have been enmeshed in her toils, and you would do well to stop your ears with wax, as Ulysses made his sailors do, to escape the Sirens" (*Alias Grace*, 71). At one point, Dr. Jordan compliments Grace on her singing, but he never gets the connection, never realizes that she has become the object of his fantasies. As he sits with her in the sewing room, he imagines the smell of her skin, "with its undertone of dampness, fullness, ripeness—what? Ferns and mushrooms; fruits crushed and fermenting. He wonders how often the female prisoners are allowed to bathe. . . . He is in the presence of a female animal" (*Alias Grace*, 90). Fantasies about Grace lead him into degrading sexual acts with his landlady as Grace's surrogate. Professionally, too, Dr. Jordan has suffered from his association with Grace; the Sirens may well have helped Ulysses's career, but a paper written about Grace doesn't help Dr. Jordan as he expected it would.

Not that Dr. Jordan deserves help, and Atwood dissolves any possible sympathy to which her wayward readers may have succumbed, by reminding us that Dr. Jordan, "while a medical student, dissected a good many women — from the labouring classes, naturally," nor does he make political connections though he notices that "their spines and musculature were on the average no feebler than those of men, although many suffered from rickets" (*Alias Grace*, 73). His interest, clearly, is not only medical: "He has opened up women's bodies, and peered inside ... he is one of the dark trio — the doctor, the judge, the executioner" (*Alias Grace*, 82).

In Atwood's fictions there is a dark trio of women as well — along with Arachne, the weaver, and Circe, the Siren, there is also Scheherazade, telling stories to stay alive. As a more perceptive male character tells Dr. Jordan of Grace: "Has she been lying to you, you ask? Let me put it this way — did Scheherazade lie? Not in her own eyes; indeed, the stories she told ought never to be subjected to the harsh categories of Truth and Falsehood. They belong in another realm altogether" (*Alias Grace*, 377). In case we have missed the inherent ambiguity of the nature of truth, which is Atwood's major thesis, Atwood begins the novel with an epigraph, a quotation from William Morris, *The Defense of Guenevere*, another heroine condemned by history and literature: "Whatever may have happened through these years, / God knows I speak truth, saying that you lie."

The paradoxical relation between truth and fabrication, fact and fiction, are at the center of all of Atwood's narratives, especially *Alias Grace*, which combines history (or truth as we know it) and the novel. Atwood weaves fiction in between court records, sketches of the defendants, ballads written around the events of the murders, and newspaper accounts, many of which were fiction as well, as Grace maintains throughout her story and Atwood also believes was the case, as she states in the "Author's Afterword." She also quotes observations by that clearly not infallible recorder of events, Mrs. Susanna Moodie, who also has an existence in historical record and whom we recognize from Atwood's earlier volume of poetry, *The Journals of Susanna Moodie*. That there was also a Grace Marks who spent twenty-nine years in the Kingston Penitentiary is documented by sources other than Atwood. But Atwood, as she writes, has "of course fictionalized historical events. . . . Where many hints and outright gaps exist in the records, I have felt free to invent" (*Alias Grace*, 466–67).

History itself is as enigmatic as any of Atwood's narrative interests, and she moves through epochs without a backward glance. The dates are all there for Grace, and she is solidly of a past which evokes horror in the twentieth-century reader. But dates are not always so dependable, as we know from *The Handmaid's Tale*, in which future becomes merged with past, one as unbearable as the other. The future Gilead is a ghost of Puritan America, in which witches still hang, sex for pleasure is forbidden, and language is subject to censorship. Grace shares with Offred the veil of history, and as Professor Pieixoto tells his audience about the irretrievability of past heroines, fictional or historical: "We may call Eurydice forth from the world of the dead, but we cannot make her answer. . . . As all historians know, the past is a great darkness, and filled with echoes" (*The Handmaid's Tale*, 324). Tony in *The*

Robber Bride is a historian by profession, and she knows that "History was once a substantial edifice, with pillars of wisdom," but these pillars are only "glimpsed here and there through the trees, on the mountain roads, among the ruins, on the long march into chaos" (*The Robber Bride*, 462). And sometimes Atwood can make history disappear altogether, as she does in the introductory paragraphs of *Cat's Eye*, where time itself is subject to the narrator's perception. A speaker not yet named Elaine tells us that she thinks "of time as having a shape, something you could see, like a series of liquid transparencies, one laid on top of another. You don't look back along time, but down through it, like water. Sometimes this comes to the surface, sometimes that, sometimes nothing. Nothing goes away" (*Cat's Eye*, 3).

So, if we cannot even depend on the reality of time as we perceive it, history and the historian are certainly not to be trusted, which is exactly the conclusion to which Atwood would like us to arrive. We certainly have no wish to doubt Atwood's veracity in her historical narratives, or even to question her evidence, even though we cannot help but contrast the "Author's Afterword" in *Alias Grace* with the ironic epilogue to *The Handmaid's Tale*, the "Historical Notes" in which Offred's terrible story is so misinterpreted in the academic jargon of professors of anthropology at an international conference at the "University of Denay, Nunavit." Truth itself, finally, is like Scheherazade's stories, "Another realm altogether." Indeed, as Sherrill E. Grace has argued so well: "Duplicity — deceit and doubleness — is a familiar Atwood subject and a fundamental Atwood concern. It informs her vision of this world, is at the root of her poetics, and is, indeed, the systemic model for her work" (55).

Thus, Atwood places herself (inadvertently or otherwise) directly in the center of current academic controversy and theoretical debate (another "Disneyland of the Soul," though not the one Atwood meant in her earlier essay) about feminism and its relation to Booth's "implied narrator," Bakhtin's "dialogic imagination," Genette's "autodiegetic" narrative, and to numerous other auto- and homodiegetic schools of thought, until we feel like the audience at the University of Denay, Nunavit must have felt. We are fortunate that Atwood herself has anticipated her critical position and characterized theories of narrative intention in simpler terms: "Why do authors wish to pretend they don't exist? It's a way of skinning out, of avoiding truth and consequences. They'd like to deny the crime, although their fingerprints are all over the martini glasses, not to mention the hacksaw blade and the victim's neck" ("Me, She, and It," 17). But fingerprints or not, we are still puzzled by Atwood's refusal to distinguish, let alone choose, between author and narrator, and who to hang in the end, since there is never, strictly speaking, an "end" anyway. It is almost always we, the readers, who are left hanging, bereft of answers, and condemned to imagine our own, longing for that post-postmodernist writer who even now may be planning a text in which Anna Karenina always jumps, Mrs. Ramsay always dies, heroines like Emma always get their man. Would we like that?

Except for the relevance of a Canadian setting to Atwood's own life, she disappears from her text as much as do the guilty authors she cites above. Who, for example, is telling Grace's story? Mostly it is Grace, but how do we know about Dr. Jordan's secret life, and who reads the news reports to us? Mostly Grace addresses her story to Dr. Jordan, to "Sir," but at other times she is alone, either thinking, or perhaps, since she and Atwood are both careful to tell us that Grace can read and write, actually writing her own story. Tense varies as well, and subjects arise seemingly spontaneously, a flight of ideas, as is sometimes the case for people who are either very young or very old or emotionally very ill. So, we can only know about Grace what she wants us to know, and Atwood is back to her narrative tricks.

In all of Atwood's novels, the author is not the only criminal, for all of her protagonists have their fingerprints on the martini glasses as well and especially on the hacksaw blades. They are bloodthirsty and sometimes violent. Marian MacAlpin of *The Edible Woman* is a cannibal who eats herself; the nameless protagonist of *Surfacing* ritualistically murders dolls in childhood, just as she later, as an adult, considers herself guilty of child murder by abortion, real or imagined or simply a lie; Joan Foster of *Lady Oracle* kills her own identity into fantasy and romance, just as Lesje in *Life Before Man* kills hers into a Disney version of prehistory; Rennie in *Bodily Harm* either imagines or engineers for herself every version of bodily harm from cancer to torture at the hands of political tyrants; Offred in *The Handmaid's Tale* is truly victimized by oppression beyond self-destruction, but she also participates in the "Salvaging Ceremony," in which a man is torn to pieces by a crowd of Maenad-like women. Mostly men do terrible things to women in Atwood's fictions, but increasingly and particularly in the most recent novels, women do them to each other: a live burial in *Cat's Eye*, mental and physical cruelty in *The Robber Bride*, and, as stated earlier, murder and (possibly) dismemberment in *Alias Grace*. Some of the poems are worse.

How, then, given such negative portrayals of women, can we construct a feminist ethic for Atwood, how infer a woman-centered poetic? Atwood's gender politics are trickier than her narrative style. If women are responsible for their own predicaments (how did Scheherazade get herself into that situation in the first place?), what can we conclude about guilt and innocence in general, the nature of human beings, the possibility of evil? Is evil merely a childhood fantasy like the Hitler games in *Surfacing*, or could there be physiological explanations, like those Dr. Jordan provides for himself, that evil has a scientific explanation, that it is "an illness due to some lesion of the nervous system, and that the Devil himself is simply a malformation of the cerebrum" (*Alias Grace*, 80)? Is the quest for power a motivating force for women as well as for men? Based on Atwood's evidence, we must agree with Roz in *The Robber Bride* that women "haven't let themselves be molded into male fantasies, they've done it to themselves" (*The Robber Bride*, 388).

A strange gender inequality exists in all of Atwood's texts, for women, more than their comparatively benign male counterparts, are capable of virtually demonic power. Atwood has always, since her early fiction and essays, claimed that writing itself is at least figuratively demonic, a function of possession, a practice akin to witchcraft, which women have traditionally practiced with greater success than men. Grace, for example, can conjure the initials of her future husband with an apple peeling and confound a room full of theologians and scientists by enacting a drama of possession and spiritualism, abetted by her doppelgänger, the peddler/gypsy, Jeremiah. Not surprisingly, this chapter in the novel is entitled "Pandora's Box," again the name of one of Grace's quilt patterns, but also a design to evoke the mythological association of Grace and women in general with the nature of evil.

Similarly, Elaine in *Cat's Eye* is a talented witch who can summon to her rescue the Virgin Mary, or some darker manifestation of her, and then summon her again in a painting of "a woman dressed in black, with a black hood or veil covering her hair. Here and there on the black of her dress or cloak there are pinpoints of light" (*Cat's Eye*, 430). This novel appropriately concludes on All Souls' Eve, that witch's festival of masked children who are really "spirits of the dead . . . come back to the living, dressed as ballerinas and Coke bottles, and spacemen and Mickey Mice, and the living will give them candy to keep them from turning vicious" (*Cat's Eye*, 409). As expected, Elaine changes her blue jogging suit for a black dress at the last moment. We know from the subjects of Elaine's paintings evoking the evils done to her in childhood that she has the "evil eye," capable of transforming her enemies to stone, or at least freezing them into paint and exposing their ugliness to curious gallery visitors. Mrs. Smeath, we agree, deserves her representation as an "imagined body, white as a burdock root, flabby as pork fat. Hairy as the inside of an ear" (*Cat's Eye*, 426–27). It is Elaine's curse and her fantasy that Cordelia, responsible in childhood for so many brutal acts, dies, finally, in obscurity and misery, while Elaine herself enjoys the success imaged in the "retrospective" of her work.

All of Atwood's writer/artist protagonists are witches to varying degrees, capable of casting spells, and all are on trial for witchcraft, if not for murder. Atwood writes in *Second Words* that writers are always under suspicion, and that they "cannot have come by their power naturally, it is felt. They must have *got it from somewhere*. Women writers are particularly subject to such projections, for writing itself is uncanny" (*Second Words*, 331). This is, of course, feminist rhetoric, for by restoring ancient powers to women, albeit symbolically, Atwood takes her characters as well as her readers above and beyond the gendered stereotypes.

Atwood also restores women to women as friends, ultimately, though they may have suffered horrors at one another's hands. In every novel, a friendship between two, or among a group, forms a center. Even Cordelia is resurrected, redeemed, and imagined as a friend, as "not something that's gone, but something that will never happen. Two old women giggling over their tea" (*Cat's Eye*, 445). The evil Zenia in *The Robber Bride* serves unwittingly to bring all her victims together in the end, when they celebrate their powers by telling stories, "That's what they will do, increasingly, in their lives" (*The Robber Bride*, 470). Offred in *The Handmaid's Tale* can have no friendships in her present life, but the words of her unknown and unnamed predecessor are the friendly message of one woman to another, "Don't let the bastards grind you down" (197).

If Atwood will not create heroines, her protagonists often fabricate their own. Offred idealizes Moira, who speaks the unspeakable that Offred is afraid even to think in *The Handmaid's Tale*; Rennie in *Bodily Harm* endows Lora with the same ability to speak and do the outrageous things that lead to survival. Not many women in the world of *Alias Grace* are capable of intimacy, but Mary Whitney, mostly because of her wild stories and rebellious language, becomes like a sister to Grace, lending her clothes, her name for Grace's alias, and thus also her identity: "She was always kind to me . . . and without her, it would have been a different story entirely" (*Alias Grace*, 102). Thus, the celebration of women's friendships and their relation to language and stories more than mitigates Atwood's cynicism about human relationships in general.

In many ways, then, Atwood's gender politics have not changed essentially during her writing career, and neither have her narrative games, which continue to be a contest between reader and author, of, to parody Atwood herself, "who can say what to whom and get away with it." But the ironic edge is stronger now than before; Atwood's narrative blades are sharpened and ready lest we sink her into sentiment. She refuses to be canonized in any area but the literary. Everything for Atwood is two-sided, and both sides are subjects for satire, satire as subtle yet as cutting as that which Jane Austen wrote. Somewhere there is a line between laughter and anguish, "cutting the heart asunder" (Woolf, 17). Atwood also writes that line exactly, and what utterly and finally redeems her tricks and games is her political sensibility, as serious as any grave.

Though Atwood as author may choose her subjects to "look" at them, as Mrs. Moodie so coldly examines Grace who sits unknowing in her prison cell, Atwood's women are not mere objects of curiosity. Grace's story is a narrative exercise, but it is also a tragedy, not a testament to the survivor ability of women, but an autopsy of a world that has killed women's spirits as well as their bodies. The real enigma of Grace is that she can resist the drama of her own story, that she can tell so simply and ingenuously the account of her emigration, as horrific as any historical or fictional recounting of the Middle Passage, that she can analyze her own poverty and servitude without hysteria, that her very hysteria becomes a revelation about the medical treatment of madness in the period and about how people must have suffered from such inhumane practices. What, then, is truly amazing about Grace is that she can see flowers from the barred windows of the madhouse. Like Atwood herself, Grace stitches on the "Tree of Paradise," "changing the pattern a little to suit my own ideas" (*Alias Grace*, 459).

Works Cited

Atwood, Margaret. *Alias Grace*. Toronto: McClelland & Stewart, 1996.

———. *Bodily Harm*. New York: Bantam, 1983.

———. *Cat's Eye*. New York: Doubleday, 1989.

———. "A Disneyland of the Soul." In *The Writer and Human Rights*. Ed. Toronto Arts Group for Human Rights. Toronto: Lester, 1983.

———. *The Edible Woman*. New York: Popular Library, 1976.

———. *The Handmaid's Tale*. Toronto: McClelland & Stewart, 1985.

———. *The Journals of Susanna Moodie*. Toronto: Oxford University Press, 1970.

———. *Lady Oracle*. New York: Avon, 1978.

———. *Life Before Man*. New York: Warner, 1983.

————. "Me, She, and It." In *Who's Writing This: Notations on the Authorial I With Self-Portraits*. Ed. Daniel Halpern. New Jersey: Ecco Press, 1995.

————. *Murder in the Dark: Short Fiction and Prose Poems*. Toronto: Coach House Press, 1983.

————. *The Robber Bride*. New York: Bantam, 1995.

————. *Second Words: Selected Critical Prose*. Toronto: Anansi, 1983.

————. *Surfacing*. New York: Popular Library, 1976.

Grace, Sherrill E. "Margaret Atwood and the Poetics of Duplicity." In *The Art of Margaret Atwood: Essays in Criticism*. Ed. Arnold E. Davidson and Cathy N. Davidson. Toronto: Anansi, 1981: 55–68.

Woolf, Virginia. *A Room of One's Own*. New York: Harvest, 1929.

Margaret Atwood: A Canadian Nationalist

Paul Goetsch (University of Freiburg)

Atwood and MacLennan

MARGARET ATWOOD HARDLY EVER mentions Hugh MacLennan in her published work. Nevertheless, she can be regarded as his successor in one respect. Among English-Canadian authors, MacLennan was the leading literary nationalist in the 1950s and early 1960s. Atwood assumed the same role in the 1970s. Since she is far superior to MacLennan as a writer, it has not been noticed how much she and her predecessor have in common.

Both writers had their cultural roots in Nova Scotia and were fully aware of Canada's regional diversity (Ingersoll 1990, 55). But both of them wanted to put their country as a whole on the literary map. Since there was no Canadian literature "as a national cultural form" in the 1940s (MacLennan 1947, 13), MacLennan hoped "to hammer out a literary pattern for Canadian life" (1942, 13). Decades later, Atwood similarly lamented the absence of a long-standing Canadian tradition in novel writing and the public's lack of interest in Canadian literature in general. She asserted: "We've been so cut off from our social mythology that we hardly know what it is; that's one thing that has to be discovered" (Ingersoll 1990, 9). Both MacLennan and Atwood readily turned to Canadian settings for their works and took up Canadian themes such as the relationship between English and French Canada or between Canada and the USA. Their attempts to define or shape the Canadian identity were successful in some ways.

MacLennan eventually won a Canadian reading audience for his fiction and essays. His novel *Two Solitudes* (1945) was adopted as a schoolbook, at least in Ontario, early on; its title served as a formula in public discussions on the two Canadas. Several of his novels were remarkable commercial successes outside of Canada. By the time MacLennan published *The Watch That Ends the Night* (1959), he was a well-known writer and, like his narrator in *The Watch*, a respected commentator on Canadian issues. He believed that Canada had left its colonial past behind in the First World War (*Barometer Rising* [1941], *Two Solitudes*) and had emerged from the Great Depression and the Second World War (*The Watch*) as a nation ready to shoulder responsibility in the United Nations and elsewhere. In the essay "Where Is My Potted Palm?" he wrote:

> The point of view from which I wrote *Barometer Rising* is now largely a thing of the past. I don't believe Canadian novelists need worry so much any longer about the problem of unfamiliarity. Before 1939 Canada was apathetic about herself, neither a colony nor a nation, and in the literary world she was little better than a dumping-ground for foreign books. Now she has become one of the most self-conscious nations in the world. That self-consciousness is, of course, a symptom of growth out of adolescence into maturity. (MacLennan 1954, 53–54)

In a letter to this writer (6 October 1959) MacLennan maintained that it was no longer necessary to draw up "literary archetypes" and "literary maps" of the country. This self-confidence was severely shaken in the course of the 1960s and 1970s, as his later novels, *Return of the Sphinx* (1967) and *Voices in Time* (1980), testify.

Wittily alluding to MacLennan's optimistic essay quoted above, Margaret Atwood once recalled that, as a young writer, she felt like a colonial when hiding behind potted palms to read MacLennan, a Canadian author, in public (Atwood 1987, 36). In her opinion, there were no grounds for national complacency in the late 1950s and the early 1960s. Canadians, she later explained in an interview, still "had the usual colonial attitude (which corresponded with the United States' in 1820), that things in their country were of negligible interest and that the important things were elsewhere" (VanSpanckeren and Castro 1988, 242). So she set out "to find what in the [Canadian] tradition is usable and use it" (Ingersoll 1990, 9). She wrote poems, short stories, and novels, and spelled out the personal poetics that underlies these works as well as her views on Canadian traditions in *Survival* (1972). This work was a huge success within Canada. It provoked and survived a controversy on thematic criticism in 1973. As late as 1988 *Survival* was called "Canada's best-selling and most influential work of literary criticism," besides being "a key guide to her [Atwood's] own work" (McCombs 1988a, 1). Judith McCombs states in her useful survey of Atwood criticism:

> By 1974, Margaret Atwood was widely recognized as English Canada's foremost writer; *Surfacing* and *Survival* had written her themes large, and had impelled as well as coincided with nationalist, feminist, and counter-cultural movements. In the newly burgeoning fields of

> women's studies and Canadian studies, which countered New Criti-
> cism by proclaiming the personal and the literary as the political and
> the national, Atwood's works were evaluated not as unique or peculiar
> artistic creations, but as voicing the hitherto-suppressed truths of
> women's and Canadians' lives. (8; see also McCombs 1989)

In order to understand Atwood's rise to prominence as a literary nationalist, it is necessary to contextualize her early work and contrast her
position with MacLennan's political view.

English-Canadian Literary Nationalism in the 1970s

Today, both MacLennan and Atwood can be seen as typical representatives of the postcolonial drive to project an autonomous national
identity by constructing a coherent culture or literature. They differ
chiefly in their identification of the imperial center.

Like other members of his generation, MacLennan, who had studied at Oxford and Princeton, defined the passage from colony to nation
as Canada's emancipation from the mother country. In his novels, a
number of Canadian characters learn in Europe, above all on the bat-
tlefield, what it means to be Canadian. Accordingly, the explosion in
the harbor of Halifax, which is the climax of *Barometer Rising*, symbolically clears the way for the Canadian war generation to throw off
the shackles of the past and forge the future Canadian nation. This future, MacLennan suggests in *Barometer Rising* and elsewhere, entails a
fusion of European and North American elements that would place
Canada in the role of mediator between Great Britain and the USA.
MacLennan thus embraces the notion of Canada as a "golden
hinge" — a concept that was popular with politicians and historians
after 1945, especially in the period when Lester B. Pearson often acted
as negotiator for the United Nations (see Goetsch 1961, 46–55).

For the young Margaret Atwood, Britain's influence as the former
imperial center still made itself felt in various ways, for instance, in the
books usually read at school (see the school scenes in *Cat's Eye*
[1988]). On the whole, however, Atwood worried much less about
Britain than about the new imperial center south of the border.
Whereas MacLennan apparently began to reflect upon his Canadian
identity when studying in Europe, Atwood did so when she worked
towards an academic degree in the United States. In an interview she
explained:

> It's not that anyone in Boston — few in the Graduate School were
> *from* that area in any case . . . — it's not that the Americans I met had

any odd or "upsetting" attitudes towards Canada. They simply didn't have any attitudes at all. They had a vague idea that such a place existed — it was that blank area north on the map where the bad weather came from — but if they thought about it at all they found it boring. They seemed to want to believe that my father was a Mounted Policeman and that we lived in igloos all year round.

And she added: "The beginning of Canadian cultural nationalism was not 'Am I really that oppressed?' but 'Am I really that boring?' You see, we had never been taught much about our own history or culture" (Ingersoll 1990, 78). This reaction was not idiosyncratic. In the 1960s many critics and writers deplored the colonial mentality and chose to measure Canada against the USA rather than Great Britain.

As I have shown in detail elsewhere (1977 and 1982), the new nationalism of the 1960s was the result of various developments. In the wake of the 1951 *Report* by the Royal Commission on National Development in the Arts, Letters and Sciences, and the creation of the Canada Council, Canadian culture received greater public attention and some long-needed financial support. Increasingly, the public became aware of the Americanization of Canadian culture. Atwood herself repeatedly drew attention to the influence of American publishers, even on the schoolbook market, the scarcity of outlets for Canadian literature, and the neglect of Canadian culture at the universities. There was an upsurge of nationalism. Rejecting the complacent nationalism of the 1950s, critics and writers demanded change. New literary journals and publishing firms sprang up, Canadian studies were institutionalized at the universities, and there was an enormous increase in readership, which presented a "cultural explosion," as Atwood put it (VanSpanckeren and Castro 1988, 242). Cultural nationalism was further intensified by pressing economic and political problems, particularly by Quebec separatism and by US imperialism, which had shown its ugly face in Vietnam and seemed to threaten Canada with an economic and political takeover. In 1964, the historian W. L. Morton declared: "The country is so irradiated by the American presence that it sickens and threatens to dissolve in cancerous slime" (Baker 1973, 71). One year later the conservative philosopher George Grant published *Lament for a Nation: The Defeat of Canadian Nationalism*. After blaming the Liberals for hastening the Canadian sell-out to the States, he concluded:

Canada has ceased to be a nation, but its formal political existence will not end quickly. Our social and economic blending into the empire will continue apace, but political union will probably be delayed. (86)

In 1970, the well-reputed historian Donald Creighton, who had long considered the United States the greatest threat to the nation, played Cassandra in his book *Canada's First Century, 1867–1967*; in 1978 he dramatized his fears in the crime story *Takeover*.

Because of the widespread fears of Quebec separatism and American influence, many critics and writers addressed the issue of Canadian identity. It may suffice here to sketch the position of three writers who anticipated or shaped the views Atwood expressed in her early poetry as well as in *Surfacing* and *Survival*.

In *The Canadian Identity* (1961), W. L. Morton pointed out, among other things, that the frontier played a different role in the Canadian and American imaginations. He emphasized the importance of the North for Canadian life in general and regarded it as the main influence on the national character. In his opinion, to be Canadian meant to unite individualism with respect for authority and moral discipline. This "psychology of endurance and survival" allows Canadians to cling to "the essentials of the greatest of civilizations in the grimmest of environments" (in Mandel 1971, 69–70). This comes very close to Atwood's main thesis in *Survival*, though she does not mention Morton's book in this context.

One influence Atwood admits to is that of Dennis Lee, who edited *Survival* and "helped create order from chaos" (Atwood 1972, 5). She praises *Civil Elegies* as the work of a man who makes himself a representative of his society and embodies its plight. Dennis Lee, she explains, deals with "the impossibility, or near-impossibility of 'citizenship' in Canada" and traces this Canadian predicament back to colonialism, whether of British or American origin:

> Because Canada was never claimed by and for the people who live there — there were, after all, foreign flags on those historic flagpoles — the citizens dwell in a kind of limbo, a state of unreal suspension. (244)

She welcomes Lee's message that Canadians should control their "own space, physical as well as cultural" (244) and is encouraged by the fact that other writers, both English- and French-Canadians, have begun to deal openly with Canadian problems: "For both groups, this 'voicing' is both an exploratory plunge into their own tradition and a departure from it; and for both groups the voicing would have been unimaginable twenty years ago" (245; see also Lee 1973).

Northrop Frye also exercised a great influence on *Survival*. Frye often formulated scruples about literary nationalism, remained unimpressed by the quality of Canadian literature, and believed that "the colonial position of Canada" was "a frostbite at the roots of the Canadian imagination" (Frye 1971, 134). But by 1965, when he wrote the "Conclusion" to Klinck's *Literary History of Canada*, he felt that writers and readers alike needed national cultural traditions, most of all when their identity was threatened. Consequently, he overcame his skepticism and associated Canadian writers with a tradition of earlier poets and novelists whom he did not greatly admire. He drew attention to some typical themes of Canadian literature and argued that the writers had left "an imaginative legacy of dignity and of high courage" (251). Atwood seems to be indebted to Frye's view of past achievements, his notion of the garrison mentality of Canadian culture (which encourages "a herd-mind in which nothing original can grow," 226), the environmental determinism Frye adopts in the "Conclusion" and previous essays, and, finally, Frye's belief in the importance of literature for the creation of a social mythology.

Before and after the publication of *Survival*, a number of similar thematic studies of Canadian literature appeared (see Goetsch 1977). If Atwood's book was more successful, this was also owing to its format, which allowed the author to respond to the national crisis and at the same time to write about issues that had preoccupied her since her early poetry.

Survival

Survival was originally intended to be "a short, easy-to-use guide to Canadian literature" for those who suddenly found themselves teaching "'Canlit', a subject they [had] never studied" (Atwood 1972, 11). It then grew into a somewhat longer book, not an academic literary history, as Margaret Atwood herself insists, but "a cross between a personal statement . . . and a political manifesto" (13).

Survival starts from the premise that Canadians are, as it were, lost in an unknown territory and are desperately in need of instruction about the country they physically and mentally inhabit. Echoing Northrop Frye's comments quoted above, Atwood writes: "For the members of a country or a culture, shared knowledge of their place, their here, is not a luxury but a necessity. Without that knowledge we will not survive" (19). Because literature presents "a map, a geography of the mind," Atwood assumes that it can engage the Canadian tendency "to emphasize the personal and the universal but to skip the national or cultural" (18). It can also offer answers to the question of "Where is here?" which perplexes the Canadian sensibility, according to Northrop Frye (Frye 1971, 220). Ultimately, then, *Survival* is more than a guide to Canadian literature; it is meant to be a contribution to national self-awareness and a guide to national survival.

This political aim informs the selection of material and the approach to literature. Atwood concentrates on twentieth-century authors, but dwells chiefly on contemporary writers because she believes that the recognition of the present situation is a more urgent task than a historical survey. Her choice of characteristic Canadian themes is determined by her preoccupation with survival. She argues that the very quality the present demands — the ability to hang on and stay alive — is the central symbol in both English- and French-Canadian literature. When compared to the role of the island in English literature, or that of the frontier in American culture, the theme of survival emerges as a negative one; the survival motif highlights a national tradition that is characterized by a colonial mentality, by the obsession with the possibility of defeat, and perhaps even by the longing for failure. Atwood classifies her material by distinguishing four basic victim positions:

> *Position One:*
>
> *To deny the fact that you are a victim. . . .*
>
> *Position Two:*
>
> *To acknowledge the fact that you are a victim, but to explain this as an act of Fate, the Will of God, the dictates of Biology (in the case of women, for instance), the necessity decreed by History, or Economics, or the Unconscious, or any other large general powerful idea. . . .*
>
> *Position Three:*
>
> *To acknowledge the fact that you are a victim but to refuse to accept the assumption that the role is inevitable. . . .*
>
> *Position Four:*
>
> *To be a creative non-victim.* (36–38)

Atwood applies her schema to poems, stories, and novels about nature, animals, natives, explorers, settlers, immigrants, artists, women, futile heroes, and other characters and topics. She admits that the majority of her examples fits into the first two categories, but she believes that a diagnosis of one's disease is better than a mere acquiescence (42). Thus, she encourages Canadians to know their cultural tradition and transform it in the direction of the third and the fourth position.

Her main hypothesis allows Atwood to deal with all kinds of power relationships and move easily from political and social violence to gender relationships. In the course of her book, however, she focuses not only on the colonial mentality and the need to survive, but also on other themes that refer explicitly to problems of Canada as a nation and link the book to her previous writings and the new nationalism of the 1960s and 1970s.

One such theme is the natural environment. In *The Journals of Susanna Moodie* (1970), which is loosely based on Moodie's autobiographical account *Roughing It in the Bush*, Atwood demonstrates how difficult it is for the immigrant to feel at home in a country that is too big to possess and civilize:

> My husband walks in the frosted field
> an X, a concept
> defined against a blank;
> he swerves, enters the forest
> and is blotted out.
>
> (Atwood 1970, 19; see Smith 1993)

In her "Afterword" Atwood ascribes a markedly double-minded attitude to Susanna Moodie:

> If the national mental illness of the United States is megalomania, that of Canada is paranoid schizophrenia. Mrs Moodie is divided down the middle: she praises the Canadian landscape but accuses it of destroying her; she dislikes the people already in Canada but finds in people her only refuge from the land itself; she preaches progress and the march of civilization while brooding elegiacally upon the destruction of the wilderness. (62)

In *Survival* she discovers similar reactions to the environment in other works and thus explains why Canadians like to seek cover in garrisons.

Like Dennis Lee (*Civil Elegies*), Atwood is also concerned about the exploitation of nature and ecological dangers (see Goetsch 1984; Roth 1998). According to her poem "Backdrop Addresses Cowboy," the star-spangled cowboy leaves "a heroic trail of desolation" behind him and desecrates the space he passes through (Atwood 1976, 70). But as *Surfacing* (1972) makes clear, not only Americans but also loud-mouthed Canadian nationalists bear responsibility for the disregard of ecological issues.

A second national theme Atwood singles out for special attention is the influence of Puritanism. Like Northrop Frye, who criticizes the sectarian roots of the garrison mentality, she believes that Calvinism and colonialism feed on each other (239). Hence, in a number of works written after *Survival*, she illustrates the difficulties of emancipating oneself from a Puritan upbringing. Whereas MacLennan suggests in *The Precipice* (1948) that a more enlightened form of Canadian Puritanism might give the secularized and materialistically minded United States guidance, Atwood chooses to set her novelistic critique of Puritanism, *The Handmaid's Tale* (1985), in the USA. As a former student of Perry Miller's, she is familiar with the importance of Puritanism for American nation-building and therefore assumes in her dystopian satire that a conservative backlash is more likely to take place in the United States than in Canada (see Tomc 1993).

Of course Canada's relationship with the United States is one of the major concerns of *Survival*. Atwood lists a number of works treating the American threat. Like MacLennan in *The Precipice*, she tends to identify the American as male and the Canadian as female; unlike MacLennan, she stresses the woman-as-victim theme in her early works and at least once conceives of America as dangerous demon lover (see McCombs 1988b, 142; Broege 1981). In *The Circle Game* (1966), and later in *Power Politics* (1971), she dramatizes the power games between men and women as a battle for dominance between two nations:

> So now you trace me
> like a country's boundary
> ...
> and I am fixed, stuck
> down on the outspread map
> of this room, of your mind's continent
> (Atwood 1976, 19)

The novel *Surfacing* suggests that the nameless Canadian heroine can perhaps avoid victimization if she resists American or, simply, male violence, comes to terms with her own nature and her environment, and tries to heal her mind-body split. However, the risk of getting the national disease, paranoid schizophrenia, remains.

In her early work Margaret Atwood also associated this disease with the national problem of separatism. The Canadian heroine in her story "Polarities" (1971) is so confused that she plays different roles, moves from the English to the French language and vice versa, and suddenly claims to have a French Protestant mother and an English Catholic father. In *Two-Headed Poems* (1978) Atwood symbolizes national self-division through Siamese twins who, though bodily linked, fight for separation. Hugh MacLennan was far more optimistic in *Two Solitudes*.

Modeling his work on Scott's historical novels, he treats Quebec as a kind of backward Scotland. Judging from Paul Tallard's development, who sheds his Catholicism and becomes a novelist interested in Canada as a nation, the problem of national unity can be solved through the modernization of French Canada.

The Controversy about *Survival*

Survival was enthusiastically accepted by some readers and harshly criticized by others. It is not necessary to discuss the controversy the book caused in 1973 at length (see Schlueter 1988). Obviously, *Survival* is not intended to be a cautious academic study. It works with sweeping generalizations and highly emotive language (see Blodgett 1992, 144) and presents a personal and political vision of Canadian literature and Canadian themes. It annoyed Marxists, who saw Atwood as entrapped in liberal, ahistorical positions, as serving the establishment, and resting content with utopian individualism (see Steele 1988). It probably even irritated some confirmed nationalists. For one thing, *Survival* offers a very negative image of Canada and its literary tradition. Secondly, Atwood's knowledge of French-Canadian literature is so limited that her reinterpretation of the French-Canadian idea of *survivance* in terms of the general Canadian need for survival may easily appear as yet another example of English-Canadian arrogance. Thirdly, the book will today no doubt appear very old-fashioned to those more recent nationalists who want to save the nation by propagating Canadian multiculturalism (see Loriggio 1987). Of course, *Survival* will also be met with rejection by those who believe that meta-narratives and nineteenth-century notions of identity have had their day (see Bennett 1993–94; Goetsch 1994).

In hindsight it is clear that *Survival* is nevertheless a crucial book which fulfilled important functions in the 1970s and met needs of the time. Its array of themes and comparisons of various works remain fascinating, even if the book instigated an interesting debate on the deficiencies of thematic studies. Atwood's main hypothesis now appears less restrictive than it did at first. While it defines negative Canadian traditions, it does not prescribe the ways in which the victim role should be overcome. Atwood's schema of victor-victim relations invites a Foucauldian approach (see Zimmermann 1998). And the role reversals and metamorphoses characteristic of her stories of individual development show that Atwood may be more concerned with questioning the concept of a monolithic, stable identity than some of her pronouncements on nationalism and national identity might warrant (see

Nicholson 1994). Last but not least, one should consider her penchant for mocking seriously-held positions. Even in her more tendentious works, nationalists and national clichés are not exempted from her mordant wit.

Atwood's Development since *Survival*

Atwood defended herself against some of the attacks made upon *Survival*, wrote a number of essays supplementing her thematic studies, and developed her views about the role of the North in a lecture series (Atwood 1982; 1995). She edited the acclaimed *The New Oxford Book of Canadian Verse in English* (1982) and co-edited the interesting collections *The Oxford Book of Canadian Short Stories in English* (1986) and *Barbed Lyres: Canadian Venomous Verse* (1986). She thus continued to promote public interest in Canadian literary traditions.

Still, Atwood told an American audience in 1985 that she would not write *Survival* today, because Canadian literature had finally come into its own. If forced to rewrite the book, she would add a great number of texts and devote new chapters to regionalism, Canadian humor, the relationship between the new literatures in English, and other topics. She would, however, again take the stand "that Canadian literature is a distinct entity, that it is informed by its colonial or post-colonial status, and that it is worthy of study" (Atwood 1987, 38).

The witty, humorous tone of her lectures on the malevolent North in Canadian literature and Atwood's awareness that she is to some extent bandying about clichés also indicate that the sense of political urgency which informs her works up to *Survival* and *Surfacing* has given way to a more relaxed and self-confident attitude. Consequently, the national themes discussed above have receded into the background of most of her works. Margaret Atwood is still a politically committed writer, as her work for Amnesty International and novels like *Bodily Harm* (1981) and *The Handmaid's Tale* (see Tomc 1993) demonstrate. But gender conflicts and problems of individual subjectivity have gained precedence over national themes in her later writings (see Nicholson 1994).

As a nationalist, then, Atwood, like MacLennan, moved from a sense of crisis to a feeling of self-confidence. Like her predecessor, she addressed a number of perennial Canadian problems. If she took a different stand on some of them, this was chiefly due to the different historical situations with which she and MacLennan were confronted. Whereas MacLennan expressed the predominant mood of the postwar era, Atwood's views were largely shaped by the new nationalism and anti-Americanism of the 1960s and 1970s. Both brands of nationalism have now become dated. If MacLennan's and Atwood's nationalistic works survive, they do so in spite of their topicality.

Works Cited

Atwood, Margaret. "After Survival . . . Excerpts from a Speech Delivered at Princeton University, April 19, 1985." *The CEA Critic*, 50 (Fall 1987): 35–40.

———. *The Journals of Susanna Moodie*. Toronto: Oxford University Press, 1970.

———, ed. *The New Oxford Book of Canadian Verse in English*. Toronto: Oxford University Press, 1982.

———. *Second Words: Selected Critical Prose*. Toronto: Anansi, 1982.

———. *Selected Poems*. Toronto: Oxford University Press, 1976.

———. *Strange Things: The Malevolent North in Canadian Literature*. Oxford: Clarendon Press, 1985.

———. *Survival: A Thematic Guide to Canadian Literature*. Toronto: Anansi, 1972.

Atwood, Margaret and Tom Denholm, ed. *Barbed Lyres: Canadian Venomous Verse*. Toronto: Key Porter Books, 1990.

Atwood, Margaret and Robert Weaver, ed. *The Oxford Book of Canadian Short Stories in English*. Toronto: Oxford University Press, 1986.

Baker, William M. "The Anti-American Ingredient in Canadian History." *Dalhousie Review* 53 (Spring 1973): 57–77.

Bennett, Donna. "English Canada's Postcolonial Complexities." *Essays on Canadian Writing* 51–52 (1993–94): 164–210.

Blodgett, E. D. "'Distinctively Canadian': Thematic Criticism of English-Canadian Literature." In *100 Years of Critical Solitudes*. Ed. Caroline Bayard. Toronto: ECW Press, 1992: 136–54.

Broege, Valerie. "Margaret Atwood's Americans and Canadians." *Essays on Canadian Writing* 22 (1981): 111–35.

Creighton, Donald. *Canada's First Century, 1867–1967*. Toronto: Macmillan, 1976.

———. *Takeover*. Toronto: McClelland & Stewart, 1978.

Frye, Northrop. *The Bush Garden: Essays on the Canadian Imagination*. Toronto: Anansi, 1971.

———. "Conclusion." In *Literary History of Canada*, vol. 3. Ed. C. F. Klinck. Toronto: University of Toronto Press, 1965: 318–32.

Goetsch, Paul. "Das Bild der Vereinigten Staaten in der anglokanadischen Literatur der Gegenwart." In *Die amerikanische Literatur in der Weltliteratur: Themen und Aspekte*. Ed. Claus Uhlig and Volker Bischoff. Berlin: Schmidt, 1982: 476–97.

———. "Der literarische Nationalismus in Kanada seit 1960." In *Literaturen in englischer Sprache: Ein Überblick über englischsprachige Nationalliteraturen außerhalb Englands*. Ed. H. Kosok and H. Prießnitz. Bonn: Bouvier, 1977: 122–40.

———. "'The Long Saga of the New New Criticism': Political and Cultural Implications of Poststructuralism and Postmodernism in Canada." *Zeitschrift für Kanada-Studien* 14.1 (1994): 75–86.

———. "Ökologische Aspekte der Werke von Margaret Atwood." In *Zur Literatur und Kultur Kanadas*. Ed. Dieter Meindl. Erlangen: Palm & Enke, 1984: 109–28.

———. *Das Romanwerk Hugh MacLennans: Eine Studie zum literarischen Nationalismus in Kanada*. Hamburg: Cram, de Gruyter, 1961.

Grant, George. *Lament for a Nation*. Toronto: McClelland & Stewart, 1965.

Ingersoll, Earl G., ed. *Margaret Atwood: Conversations*. Princeton, N.J.: Ontario Review Press, 1990.

Lee, Dennis. "Cadence, Country, Silence: Writing in a Colonial Space." *Open Letter* 2 (Fall 1973): 34–53.

Loriggio, Francesco. "The Question of the Corpus: Ethnicity and Canadian Literature." In *Future Indicative: Literary Theory and Canadian Literature*. Ed. John Moss. Ottawa: University of Ottawa Press, 1987: 53–69.

McCombs, Judith. "Country, Politics, and Gender in Canadian Studies: A Report from Twenty Years of Atwood Criticism." In *Literatures in Canada*. Ed. Deborah C. Poff. Montreal: Association for Canadian Studies, 1989: 27–47.

———, ed. *Criticial Essays on Margaret Atwood*. Boston: Hall, 1988 (a).

———. "Politics, Structure, and Poetic Development in Atwood's Canadian-American Sequences." In VanSpanckeren and Castro 1988 (b): 142–62.

MacLennan, Hugh. "Culture, Canadian Style." *Saturday Review of Literature* 25, 28 March 1941, 13.

———. "Do We Gag Our Writers?" *Maclean's Magazine* 60, 1 March 1947, 13.

———. *Thirty and Three*. Ed. Dorothy Duncan. Toronto: Macmillan, 1954.

Mandel, Eli, ed. *Contexts of Canadian Criticism: A Collection of Critical Essays*. Chicago: University of Chicago Press, 1971.

Morton, W. L. *The Canadian Identity*. Madison: University of Wisconsin Press, 1961.

Nicholson, Colin. "Living on the Edges: Constructions of Post-Colonial Subjectivity in Atwood's Early Poetry." In *Margaret Atwood: Writing and Subjectivity: New Critical Essays*. Ed. Colin Nicholson. New York: St. Martin's Press, 1994: 11–50.

Roth, Verena Bühler. *Wilderness and the Natural Environment: Margaret Atwood's Recycling of a Canadian Theme*. Tübingen/Basel: Francke, 1998.

Schlueter, June. "Canlit: Victimlit: *Survival* and *Second Words*." In Van-Spanckeren and Castro 1988: 1–11.

Smith, Erwin. "Gender and National Identity in *The Journals of Susanna Moodie* and *Tamsen Donner: A Woman's Journey*." *Frontiers* 13.2 (1993): 75–86.

Steele, James. "The Literary Criticism of Margaret Atwood." In *In Our Own House: Social Perspectives on Canadian Literature*. Ed. Paul Cappon. Toronto: McClelland & Stewart, 1988: 73–81.

Tomc, Sandra. "'The Missionary Position': Feminism and Nationalism in Margaret Atwood's *The Handmaid's Tale*." *Canadian Literature* 138–139 (1993): 73–87.

VanSpanckeren, Kathryn, and Jan Garden Castro, ed. *Margaret Atwood: Vision and Forms*. Carbondale, Edwardsville: Southern Illinois University Press, 1988.

Zimmermann, Hannelore. *Erscheinungsformen der Macht in den Romanen Margaret Atwoods*. Frankfurt: Lang, 1998.

Margaret Atwood, the Land, and Ecology

Ronald B. Hatch (University of British Columbia, Vancouver)

MENTION THE NAME of Margaret Atwood to students of Canadian literature, and one of the first associations is likely to be with the land. This is not surprising, since Atwood's popular critical study *Survival* (1972) has become one of the central texts in the teaching of Canadian literature, especially among high school teachers. Atwood's theory that Canadians are survivalists in the midst of a vast, unknowable land has in fact become an influential if somewhat dubious origin myth for Euro-Canadians. Only a few years ago, Atwood herself consolidated this survivalist view with the publication of her Oxford lectures, under the title of *Strange Things* (1995), in which she argues once again that "the malevolent north" appears as a *femme fatale* hypnotizing males and leading "them to their doom" (*Strange Things*, 3). Atwood's own early upbringing has also helped to create the image of her close connection to the land. The publishers' notes on her early novels frequently mention the many summers she spent in the north with her parents when her father, an entomologist, made field trips into northern Quebec and Ontario. In fact these trips turn up in a number of her novels in different forms. Then, too, since the publication of the two recent biographies by Cooke and Sullivan, Atwood's years living on a farm at Alliston, north of Toronto, with her partner Graeme Gibson have also become well known, as has her time working with children at Camp Hurontario (Cooke, 81, 212–13). Certainly, her own poetry and fiction draw on the land in powerful ways, as when the protagonist in *Surfacing* determines to throw off her social exterior and merge for a time with the wilderness, or when Atwood's Susanna Moodie, in *The Journals of Susanna Moodie*, finds the land is transforming her. In addition, Atwood herself has become a strong proponent of the need to safeguard the remaining wilderness, and has numerous times lent her name to environmental causes.

On the surface, then, the connection between Atwood, her work, and the land seems straightforward, almost overwhelming. Yet one can easily overestimate Atwood's connection to the land and assume that the wilderness has been her main theme. On the contrary, many of Atwood's works — among them her best — have virtually nothing to do with the land. Many of her readers will tell you that her work is essentially urban, often intimately connected with the geography of Toronto. One has only to recall the settings of *The Edible Woman, Lady Oracle, Life Before Man, The Robber Bride*, or most of her short stories to recognize that there is a good deal of truth in this picture of Atwood as an urban novelist. Even in *Alias Grace* (1996), her most recent novel, set in nineteenth-century Canada, when there was a great deal more wild countryside than at present, Atwood's concern with character leads her to say little about the land. Indeed, most of Atwood's novels and much of her poetry develop as mordant irony leveled against contemporary civilization and its distortions, an ironic mode that exists with difficulty alongside renderings of the "natural."

At times, one hears the view that Atwood's writing simply outgrew the topic of the land (just as the Quebec novel outgrew the *terroir*), and that her later work has helped to take the Canadian novel in new directions. This view is partially correct, but needs to be treated with caution. Verena Bühler Roth has recently taken issue with the categorization of Atwood's writing into early work, concerned with the land, and later work, concerned with the urban scene, and has shown that the land is still an important element in Atwood's later work, playing a significant role in *Cat's Eye, Wilderness Tips*, and even *The Handmaid's Tale*. While Roth's argument is an interesting corrective, she also tends to exaggerate the influence of the land in the later novels while neglecting the crucial fact that much early work, such as Atwood's first novel, *The Edible Woman*, has nothing to do with the land. What is needed is an assessment of Atwood's developing use of the land in her work. As will become apparent, Atwood has something in common with recent ecocentrist writers in their rejection of the anthropomorphic viewpoint and their struggles to re-position humanity as one species among many in a web of natural connections. Yet Atwood can hardly be called ecocentrist, since she rarely focuses on the natural world as her *principal* subject. What she does, however, is to break down the too easy assumption that the individual is a being entirely separate from his or her environment. Thus the environment — whether it be the land or the urbanscape — plays a crucial role in revealing the problems associated with individualism.

Roth asserts that Atwood's focus on the land begins with her Susanna Moodie poems, but in fact the land is there even earlier in *The Circle Game* (1966), *The Animals in That Country* (1968), and *Procedures for Underground* (1970). All these books include poems that refer to the land, at least occasionally. In reading these poems one has no difficulty in recognizing features of the glaciated Shield country of northern Ontario and Quebec where Atwood spent summers with her family. For example, water figures prominently, as it does in the Shield area. But instead of merely representing the area, Atwood uses the landscape to write about representation in general. For example, in "This is a Photograph of Me" the speaker reveals that she has drowned, and thus the lake and the drowning must also be understood figuratively. As we become aware that the speaker has lost her individuality to such an extent that she has become submerged in the landscape, the actual landscape of lakes and trees and cottages gradually transforms into the landscape of language through which we can see the individual — if we look "long enough" (*Circle Game*, 11).

Because Atwood's early poems locate themselves within the supposed binary of individual and environment, both the psyche of the speaker and the landscape itself take on distorted forms. The landscape is frequently presented as primitive and uncontrolled, a presence in sharp contrast to those who attempt to control their lives through reason or logic. In "An Attempted Solution for Chess Problems," for instance, the speaker imagines her sister pondering "her next move / the arrangement of her empire" (*Circle Game*, 17). She sees her sister "obsessed by history," struggling to maintain control while "outside the windows of this room / the land unrolls without landmark / a meshing of green on green." The sister embodies a rationalist or Enlightenment view in which order is paramount, but this ordering principle is placed in sharp contrast to the natural world, resulting in a "stalemate" with "vestiges of black and white / ruled squares on the green landscape" (*Circle Game*, 18). As should be apparent, Atwood's project in these poems does not demand that she represent the land in any great detail. In fact, it is the lack of detail which gives the land such force in subverting the Cartesian sense of mind-body duality.

The early poems frequently draw on a kind of magic realism as Atwood enforces the point that social constructs depend upon a natural world that is always in the process of undermining the social. In "The City Planners" it is suggested that the houses will eventually capsize, "will slide / obliquely into the clay seas, gradual as glaciers" (*Circle Game*, 27). Atwood depicts modern civilization as being afraid of the land, with individuals cutting themselves off from the natural forces of the forest and dancing inwards in "the circle game." For Atwood there is also a good deal of irony in the situation, since people use the "natural" to fend off the "natural." For example, the protagonists in "Spring in the Igloo" are living inside an igloo they have built, unaware of the existing primal energies except when the sun "seared itself through the roof." At the end of the poem they are drifting "into a tepid ocean / on a shrinking piece of winter," the image creating brilliantly the sense of impending destruction, with "ice the only thing / between [them] and disaster" (*Circle Game*, 48). The pair find themselves caught in a double bind, for they depend upon the ice for survival, but ultimately the ice has no nurturing ability. Thus Atwood uses the description of Canada as a northern nation to reflect the alienation of the late 1960s, where the ice of civilization is being destroyed by natural forces, but these forces are seen by the protagonists as dangerous.

As has come to be recognized in the environmental literature, the very idea of "wilderness" is highly problematic (Cronon). Atwood herself points to some of the difficulties with the concept in her poem "Migration: C.P.R.," when her speaker decides to journey across the land from the relatively civilized east to what is seen as the more primitive west (Atwood taught at the University of British Columbia on the west coast in 1964, so she knew something about living on the edge of the world). But the west cannot yield true wilderness, since "in the forest, even / apart from the trodden / paths, we can tell (from the sawn / firstumps) that many / have passed the same way" (*Circle Game*, 55). The land as a kind of *terra incognita* has been a strong influence in Canada's past, but Atwood recognizes that such a notion ignores the fact that the land has been inhabited for more than 10,000 years. For Atwood, however, the historical situation often takes a back seat to the psychological, for after her speaker migrates to the west coast, not only does she find signs of habitation, but the vegetation itself appears unnatural: "Things here grow from the ground / too insistently / green to seem / spontaneous." While it is possible to argue that Atwood the easterner cannot accept the remarkable growth of vegetation in the rainforest, this is to see the poems in too referential a mode, for the poems ask to be read not as poems about the land, but about a protagonist who is so accustomed to social geometries that the natural appears hallucinatory. As Dieter Meindl has observed, Atwood's representation of the land owes something to Faulkner in its use of the grotesque (Meindl, 306), for the binary of individual and environment eventually causes even the natural to appear unnatural.

The land in Atwood, then, becomes a metaphor by which the plight of the contemporary individual can be explored. In "Journey to the Interior," Atwood uses the British Columbia term "the interior," which refers to everything that is not the coast or the lower Fraser Valley, as an image for the interior of the self. The literal journey up the Fraser and the Thompson rivers quickly passes over into a figurative search for the self. The actual physical journey into the interior is only sketchily described, the language moving us away from a determinate landscape, so that at the end of the poem the speaker can say, "Whatever I do I must / keep my head. I know / it is easier for me to lose my way / forever here, than in other landscapes" (*Circle Game*, 58). The physical landscapes are alluded to but not filled in, since the emphasis falls on the way the outer journey is a metaphor for the internal one.

With *The Animals in That Country* (1968) Atwood continues many of her earlier themes, but one also detects a shift in emphasis, for as the title indicates, the animals in "that" country are the animals of England, and Atwood maintains that they are different from those in her own country, Canada. The reason is that the animals in "that" country have been incorporated into a human construct and given human meanings and even "the faces of people" (*Animals*, 2). For Atwood, the cats, the foxes, the bulls, and the wolves of Europe all have a place in human mythology. She imagines the wolves "holding resonant / conversations in their / forests thickened with legend" (3). Similarly the fox is run "politely to earth, the huntsmen / standing around him, fixed / in their tapestry of manners" (2). But, Atwood states, "In this country the animals / have the faces of / animals. // Their eyes / flash once in car headlights / and are gone. // Their deaths are not elegant. // They have the faces of / no-one" (*Animals*, 3). Atwood is here pushing towards the recognition that the natural world in Canada is not something that can be easily incorporated into the human domain to create a seamless unified field. By denying the animals a human face, the totemic qualities of unity are destroyed, and the individual is left with a feeling of brokenness. This sense of exile is repeated in the individual's own being when she observes that the animals have all left her and her mind is now "crowded with hollow totems" (*Animals*, 22).

As Atwood portrays the wilderness, it is something that people fear because it seems to deny the importance of their own existence. "Progressive Insanities of a Pioneer," one of Atwood's best known poems, describes the pioneer becoming progressively more insane as he attempts to assert his centrality in a wilderness wholly indifferent to him. At the opening, "He stood, a point / on a sheet of green paper / proclaiming himself the centre" (*Animals*, 36). The situation resembles that of Pascal, with the silence of the universe and the infinite spaces presenting the individual with a dizzying sense of inconsequentiality. The pioneer, Atwood indicates, lives in a world "with no walls, no borders," yet he shouts, "Let me out!" (36). Throughout, the pioneer attempts to impose himself on the landscape, to assert his importance, fearing that he is not central but "random." But in each case the land

responds in ways that he cannot understand. Thus, in answer to his as-
sertions, "the ground / replied with aphorisms": only in this case, the
aphorisms are "a tree-sprout, a nameless / weed, words / he couldn't
understand" (36). The fascinating point here is that Atwood envisages
the land possessing its own kind of language, the vegetation itself, but
not a language that the pioneer can understand.

One of the features that any farmer or gardener knows well, but
which is intensified in a pioneer situation, is that cleared land quickly
reverts to the wild. Atwood notes how "in the darkness the fields /
defend themselves with fences / in vain: / everything / is getting in"
(*Animals*, 37). Thus the vegetation and the animals are always en-
croaching upon the pioneer's patch of cultivated land, threatening to
overtake it. To the pioneer, the wilderness is something of a monster,
and the fences have to defend themselves against the forces of the
"other." While the pioneer can work only by daylight, the forces of the
wild work both day and night. Looking around him, the pioneer sees
the wilderness as "the absence / of order," a common complaint that
one hears farmers and ranchers voicing even today. He looks at "the
swamp's clamourings and the outbursts / of rocks" and finds he is disgusted. To the settler, "raw land" is merely swampy waste or rocky
bush until it is transformed by the "civilized" developer. Atwood extends the situation one step further when she has the forest itself responding to the pioneer: "He was wrong, the unanswering / forest
implied: / It was / an ordered absence." This phrase "an ordered absence" is intriguing. Atwood's emphasis on "order" is surely right,
since most ecologists today find an ecological order or balance in the
natural world. But if the "other" is also an absence, then it cannot reflect the pioneer, for the binary within which he has defined himself has
been broken.

What the pioneer wants, at least in Atwood's rendering, is some
grand narrative or "vision" that will allow him to stand back and com-
prehend his relation to the land. Atwood shows how the pioneer dan-
gles "the hooks of sown / roots under the surface / of the shallow
earth," fishing for a vision (*Animals*, 38). But such natural husbandry
does not do justice to the nature of the land. As she says, "It was like /
enticing whales with a bent / pin." The idea of fishing for a "great vision" has clear religious overtones and is connected to Jesus as a fisher
of men. But in this case the religion of farming is unequal to the force
and extent of the wilderness itself. The hooks of the farmer cannot
hook the whales of the land. What the pioneer actually needs is the experience that the "unstructured space" of the wilderness is "a deluge."
Then he would be able to stock "his log house- / boat with all the

animals // even the wolves." In this way he would not have stood out-side his vision, but would have become part of it, would have taken on board everything in the land, and would have been able to escape drowning. But instead of joining with the forces of the land, the pio-neer continues to struggle to hold himself aloof, a struggle that he is bound to lose. "In the end / through eyes / made ragged by his / ef-fort, the tension / between subject and object, // the green / vision, the unnamed / whale invaded" (39). The invasion presumably refers to the experience of going "bushed," of going crazy as a result of being too long alone in the woods, and reminds one of other Canadian po-ems about going bushed, poems such as Earle Birney's "Bushed" and Charles Lillard's "Bushed."

Where Atwood differs from Birney and Lillard is that she does not valorize the position of sanity, but implies that the pioneer should not have attempted to retain the distinction between subject and object, between himself and the land. Atwood's poem comes out of a period when various intellectuals were advising that the ego merge with the surrounding world. R. D. Laing's work comes to mind as does that of Alan Watts. For such writers, individuals go mad because they attempt to keep themselves isolated from their environment. Unlike Birney and Lillard, who show people going insane after being too long in the bush, Atwood indicates that the pioneer needs to create a closer rela-tion to the wilderness in order *not* to go insane.

In some ways an even more interesting poem showing Atwood breaking down the binary of the individual and the environment is "Backdrop Addresses Cowboy." Using the situation of movies, in which cowboys act out their role of hero against the land, Atwood in this poem first reveals the land of the movies to be a mere painted backdrop. Then she goes one step further. As the title indicates, At-wood has the backdrop speaking to the cowboy, who does not see the environment he travels through as something important in its own right, but as a simple backdrop for his actions. Clearly drawing on the Western film, Atwood depicts the "Starspangled cowboy / sauntering out of the almost- / silly West, on your face / a porcelain grin, / tug-ging a papier-mâché cactus / on wheels behind you with a string" (*Animals*, 50). The point is that the cowboy (in this case clearly an ac-tor) in his apparent innocence and self-centeredness creates the ene-mies, "the other," against which he then fights. But Atwood adds another dimension when she also notes that "you leave behind you a heroic / trail of desolation: / beer bottles / slaughtered by the side / of the road, bird- / skulls bleaching in the sunset." Here she is point-ing not only to the way that the cowboy of Western fame creates his own enemies, but also desolates the landscape through which he moves. The poem has moved the central intelligence away from the individual cowboy to the "backdrop" against which the individual operates. Indeed, in the second half of the poem, Atwood notes that although, given the conventions of the Western film, the backdrop ought to be watching "in admiration" once the shooting begins, instead the backdrop is now "elsewhere," no longer in a submissive attitude of adulation, and, indeed, no longer just a backdrop, but "the horizon / you ride towards, the thing you can never lasso" (*Animals*, 51).

In the final lines of the poem, the voice of the "backdrop" takes on a new quality when it/she/he says, "I am also what surrounds you: / my brain / scattered with your / tincans, bones, empty shells, / the litter of your invasions. // I am the space you desecrate / as you pass through" (*Animals*, 51). In other words, the reader now views the land as a sentient, existing being, and Atwood here comes close to creating an ecocentric or ecological view of the land. The land itself becomes the center and the human being merely a part of the larger whole. Yet one hesitates to use the term "ecocentric" in this case, since she does not recreate the landscape. The poem gains its strength and wit by giving voice to the backdrop and forcing us to see that the backdrop has its own dimensions. In a way, Atwood is here using some of the same techniques as in her presentation of feminist values in her poems about power politics. She shows the male assuming that the female is a willing mirror of himself, and then gives the mirror a voice, allowing the reader to experience the situation from the mirror's point of view. In "Backdrop Addresses Cowboy" the landscape speaks and expresses an ecocentric perspective, but the backdrop never transforms into the land itself.

The volume of poetry which has made the greatest impact in terms of Atwood's depiction of the land is *The Journals of Susanna Moodie* (1970). With even greater force than in her earlier poems, Atwood turns the Canadian landscape into a metaphor by delineating the process by which the nineteenth-century pioneer Susanna Moodie learns, or almost learns, not to distance herself from her environment but to become part of it — something that Atwood clearly believes the contemporary world needs to learn. In Moodie's famous prose collections *Roughing It in the Bush* (1852) and *Life in the Clearings* (1853), she uses two different kinds of rhetoric to describe the Canadian land: the sublime of late eighteenth-century romance and the gritty realism of the settler's own experience. For Atwood, these two conflicting language bases created a "violent duality," and she set out to frame in contemporary language the thoughts and feelings that lay beneath or between this duality. Atwood, however, also sharpens Moodie's feelings of alienation towards her adopted country and makes it appear as though Moodie is far more distanced from the wilderness than she actually was. In other words, Atwood imposes on Moodie a view of the land that comes from our own time, when urbanites tend to find any contact with the wilderness frightening.

While historically what Atwood does with the Moodie-land relationship is questionable, there is no doubt that she offers through Moodie's voice a view of the wilderness that speaks to contemporary readers. Atwood herself designed the cover and the collages that are included with the poems. The cover art shows a historical picture of Susanna Moodie in an oval frame, turned on its side, with stylized trees to each side of it. The picture is set against a white background with a wide band of black below it. The effect is to suggest that the historical Moodie is very much out of place, out of kilter in her environment. Throughout the book the Atwood collages, crude as they are, suggest that the historical figures do not fit with the land. They are imposed upon the land. Indeed, this is the central theme of the book — how Moodie comes to realize that she does not fit into the land, and that it is not she who must transform the land, but the land which must transform her. To some degree, of course, this is what the historical Moodie also learned: she had to leave behind many of her learned English attitudes and create new attitudes determined in large part by the situation in the new land.

Where Atwood excels is in allowing the reader to observe Moodie's transformation as a result of coming to terms with the wilderness. In the opening poem, "Disembarking at Quebec," Moodie is shown as being acutely aware that the new space is ignoring her. Atwood gives the land itself a presence and a life of its own. In older terms it would be said to be animist. Moodie is aware that "the moving water will not show me / my reflection" (*Journals*, 11). And when Atwood has Moodie say, "The rocks ignore," omitting the object "me," it appears as though Moodie has been erased by the new land. She has become "a word / in a foreign language," and it is apparent that she will have to learn the language of the new land, and in fact become a part of that new land.

Curiously enough, Atwood has little to say about the actual qualities of the new land, and if one wants an account of the Canadian backwoods, one would do much better to return to Moodie's own *Roughing It in the Bush*. Atwood's interest lies not in the actual representation of the wilderness, but in showing how Moodie as a representative of modernity has to rid herself of her binary way of seeing herself and what lies around her. For Atwood, the point is to break down the socially constructed armor and to allow self and world to blend. Much of the philosophical thrust here can be traced to Wilhelm Reich, and the notion that individuals must lose their artificial ego boundaries and learn to exist in an authentic present. Thus, Atwood soon has Moodie learning that she needs "wolf's eyes to see / the truth" (*Journals*, 13), the wolf being symbolic of the dangers of the forest, and Atwood reversing the fairy tale motif.

As Atwood portrays it, the wilderness becomes the desired place in which none of the ideological concepts of civilization apply. The wilderness is the unorganized, chaotic present in which the civilized mind takes no part. Perhaps the finest poem to present this idea is "The Planters," in which Atwood portrays Moodie watching her husband and some other workers as they labor to clear land and plant a crop. This was the quintessential job of nineteenth- and early twentieth-century pioneers in North America, many of whom were deeded a quarter section of wilderness, a homestead, in return for clearing a small acreage and building a house and barn. Yet it is not the experience of pioneer life that fascinates Atwood; she is concerned with how people forget the living present of what might be thought of as Heideggerian Being, and live for a fabricated future. Atwood has Mrs. Moodie say, "I see them; I know / none of them believe they are here. / They deny the ground they stand on, / pretend this dirt is the future" (*Journals*, 16–17). As Atwood presents the situation, the truly important element is that Mrs. Moodie becomes aware of the possibility of living in the immediate present without any of the rational means of keeping that present at bay. Such a state of being is both liberating and potentially terrifying. Caught between both reactions, Mrs. Moodie believes that the men are right to hold onto their illusions, for if they do not, and they "open their eyes even for a moment / to these trees, to this particular sun / they would be surrounded, stormed, broken // in upon by branches, roots, tendrils, the dark / side of light / as I am." Even as the uncultivated forest breaks in upon the cleared land, so does the "natural" break in upon the civilized.

In Atwood's portrayal, Mrs. Moodie almost learns the lesson of the land, but when she and her husband leave the bush, she loses the opportunity. The final poem of Journal I has Moodie reflecting how she "was crept in / upon by green" and how "the animals / arrived to inhabit me" (*Journals*, 26), the suggestion being that slowly she is becoming attuned to a more natural self. But when she travels to Belleville to meet her husband and begin town life, she recognizes that

"There was something they almost taught me / I came away not having learned" (27). Journal II takes up this idea of incompletion and Moodie reflects on how she adapted to her new country, learning much about it, but in the end always speaking with two voices. As she says: "Two voices / took turns using my eyes" (*Journals*, 42). For Atwood, this dual voice attempting to put Canada into words is something that she believes is typical of all Canada, not just in Moodie's time, but even today. As she says in her "Afterword" to the collection:

> We are all immigrants to this place even if we were born here: the country is too big for anyone to inhabit completely, and in the parts unknown to us we move in fear, exiles and invaders. This country is something that must be chosen — it is so easy to leave — and if we do choose it we are still choosing a violent duality. (*Journals*, 62)

Atwood suggests that the ghost of Mrs. Moodie still inhabits Canadians in their struggle to be a part of the natural world — even though most Canadians now live in urban centers (perhaps *because* most Canadians live in urban centers). The final lines make this clear: "Turn, look down: / there is no city; / this is the centre of a forest // your place is empty" (*Journals*, 61). The collection is a superb series of poems — the favorite book of a great many Atwood readers. It succeeds so well on its own terms because the land is worked superbly as a metaphor to explore a potentially new paradigm of the individual. There is not space to deal with Atwood's later poems about the land, but *Two-Headed Poems* (1978) and *Interlunar* (1984) both open up new directions, many of which are developed in the novels.

Of all Atwood's novels, the one that deals most thoroughly with the land is *Surfacing*, published only two years after *The Journals of Susanna Moodie*. Her publisher initially thought it would prove a harder sell than *The Edible Woman*, but it quickly became a best seller and has often been claimed as a defining novel for Canadians' sense of their selves. Like many of Atwood's early poems, *Surfacing* is concerned with a death-in-life situation, psychological anomie, and the regeneration or resurrection that may be possible. It also contains a search for the missing father of western civilization, but when the father is discovered to be dead, the novel moves out and beyond the logocentrism of patriarchy.

Unlike the poems which tend to recreate the land largely as metaphor, *Surfacing* also gives a graphic and gritty view of the northern landscape, one that is easily recognizable in its details. George Woodcock has said that "the environment is the great theme of *Surfacing*" (Woodcock, 69). Since the novel portrays its four main characters trav-

eling from southern cities into the Canadian north, it might seem that
the landscape is intended to have a healing effect. In part this is true,
but Atwood by no means paints an idyllic Bliss Carman view of the
land. It is not the "true north strong and free," as the Canadian national anthem would have it. In fact there is little wilderness on this
journey. The marks of contemporary civilization, with its power to in-
trude into the land, to destroy and desacralize, are everywhere. Not far
from the city limits the unnamed protagonist notices that "the white
birches are dying, the disease is spreading up from the south" (*Surfacing*, 9). As they travel north, they move through "flattened cow-
sprinkled hills and leaf trees and dead elm skeletons, then into the nee-
dle trees and the cuttings dynamited in pink and gray granite and the
flimsy tourist cabins" (*Surfacing*, 11). The protagonist points to what
appears an innocent hill, but it turns out that it is a "pit the Americans
hollowed out" for a rocket site. The local people have participated in
this despoliation; they have even denatured the animals. At a gas station, the foursome discover three stuffed moose dressed in human
clothes and another on the roof — "a little girl moose in a frilly skirt
and a pigtailed blond wig, holding a red parasol in one hoof" (*Surfacing*, 16). The land and its wildlife has been transformed into a kind of
mini-Disneyland.

In fact the degradation of the wilderness has been going on for decades, as we learn when the protagonist and her friends reach the lake
where her parents built their cabin. She recalls that even as a child when
she came to the lake with her parents, a dam had already been built and
the level raised to facilitate logging. The entire area seems now to have
been logged over and what remains are scrub trees. There is no longer
much logging near the lake, the second growth apparently not ready to
be logged or not worth logging. What is left is a very poor, small community entirely dependent on tourists. In the local bar there is a picture
that attempts to capture a sporting, outdoors image, but it has nothing
in common with the reality of this "wilderness" situation. It is in a

> scrolled gilt frame, blown-up photograph of a stream with trees and
> rapids and a man fishing. It's an imitation of other places, more
> southern ones, which are themselves imitations, the original some-
> one's distorted memory of a nineteenth-century English gentleman's
> shooting lodge, the kind with trophy heads and furniture made from
> deer antlers. (*Surfacing*, 32)

The recognition in *Surfacing* that the wilderness no longer exists —
if ever it did — appears to have had profound implications for Atwood
as a writer. Much of the novel sets out to disabuse her contemporaries

of some of their most dearly beloved myths about the wilderness and to show that Canadians have been fully complicit in the destruction of the land. The incident showing this most forcefully is the senseless slaughter of the heron, an act that recalls the shooting of the albatross in "The Ancient Mariner." At first the killing of the heron is blamed on the Americans, the protagonist and her friends preferring to believe that Canadians still retain something of an uncorrupted nature. When it is later learned that Canadians were responsible, it becomes apparent that the malaise of modernity — which sees the entire natural world as potential products to be used instrumentally — ultimately involves everyone. There is no safe place to stand apart.

Yet Atwood at this stage in her writing career is still very much involved with the narrative of personal liberation, and it becomes apparent that she is loathe to give it up. Thus she portrays the protagonist continuing in her search for an authentic state of being. In part the solution comes when she dives deep into the lake/herself and recovers lost memories of an abortion she had had some years before. The narrative also suggests that she makes contact with the memories of her dead parents and renews a contact that had been broken. On the psychological level, these discoveries make eminent sense and help to account for the protagonist's earlier emotional frigidity. But Atwood clearly wants something more than straightforward psychological renewal, since she also portrays the young woman refusing to return to civilization, throwing off her clothes and attempting a literal merging with the natural world. The protagonist has learned from her parents at an early age how to live in the bush and, as the novel draws to a close, she undertakes to go well beyond the survival skills her parents taught her. However, since the forest has already been shown to be degraded, an attempted fusion with the natural world will not in itself be persuasive, and Atwood is compelled to extend the situation one stage further, which she does by portraying the young woman experiencing a mystical vision — seeing in her parents' garden the figure of an antlered man. This vision develops from her discovery that her father at the time of his death had been studying ancient Native rock paintings. The appearance of the antlered man — a figure presumably painted by the Natives at a time when they were still in touch with their original religion — puts the protagonist in touch with a spiritual dimension that seems to integrate the natural and the human, but also to represent the essence of the land at a pre-historic level. As in the earlier poems, the land has again been transformed into a metaphor, in this case of spiritual unity between humanity and nature. In a novel, of course, even as imagistic a novel as *Surfacing*, it is difficult to end with the poetic epiphany of the antlered man, and Atwood soon after has to depict her protagonist returning to civilization, but carrying with her the memory of her vision to help channel her imaginative energies in new and more satisfying directions.

In the same year that *Surfacing* appeared, Atwood published *Survival: A Thematic Guide to Canadian Literature*. The book has exerted an extraordinary influence. It follows up on Northrop Frye's view in the "Conclusion" to the first edition of the *Literary History of Canada* (1965), that the early settlers to Canada were afraid of the wilderness and tended to position themselves in physical and psychic garrisons. Frye introduced the stunning image of early settlers to Canada traveling up the St. Lawrence and finding themselves in the middle of a dark continent, a Canadian version of *Heart of Darkness*. The problem with the Atwood-Frye thesis is that it has little basis in fact. The fear of the wilderness seems to be much more of an urban phenomenon of the twentieth century. In reading the early settler accounts right up until the 1940s, one finds that the land is generally seen as an opportunity. When Peter Evans, an old homesteader in the Prince George region of British Columbia (his parents started clearing the land in 1903), read Eric Collier's book *Three Against the Wilderness* (1959), he laughed and said that Collier was a city person who failed to understand that the wilderness was not *against* him. Collier simply needed to learn how to use some simple hand tools, such as a froe and an adze, and the land would supply his needs. The old homesteaders, he maintained, had not seen themselves *against* the wilderness, but *with* it.

In this respect, it is interesting to note that Atwood's own poetry and fiction about the land emphasize the need to gain a closer connection to the land. It may well be that she unconsciously exaggerated the alienation experienced in the historical situation in order to valorize her own belief that one needs to merge with the natural landscape. Certainly her own early life, when her parents taught her to live in the woods, would indicate that she herself did not fear the wilderness, a point she confirms in several poems in *Morning in the Burned House* (1995).

In the novels following *Surfacing* — *Lady Oracle* (1976), *Life Before Man* (1979), and *Bodily Harm* (1981) — Atwood pays little attention to the land. One wonders if the writing of *Surfacing* had perhaps taught her that a direct attempt to delve ever deeper into the wilderness in search of a natural purity is something of a dead end. Certainly she becomes ever more interested in the social dimension as a site of contention which needs to be unraveled in its own right. By the 1980s, however, there was a growing public awareness of the danger to the environment (many people place this awareness as beginning with the publication of Rachel Carson's *Silent Spring* in 1962), and Atwood with her highly sensitive antennae for social issues, began to introduce this environmental concern. *The Handmaid's Tale* (1985) is a dystopian novel set in a future where it is evident that the environment has been destroyed. The thrust of *The Handmaid's Tale* is to bring out the implications of the trends of present day civilization. Not only are women the handmaids of men, but the natural world has been devastated, with no clean water left and only a few parks for recreation. As dystopian fiction, *The Handmaid's Tale* does not emphasize the land, the point being that our present policies of patriarchy, growth, and domination of the natural world are leading us to a doomsday end.

By the time of *Cat's Eye* in 1988, one can see how Atwood's portrayal of the land has changed. Here Atwood uses Elaine Risley's childhood memories of her life with her parents on summer trips to the north as a measure of normality and innocence in contrast to the artificiality of life in the city — especially for women. At one point Elaine describes their return to Toronto in her parent's car as being

> like coming down from a mountain. We descend through layers of clarity, of coolness and uncluttered light, down past the last granite outcrop, the last small raggedy-edged lake, into the thicker air, the dampness and warm heaviness, the cricket noises and weedy meadow smells of the south. (*Cat's Eye*, 73)

While this contrast between country innocence and urban experience is effectively rendered in the novel, the narrative employs the country more as a simple counter to highlight the compelling artistic and psychological dilemmas of urban people concerned with time, memory, and the imagination. Moreover, Atwood has not forgotten that although the child may experience the countryside as natural wilderness, the adult sees things differently. Reflecting on her home in Vancouver, Elaine remembers how the wilderness near Vancouver looks almost unreal in its beauty. But she also knows that, "go a few miles here, go a few miles there, out of sight of the picture windows, and you come to the land of stumps" (*Cat's Eye*, 43–44). Here Atwood reminds us that behind the scenic corridors there lies the reality of clear-cutting. The novel introduces the point almost as an aside, but the implication is that the memory of the child's experience of the wilderness is not to be taken at face value. You may not see the forest for the trees. In fact there may not be a forest, only a screen of trees.

Wilderness Tips (1991) contains at least three important short stories dealing with the wilderness, but as with *Cat's Eye*, Atwood tends to situate the wilderness in the past. It is as if she recognizes that Canada has become an urban nation, and that most readers will have no immediate experience of the wilderness. The protagonists now "read" past narratives of the land for what they tell us of our current situation. In "The Age of Lead," Atwood presents her protagonist Jane watching a television program about the Franklin expedition of the nineteenth century. The program is filming the unearthing of the body of John Torrington, one of the expedition members, which has been remarkably well preserved in the permafrost. Once the body is thawed out and examined, it is discovered that Torrington and the other members of the expedition died not of the extreme conditions of the arctic, as had been believed, but of lead poisoning, the lead having been used in the new technology of sealing cans of foods. The lead poisoning may also have caused the men to become disoriented and would explain their strange behavior at the end, when they attempted to go overland with massive amounts of unnecessary goods which they discarded on the way. As Jane watches the program it occurs to her that, for the men on the Franklin expedition, there was only one source of poison, the lead used to solder the cans, but in the late twentieth century, there are a multitude of poisons and they are everywhere:

> Jane began to notice news items of the kind she'd once skimmed over. Maple groves dying of acid rain, hormones in the beef, mercury in the fish, pesticides in the vegetables, poison sprayed on the fruit, God knows what in the drinking water. She subscribed to a bottled spring-water service and felt better for a few weeks, then read in the paper that it wouldn't do her much good, because whatever it was had been seeping into everything. Each time you took a breath, you breathed some of it in. She thought about moving out of the city, then read about toxic dumps, radioactive waste, concealed here and there in the countryside and masked by the lush, deceitful green of waving trees. (*Wilderness Tips*, 166–67)

Atwood employs the Franklin expedition and the arctic wilderness as a telling example of how, in the midst of nature, the technological innovation which seems to be the expedition's salvation — canned food — is also what drives the men mad and eventually kills them. The chilling feature is that they are never aware of the lead poisoning. It is the hidden killer. The application to our own society is evident. The title "The Age of Lead" refers not only to the lead used to solder the tins shut but also to the Greek idea of the four ages — gold, silver, bronze, and lead — with lead being the most degraded. Atwood implies that we are living in an age of lead, with spreading madness in the population and a civilization consumed by its own apparent mastery of the environment.

In "Death by Landscape" the land is again something to be read in the past. The protagonist Lois, an older woman, has recently moved to a waterfront condominium and appears not to miss the natural world: "The only plant life is in pots in the solarium" (*Wilderness Tips*, 101). Ironically, her walls are covered with landscape paintings by the Group of Seven and David Milne. Nor is this fascination with landscape mere nostalgia for a time past or even an investment strategy.

> She bought them because she wanted them . . . although she could not have said at the time what it was. It was not peace: she does not find them peaceful in the least. Looking at them fills her with a word-less unease. Despite the fact that there are no people in them or even animals, it's as if there is something, or someone, looking back out. (*Wilderness Tips*, 102)

What this "something" or "someone" is, we learn when Lois thinks back to an early childhood camping experience, when her friend Lucy mysteriously died on a wilderness canoeing trip. As Atwood showed in "The Grey Owl Syndrome" (an essay in *Strange Things*), Canadians at one time delighted in emulating the Native people. In Lois's case what particularly impressed her about her camping experience was the way in which the camp counselors encouraged them to imitate the Indians. Indeed, on the night they are to leave on the canoe trip the campers have their faces painted and are infused with the desire to do something wonderful and great. Lois wants to be "an Indian," and even though she now realizes that all of that was hokum, "a form of stealing," at the time it meant a great deal to her. As she says, "She wanted to be ad-venturous and pure, and aboriginal" (*Wilderness Tips*, 110). At the same time, however, the canoe trip allows her to experience the wilder-ness in all of its vast empty space. Once they are in the canoes, she feels as though "an invisible rope has broken. They're floating free, on their own, cut loose. Beneath the canoe the lake goes down, deeper and colder than it was a minute before" (*Wilderness Tips*, 112). And soon afterwards Lucy disappears without a trace.

Clearly Atwood is here drawing on the opposing senses of the wil-derness as both liberating and horrifying. For Lois, this paradox has never been lived through and resolved. She has never again gone up north "or to any place with wild lakes and wild trees and the calls of loons" (*Wilderness Tips*, 120). Yet she still lives with the awareness of "this empty space in sound" (120), and recognizes that she needs to keep the paintings of the Canadian wilderness near her. Moreover, she realizes that the Canadian landscape paintings are not "landscape paintings. Because there aren't any landscapes up there, not in the old, tidy European sense, with a gentle hill, a curving river, a cottage, a mountain in the background, a golden evening sky" (*Wilderness Tips*, 121). Instead, there is a maze, and she intuits that Lucy is hidden in the paintings, that she is still alive in the apartment. There are many echoes here of Atwood's other works, but the crucial point for Atwood is that even in contemporary times, when people seem to be cut off entirely from the wilderness, it still haunts them as the absence at the heart of being, the absence that has not been adequately dealt with.

The title story of the volume, "Wilderness Tips," offers even more of a "reading" of past wilderness motifs. The setting is at Wacousta Lodge on a northern lake. The name Wacousta derives from Major John Richardson's novel of the same name, as the characters remind us. Moreover, just as Richardson's novel is about war, so too is Atwood's story — about the war of the sexes. Indeed, it is the story of three daughters who all fight over a Hungarian émigré, George, who is married to the younger daughter Portia but who has an affair from time to time with the second daughter Prue, and who in this incident begins to have an affair with the older daughter. Yet this story contains another old book that must be read — this time from 1905 — that gives tips on how to survive in the wilderness. "These instructions were interspersed with lyrical passages about the joys of independence and the open air, and descriptions of fish-catching and sunsets" (*Wilderness Tips*, 202). As was the case with "Death by Landscape," Atwood develops the two opposing views of the landscape: peaceful, gentle, and inspiring; nasty, brutish, and short. The characters enjoying a holiday at Wacousta Lodge imagine that they are dealing with a poster image of Canada's pristine wilderness, and that civilization has removed them from any idea of darkness and warfare. Yet the return of the natural is always incipient, always threatening to break through the civilized patina. As one of the characters notes, the title "Wilderness Tips" can also be read as meaning that the wilderness is tipping, and that everyone will be caught up in this tipping motion and drown.

Atwood herself has many times taken the opportunity to speak out on the need to protect the remaining wilderness areas. For an author who has spent so much time plumbing the metaphoric qualities of the land, it is surprising to see how pragmatic Atwood is about wilderness preservation. But then this may well be a good strategy for a writer of poetry and fiction. In the summer of 1987, she wrote an article for the Saturday Magazine section of the *Toronto Star* about a trip she made through the Temagami. As Atwood described it, she "took part in an old Canadian summer ritual. I went wilderness canoeing in the north" (*Toronto Star* M-1). In the article, she talks about why people put themselves through the difficulty of canoeing and portaging and comes up with the fairly straightforward notion that the scenery is worth it. The point of writing the essay is that "the area needs help." Although the central part of Temagami is a park, the government of Ontario was considering the granting of permits to extend logging roads into the area immediately to the south and this would endanger the entire area through fragmentation. Atwood takes pains to point out that although "this issue is often presented as a fight between tree-huggers or 'environmentalists,' seen as woolly headed, impractical nature lovers who want public money to be put into frivolities like parks, versus hard-headed private-sector businessmen logging-company folks who have the real interests, that is, the jobs, of the local community at heart," in fact there are other arguments against allowing logging in the area. Her main point is that "there is a very sound economic argument for preserving this land as wilderness, or as a heartland wilderness with a buffer zone around it." The arguments are that more and more people want to visit wilderness areas and these people create a soundly based economic industry. Making the point that the Temagami is close to both Toronto and the cities of the United States, Atwood argues: "Destroy it and you've denied the wilderness experience to a lot of people who can't afford to get it any other way." As the headline writer for the article understood all too well, Atwood's main argument is that preservation makes good economic sense. "Profiting by Our Wilderness" is the headline. One should not make too much out of this short newspaper article, but it is interesting to see Atwood downplaying the ecological argument and playing up the economic one.

In 1989 Atwood again returned to the environmental scene, writing a two-page preface to *The Canadian Green Consumer Guide* in which she urged consumers "not to buy polluting products" (3). Two years later Atwood contributed a small piece to the collection of essays by Jonathon Porritt entitled *Save the Earth*, with a foreword by the Prince of Wales and introduction by David Suzuki. The book was published to raise money for Friends of the Earth International. It is a semi-serious large format coffee table book with a number of substantive articles and a great many small pieces by famous people. For example, there is a poem by Ted Hughes and a short piece by the Dalai Lama. Atwood's piece is only about fifty words and appears on the same page as a piece by Al Gore, at that time a senator from Tennessee. Atwood concentrates on the fact that pollution is becoming a serious issue for everyone. As she says:

> Concern for the environment is no longer the preserve of a small, eccentric minority. It cuts across the political spectrum from left to

right . . . Once, we were threatened with disaster in the time of our children, or our children's children; we shrugged and kept on polluting. But now, we're told, all these unpleasant things are going to happen to us. No wonder people are worried. (in Porritt, 194)

Again in 1995, responding to the largest civil disobedience movement in Canada's history, Atwood volunteered to lend her voice to the campaign to save Clayoquot Sound from clear-cut logging. She crafted a quotation that Greenpeace and other environmental organizations have often used on their brochures:

> We would never buy paper made from dead bears, otter, salmon and birds, from ruined native cultures, from destroyed species and destroyed lives, from ancient forests reduced to stumps and mud; but that's what we're buying when we buy paper made from old-growth clearcut trees.

Along with Timothy Findley and other well-known authors, she also spoke at length for Greenpeace about the need to protect endangered wilderness areas.

It is interesting to speculate whether the environmental movement has not helped to move Atwood's writing in new directions. And by this it is not meant that she now introduces environmental issues into her writing. Environmentalists, as John Livingston has remarked, are often well intentioned, but by emphasizing the need for parks and protected areas, they also re-institute systems of thought which are controlling, which place the natural world under the umbrella of human instrumentality. In *Wilderness Tips*, Atwood depicts the revenge of the natural world on those who imagine that they are eco-friendly but who actually subvert the natural by denying its fullness. This is not to say that Atwood is an ecocentrist or ecological writer in the same vein as Sharon Butala, Harold Rhenisch, or Don Gayton. But her earlier writing has made her deeply aware of our own contradictory attitudes towards nature, and now when she writes of the effect of the land on individuals, she conjures shadows and absences threatening to overwhelm us as we continue with our childish ideas of domination.

Works Consulted

Atwood, Margaret. *Alias Grace*. Toronto: McClelland & Stewart, 1996.

———. *The Animals in That Country*. Toronto: Oxford University Press, 1968.

———. *Bluebeard's Egg*. Toronto: McClelland & Stewart, 1983.

———. *Cat's Eye*. Toronto: McClelland & Stewart, 1988.

———. *The Circle Game*. Toronto: Anansi, 1967.

———. "A Double-Bladed Knife: Subversive Laughter in Two Stories by Thomas King." *Canadian Literature* 124–125 (1990): 243–50.

———. *Good Bones*. Toronto: Coach House Press, 1992.

———. *The Handmaid's Tale*. Toronto: McClelland & Stewart, 1985.

———. *Interlunar*. Toronto: Oxford University Press, 1984.

———. *The Journals of Susanna Moodie*. Toronto: Oxford University Press, 1970.

———. *Morning in the Burned House*. Toronto: McClelland & Stewart, 1995.

———. Preface to *The Canadian Green Consumer Guide*. Toronto: McClelland & Stewart, 1989.

———. *Procedures for Underground*. Toronto: Oxford University Press, 1970.

———. *Second Words: Selected Critical Prose*. Toronto: Anansi, 1982.

———. *Strange Things: The Malevolent North in Canadian Literature*. Oxford: Clarendon Press, 1995.

———. *Surfacing*. New York: Fawcett Popular Library, 1972.

———. *Survival: A Thematic Guide to Canadian Literature*. Toronto: Anansi, 1972.

———. *True Stories*. Toronto: Oxford University Press, 1981.

———. *Two-Headed Poems*. Toronto: Oxford University Press, 1978.

———. Untitled comment in *Save the Earth*. Ed. Jonathon Porritt. Toronto: McClelland & Stewart, 1991: 194.

———. *Wilderness Tips*. Toronto: McClelland & Stewart, 1991.

———. *You Are Happy*. Toronto: Oxford University Press, 1974.

Collier, Eric. *Three Against the Wilderness*. New York: Dutton, 1959.

Cooke, Nathalie. *Margaret Atwood: A Biography*. Toronto: ECW Press, 1998.

Cronon, William. "The Trouble with the Wilderness or, Getting Back to the Wrong Nature." In *Uncommon Ground: Toward Reinventing Nature*. Ed. William Cronon. New York: Norton, 1995.

Frye, Northrop. "Conclusion" to *The Literary History of Canada*. Ed. Carl F. Klinck. 1st ed. Toronto: University of Toronto Press, 1965: 819–49.

Glotfelty, Cheryll and Harold Fromm, ed. *The Ecocriticism Reader: Landmarks in Literary Ecology.* Athens/London: University of Georgia Press, 1996.

Grace, Sherrill. *Violent Duality: A Study of Margaret Atwood.* Montreal: Véhicule Press, 1980.

Howells, Coral Ann. "'It all depends on where you stand in relation to the forest': Atwood and the Wilderness from *Surfacing* to *Wilderness Tips.*" In *Various Atwoods.* Ed. Lorraine M. York. Toronto: Anansi, 1995: 47–70.

Keith, W. J. *Margaret Atwood's* The Edible Woman*: A Reader's Guide.* Toronto: ECW Press, 1989.

Livingston, John A. *Rogue Primate.* Toronto: Key Porter, 1994.

MacDonald, Judy. "The Bug's the Thing." *The Canadian Forum* (April 1999): 24–25.

Meindl, Dieter. "Between Eliot and Atwood: Faulkner as Ecologist." In *Faulkner, His Contemporaries, and His Posterity.* Ed. W. Zacharasiewicz. Tübingen/Basel: Francke, 1993: 301–8.

Moodie, Susanna. *Life in the Clearings versus the Bush.* Toronto: Macmillan, 1976.

———. *Roughing It in the Bush.* Toronto: McClelland & Stewart, 1997.

Roth, Verena Bühler. *Wilderness and the Natural Environment: Margaret Atwood's Recycling of a Canadian Theme.* Tübingen/Basel: Francke, 1998.

Scholtmeijer, Marian. *Animal Victims in Modern Fiction: From Sanctity to Sacrifice.* Toronto: University of Toronto Press, 1993.

Sullivan, Rosemary. *The Red Shoes: Margaret Atwood Starting Out.* Toronto: Harper Flamingo, 1998.

Woodcock, George. *Introducing Margaret Atwood's* Surfacing. Toronto: ECW Press, 1990.

Recycling Culture: Kitsch, Camp, and Trash in Margaret Atwood's Fiction

Lorna Irvine (George Mason University, Fairfax, Virginia)

As *LADY ORACLE'S* Joan Foster begins to acquaint herself with England, a country that, unlike her home country, Canada, has a long and varied history, she wanders about London's Victoria and Albert Museum and, more damaging to her relationship with Paul, the endless stalls of used clothing, jewelry, furniture, and knickknacks that have made the Portobello Road famous. There, she discovers an obsession that before long feeds into the costume Gothics that she begins to produce at an alarming rate. Apart from any writer's fascination with language, for example with old-fashioned words like "'fichu' and 'paletot' and 'pelisse'" (175), Joan finds that learning more about archaic language, nineteenth-century clothing and, in general, antique material objects helps her to create what she imagines to be more authentic literary characters. In her first costume Gothic, she evokes the nineteenth-century Crystal Palace — according to Celeste Olalquiaga, a structure that tamed industrial production by making machines appear as "products of nature rather than of human labor" (39) — as the background for one of Samantha and Sir Edmund's meetings and, in another of her Gothics, a maze that, as one of the housemaids assures the main character, Charlotte, was *"planted by the Master's forebears, hundreds of years ago, in the reign of Good Queen Bess"* (208).

Discovering the sensuous pleasure of past material cultures is one of several realizations discussed in *In Search of Alias Grace*. In this short essay, Atwood explains the rationale for some of the research relevant to the writing of her 1996 novel, *Alias Grace*. She confesses that part of her fascination with the nineteenth century (the century in which *Alias Grace* is set) is occasioned by the emphasis placed by that century on memory and certain concomitant emotions: "Nostalgia for what once was, guilt for what you once did, revenge for what someone else once did to you, regret for what you once might have done but did not do" (10). Apart from the fact that nostalgia, guilt, revenge, and regret are at the heart of most works of fiction, Atwood's emphasis on the tension between forgetting as a central act of the late twentieth-century imagination and the nineteenth-century emphasis on memory permeates her work. She believes that today, because of our "postmodern conscious-ness" (13), time and therefore identity seem to be "a collage of freeze-frames, jumbled fragments, and jump-cuts" (12), and that Canada, suffering from what Earle Birney has referred to as a "lack of ghosts" (17) and, Atwood suggests, from any interest in discovering "the ap-propriate clothing" (14) for the genre of historical romance, has only recently begun to find the reconstruction of Canada's past significantly rewarding.

In *Lady Oracle*, Joan also discovers a way of increasing the patina of age that a Canadian writer, suffering, according to Paul, a new world lack of history, might fail to develop persuasively. Burying herself in the Portobello stalls, where "waves" of age wash over her, Joan becomes obsessed with "worn necklaces, sets of gilt spoons, sugar tongs in the shape of hen's feet or midget hands, clocks that didn't work, flowered china, spotty mirrors and ponderous furniture" that are, as she also re-alizes, the "flotsam left by those receding centuries in which, more and more, I was living" (178–79). She becomes fascinated with how the discarded objects of former lives continue to circulate in the present. People die; their possessions do not, often becoming "more valuable, harder and more brilliant, as if they had absorbed their owners' suffer-ings and fed on them" (179).

In these two passages from *Lady Oracle* several significant issues surface. While, as Atwood admits in *In Search of Alias Grace*, we are all "trapped by time and circumstance" (4), writers learn to evoke the past for their readers by recycling images and language and, in the process, transform both. Such transformation is important to Marie Vauthier's argument in *New World Myth*, her study of the many ways in which new world countries such as Canada use traditional myths for their own purposes, changing traditional stories about life into ones more in keeping with a different and more contemporary world view. She quotes Jacques Godbout: "'Toute entreprise d'écriture est une entre-prise pour masquer, transformer, transmuer les choses, et non pas pour les dire comme elles sont . . . [Ecrire, c'est] briser la chronologie, briser la représentation'" (61). Often in Atwood's fiction, used objects con-nect the past with the present, compensating for the freeze-frames that postmodernism offers in the place of historical continuity and keeping the dialogue open between the old world and the new. In other words, Atwood offers the mystique of kitsch. In *The Artificial Kingdom*, Olalquiaga argues that

> kitsch is nothing if not a suspended memory whose elusiveness is made even more keen by its extreme iconicity. Despite appearances,

kitsch is not an active commodity naively infused with the desire of a
wish image, but rather a failed commodity that continually speaks of
all it has ceased to be. . . . Kitsch is a time capsule with a two-way
ticket to the realm of myth. . . . Here, for a second or perhaps even a
few minutes, there reigns an illusion of completeness, a universe de-
void of past and future. . . . Kitsch assures that this lost time is mo-
mentarily found. (28–29)

Time capsules, kitsch objects carry their histories with them, leading to
the creation of liminal spaces. Throughout her fiction, Atwood holds
time in odd suspensions so that her characters frequently seem to exist
in a kind of limbo, a visual space that Elaine Risley, in *Cat's Eye*, describes as a "series of liquid transparencies, one laid on top of another."
"Nothing," she says, "goes away" (3). In *Lady Oracle*, time capsules
become literal, life is suspended, and death and life unite. Indeed, at
the beginning of the novel, Joan describes her existence as seeming to
scroll and festoon "like the frame of a baroque mirror" (3), an image
that, like so many Atwood images, captures the dynamics of the ensuing novel.

The recycling of culture, while aesthetically appealing to Atwood, is
politically interesting to her as well. In the second of the passages
quoted from *Lady Oracle*, Joan becomes fascinated with the way in
which objects from the past continue to circulate in the present. By
drawing attention to the circulation of commodities, she raises questions about commerce and, as Jon Goss argues in his article "Once-
upon-a-Time in the Commodity World," the "commercialization of
aesthetics" (72). At the end of his discussion, he writes: "Collective
identity forged in consumption is kitsch, a self-conscious sharing of
faith in material signs of a 'real' community that is felt in its absence,
but it also provides glimpses of imagined authenticity and keeps alive
dreams of utopian possibility, a vital political function" (72). Apart
from using the rather morbid image of objects feeding on their owners
in the above passage from *Lady Oracle*, Atwood openly criticizes certain
aspects of contemporary capitalist commerce. In *The Edible Woman*,
Seymour Surveys, the marketing firm for which Marian MacAlpin
works, is the butt of Atwood's satire, partly because it creates a commercial definition of a shared Canadian identity. Its jingle, created to
sell Moose Beer, suggests that drinking the beer is a wilderness experience, and while Atwood's attack is certainly directed at the crassness of
advertising, this example also underlines the commercialization of nature, and the confusion between natural objects and the products of
human labor. Further, by plotting the main character's attempt to escape the rule of commerce, Atwood emphasizes the destructive effects

of consumerism, even upon Canadian nationalist objectives. *Surfacing* hits all of these messages home by likening the "secondhand American" spreading over one of the characters to "mange or lichen," and a conflation of "handbills, pages from magazines, *affiches*" (178–79) from the world of commerce with the natural world.

Apart from raising issues about memory, nostalgia, liminality, and consumerism, kitsch also highlights decay and, ultimately, death. Olalquiaga turns to Walter Benjamin who, in his discussion of kitsch, "employs the metaphor of dust to describe the rundown state of dreams in modernity" (87). Kitsch, with its layer of dust, becomes an opaque phantom of itself, a sort of trashy oracle, not unlike the reincarnation of Joan Foster as "lady oracle" whose trance-like dreams of a "*death boat*" (247) become both a "modern" novel and a costume Gothic with its obviously recycled past, "the debris of the aura" (Olalquiaga, 94), "a fragment of its former existence" (ibid., 95). Atwood's fascination with hauntings, and with the return of the repressed, permeate her writing, reaching their apex in the vampire character Zenia of *The Robber Bride* who, recycled, inhabits a body on which "the Frankenstein doctors have been at work" (118). The ultimate "mechanical reproduction" (Benjamin), Zenia sucks the life out of the novel's male characters, a visceral evocation of what Nate, in *Life Before Man*, finds in the "abstractions of paper, torts and writs, the convolutions of a language deliberately dried," objects of contemporary life that are losing all "sensuous values" (40).

While kitsch invokes certain melancholic aspects of the past as it draws attention to the circulation of goods, not all recycled culture emphasizes memory and death. A later series of episodes from *Lady Oracle* revels in an imaginative, excessive, and witty playfulness that has been termed "camp." Joan, somewhat older, married and back in Canada, gets involved with a man who calls himself the Royal Porcupine. When she meets him, he is "wearing a long black cloak and spats, and carrying a gold-headed cane, a pair of white gloves, and a top hat embroidered with porcupine quills" (266). He invites Joan to the opening of his show at a gallery called The Takeoff, an example of Atwood's frequent use of witty nomenclature to undercut the excesses of contemporary culture. The title of his show exaggerates this proclivity; it is SQUAWSHT. The man explains his name. The Royal, as do descriptions of the artifacts of the Portobello Road and Victoria and Albert Museum, connects Canada and England; the porcupine pokes fun at Canada's national symbol. He argues that the beaver is too dull a symbol of Canada ("too nineteenth-century," 267), while the porcupine, being prickly and of odd tastes, represents the country much better.

The show itself is made up of glass cases filled with fast-frozen roadkill, an art form that parodies contemporary art while giving the critique an ecological spin. The influence of that peripatetic guru, Marshall McLuhan, is also apparent. The Royal Porcupine describes his show as an example of culture as a rearview mirror, echoing McLuhan's conviction that "our educational system is totally rearview mirror. It's a dying and outdated system founded on literate values and fragmented and classified data totally unsuited to the needs of the first television generation" (Benedetti, 124). The Royal Porcupine believes that "the new poetry is the poetry of *things*" (268–69). He has yet to sell any of his "con-create" (268) poetry in Canada, although he assumes he would have much better luck in the United States where, he assures Joan, people are less cautious than in Canada.

It is tempting to suggest that, on the whole, camp may be of greater interest to United States popular culture than kitsch with its historical connotations and its melancholic overlays. After all, Canada does have a considerably more complex modern relationship with England than the United States does. Yet Atwood clearly delights in the absurdities of camp and its parodic potentialities. It is camp that allows her to skewer some of contemporary culture's more absurd extravagances. In *Lady Oracle*, the Royal Porcupine's show is being picketed by the SPCA, people bearing signs saying "SAVE OUR ANIMALS." The artist dismisses their picketing: "'They missed the *point*,'" he announces. "'I don't squash them, I just recycle them, what's wrong with that?'" (269). Recycling takes many forms. The Royal Porcupine's exhibition illustrates the distinction he makes between dead bodies in natural environments and dead bodies framed and transformed into art. As Pierre Bourdieu comments: "Intellectuals and artists have a special predilection for the most risky but also most profitable strategies of distinction, those which consist in asserting the power, which is peculiarly theirs, to constitute insignificant objects as works of art" (282). Like Joan, the Royal Porcupine is also interested in old clothing, although with a difference. His bizarre tastes are aimed at humor; he uses parody to get a laugh. When Joan goes home with him, they pass a series of old stores that are in the process of being turned into boutiques, a contemporary form of recycling that Atwood often illustrates. The Royal Porcupine lives in a downtown warehouse that has been converted into artists' studios. The bed in his studio is covered by a "tattered red velvet canopy with tassels" (271). Most appealing of all to Joan, as their affair progresses, is that he likes frequenting junk shops as much as she, searching for articles such as "formal gowns of the fifties," "button boots" from 1905, and "black net stockings" (284). She confesses: "I soon discovered that my own interest in nineteenth-century trivia was no match for the Royal Porcupine's obsession with cultural detritus" (284). In fact, he is a "walking catalog of ephemera, of the irrelevant and the disposable" (284). He loves to perform, to camp; his passion for trivia results in parodic performances that are meant both to shock and amuse.

The allure of artificiality informs all of Atwood's writing. Partly, she uses the distance afforded to laugh at cultural pretensions, turning the potentially serious into exaggerated frivolity — the death of animals on the road, the SPCA's activities, marital infidelity. She often sets style above content and, in the process, undercuts institutionalized traditions. Sometimes the calculated flatness can make Atwood's work seem passionless, a game that denies intense involvement. For example, her reliance on the game of Clue in *Bodily Harm*, or Scrabble in *The Handmaid's Tale*, dramatizes this proclivity, and reminds us of the emphasis on performance in much of Atwood's writing. In *The Edible Woman* and *Surfacing*, she laughs at the pretensions that surround certain lifestyles — those of lawyers, for example, or Canadian nationalists, or sixties survivalists. Yet she is equally capable of lambasting the pursuit of trivia. In *Surfacing*, David, a thoroughly unpleasant character, films the elitist and sexist "Random Samples," a collection of recycled trivia that callously makes fun of bad taste and suggests this elitist stance as a nationalist, anti-American one.

According to Susan Sontag, "the whole point of Camp is to dethrone the serious" (288). In a mass-culture age, camp styles and camping draw attention to the unusual, the odd, in an effort to halt the dreadful flatness of anonymity. *Bodily Harm* is replete with descriptions of exotic and eccentric clothing, activities, and spaces: "Garters, merry widows, red bikini pants with gold spangles" (20); "drain-chain jewellery" that was the latest "Queen Street thing," an example of "*nouveau wavé*" (23–24); Jocasta's store, "Ripped Off," which specializes in the clothes of the underground, mostly violently ugly fifties memorabilia. Rennie and Jocasta shop at the Sally Ann for used clothing. When Rennie goes to the Caribbean, she discovers further examples of camp culture: orange T-shirts with pictures on them, extravagant advertisements for rum, massive bushes with "flamboyant red and pink flowers dangling from them like Kleenex flowers at a high-school dance" (39). The market on St. Antoine is filled with gadgetry, "the spillover from Japan" (75), a St. Antoine taxi is "upholstered in mauve shag . . . A St. Christopher doll and a pair of rubber dice swing from the mirror" (118), a visually overdetermined linking of chance and religion that is further impressed on the reader by the orange T-shirts emblazoned with the words, "PRINCE OF PEACE," a reference not to Christ but to a political candidate. In these ways, Atwood uses exaggeration and artifice, in Sontag's words, as "something of a private code, a badge of identity even, among small urban cliques" (275).

While camp is indeed humorous — a bold celebration of bad taste — it can be used quite effectively to make serious problems resonate more dramatically. *Bodily Harm* and *The Handmaid's Tale* demonstrate exaggerated styles that threaten the integrity of women's bodies. Take the mermaid light in Rennie's motel room, "with her arms over her head, holding up the bulb. Her breasts aren't bare, she's wearing a harem jacket open at the front, its edges grazing the nipples" (47). While the light, like many other objects in *Bodily Harm*, reflects the novel's attention to breast cancer, it also connects with all the other objects and occurrences in the novel that transform women's bodies into objects. For example, a sculptor friend of Rennie's uses life-size mannequins to construct his furniture: "The women were dressed in half-cup bras and G-string panties, set on their hands and knees for the tables, locked into a sitting position for the chairs. The ropes and arms were the arms of the chair, her bum was the seat" (208). *Visor's* managing editor interprets this work as "sort of fun," possessing an "element of playfulness" (207), upstaging the heavy-handed approach to pornography apparent in feminist writing. The sculptor tells Rennie that his work is "a visual pun," and shows her another of a woman "harnessed to a dogsled, with a muzzle on." He titles this work "*Nationalism is Dangerous*" (208), resonating with a comment made by Atwood in her testimony before the Parliamentary Commission on Free Trade: "Canada as a separate but dominated country has done as well under the US as women, worldwide, have done under men. . . . I guess that's why the national wisdom vis-à-vis Them has so often taken the form of lying still, keeping your mouth shut, and pretending you like it" (quoted in Flaherty and Manning 1993, 4).

Rennie's experiences operate on different levels. While she is a travel writer of superficial, although catchy, articles on lifestyles, and, as such, lives a life of camp styles and behavior, both in Canada and in Central America, various kinds of visual punning mask serious and potentially life-threatening problems. The body camp displayed in the furniture constructed by Rennie's friend, as well as in Jocasta's boutique, covers up the underlying cancer. On the islands, Rennie's definition of bad taste is an "exceptionally tacky movie" (159), a mistake that lands her in the middle of a dangerous revolution. In this novel, camp and kitsch highlight contrasts between superficiality and depth, interiority and exteriority. *Lady Oracle* focuses on the melancholy of kitsch, and uses camp to parody the excesses of contemporary culture; *Bodily Harm* increases their political possibilities. It insists on depth in a superficial, postmodern landscape.

In his book *The System of Objects*, Baudrillard glimpses the "coming end" of the order of Nature, and offers the "notion of a world no longer given but instead produced — mastered, manipulated, inventoried, controlled: a world, in short, that has to be *constructed*" (29). *The Handmaid's Tale* speaks to Baudrillard's concerns by presenting a controlled and constructed world, using examples of recycled culture both as escape and as a method to control and silence a population. Isolated and forlorn, Offred uses her memories of Moira to lift her out of the bland, puritanic, totalitarian Republic of Gilead. There Moira suddenly is, a flash of sexuality in an otherwise rigidly stratified landscape, "legs crossed, ankle on knee, in her purple overalls, one dangly earring, the gold fingernail she wore to be eccentric" (47), a recycled version of *Bodily Harm*'s Jocasta. Moira represents a decadent but vibrant past and extends, into Gilead's Republic, the questions raised in *Bodily Harm* about pornography's effects on women. Here, more clearly than in the earlier novel, Atwood raises issues about censorship, and uses camp and kitsch to illustrate certain kinds of freedom — the ability to make personal choices, for example. Yet Gilead's leaders understand that recycling a culture cleansed of its playfulness and radical potential will help control a fearful population. The gymnasium where the handmaids are trained is only a heartbeat away from the same space in which high school dances were held, with their "undercurrent of drums, a forlorn wail, garlands made of tissue-paper flowers, cardboard devils, a revolving ball of mirrors" (13). Offred's commander, in his former life a market researcher, recycles the names of commodities from the past, "cosmetic lines, cake mixes, frozen desserts, and even medicinal remedies" (321) in the names given to Gilead's Aunts.

Ostensibly, the Republic has banned all examples of kitsch and camp, prohibiting even their visual representation in magazines. Atwood creates Jezebels to suggest their radical nature in a totalitarian regime. Entering the nightclub, Offred and the Commander pass through a simulated birth canal, a softly-lit mushroom-colored corridor leading into a courtyard that sports an artificially constructed natural world: a fountain, "potted plants and trees" (246), and vines. Dressed in banned clothing, a "garment" with "cups for the breasts, covered in purple sequins" (242) and with feathers around the holes for her legs, Offred discovers a roomful of "tropical" women in "festive gear" (246) reminiscent of masquerade parties. This clothing, recycled from a freer time, is out-of-place and therefore erotic and radical — old-fashioned

lingerie, baby doll pajamas, every kind of bathing suit, and exercise and
cheerleading outfits. Most important, Moira reappears at Jezebels.

> She's dressed absurdly, in a black outfit of once-shiny satin. . . . It's
> strapless, wired from the inside, pushing up the breasts. . . . There's a
> wad of cotton attached to the back. . . . Attached to her head are two
> ears. . . . She has a black bow tie around her neck and is wearing black
> net stockings and black high heels. (250–51)

The costume does not fit her. As a result, she simultaneously parodies
the demeaning nature of the female outfits in Hugh Hefner's former
bunny clubs, while she also stands for the irrepressible return of everything the Republic has attempted to obliterate.

Lady Oracle dramatizes recycled culture as a *mise en abyme* for the
writer. *Bodily Harm* and *The Handmaid's Tale*, in different ways, show
how recycled clothing, furnishings, and objects can point to political
repression. *Cat's Eye* and *The Robber Bride* are deeply invested in an
analytic world where repression returns, revealing deep personal and
cultural traumas. In these latter novels, as Olalquiaga suggests, "the
temporal dimension, represented as narrative, shapes the spatial one
into a three-dimensional scenography . . . where time, however suspended, is the underlying motif" (122).

In *Cat's Eye*, Elaine Risley observes that "somewhere in Limbo, all
the old devices and appliances and costumes are lined up, waiting their
turn for re-entry" (386). Imagining time as spatial, Elaine turns her
past into a series of kitschy icons — sweater twin sets and print house-
dresses; Valentine hearts, Easter eggs, and Halloween decorations;
"pictures of women, from *Good Housekeeping, The Ladies' Home Journal, Chatelaine*" (148). These and many more objects are recycled in
Elaine's paintings which, as the retrospective her work is undergoing
suggests, are present in the gallery Sub-Versions throughout the narrative. Dredging up images out of Limbo, Elaine has painted "a silver
toaster, the old kind, with knobs and doors . . . a glass coffee percola-
tor, with bubbles gathering in the clear water . . . a wringer washing
machine," images that appear to cross her mind "detached from any
context" (357). They appear, therefore, as kitsch does, "fetishistically"
endowed with "metaphysical attributes" (Olalquiaga, 233). Reviewers
of the show find, for example, much "female symbolism," "the charis-
matic nature of domestic objects," and even parodies of the paintings
of the Group of Seven that reconstruct "their vision of landscape in the
light of contemporary experiment and postmodern pastiche" (427).

In this novel, kitsch and camp evoke broad cultural desires and repressions. They demonstrate how deeply objects retain their power to

affect people. Elaine, for instance, recalls her belief that the horror comics Cordelia has stolen from the drugstore are actually alive, "glowing in the dark, with a lurid sulfur-yellow light . . . curling wisps of mist coming out of them" (227). It is the uncanny power of the objects of Elaine's world that gives them a life of their own. Far from being left over and extraneous, objects control *Cat's Eye* so that even their representations are filled with uncontrollable energy; they are from "the land of the dead people" (431). Susan Stewart suggests in *On Longing* that "kitsch objects are not apprehended as the souvenir proper is apprehended, that is, on the level of the individual autobiography; rather, they are apprehended on the level of collective identity. They are souvenirs of an era and not of a self" (167). Both camp and kitsch signify an "exaggerated display of the values of consumer culture" (Stewart, 168). The toasters, washing machines, clothing, marbles of Elaine's past, all are self-consciously made into icons and thus denaturalized.

Denaturalization occurs again in *The Robber Bride*, where characters and objects are repeatedly recycled. The uncanny unfolding of the vampire story, retold with a female vampire, encourages images that are flagrantly trashy; they evoke kitsch melancholy. The novel dramatizes the psychological hold the past has on the present both in the lives of individuals as well as in the passing decades of the latter part of the twentieth century. Indeed, the passing of time is dramatically rendered by a focus on the ever-moving flow of consumer goods with their pretense at change, and their intimate connection with the rapidly changing lifestyles of those who can afford to think of their lives as "styles." Bourdieu argues that "the new bourgeoisie is the initiator of the ethical retooling required by the new economy from which it draws its power and profits, whose functioning depends as much on the production of needs and consumers as on the production of goods" (310). Atwood is caught up in exploring how consumers are created, how, for example, Jocasta of *Bodily Harm* can turn drain chains into lifestyle artifacts, an example of "trends that didn't really exist" (*Bodily Harm*, 25) until Rennie writes articles about them. *The Robber Bride* further dramatizes the intimate connections between product and consumer.

In this novel, one central space is the shop in which Charis works; it concentrates on restructuring itself to keep up with the rapidly changing styles of its mainly female consumers. In the sixties, it was called "The Blown Mind Shoppe" and sold "hash pipes and psychedelic posters and roach clips and tie-dyed undershirts and dashikis." Later, it became "Okkult," a shop that expressed the seventies. Then, it carried books on demonology and women's ancient religions. In the early eighties, it became "Radiance," concentrating its commodities on crystals, "Japanese lacquered bowls; tapes of loon calls." Now, in the novel's present, it is about to be transformed once again, this time into "Scrimpers," and will sell the "cheap stuff" that used to be the purview of the five-and-dime stores (66–67). Outfits change too, as the shop goes through its various reconfigurations. For Scrimpers, the female staff will turn the flowered pastels of Radiance into carpenter's aprons so that they will look like "they mean business." The interior of the shop will feature such homemade accessories as brown paper and twine, and the "hand-rubbed maple display cabinets" (485) will be sold to make room for cupboards made out of raw boards with the nails showing. Indeed, every detail of the shop's design and merchandise aims to emphasize all that is handmade and affordable. The artificiality of the "sell" leads, in Baudrillard's words, to "manipulated personalization" (153).

As they are in other Atwood novels, bodies, too, get recycled in *The Robber Bride*. Roz reconstructs herself, sticking on layers of language "like posters on a fence" (401). As a result, she thinks of herself as a "pastiche," a person constructed from the odds and ends of other people's lives. She even makes a career of reconstructing women, feeding them desires about perfection, and selling them cosmetics to help effect the necessary reconstruction. As the novel opens, though, it is clear that a recession has set in. The poor wandering Toronto's Queen Street contrast uneasily with the trendy boutiques that sell "fringe" fashions. Kitsch has been devalued: "The glistering dresses on the blank-faced or headless mannequins are no longer what they seemed, the incarnation of desire. Instead they look like party trash" (30–31). Drained of glamour in this economic downturn, that which is not necessary for survival seems tawdry.

No matter at what point one looks into Atwood's work, one is presented with an array of recycled culture, stories, spaces, and characters. Atwood is particularly drawn to the playfulness of camp, the melancholy and exoticism of kitsch, and the class and economic issues apparent in trash. "True Trash" (*Wilderness Tips*) elaborates on trashy "True Romance" comics being read by the mostly upper-class waitresses working at a boy's summer camp: "Every one of these magazines has a woman on the cover, with her dress pulled down over one shoulder or a cigarette in her mouth or some other evidence of a messy life. . . . Their colours are odd: sleazy, dirt-permeated, like the hand-tinted photos in the five-and-ten" (11). This story, like *Lady Oracle* with which I started this discussion, gives Atwood a chance to write "true trash" while, at the same time, critiquing the dissociation between popular objects of consumption and their consumers. She also critiques the class issues evident in the artificial distinctions between elite and popular culture. All of her attention to culture's desiderata confounds this distinction. Her concern explains other stylistic elements in the fiction. Sometimes her characters seem stilted, repetitive, and emotionally flat. I'm tempted to say they function as icons. In "True Trash," the nine waitresses seem, to one of the campers, entirely interchangeable, their number, nine, the only constant. As with Joan Foster, whose identity keeps shifting and who writes one of her novels in a trance, the female characters of "True Trash" perform their tasks like robots. The one waitress, Joanne, through whose eyes and ears we experience the story, makes its point. One rift is between the private-school, snobbish women who are waitressing for a lark, and the one working-class woman, Ronette, who needs the money. In spite of her privileged status, Joanne makes it clear that she wants "what Ronette has: the power to give herself up, without reservation and without commentary. It's that langour, that leaning back. Voluptuous mindlessness. Everything Joanne herself does is surrounded by quotation marks" (25).

It is this kind of disjunction that Atwood targets, the late twentieth-century malaise that has partially resulted from what Andreas Huyssen suggests are the parasitic tendencies of conformism to all but obliterate "the original iconoclastic and subversive thrust" (3) of the avant-garde. Atwood is persistently searching for ways to reinvest the past with meaning and the present with desire. Like Bourdieu, she is a theoretician of culture, seeking to investigate the cultural distinctions between "high aesthetics" and vulgar taste; she too wants to "abolish the sacred frontier which makes legitimate culture a separate universe" (Bourdieu, 6). In her work, although the past often seems "both darker and more brightly intense than the present" ("True Trash," 37), Atwood is deeply concerned with contemporary popular cultural trends. In the late twentieth century, when everything has been "domesticated" and is "*cool*," Atwood constructs stories that have not been "stripped of the promised mystery" ("True Trash," 37), stories that are often "allegorical and fragmentary" (Olalquiaga, 298), "mosaic artifacts" ("True Trash," 37) that bring back and reinvest with life the "flotsam" (*Lady Oracle*, 179) of the past so that it can invigorate the present. The academics at the Twelfth Symposium on Gileadean Studies, like all of us, need such lessons.

Works Cited

Atwood, Margaret. *Alias Grace*. Toronto: McClelland & Stewart, 1996.

———. *Bodily Harm*. Toronto: McClelland & Stewart, 1981.

———. *Cat's Eye*. Toronto: McClelland & Stewart, 1988.

———. *The Edible Woman*. New York: Random House, 1969.

———. *The Handmaid's Tale*. Toronto: McClelland & Stewart, 1985.

———. *In Search of Alias Grace*. Ottawa: Ottawa University Press, 1997.

———. *Lady Oracle*. New York: Random House/Ballantine Books, 1976.

———. *Life Before Man*. New York: Random House, 1979.

———. *The Robber Bride*. Toronto: McClelland & Stewart, 1993.

———. *Surfacing*. New York: Random House, 1972.

———. *Wilderness Tips*. Toronto: McClelland & Stewart, 1991.

Baudrillard, Jean. *The System of Objects*. Trans. James Benedict. London: Verso, 1996.

Benedetti, Paul and Nancy DeHart, ed. *Forward Through the Rearview Mirror: Reflections on and by Marshall McLuhan*. Toronto: Prentice-Hall, 1996.

Bourdieu, Pierre. *Distinction: A Social Critique of the Judgement of Taste*. Trans. Richard Nice. Cambridge: Harvard University Press, 1984.

Flaherty, David and Frank Manning, ed. *The Beaver Bites Back: American Popular Culture in Canada*. Montreal & Kingston: McGill-Queen's University Press, 1993.

Goss, Jon. "Once-upon-a-Time in the Commodity World: An Unofficial Guide to Mall of America." *Annals of the Association of American Geographers* 89.1 (March 1999): 45–75.

Huyssen, Andreas. *After the Great Divide: Modernism, Mass Culture, Postmodernism*. Bloomington: Indiana University Press, 1986.

Olalquiaga, Celeste. *The Artificial Kingdom: A Treasury of the Kitsch Experience*. New York: Pantheon, 1998.

Sontag, Susan. *Against Interpretation*. New York: Dell, 1961.

Stewart, Susan. *On Longing: Narratives of the Miniature, the Gigantic, the Souvenir, the Collection*. Durham: Duke University Press, 1993.

Vauthier, Marie. *New World Myth: Postmodernism and Postcolonialism in Canadian Fiction*. Montreal & Kingston: McGill-Queen's University Press, 1998.

Mythological Intertexts in Margaret Atwood's Works

Sharon R. Wilson
(University of Northern Colorado, Greeley, Colorado)

F ROM HER EARLY WORK, such as *Double Persephone*, to recent texts such as *Good Bones* and *The Robber Bride*, Margaret Atwood has used mythology in much the same way she has used other intertexts, or texts within texts. Folk tales, fairy tales, and legends are widely assumed to "contain an equally great concentration of mythical meaning" (Frye, 188; Wilson 1993, 10). Atwood intertwines these and other cultural master narratives with radio, television, and film stories, not only to provide mythic resonance and polyphonic melody, but to parody or undercut narrative authority in a postmodern way. Greek mythological intertexts in Atwood's visual art, poetry, and novels have frequently evoked both well-known and submerged aspects of the Great Goddess or Mother Goddess widely worshipped throughout the Neolithic and Bronze Ages around the world: Diana or Persephone, Venus or Demeter, and Hecate Crone. Whether explicitly named or simply implied, Atwood's varied mythological intertexts are central to her images, characterization, and themes. Despite hundreds of articles on Atwood published in the last few years, scholars are only beginning to recognize the variety and significance of her mythic intertexts.

Critics acknowledge that Atwood's female creators tend to be engaged in artistic quests. In Canadian poetry, such quests often parody those of male archetypal heroes such as Perseus or Odysseus. As Annis Pratt notes in reference to the Perseus and Medusa myth, males as well as females may sympathize with Medusa: "The hero, or Perseus, fades into the background in Canadian poems about stones and stone/women" (93). Many of the images recognized as central in Atwood's visual art, fiction, and poetry — including the flower, circle, spiral or maze, water, mirror, reflection, moon, tree, bird, flight, wings, tower, eye, womb or cave, snake, breast, dismemberment, dance, the double or the number two, and the number three — evoke well-known Greek and Egyptian myths including the Demeter and Persephone, Isis-Osiris-Seth, Theseus and the Minotaur, Daedalus and Icarus, Orpheus and Eurydice, and Narcissus and Echo stories. The apocalyptic, demonic, and analogical imagery of Frye's theory of myths (or parodies of this imagery) are as apparent in Atwood novels, such as *The Handmaid's Tale*, as are his mythoi of seasons (131–239; Wilson 1993, 274). Egg images in *The Edible Woman* (1969), *Bluebeard's Egg* (1983), *The Handmaid's Tale* (1985), and *The Robber Bride* (1993) suggest the cosmic eggs of numerous creation myths. Atwood's widespread use of metaphoric cannibalism and ritualistic eating in *The Edible Woman*, *Surfacing* (1972), *The Robber Bride*, and even *The CanLit Foodbook* (1987) — evident in the *Decameron*, the Grimms' "The Robber Bridegroom," "The Juniper Tree," "Little Red-Cap," and "Hansel and Gretel" (Wilson 1993, 83, 86) — were prefigured in two creation stories: the Egyptian myth of Nut's swallowing the sun every night and eating her offspring every morning, and the Greek myth about Cronos eating his sons (Harris and Platzner, 57, 60). Similarly, major motifs about creation and the life cycle of birth — death — rebirth, including associated transformation, dismemberment, and re-memberment, not only suggest fairy tales such as the Grimms' "Fitcher's Bird" and Christian myth, but Triple Goddess myths all over the world (Wilson 1993, 4–23).

Atwood's recently published visual art (Wilson 1993, 39–79), including cover designs and illustrations for her literary works, highlights the mythological intertexts most significant for particular volumes, and makes the impact of Great Goddess mythology throughout Atwood's work immediately evident. Not only the covers of her first published, rare work, *Double Persephone* (1961), but the whole series of poems, is about the Greek myth of Demeter and Persephone. Linocuts Atwood herself put into a flatbed printing press, the covers depict in black and white the Eve-Snake-Trees of Great Goddess, Hebrew, and Christian mythology. Departing from the Syrian sculpture of Atargatis or Dea Syria in which goddess and tree are embraced by the serpent (Harris and Platzner, 87), the goddess's body in the cover art is simultaneously the Tree of Life and the snake symbolizing life mysteries, immortality, and healing. Atwood critics have usually associated this Snake Goddess with the negative, patriarchal version of Medusa, and thus viewed Atwood's first female creator as a gorgon with freezing touch. In earlier, matriarchal stories, Medusa was part of Athena, not opposed to her, and hard to look at only because she was so beautiful. Like other Snake Goddesses such as Lamia, Kali, and Lilith, and like Atwood personae or characters based on them in "Snake Poems" (*Interlunar* 1984) and *The Robber Bride*, this Persephone, too, encompasses the life cycle, the powers of life and beauty as well as death and stasis. Although the final, title poem ends with trampling and "letters grown from branch and stem [that] / Have no green leaves enclosing them," the lost mother who appeared earlier in "Iconic Landscape" is always evident in the volume's title. In the poems as well as the covers, here, as everywhere in Atwood's texts, the double Persephone implies the entire cycle of life and creation Atwood discusses in *Survival*: Triple Goddess as Diana or crescent new moon, Venus or full moon, and Hecate Crone or old moon. "Hecate, the most forbidding of the three, is only one phase of a cycle; she is not sinister when viewed as part of a process, and she can even be a Wise Old Woman" (Wilson 1993, 59–61; *Survival*, 199). Like the brides of the "Fitcher's Bird" and "Robber Bridegroom" fairy tales, Persephone is literally married to death, but she also signifies new life. Some of Atwood's creator-goddesses are failed or parodic; all endure the female artist's double or triple bind (Wilson 1993, 16). But it is always the creator, not the White Goddess muse role, that Atwood and her characters choose.

Quite a few other Atwood covers and illustrations use mythological goddess figures or images, including parodic ones. As von Franz points out, all female deities are Great Goddess archetypes, with female demons and other "evil" mythological figures representing the shadow side (105). In Atwood's visual art the female crescent moon (*Moon* 1958), *Termite Queen* (undated), a spiral (*Circle Game* cover 1966), and several harpies — *Mother Harpy and Chics* (1974), *Male Harpy* (1970), a harpy collage (*Good Bones* 1992) — are all goddess images. Harpies or Valkyries, originally represented as beautiful, winged maidens, were children of Electra, who avenged her father's murder. As "the robbers" who carry off those who disappear without a trace, harpies suggest Atwood's many serious and parodic Robber Brides and Grooms. A number of provocative illustrations for *Good Bones and Simple Murders* (1994) also are associated with the goddess: the cover based on *Termite Queen*, a female bird, a female, a toothed stump, a female Medusa snake, a Pumpkin Woman, a trilobite and two cephalopods with female heads, a woman with a two-faced body, an angel, a flower, and an earth goddess. In addition to goddess archetypes, several of Atwood's art works also suggest the woman as nature and the nature as monster theme in Canadian literature (Atwood, *Survival*, 45–68): *Sphinx* (1970), *Angel* (undated), a Hecate Crone (*Moodie Underground* 1970), and sliced mushroom-womb (*Amanita Caesarea, Egg, Cross-Section on Cloud*, undated). The heart enclosing a running egg on the cover of *True Stories* (1981) not only implies the atrocities of human rights violations and sexual politics, but the dismemberment associated with the Isis-Osiris myth. In addition to the Demeter-

Persephone duality, the cover of *Two-Headed Poems* (1978), like the poems of this volume, recalls a number of myths about two heads or faces, such as Deceit (one of the miseries released from Pandora's box), the Janus heads facing past and future, and the two-headed Sphinx as goddess of birth and death. These heads could even suggest the decapitation or splitting, also depicted in the two *Mary Queen of Scots* watercolors (1969), of Isis, Medusa, or any entity — such as Canada. As we shall see, the split into threes, as in *Mother Harpy and Chics* and the mirrored faces of the mother in *Lady Oracle* (1976), explicitly suggests the goddess trinity. The *Fitcher's Bird* watercolor (1970) is also based on the ability of Isis and other goddesses to re-member severed or dismembered pieces in the "Fitcher's Bird" fairy tale. The marriage test, forbidden or selected door, and bird and disguise motifs of this tale and of the literature to which it is connected, such as "Bluebeard's Egg" and "Hesitations Outside the Door," also appear in many other kinds of myths.

Atwood's visual art also suggests creation, transformation, heroic quest, and trickster myths. All creation myths feature gods making beings from materials at hand, such as clay or corn meal. Such creatures are often destroyed because they are flawed, like the wooden beings of *Popul Vuh*, or modified so that they won't rival the gods, like the four First Fathers of this epic (Rosenberg, 482–83). Atwood's two *Frankenstein* watercolors (1970) clearly embed mythological texts connected not only to Atwood's early poem "Speeches for Dr. Frankenstein" (published with Charles Pachter's woodcuts 1966, *The Animals in That Country* 1968), but to Mary Shelley's modern Prometheus and to all Atwood characters who feel or appear like monsters, are afraid of creating them, or project monster images onto others. Unlike the Yoruba creator Obtala, who protects creations he deforms while drinking too much palm wine ("The Creation of the Universe and Ife," Rosenberg, 406), Atwood's Dr. Frankenstein, like Shelley's, rejects his flawed creature and his monster self.

Among other watercolors, drawings, collages, and comic strips with mythological themes is *Dream: Bluejay or Archeopteryx* (1968), Atwood's visual counterpart to the poem of this name in *Procedures for Underground* (1969) — about the kind of transformation from one order of being to another that is accomplished by Proteus, Zeus, and Circe, among others. The bluejay designation suggests not only the jays the mother of *Surfacing*'s narrator seems to turn into, but the goddess association with birds evoked in *Surfacing*, *Bodily Harm* (1981), and *The Robber Bride*; the Bluejay tricksters of NW First Peoples; and the Toronto Bluejays team. The *Hanged God* cover (1970) Atwood designed for *Power Politics* (1971) implies not only the Tarot card but the "book of Thoth," the pack of cards believed to be an adaptation of Egyptian hieroglyphics associated with the magician-god Thoth (Leach, 1110). The two *Drowned Figures* (undated) also for *Power Politics*, the second for the volume's final poem, "He is Last Seen," suggest mythological rebirth through descent to the underworld, as in the drowning and transformation of Narcissus into a white flower. The soft, natural setting of the *Interlunar* cover (1984), which, like the title poem, doubles everything, invites mythologizing of the natural world. Even the *Undersea* (undated), *Portrait of Graeme Gibson* (1974), and *Microscope Image* (undated) watercolors, and *Tarte au Salesman Kilodny* (1987) drawing, *Murder in the Dark* (1983) and Moodie collages (1970), and *Survivalwoman* comic strip (1979) either present folklore motifs or archetypal figures and processes that parallel mythic ones.

As is widely recognized, Atwood's novels are usually quest-romances (Campbell, 17–28; Wilson 1993). According to Northrop Frye, one of Atwood's teachers at the University of Toronto, "the quest-romance is the victory of fertility over the waste land." Atwood's novels often end with fertility (*Surfacing, The Handmaid's Tale, Life Before Man*) or marriage (*Alias Grace*), or even dissolution of the expected marriage to "death" (*The Edible Woman*). There are four aspects to the quest myth:

> First the *agon* or conflict itself. Second, the *pathos* or death, often the mutual death of hero and monster. Third, the disappearance of the hero, a theme which often takes the form of *sparagmos* or tearing to pieces. . . . Fourth, the reappearance and recognition of the hero. (Frye, 192)

Except for *The Handmaid's Tale*, where the *sparagmos* is literally enacted on an alter ego scapegoat but symbolically significant for the protagonist, the *sparagmos* in Atwood's novels is symbolic. Death is either symbolic or, as in *Lady Oracle*, parodic; such quest-romance motifs as the search for buried treasure and the bride as reward are ironic or parodic, often through gender reversal. *Surfacing*'s Persephone narrator quests for her Demeter mother, her own lost "child," her father, and herself; she recognizes the many ways in which she has been symbolically fragmented or torn apart; and she experiences both symbolic death and rebirth. Like Melampus, cousin of Bellerophon in Greek mythology, and like the servant in the Grimms' "The White Snake," learning animal speech helps the narrator understand the secrets of the earth, in this case through shamanic eating identified with First People's mythology. Elaine of *Cat's Eye* (1988) quests for the blacked-out space and time of her childhood "bad time," and for lost "pieces" of herself; and Grace of *Alias Grace*, who may literally have a split personality, quests seriously or duplicitously for the lost time of a nineteenth-century crime. Though some of Atwood's mythic characters initially function ironically (e.g. female creators as Proteus in the novels) or parodically (the female hero, Phoenix, Fisher King, and grail quests in *Surfacing*) because of gender reversal or shifted context, many are simultaneously serious and parodic, tragic and comic.

As titles such as *Procedures for Underground* indicate, mythic underworlds proliferate in Atwood's poetry and fiction: the lower floor of Marian's boarding house in *The Edible Woman*; in oceans, lakes, or streams in "This is a Photograph of Me," *Power Politics, Surfacing, Lady Oracle,* and *Cat's Eye*; in the ravines of many novels and stories; in prehistory in *Life Before Man*; and across the harbor and through a mirror in *The Robber Bride*. Mythic returns in Atwood's works are often only suggested and sometimes left deliberately unresolved, as in the case of *Bodily Harm*, where Atwood changed a manuscript version of the novel in order to leave the narrator on a plane in the air, in future tense (Wilson 1993, 228). Still, the narrators or personae of virtually all Atwood texts join readers on quests for self and national identity, and for understanding of the past.

So evident are mythological and other folklore intertexts in Atwood's literary art that one might question whether any of her texts lacks such reference. Characters, themes, plots, structures, motifs, images, settings, and even costumes and props may indicate mythic patterns. Mythic characters include heroes and/or mock-heroes, such as fragmented "goddesses" and tricksters. As we have seen, such heroes go on "quests," including descent to the underworld, face monster alter egos and selves, and "magically" transform, returning "whole," with improved vision, touch, and other senses. Although people commonly think of Native American, New Zealand, or African tricksters such as Raven, Coyote, Bluejay, Rabbit, Maui, and Spider, tricksters in *Lady Oracle, Good Bones, The Robber Bride,* and *Alias Grace* (1996) also suggest tricksters of Greek mythology, such as Hermes. Joan Foster in *Lady Oracle*, her own Triple Goddess, sets the pattern for all of Atwood's tricksters. She plays at being a Delphic oracle and sibyl, manufactures her own labyrinths and minotaurs, and enacts a *Red Shoes* script. Characters in other Atwood texts also play mythic parts in mythic plots. The characters of *Life Before Man* leave Danae towers of isolation for the green world; and the novel embeds Isis, Orpheus, "The Girl Without Hands," *Wizard of Oz*, and numerous nursery rhyme and literary intertexts. *Cat's Eye* alludes to eye goddesses as well as the Snow Queen, Rapunzel, and the Madonna aspect of the Great Goddess (Wilson 1993, 166–67, 310); and *The Handmaid's Tale* suggests the Triple Goddess, the Moirae or fates, Maia, as well as the biblical Jacob-Rachel-Leah-Bilhah, Madonna, werewolf, "Fitcher's Bird," and "Little Red-Cap" stories. *Bodily Harm* offers a Jocasta prophet and a Pandora's box in addition to "The Robber Bridegroom," "The Girl Without Hands," Grail, and goddess intertexts; and even *Alias Grace* has its Tree of Life, Pandora, and Pan. In *Morning in the Burned House* (1995), Helen of Troy, Daphne, Athena, and Sekhmet survive a phallocentric culture that dismembers and burns goddesses while still expecting them to heal and caress. The Circe section of *You Are Happy* (1974) is one of Atwood's best examples of re-visioned mythic intertext, and the second "Orpheus" poem in *Interlunar* illustrates a rare, unparodied use of heroic myth.

In *You Are Happy*, the Circe / Mud Poems section follows the "Songs of the Transformed," about people or creatures who have changed, naturally and mythologically. As Atwood knows from her childhood experiences with her entomologist father, seemingly magical transformation is part of life. Like the Siren of "Siren Song," who is part of a duplicitous trio whose cry for rescue "works every time" (39), Circe is a trickster and a shape-changer in more than one way. Tired of being the mud woman, beginning at the neck and ending at the knees and elbows, that Atwood's Odysseus and other men would make her, Circe anticipates Zenia of *The Robber Bride*. She constructs herself in her own image (self text) and also reconstructs the mythic text, re-visioning Homer's *Odyssey*. In *The Odyssey* and Ovid's *Metamorphoses*, Circe is the temptress who transforms men into swine, Odysseus exempt only because he is protected by a magic herb Hermes gives him. In *You Are Happy*, Circe is healing snake and moon goddess and transformer artist whose genre is words, poetry (49, 51). Rather than either Homer or Tennyson's hero, Atwood's Odysseus is an adulterous, very human, killer and colonizer. In the last poem in this section, which is not closed by a period, Circe imagines another island and a different, open story that might continue into the rest of this volume. Characteristically for Atwood, *You Are Happy* ends beyond the demands of gods or history: with touch, with two people opening themselves to one another, and with the word *whole*.

In *Interlunar*, the first two Orpheus and Eurydice poems, "Orpheus (1)" and "Eurydice," re-vision the myth, especially the Eurydice character, in a way resembling *You Are Happy*'s reconstruction of the Circe and Odysseus myth. In usual tellings or artworks based on the Orpheus myth, including the Camus film *Black Orpheus* and the Cocteau film *Orphee*, Eurydice is important only as the person the artist Orpheus loves. In the myth, Orpheus is such a wonderful musician that he charms wild beasts and makes trees and stones move. Eurydice is supposedly killed by a serpent bite, and Orpheus descends into Hades to bring her back, only to lose her forever by looking back. In most versions, Orpheus is torn to pieces and possibly his flesh is consumed in Bacchic orgies; his still singing head is carried to the island of Lesbos. In the first two of Atwood's poems based on this myth, however, Eurydice is the focus, and the archetypal journey of Persephone is also hers. Rather than the image of matriarchal goddess power, this Snake Goddess, killed by the world, sees Orpheus's love as a leash and recognizes that "it is not through him / you will get your freedom" (61). In "Orpheus (2)," however, Atwood gives this traditional hero myth, including the Orphic cults of the Orpheus myth, a political edge by telling the story of Victor Jara's courageous defiance of the Pinochet regime in Chile. Jara continued singing resistance songs, including "Chile Stadium," after his guitar was splintered and his hands were smashed, until he was beaten to death (Wilson 1993, 249). The basis for the Orpheus figure in Atwood's poem, Jara and his heroic actions remind readers of the Orpheus head that continues singing after decapitation.

Brief investigation of Medusa and Snake Goddess imagery in *Good Bones*, *The Robber Bride*, and *Alias Grace* indicates that, apart from differences of genre, style, and tone, and a growing use of postmodern techniques and postcolonial themes (Wilson 1995), Atwood's treatment of particular myths and myth types remains fairly consistent from early to recent texts.

In addition to harpy and siren stories linked to the Great Goddess, the prose poems and pieces in *Good Bones* use such traditional intertexts as Diana of Ephesus, Pandora, and Eden myths; "Bluebeard," "Rapunzel," "Cinderella," and "Hansel and Gretel" fairy tales; and Dracula and stump folklore. Often evoked through the visual art of this and its companion volume as well,[1] these folkloric references deconstruct stereotypical conceptions of men, women, nature, stories, literary tradition, and reader expectations. The volume opens with both reader and the Medusa harpy of "Bad News" awaiting an event: "Bloodlessness puts her to sleep" (9). Characters are mostly parodic versions of ones

---

[1] *Good Bones and Simple Murders* (1994), a compilation, reprints eleven pieces from *Murder in the Dark*, twenty-three from *Good Bones*, and adds one new story. See also the discussion of the "Snake Poems" section in *Interlunar* (Wilson 1993, 232–39).

already familiar to us from literature, mythology, and popular culture: the red hen, Gertrude, the ugly stepsister, the witch, the stepmother, Eve, Pandora, Red Cap, the Muse, the Pumpkin Woman, Rapunzel, created Gingerbread and biblical men, Bluebeard, Dracula, and an angel. But here we often get to hear the story from the usually submerged points of view of "shadow" or Medusa selves, including the sometimes nameless, unlucky, and unloved "unpopular gals." Animals disguised as stumps, airheads whose ignorance causes harm, male and female bodies, aliens, and bats all have their say. The Snake Goddess harpy underlying all the pieces, and on the cover of *Good Bones*, is ultimately the trickster, as deceptive as Persephone in *Double Persephone*, both dancing girl and withered crone, whose own breath, rather than that of Hades or his horses, is "impatient for her death" ("Persephone Departing," "Double Persephone").

The Snake Goddess is both comic and serious in *The Robber Bride*.[2] Zenia's three friends form a trinity resembling the alternate identities of Joan in *Lady Oracle*; of Offred's daughter, Offred, and Serena Joy in *The Handmaid's Tale*; and of both "friends" and mothers in *Cat's Eye*. Here the trinity could be conceived as head, body-heart, and spirit (Jacobsen); rationality, emotion, and spirituality; past, present, and future; or similar divisions. Tony is the goddess of memory, Mnemosyne, mother of the nine muses (462), and Athena, goddess of war and wisdom. Roz is the obvious lush-bodied earth, mother goddess, and protecting angel of the other characters. Since Charis's name suggests the wife of the lame craftsman, Hephaestus, maker of magical things but lord of the underworld,[3] and since she, like Charon, not only ferries across a figural River Styx but is the first to recognize Zenia's return, Charis represents the underworld and spirit world. Since she "dies" as Karen, is reborn as Charis, and finally reclaims Karen, Charis is the whole cycle in herself. The point is not that the characters are fundamentally different or that they represent only one or a particular quality, but that they are, as the merging dreams, clothing, and pasts in Chapter 50 suggest, all multiple or "twinned," all part of one another, and, thus, all "Medusas" as well as Isis regenerators of dismembered aspects of the self.

[2] Compare to the bride of the much later "The Robber Bridegroom" poem, whose hands hold the approaching death of the robber, rather than her own (*Interlunar*, 62).

[3] In Book 18 of *The Iliad*, Charis, rather than *The Odyssey*'s Aphrodite, is the wife.

Like Offred of *The Handmaid's Tale* and Grace of *Alias Grace*, Zenia of *The Robber Bride* is herself a story, a myth, "insubstantial, ownerless . . . drifting from mouth to mouth and changing as it goes" (461). Attempting to trace the meaning of "Zenia," Tony finds divergent, multi-cultural possibilities: the words for *hospitable*, a Hebrew shadow, and the action of a foreign pollen on fruit; the name "Zenaida" (daughter of Zeus); and the names of two early Christian martyrs, a Syrian warrior queen, a Hindu harem, a Japanese religion, and an Eastern practitioner of heretical magic (461). This postmodern Snake Goddess of indeterminate national, racial, or ethnic identity even uses plastic surgery and apparent excursions into drugs, explosives, and spying to construct stories of herself. Her contradictory roles as Circe *femme fatale*, seductress-goddess, devouring vagina, harpy, sex object, abused child, career woman, and friend — only slightly more diverse than those of a Joan Foster — suggest not only the contradictory roles a woman is imagined to play or does play, but the endless number of goddesses who are all part of the global Great Goddess. The Robber Bride of the title, Zenia, is a cannibal and vampire; she dismembers friends, lovers, and possibly chickens for fun; yet she is the mythical Helen of Troy, biblical Jezebel, and historical empress Theophano. Still, she is subject and inspiration for all the stories characters tell and readers read, both preeminent muse and postmodern text.

As the patriarchal version of Medusa who reappears at the Toxique Restaurant, Zenia is — or seems to be — poison, evil. But like the other characters, she symbolizes the entire cycle, not just the third or Hecate phase culminating in cancer, accidental death, suicide, or murder. According to Atwood, Zenia is the shadow self that we must know in order not to be controlled by it, "the Mr. Hyde to our Dr. Jekylls" that we dare not lose (Terkel, qtd. Graeber, 22). But she is also the Dr. Jekyll who unearths the dark selves, projection, and lack of responsibility the other characters must face. In all versions of her past, she is also an innocent, abused or prostituted child, a Diana Maiden of the crescent moon. As the lover who robs the other women of their mates, she is the Venus of the full moon. And even as petrifying and decapitated Medusa, she is also the Cretan Snake Goddess, guardian of the mysteries of life and healing, but still the human woman who dies sick and rejected by her best friends. As the Grimms' Robber Bride of the novel's title, Zenia, like the other characters, thus plays all the parts of the "Robber Bridegroom" fairy tale in the way that Roz's twins prefer: the cannibal Robber Bridegroom; robbed, chopped up, and eaten brides; and bride who tells the story and avenges the crime. At the end of the novel, when the three women gather to tell the story of Zenia,

Tony, the military historian, recognizes that there may not have been a side in the "war" in which they and Zenia were engaged. Zenia is an artifact:

> Tony stares up at Zenia, cornered on the balcony with her failing magic, balancing on the sharp edge, her bag of tricks finally empty. Zenia stares back down. She knows she has lost, but whatever her secrets are she's still not telling. She's like an ancient statuette dug up from a Minoan palace: there are the large breasts, the tiny waist, the dark eyes, the snaky hair. Rony picks her up and turns her over, probes and questions, but the woman with her glazed pottery face does nothing but smile. (470)

Although *Alias Grace* is a historical novel, based on a nineteenth-century crime, history is as much a construction in this postmodern and postcolonial novel as it is in *The Robber Bride*, and has been since Atwood's early use of Mary Queen of Scots and Anne Boleyn stories in her visual art. Again, the novel depicts a woman and even a comically doubling psychiatrist with contradictory "multiple personalities," including snaky shadow selves, and uses folklore alongside literature and history. In this case, Atwood uses the traditional female folk activity of quilting, and illustrations of "metaquilts," to comment on the novel's metafiction and its questioning of master patterns (see Wilson, "Quilting"). Another trickster, Grace emphasizes the oral quality of her tale, which is juxtaposed with differing historical, literary, medical, newspaper, religious, prison, and personal accounts of the murder, and alludes to myths about Perseus, St. George, Ulysses and the Sirens, Pan, Eurydice, Lot's Wife, Jeremiah, Job, Simon, Rachel, and Jonah. Provided with a different quilt pattern block for each chapter, the reader must "quilt" the pieces together, including Solomon's Temple, Pandora's Box, and Tree of Paradise patterns. Significantly, Grace, who sews while she speaks, decides to put a "border of snakes intertwined" on her Tree of Paradise quilt. Although the snakes will look like vines or a cable pattern, "without a snake or two, the main part of the story would be missing"; Grace's interpretation, of course, is "not the approved reading," (459–60) and, in postmodern fashion, the gaps are at least as important as the events. Atwood, too, plays trickster as she throws in a few embroidered snakes in her pretty pattern. Whether *quilt* spells *guilt* is left entirely to the reader (Wilson, "Quilting").

As can be seen in Atwood's use of fairy tales and other folklore, myth intertexts generally serve at least five connected purposes throughout Atwood's works. One, they indicate the quality and nature of characters' cultural contexts; two, they signify characters' — and readers' — entrapment in pre-existing patterns; and three, they comment self-consciously on these patterns — including the embedded myths, fairy tales, and related popular traditional stories — often by deconstructing constricting literary, folkloric, and cultural plots with transgressive language, thus filling in the gaps of female narrative. Four, myth and other intertexts comment self-consciously on the frame story, on themselves, and on other intertexts. When used in metafiction, intertexts call attention to themselves as intertexts, highlighting their shortcomings or celebrating the power of language and story. Finally, five, and most important, mythic intertexts structure the characters' imaginative or "magical" release from externally imposed patterns, offering the possibility of transformation for the novel's characters, for the country they partly represent, and for all human beings (Wilson 1993, 34). Since the culture and country in which characters reside is Canada, and since many of the main characters are women, mythic intertexts highlight national, political, postcolonial, and gender themes.

Like the plots, motifs, images, themes, and characters of other folkloric narratives, Atwood's work uses myth and other folklore patterns archetypally, ironically, and parodically, often recalling Jungian or Freudian dream analysis in which the dreamer plays all of the parts; i.e. the parts are interchangeable. Although themes of sexual politics predominate, and patriarchal oppression is everywhere apparent, Atwood is always ready to reverse genders, giving us female "oppressors" and male "victims." Mythic figures are almost never simple images of heroism, villainy, or greatness, however. Like the Persephone of *Double Persephone*, both Circe and the Siren of *You Are Happy*, and the Zenia Snake Goddess of *The Robber Bride*, they are at least double and often tricksters or figures of duplicity and ambiguity. As early as *Power Politics*, whether parodied, serious, or, most frequently, both parodied and serious, mythic intertexts not only undercut the authority of the very master narratives they embed, but they usually still imply rebirth. As I have previously suggested, Atwood's re-visioning of patriarchal myths creates a new feminist mythology (1993, 80), but it is always one as unafraid to laugh at itself as at literary tradition, institutions, history, and patriarchy.

Works Cited

Atwood, Margaret. *Alias Grace*. Toronto: McClelland & Stewart, 1996.

———. *The Animals in That Country*. Toronto: Oxford University Press, 1968.

———. *Bluebeard's Egg*. London: Cape, 1987.

———. *Bodily Harm.* London: Bloomsbury, 1992.

———. *The CanLit Foodbook: From Pen to Palate — a Collection of Tasty Literary Fare.* Don Mills, Ont.: Totem Books, 1987.

———. *Cat's Eye.* London: Virago, 1990.

———. *Double Persephone.* Book One, Market Book Series. Hawkshead Press: Toronto, 1961. Margaret Atwood Papers. Thomas Fisher Rare Book Library, University of Toronto, Toronto.

———. *The Edible Woman.* Toronto: McClelland & Stewart, 1969.

———. *Good Bones.* Toronto: Coach House Press, 1992.

———. *Good Bones and Simple Murders.* New York/Toronto etc.: Talese/Doubleday, 1994.

———. *The Handmaid's Tale.* London: Cape, 1980.

———. *Interlunar.* London: Cape, 1984.

———. *Lady Oracle.* New York: Simon & Schuster, 1976.

———. *Life Before Man.* London: Cape, 1980.

———. *Morning in the Burned House.* Toronto: McClelland & Stewart, 1995.

———. *Power Politics.* Toronto: Anansi, 1996.

———. *The Robber Bride.* London: Bloomsbury, 1993.

———. *Surfacing.* New York: Simon & Schuster, 1972.

———. *Survival: A Thematic Guide to Canadian Literature.* Toronto: Anansi, 1972.

———. *You Are Happy.* New York: Harper & Row, 1974.

Campbell, Josie. "The Woman as Hero in Margaret Atwood's *Surfacing.*" *Mosaic* 2.3 (1978): 17–28.

Franz, Marie Louise von. *Shadow and Evil in Fairy Tales.* Dallas, Tex.: Spring Publications, 1987.

Frye, Northrop. *Anatomy of Criticism: Four Essays.* Princeton, N.J.: Princeton University Press, 1957.

Graeber, Laurel. "Zenia is Sort of Like Madonna." *New York Times Book Review*, 31 October 1993, 22.

Harris, Stephen L. and Gloria Platzner. *Classical Mythology: Images and Insight.* 2nd edition. Mountain View, Calif.: Mayfield, 1998.

Jacobsen, Sally. "Daughters of the Dark Goddess: *Tales of Hoffman*, 'Pop Goes the Weasel,' and the Manuscript of *The Robber Bride.*" Margaret Atwood Society, MLA Convention. San Diego, Calif., December 1994.

Leach, Maria and Jerome Fried. *Funk and Wagnall's Standard Dictionary of Folklore, Mythology, and Legend.* San Francisco: Harper & Row, 1984.

Pratt, Annis. *Dancing with Goddesses: Archetypes, Poetry, and Empowerment.* Bloomington and Indianapolis: Indiana University Press, 1994.

Rosenberg, Donna. *World Mythology: An Anthology of the Great Myths and Epics.* 2nd edition. Lincolnwood, Ill.: NTC, 1994.

Terkel, Studs. Radio interview with Margaret Atwood on *The Robber Bride.* Broadcast WFMT-FM, Chicago, 15 March 1994.

Wilson, Sharon Rose. "Atwood's Metafairy Tale, *The Robber Bride*: Feminist, Postmodern, and Postcolonial Contexts." Association for Canadian Studies in the US. Conference. Seattle, November 1995.

———. *Margaret Atwood's Fairy-Tale Sexual Politics.* Jackson: University of Mississippi Press, 1993.

———. "Quilting as Narrative Art: Metafictional Construction in Margaret Atwood's *Alias Grace.*" Association for Canadian Studies in the US. Conference. Minneapolis, November 1997.

Re-Constructions of Reality in Margaret Atwood's Literature: A Constructionist Approach

Klaus Peter Müller (University of Stuttgart)

Why a Constructionist Approach?

CONSTRUCTIONISM IS AN INTRIGUING APPROACH employed in understanding reality, and it is particularly attractive because it is used in the humanities and the arts, as well as in the sciences. Bluntly stated, it means that reality is not simply out there in the world waiting for human beings to look at it properly and thus understand it. Constructionism rejects such simple forms of realism, empiricism, and positivism. In contrast to these approaches, it underlines the importance of the human mind for any understanding of reality, and claims that reality is not only obviously there, but is also constructed by human beings, who give value and meaning to it. This construction of reality, however, must not be seen as an act of solipsism or idealism. Constructionism avoids the one-sidedness of idealism, as well as that of materialism or any form of predetermination. Reality is there, but the way in which human beings look at it, and the meaning they attribute to it, depend on many complicated individual, biological, and cultural factors.

The most convincing introductions to constructionism have been Maturana and Varela (1984) and Varela, Thompson, and Rosch (1991). The first book shows how seemingly obvious properties such as color and smell are actually constructed by human beings because of the biological and physical faculties humans have for perceiving such elements of reality. The second book enlarges upon these findings of biological research and reveals that reality as a whole should be regarded as "the embodied mind." Reality is that which human beings can become aware of and to which they give meaning. This second element of giving meaning to things reinforces the importance of the arts, a fact which is explicitly recognized in this book (see also Müller 1996). Constructionism may thus bring the arts and the sciences closer together again. It also makes it essential to pay close attention to culture whenever reality is discussed or described, because its emphasis on looking both at facts and the meanings or values attributed to them by human beings echoes one of the best definitions of culture, a definition Stuart Hall (1996, 38) adopted from Raymond Williams and E.P. Thompson. It defines "'culture' as *both* the meanings and values which arise amongst distinctive social groups and classes . . . *and* as the lived traditions and practices through which those 'understandings' are expressed and in which they are embodied." Any culture, and I would claim any reality, can adequately be described only when both of these parts are taken into account. And this is what constructionism does.[1]

Atwood's Concern with Reality, or Literature as a Form of Creating Authentic Seeing

Atwood repeatedly warns her readers not to confuse her fiction with the facts of her own life, and she often emphasizes that a work of art has its own arrangements (cf., e.g., the warning label in *Cat's Eye*). But she also underlines the fact that people need to be defined by what they do rather than by who they are supposed to be. She thus refuses a simple identification of the writer and her work:

> We have a somewhat romantic notion on this side of the Atlantic about what an author is. We think of "writing" not as something you do but as something you are. The writer is seen as "expressing" herself; therefore, her books must be autobiographical. If the book were seen as something made, like a pot, we probably wouldn't have this difficulty. (Atwood in Oates 1990, 72)

Similarly, constructionism says reality does not simply exist, but is always connected with what people do. In this context, I will investigate what the characters, narrators, and poetic personae in Atwood's work

---

[1] Constructionism has been of particular influence in sociology, where, according to Delanty (1997, 114), it was *the* "social scientific methodology of the 1980s," and, he claims, "there is little sign of it abating." Holstein / Miller (1993) confirm this, but the approach has been used more generally for researching identity (Kitzinger 1987; Michael 1996; Shotter / Gergen 1989), reality (Arbib / Hesse 1990; Potter 1996) or culture comprehensively (Strauss / Quinn 1997). It can be regarded as "making natural knowledge," providing new understanding for "the history of human engagement with the material world and . . . the embeddedness of knowledge in time" as well as for "the fundamental categories of human experience." (Golinski 1998, 205–6.)

do toward creating a specific reality. In Atwood's words, I will look at her work "like a pot."

Atwood is sometimes quite explicit about reality being a construct. This applies, for instance, to interviews, where some people expect to be presented with the truth about a person:

> Interviews are an art form in themselves. As such, they're fictional and arranged. The illusion that what you're getting is the straight truth from the writer and accurate in every detail is false. . . . Interviews as the truth, the whole truth, and nothing but the truth are suspect. They're fictions. (Atwood in Ingersoll 1990, 191)

She also agrees with Eli Mandel's evaluation of criticism as a type of novel: "They *are* imaginative constructs" (Atwood in Ingersoll 1990, 53). She thus significantly relativizes the traditional roles of fact and fiction.

She often emphasizes, however, the importance of the truth one should expect in literature: "The literature of one's own country is not escape literature. It tells truths, some of them hard" (in Ingersoll 1990, 52). And: "For me it's axiomatic that art has its roots in social realities" (53). "It could mean that art is a way of explaining or controlling the environment." (ibid.) The characters she selects for her creative work are "outgrowths of their society," so that even Atwood says that her writing is "largely realism" (in Ingersoll 1990, 54–55).

Atwood also underlines the importance of culture in her work: "Cultural attitudes in novels are not usually invented by the novelist; they are reflections of something the novelist sees in the society around her" (Atwood in Oates 1990, 72–73). As a postcolonial writer, she is much concerned with adapting the "cultural environment," i.e. the concepts and criteria people have in their minds, to the "physical environment." The discrepancy between the two is

> what Canada and Australia have in common — that they have had a physical environment which has been out of sync with their cultural environment, because their cultural environment has come from elsewhere. And it seems to me that the job in a colony for writers, not imposed by anybody but simply one they come to recognize, is to somehow get these two things together. The perception of their physical environment and the cultural rendering of it somehow have to be welded in a way that the artist in other kinds of countries doesn't have to face. (Atwood in Ingersoll 1990, 91)

Although Atwood often denies that there is one "real" reality (Ingersoll 1990, 108), she nevertheless speaks of authenticity and of avoiding arbitrariness. Davidson's (in Ingersoll 1990, 90) suggestion that her work is "much concerned with changing ways of seeing" is intensified by her defining an objective in her writing, which is "that the seeing becomes authentic." Authenticity, for her, is connected with the fact that one lives in a particular country at a specific time and in certain contexts which shape the political and economic aspects of reality: "In Canada you're involved because the climate is political." Thus, "social and political forms get translated into poetry" (Atwood in Ingersoll 1990, 119) and into literature in general. Canada's economic dependence on America, for instance, is a simple fact for Atwood:

> We *are* dominated by American unions. I didn't invent these facts; they are part of the society in which I live. . . . Of course, I'm taking a position by choosing to describe that reality, rather than some other reality. However, I did not invent the reality I describe, and I cannot make it go away. (in Ingersoll 1990, 138)

She concludes her special consideration of reality in this way: "Novels have people; people exist in a social milieu; all of the cultural milieu gets into the novel" (137).

Atwood's intention to lead readers to "authentic seeing" is thus based on the assertion that there are important aspects of reality which people need to be aware of. In addition, Atwood underlines the relevance of mature moral behavior in contemporary societies, which is also connected with an authentic life: "I do think that 'morality' is going to come back in now. Unfortunately most people still aren't too equipped to think ethically!" (Atwood in Twigg 1990, 123). Lack of authenticity is also strongly connected with what Twigg rightly calls "the main form of censorship in our society": "self-censorship" (Twigg 1990, 126). Authentic seeing is based on what Atwood claims are the basic elements of feminism and desiderata of human life as a whole, namely, "human equality and freedom of choice" (Atwood in Ingersoll 1990, 142).

This freedom implies a conscious involvement with reality and literature that provides no escapism. In "Women's Novels" (*Murder in the Dark*, 57–62), the narrator speaks about the kind of novels Atwood does not write, namely, romantic fairy tales with "happiness, guaranteed, joy all round." For this narrator, "real life is bad for you, hold it in your hand long enough and you'll get pimples and become feebleminded. You'll go blind" (60). It is in this sarcastic sense, too, that Atwood's texts are about "real life." As she said in an interview: "I never make Prince Charming endings because I don't believe in them. But I do believe that people can change. Maybe not completely, but some" (in Twigg 1990, 125).

The freedom Atwood claims for an authentic seeing is never absolute. To believe in absolute freedom is to be subject to a destructive illusion, a childish myth, or to be an American:

> The Americans believe in free choice, and they think that what that means is that you have a choice of everything. You don't. You have a very limited smorgasbord. You have a choice between A, B, or C, and that is it in your own life. And anybody who thinks otherwise is just indulging in the most wishful thinking. Utopian. Millennialist. To me, American thinking. (Atwood in Ingersoll 1990, 189)

Atwood rejects any kind of absolutism and one-sidedness, too, and emphasizes that reality is far too complex for simple answers, even though these are often provided by society. Authentic seeing is connected with the awareness of the dominant factors involved in any construction of reality. These factors include much more than just the visible facts, namely, the things people have in their minds:

> Even in the "real" world, the tangible and visible is not for most people the only reality. There are also dreams, visions, beliefs, emotions, . . . and these invisible elements are often just as important to people, or more important, than their mortgage or their new car; I'd say if this isn't so there is probably something a little wrong with the emotional construction of a person. In life as in literature, the so-called real world is not the only real world; and narrow realism quite frequently misses the point. (Atwood, "Southern Ontario Gothic" [CBC Radio Program, January 1986], quoted in Vespermann 1995, 202)

Atwood's awareness of the importance of people's minds for the construction of reality is not only a significant link to constructionism, but can be seen as a typical element of modern understanding. For Atwood, reality is indeed both fact and fiction, the material world as well as the mental world, which is often manifested in books and writing, and constitutes "this paper / world which is the real world / also" ("Reading A Political Thriller ..." in *Interlunar*, 79). John Fowler developed his concept of the "mind-style" as an important way of describing this paper world through the realities depicted in texts by the minds of characters. The mind-style, he says, is "the systems of beliefs, values and categories by reference to which a person comprehends the world" (Fowler 1977, 130). Reingard M. Nischik (1991) and Hilde Staels (1995) have extended this perspective to Atwood's work and have, in this way, further emphasized the construction of reality through the mind and through language.

With this in mind, I now want to outline the basic areas in which such constructions are most evident in Atwood's literary texts, namely, people's biographies, landscapes, myths, and language.

Reality Constructions in Atwood's Literary Texts

The rewriting of one's own life, or of the lives of others, is a predominant motif in Atwood's work. It runs through her novels from *The Edible Woman* or *Surfacing* to *Alias Grace*, and it is as frequent in her poetry, as, for instance, *The Circle Game, Power Politics, The Journals of Susanna Moodie, Interlunar*, or *Morning in the Burned House* can testify. Feminist, postcolonial, and postmodern perspectives are conspicuously and idiosyncratically connected with one another in this endeavor, as are the four areas focused on in this article. Any identity requires language for its constitution, involves myths, and is inseparable from the landscape, the social and geographical environment of the individual person. A landscape, on the other hand, can never be neutral when it is described through language, and in Atwood especially it is always intricately related to human beings.

Re-Constructions of Biographies

Re-Constructing One's Own Biography

Totally independent and autonomous constructions of oneself are the results of solipsism and always an illusion for Atwood. "Solipsism While Dying" (*Moodie*, 52–53) ridicules the idea of absolute self-creation and of the world existing only because of any individual person. The lyrical "I" assumes at first that "what I heard / I created . . . I said I created / myself . . . the world [is] touched / into existence" (52) by the speaker's hands. But then these assumptions are questioned and finally derided: "Or so I thought, lying in the bed / being regretted // added: What will they do now / that I, that all / depending on me disappears? // Where will be Belleville? // Kingston? // (the fields / I held between. the lake / boats // tor o N T O" (53). Atwood shows that one always constructs one's life with the elements provided by society. The key questions are: a) What choice or how much freedom does one really have? b) Which positions and roles in society can one achieve?

The female protagonist in *Surfacing* at first, and unconsciously, adopts the colonial role traditionally provided for her by society. It is a role connected with her country and gender: as a Canadian woman she is a double victim.[2] Driving back to the North and literally immerging into the country, she eventually learns to reject this identity and to accept a new role, which is much more difficult, as it is less clearly defined and more open to self-creation. It explicitly involves constructions and changes in her mind:

> This above all, to refuse to be a victim. Unless I can do that I can do nothing. I have to recant, give up the old belief that I am powerless and because of it nothing I can do will ever hurt anyone. A lie which was always more disastrous than the truth would have been. The word games, the winning and losing games are finished; at the moment there are no others but they will have to be invented, withdrawing is no longer possible and the alternative is death. (*Surfacing*, 191)

Joan in *Lady Oracle* adopts another, but similarly negative identity which is connected with the literary genre of Gothic romance and is, for Atwood, explicitly a myth offered to women. Joan is "someone who is attempting to act out a romantic myth we're all handed as women in a non-romantic world" (Atwood in Ingersoll 1990, 107). In order to comply with this myth, Joan needs to act in certain ways; she thus constructs herself quite consciously and says: "I fabricated my life, time after time: the truth was not convincing" (*Lady Oracle*, 150). In order to escape from an unconvincing, disappointing reality, she adopts a role which society provides for her and which is connected with her desire for fulfillment and happiness. All the time she hopes for "magic transformations" (46), which, of course, never happen.

Atwood's protagonists usually construct inhibiting identities for themselves or allow others to do this to them. All of her main characters need to learn that they are not simply who they are told to be or want to be, but that they are what they make of themselves or allow others to make of them. In *The Circle Game*, the lyrical "I" often speaks of trying to avoid becoming reified, of wanting to get out of all those imprisoning circles provided by society. The lyrical "I" usually tries to escape from an enforced identity and never actually envisages

---

[2] Cf. Atwood in Ingersoll (1990, 13): "What I'm really into in that book is the great Canadian victim complex. If you define yourself as innocent then nothing is ever your fault — it is somebody else doing it to you, and until you stop defining yourself as a victim that will always be true. It will always be somebody else's fault, and you will always be the object of that rather than somebody who has any choice or takes responsibility for their life. And that is not only the Canadian stance towards the world, but the usual female one. 'Look what a mess I am and it's all their fault.'"

the positive creation of a new self. The ending of "Camera" is typical of this: "That small black speck / travelling towards the horizon / at almost the speed of light / is me."[3] Like most contemporary writers, Atwood avoids characters who achieve positive constructions of themselves. There are at least two reasons for this: a) there are not many to be found in reality; b) they might make for boring literature.

The escape from reality, which characterizes the protagonists in Atwood's early novels, is noticeable in the later ones as well. Reality is always so complicated, demanding, and unconvincing that people construct roles for themselves which promise more happiness and peace. These roles are provided by society and especially by the media, which are often sign systems promising fulfillment. Such promises, however, are always revealed as an illusion. Wanting to be good, loved, and accepted as well as being free from pain are presented as general desires, and it is never quite clear whether these are ordinary human wishes, or desires created by society for the purpose of exercising power. Atwood makes it quite clear, though, that these desires lead to enormous dependence on others. They induce Offred, the handmaid, and her colleagues to come to terms with their imprisonment;[4] they make Elaine, who still wants to "look good" (*Cat's Eye*, 6) when she narrates her story, comply with the cruel absurdities of Cordelia and her friends: "They are my friends, my girl friends, my best friends. I have never had any before and I'm terrified of losing them. I want to please" (127). Similarly, in *The Robber Bride*, Tony, Charis, and Roz desire to "successfully avoid the present" (34) as they, in various ways, are always "trying to avoid being the victims" (24), and each one of them succumbs to "her willed illusion of comfort and stability" (40). Grace Marks in *Alias Grace* also shows that reality or the truth is not as important as preserving appearances, or, as Grace puts it, "to keep hold of your dignity if at all possible" (38).

All of Atwood's novels reveal that trying to be as others or society want you to be is never successful, nor even possible. But employing the opposite solution and wanting to define oneself by dominating others is also not advisable. Elaine's story, for example, shows that her independence from Cordelia and from what others think of her is combined with her lack of concern for others. Eventually, Elaine learns that

---

[3] (57). Another good example is "She Considers Evading Him" in *Power Politics*, 4.

[4] "Already we were losing the taste for freedom, already we were finding these walls secure" (143). Cf. also *Surfacing* (165) for examples of captivating media images and roles.

this phase of "ill will" (422) has been the result of the same ignorance as her former dependence and has led to further cruelty and destruction, but not to a better understanding of her life: "I have not done it justice, or rather mercy. Instead I went for vengeance. An eye for an eye leads only to more blindness" (427).

Atwood describes common failures of human beings in their endeavor to construct identities for themselves. Jean-Paul Sartre (1977: 413–63) expressed these failures with the image of people being either prostitutes or murderers. If you try to define yourself simply by doing what others expect of you, you are a prostitute; if you determine yourself by forcing others to do what you want, you are a murderer. In either case, freedom is destroyed, either your own, or that of others, and without freedom there is no human life.[5] The basic and general problem in human life is precisely to be neither a prostitute nor a murderer. This is also the main problem treated in Atwood's work, and she has described it with reference to her first novels:

> The ideal would be somebody who would neither be a killer or a victim, who could achieve some kind of harmony with the world, which is a productive or creative harmony, rather than a destructive relationship towards the world. Now in neither book is that actualized, but in both it's seen as a possibility finally, whereas initially it is not. (in Ingersoll 1990, 16–17)

The same can be said about her later work, where her solution to this perennial problem is more specific than Sartre's. Atwood requires people not only to avoid being prostitutes or murderers and to accept their own as well as other people's freedom (as Sartre did), she also demands that they accept duality, even multiplicity and uncertainty (which is a more prominent postmodernist element in her work than it was for Sartre).

Speaking about Gwendolyn MacEwen, Atwood (1995a, 58) says that for MacEwen "tricksters and illusionists — those who live two realities — are not emblems of the ersatz, the phoney, but true expressions of human doubleness, of two-handedness, of a sometimes tragic but always necessary duality." This duality is still a problem in *Two-Headed Poems*, where people's desires and "dreams" of absolute "freedom," of complete happiness, an "effortless" "song," etc. are "our double," but are not yet constructively connected with their reality.

---

[5] Cf. Sartre (1977, 60, 495): "être c'est être libre" and "être c'est se choisir," which expresses the strong constructionist element in Sartre, who also says that every human being needs to invent him-/herself anew every day (1972, 352).

That is why a section of "Two-Headed Poems" (74) reads: "Dreams are not bargains, / they settle nothing." The duality of this stage in Atwood's work offers only a very limited choice: "I can choose to enter / this room, or not to enter." Or: "Nasturtium is the flower / of prophecy; or not, / as you choose" ("Nasturtium," 78–79). The choice includes what Atwood has already said about her first two novels:

> To a large extent the characters are creating the world which they inhabit, and I think we all do that to a certain extent, or we certainly do a lot of rearranging. There is an objective world out there, I'm far from being a solipsist. There are a lot of things out there, but towards any object in the world you can take a positive or a negative attitude or, let us say, you can turn it into a positive or a negative symbol, and that goes for everything. . . . Evil obviously exists in the world, right? But you have a choice of how you can see yourself in relation to that. (in Ingersoll 1990, 14)

This dualistic and almost Manichaean attitude has become more open to allow a more comprehensive mixture in the necessary acceptance of duality, multiplicity, and even uncertainty. This new sense of duality, which is far better expressed by the term "hybridity" often used in *The Robber Bride*, implies being able to "tell fantasy from reality" (*Murder in the Dark*, 48), but also to combine both productively and not in an illusionary one-sided way. Thus something, namely reality, is made out of what the characters often look at as being nothing, which, however, is indispensable for reality and is in fact an ordinary element of human life.[6] Existentialist nothingness, or simply the feeling of being nothing, are important and frequent motifs in Atwood's work. Offred sees herself as "a blank" (240) and a "*Zilch*" (193); Elaine has "*Nothing*" to say for herself and connects that word with her life, "as if I was nothing, as if there was nothing there at all" (43); Zenia is called "*nothing*" (78); and the poems "Nothing New Here" (*Two-Headed Poems*),

---

[6] Both forms of doubleness, the antagonistic and the comprehensive, are often connected with the twin motif in the novels and poems. In *Surfacing*, the protagonist tries to retrieve her "other half, the one locked away, . . . the only one that could live" (108), from the country; in *The Robber Bride*, Charis is forced to acknowledge Karen (47, 265ff.), Roz's twin children make her muse about "whether they have a life of their own each, or just one between the two of them" (83), Tony creates herself a "twin" identity as "Ynot" (160); and *Alias Grace* explicitly discusses "*double consciousness*" (462), the existence of "two persons . . . in one brain" (463). "The Signer" (*Morning in the Burned House*, 114–15) is just one example of the motif in Atwood's poetry.

"Nothing," "Notes Toward a Poem That Can Never Be Written" (*True Stories*) are just some of the many examples where "nothing" is an important topic. What is always emphasized is the need for every human being to make something of themselves, virtually out of nothing, not to be dismayed by the seeming emptiness in themselves, but to be constructive and creative: "Hope comes from the fact that people create, that they find it worthwhile to create. Not just from the nature of what is created" (Atwood in Ingersoll 1990, 220).

Atwood warns against simply taking over the roles and criteria of one's society for one's own biography: "People see two alternatives. You can be part of the machine or you can be something that gets run over by it. And I think there has to be a third thing" (in Ingersoll 1990, 19). This "third thing" is obviously something that needs to be constructed, in order to avoid the deadly trappings of "the lonely crowd" (Riesman 1953) or any mass society. A simple adaptation to the dominant social system or "machine," called "the death machine, emptiness machine" in *Surfacing* (162), is as insufficient as allowing the system to kill you or as defining yourself simply in opposition to it.[7] This is one of the reasons why Atwood is against one-sided feminism and postcolonialism: she demands the creation of a hybrid construct, where opposites are not denied but integrated, or transformed into something new.

The transformation always includes elements that already exist. There is thus never any pure construction, but always a re-construction or metamorphosis. The product, too, is never absolute and definitive. All of Atwood's texts reveal why this is so, but *The Handmaid's Tale* makes the reason explicit: "Context is all" (154, 202). Reality and a specific biography are always defined by particular contexts and are not things that exist on their own.[8] *Cat's Eye* expresses the same idea by revealing that a human biography is — like time — "not a line but a dimension" (3), i.e. it is something that cannot easily be pinned down chronologically, but depends on the contexts that are relevant for a certain person in a particular situation and in a specific relationship. Elaine, the painter, puts it this way: "So much depends on the light, and the way you squint" (5).

[7] The third way is also alluded to in *Surfacing* (189): "To immerse oneself, join in the war, or to be destroyed. Though there ought to be other choices."

[8] They are thus defined in the same way as meaning generally, when a pragmatic approach is used. Cf. Wittgenstein (1969, § 43). Constructionism is extremely pragmatic, as it is concerned with cognition, which for Varela (1993, 110–11, 121) is quite generally "effective behaviour."

One of the characters who most consistently and absolutely construct themselves in Atwood's work is Selena in "Isis in Darkness" (*Wilderness Tips*). She has chosen a new name for herself, "Selena," just as "she'd appropriated everything else that would help her to construct her new, preferred identity" (60). She wants to be a poet, and in her poems she "was creating the universe by an act of love" (65). The result of her poetry is stupendous: "For a moment she had transformed reality, and it took them [the audience] a breath to get it back" (66). But she is also described by Richard, the other protagonist, as "a child sleepwalking" (68), and she writes about people who, for Atwood, are not "real," but one-sided constructions: "regal, tricky women, magical, shape-shifting men" (68). She creates a "mythology" of her own (82), but one without any connection to reality. In the end, however, reality catches up with her, reduces her to a nondescript person who hates poetry and sees only "decay in all around": "I hate poetry. It's just this. This is all there is. This stupid city" (81). Her mythology is reduced to very bleak, ordinary, everyday standards, and the Isis-Osiris-myth is reversed after her death, when Richard puts together the pieces of the dead woman:

> It will not be what he once wanted: not Osiris, not a blue-eyed god with burning wings. His are humbler metaphors. He will only be the archaeologist; not part of the main story, but the one who stumbles upon it afterwards, making his way for his own obscure and battered reasons through the jungle .... He is the one who will sift through the rubble, groping for the shape of the past. He is the one who will say it has meaning. That too is a calling, that also can be a fate. (82)

The story is actually less about Isis or Selena than about what Richard sees in Selena and makes of her. He is most of the time "*fatuously romantic*" (80) and, therefore, very inefficient, but in the end he is at least constructing something when he writes about Selena. Even though he has given up his hopes for romantic absolutes, he remains involved in constructing a new myth, a new "*Genesis*" about "*Isis in Darkness*" (82). It will hopefully be a more balanced myth consisting of the "real" duality of him and her: "He will exist for her at last, he will be created by her, he will have a place in her mythology after all" (82).

Re-Constructions of the Biographies of Others

Biographies are always stories and, therefore, part fiction, but Atwood emphasizes the need not to disregard reality too much. A healthy biography should include both fact and fiction. Lives which neglect this duality are always in danger of becoming self-destructive or damaging to others. Just as it is not possible to construct oneself in any absolute way, one cannot construct others either. Atwood thus uses Susanna Moodie quite creatively, not in order to write a "true" biography of her, but because her life and personality "reflects many of the obsessions still with us" (*Moodie*, 62). Similarly, the "Five Poems For Grandmothers" claim that one can understand and know others ultimately only through oneself: "Finally I know you / through your daughters, / my mother, her sisters, / and through myself" (*Two-Headed Poems*, 38). There is thus no way of understanding others than through oneself.

But just as we live in a world of dualities where one perspective can be only half of the whole, the opposite is equally true, namely, that for defining oneself one needs others, too. Without them, there would be only solipsistic constructions. These can be overcome by communication. *Cat's Eye* emphasizes the specific communicative function of art, in particular painting and literature, as ways of overcoming one-sided versions of oneself or others. The novel is quite explicit about the use of others for an adequate knowledge of reality through the motifs of "Half A Face" (209–37), twins, and reflections, which offer alternative stories to the ones every individual person will narrate about his/her life. Thus, Elaine knows that Cordelia's story will be different from her own:

> She will have her own version. I am not the center of her story, because she herself is that. But I could give her something you can never have, except from another person: what you look like from outside. A reflection. This is the part of herself I could give back to her. We are like the twins in old fables, each of whom has been given half a key. (434)

Very often, however, this communication does not take place. Nevertheless, people write biographies for and of others all the time, frequently by giving them roles that are more indicative of the writer than of the person described. In *Alias Grace* this telling of stories and their relation to truth is the dominant issue right from the beginning, and the title already refers to this problem. Who is Grace Marks, and what has she done? There are instantly very different constructions or stories of her life, which depend on the people who make them and on the media or genres employed. In Susanna Moodie's autobiography, Grace is "the celebrated murderess" (3), the mad woman providing "the potential for literary melodrama" (528); in the ballad (11–15), she is involved in a crime of passion; when seen from the perspective of Emily Brontë's poem "The Prisoner" (19), she has been given by human beings, particularly by "man," "a sentence, unapproved, and overruled by Heaven" (Wise and Symington 1989, 14). Her lawyer made "an idiot" (23) of her, in order to save "her from the gallows" (3), and he has thus turned her into a person that Grace herself does not recognize (24). The governor's wife claims that "one must feel pity for these poor benighted creatures," and as Grace "was trained as a servant, . . . it's as well to keep [her] employed" (24). Grace was also looked upon as mad, so "she has spent time in the Lunatic Asylum in Toronto" (24). The governor's daughters, though, see her as "a romantic figure," and as Grace knows that "romantic people are not supposed to laugh," she does not do it. She herself gives two very important reasons for not laughing: "If I laughed out loud I might not be able to stop; and also it would spoil their romantic notion of me" (25). Whether Grace laughs in despair or because she is amused by what has happened to her, the reader does not know. But one learns here that Grace sometimes acts in a certain way because she knows or thinks it is expected of her, and that it serves a specific function. Like all other characters in the novel, Grace constructs her reality in accordance with the criteria that are available to her and that she finds useful.

It is thus obvious from the beginning of the novel that people's versions of reality, what they call the truth, and how they see other people, are always constructions strongly influenced by the criteria applied and by the interests involved. The novel scrutinizes not so much Grace, as the stories people construct about her and "the mechanisms at work" (94) in these constructions. These mechanisms include politics and love, carnal desires, and scientific endeavors, religion, and in fact everything that animates human beings. It becomes obvious that reality is not the truth, but a construct people believe in. It often implies behaving "as if in a book" (524), i.e. conforming to accepted and well-known roles, as this comforts and satisfies people. People are particularly haunted by the experience "*Not to know*" (482), and when that happens they are keen to invent believable stories of themselves and others. Society wants absolute certainty and its desires fulfilled. This is revealed as a weakness responsible for most of "the sorrow in the world" (523). Grace's notion that these weak people "need to be forgiven" (523) is a slightly surprising but consistent conclusion in her life and the way in which it has been constructed for her by those weak people who together constitute contemporary society. The novel also shows that forgiveness is not everything; a stronger society allowing for more diversity, freer, and even contradictory constructions of identity is much more needed.[9]

But in Atwood's work, as in reality, negative constructions predominate, and people are usually used for very personal interests, their biographies often re-written in order to satisfy selfish desires. People are thus turned into icons, which have no relationship to themselves and are forced to be as others want them to be: "He wants her arranged just so. He wants her, arranged. He arranges to want her" ("Iconography" in *Murder in the Dark*, 89). "The most important thing is making her. Over, from nothing, new. From scratch, the way he wants" (90). Such negative constructions, which reveal how human beings are exploited and abused, are always strongly connected with language and power over it: "He has the last word. He has the word" (90).

Love in Atwood is often such a negative rewriting of others: "The love / of one statue for another: tensed / and static. General, you enlist / my body in your heroic / struggle to become real" ("They Eat Out" in *Power Politics*, 7) The struggle is always lost ludicrously. "A Women's Issue" (*True Stories*) describes women tortured and raped, and ends with the question, "Who invented the word *love*?" (55). The word is clearly an invention, and Atwood emphasizes the enormous discrepancy between its meaning and reality. "Christmas Carol" (56–57) again claims that people should not only speak and sing about love but also practice it in its complete sense. There is no alternative: "This word is not enough but it will / have to do." "You can / hold on or let go." But if you let go, you will fall down the "cliffside" ("Variations on the Word *Love*," 83).

All too often, love is connected with choosing "in advance what to kill" ("He shifts from east to west" in *Power Politics*, 35). Love is thus a mere strategy in a war between so-called lovers, who "attempt merely power / [and] accomplish merely suffering" (32). These lovers mutilate each other, even though the other person is perhaps "the / last chance for freedom" ("They Are Hostile Nations," 46). So the "I" in this poem ends by asking, "How can I stop you // Why did I create you" (47), and reveals in these lines that there is always an extremely intricate relationship between the I and the you.

This relationship is developed extensively in *The Robber Bride*, which abounds with war imagery and uses metaphors in its title that reveal the kind of war going on in everyday life: people trying to rob others of their possessions (404). But, the novel claims, they can only do

---

[9] The same could be said about *The Handmaid's Tale*, where forgiveness is prominently discussed on pp. 144–45.

this when there is a strong relationship between the robber and the victim. Thus Zenia, the robber bride, is in the sense of the poem created by the three other women, who through her are forced to acknowledge those aspects of their lives they would have preferred to neglect. She also represents their desire for wholeness, happiness, and success.[10] When Zenia meets Roz, for instance, she presents herself by telling an inspirational "success story. A story about overcoming fears and obstacles, about facing up to yourself and becoming a whole person" (423). Even after Zenia has stolen Roz's husband, and Roz in her despair has tried to commit suicide, Roz is obviously not content with herself, "she would like to be somebody else," but "not just anyone," "she would like to be Zenia" (457).

The intricate relationships between Zenia and the three women, as well as their various constructions of each other, is the stuff of this novel, which reveals the complexity and war-like nature of everyday reality, and makes it obvious that desperately clinging to just one whole and happy story of one's own or other people's life hardly ever gets to the core of any life. This much, it seems, the characters have learned, because this is what they "will do, increasingly in their lives: tell stories." The main question connected with these stories and Zenia is expressed again at the very end: "Was she in any way like us? thinks Tony. Or, to put it the other way around: Are we in any way like her?" (546). The novel shows how they are indeed like her and confirms Tony's statement to her students, "*The end of any history is a lie in which we all agree to conspire*" (540), because, in reality, there is no end. Reality ends only with death, but Atwood's literature is about life and the various contexts that can be used for writing it.[11]

---

[10] In "Wilderness Tips," Portia calls her husband "a robber king" (218). Gender is obviously not important for being a robber; the relevant characteristic is found in people's minds and connected with their intention of exploiting or "murdering."

[11] Cf. "Happy Endings" (*Murder in the Dark*, 57–70): "The only authentic ending is the one provided here: *John and Mary die. John and Mary die. John and Mary die*" (69). Atwood's work is about "the stretch in between" birth and death, which is actually for "True connoisseurs," "since it's the hardest to do anything with" (70). The statement applies equally to constructions of fiction and of everyday factual life.

Re-Constructing Landscapes, Cities, and Environments

Individuals in Atwood's work are very often identified with the country.[12] "This Is A Photograph Of Me" in *The Circle Game* is a good example, because it highlights the fact that this identification is only possible through a medium. The basic medium is language, but in this poem photo-graphy, i.e. writing with light, is added. Whenever language is used to describe a country, the landscape is already the "embodied mind." Landscape can only be understood in relation to human beings, and people may use very different perspectives, languages, or media. Elaine's statement on the importance of light and darkness, seeing and not seeing, for the constitution of reality, her "squinting," is expressed in the poem, too, but in a different way: "It is difficult to say where / precisely, or to say / how large or small I am: / the effect of water / on light is a distortion // but if you look long enough, / eventually / you will be able to see me" (17). One needs to take into account the distortions of water or the contexts of history and society, as well as all the difficulties connected with language ("It is difficult to say"), but one will, in the end, find in the photograph and the landscape a human identity.

The identity of the landscape, the cities, and environments is strongly influenced not only by their present material forms but also by the past, the people who have lived there, and by the understanding, the mentality of the people looking at the landscape today. "The Settlers" reveals how findings of skeletons, etc. are always stuff for new stories about the country and its past, and are even literally the material on which present life is founded. In *Moodie*, too, the dead people are in the land and influence the living people like language (cf. "The Deaths of the Other Children"). The collection emphasizes the power of the country to change human beings more than that of humans to shape the countryside, though both aspects are evident (cf. "The Wereman" and "Paths and Thingscape"). But the constructions made by human beings are never satisfactory. While the statement that Belleville was "still no place for an english gentleman" (55) in Moodie's time may be explained as being connected with a colonial attitude, the collection clearly ends with scorn and pity for what has been built since. The "closed senses" (57) of the people and their promise, "We will build / silver paradise with a bulldozer" (60), have made them construct only

---

[12] In addition to the examples discussed, cf., for instance, *Surfacing* (181, 187); "The Circle Game" and "The Explorers" in *The Circle Game*; "Autobiography" in *Murder in the Dark*; "Death By Landscape" in *Wilderness Tips*.

new prisons. The conclusion is devastating: "Turn, look down: / there is no city; / this is the centre of a forest // your place is empty" (61). What has been constructed in contemporary Canada is revealed as emptiness in spite of abundant material, and it is still the emptiness of the one-sided desire for absolutes. There is no paradise in Canada and the gardens described by Atwood are full of "blood" (34).

For Atwood, human beings can at best construct a "rock garden" ("Daybooks I" in *Two-Headed Poems*, 29). Human constructions of landscapes, cities, and environments like all "things manmade split & erode / as usual, but faster" ("One More Garden" in *True Stories*, 17). But even though the characters confess, "this is what we have made, / this ragged place, an order / gone to seed," they must at the same time admit, "this is also what we have / in common; this broken / garden, measure / of our neglect and failure, still / gives what we eat" ("Nothing New Here" in *Two-Headed Poems*, 26). There is again nothing beyond that which human beings have constructed, the landscape is indeed the embodied mind. That is why there is a very strong emphasis in Atwood's work on the responsibility of human beings for their constructions of landscapes, cities, and environments. The dangers of excessive tourism or industrial pollution that critics have detected in her writing are two of many examples where human beings on the land are an "extra, / a mistake, something found: / a gift, a contradiction" ("Petit Nevis" in *True Stories*, 22).[13] Duality is expressed here again, and Atwood strongly writes in favor of human beings behaving like a gift to the land and not like a contradiction that might end in a final fatal mistake. One could even imagine her complying ironically with the lyrical "I" in *Moodie*, saying "at the last / judgement we will all be trees" (59), as there is an inseparable relationship in her work between humans and their environment.[14]

Re-Constructions of Myths

A myth is basically a story giving meaning to human life and helping to explain significant and often confusing or mysterious phenomena. Its

[13] Cf. Goetsch (1984), Howells (1996, 20–21), and Karrasch (1995, 33–42) for such criticism.

[14] Cf. also Atwood (1995a, 60): "If white Canadians would adopt a more traditionally Native attitude towards the natural world, a less exploitative and more respectful attitude, they might be able to reverse the galloping environmental carnage of the late twentieth century and salvage for themselves some of that wilderness they keep saying they identify with and need."

constitution as a narrative people believe in is as important for its definition as its opposition to what people accept as fact. Myths are strongly connected with people's ideologies because they express people's beliefs and desires.[15] The "firm ground and safety" yearned for by Atwood's characters is only a myth "carrying a new death" (*Power Politics*, 56) and never providing life. Not to have any myth, however, is an impossible alternative. All human beings need one in their lives, they need a story for their biography that gives meaning to their existence.[16] The only possible alternatives are to have a constructive myth or a destructive one:

> I think most people have unconscious mythologies. Again, I think it's a question of making them conscious, getting them out in the place where they can be viewed. And I don't believe that people should divest themselves of all their mythologies because I think, in a way, everybody needs one. It's just a question of getting one that is livable and not destructive to you. (Atwood in Ingersoll 1990, 32)

Traditional myths are destructive for Atwood because they annihilate human freedom and the possibility of creating something new. The old, well-known myths include predetermined roles and conclusions, they imply essential, unchangeable characteristics described by Atwood as reifying human beings and giving them the quality of "thinghood."[17] She presents traditional myths as stifling chains and dead stories. Atwood criticizes the strong influence they have had on people's perceptions of reality, and adds new perspectives and new possibilities by reversing roles, changing solutions, etc. Thus Bluebeard in "Hesitations Outside the Door" (*Power Politics*, 48–55) still tries to "twist all possible / dimensions into [his] own," as in the traditional story, but the woman in Atwood's poem suggests several "alternate version[s]" (49), admonishing the man to change "while [he] still can" (50), and stating

[15] Cf. Althusser (1971), Barthes (1957), Eliade (1963).

[16] Cf. Dennett (1988) for a constructionist variety of this basic need.

[17] Cf. her essay "The Curse of Eve — Or, What I Learned in School" (Atwood 1982a, 222): "This quality of thinghood . . . appears most frequently in stories about male heroes, especially the travelling variety such as Odysseus. In such stories, the female figures are events that happen to the hero, adventures in which he is involved. The women are static, the hero dynamic. He experiences the adventure and moves on through a landscape that is a landscape of women as well as one of geographical features. This kind of story is still very much with us, as anyone who has read the James Bond stories, Henry Miller or, closer to home, Robert Kroetsch's *The Studhorse Man* can testify."

that "There is no way I can lose you / when you are lost already" (54). In the end, Bluebeard persistently follows the woman, but he is "crippled," his "face corroded by truth" (55), the truth being that his pursuits have been unsuccessful and destructive, especially for himself.

Another woman who rejects her traditional mythological role is Eurydice, who refuses to follow Orpheus back into the world because of her final awareness that "it is not through him / you will get your freedom" (*Interlunar*, 61). She is only a negative construct of Orpheus, made in the tradition of abusive "love," which is in reality an "old leash" (58) turning humans into commodities. This is why she says of their relationship, "I was your hallucination" (59). She was sung into existence by him, but not as a free person, only as his "echo." Eurydice, however, claims her own identity and refuses to have her life written by somebody else. Orpheus, who is ensnared by his own mythical role, cannot understand this, and the poem concludes: "You could not believe I was more than your echo" (59).

There is a noticeable shift in Atwood's work from characters who refuse confining traditional myths to persons who consciously change them into positive constructions. This is most evident in "Unpopular Girls" and "Let Us Now Praise Stupid Women," where such women claim their significance for good stories and their relevance in fiction. Again, Atwood and the important concept of duality maintain that such women are both fiction and fact at the same time, i.e. they are not only important in "Literature" (*Good Bones*, 37), but also in real life, where myths of ugly and stupid women have had an enormous influence on people's perceptions and behavior.

Changing traditional myths is just one aspect of Atwood's re-construction of mythology. It needs to be combined with the other perspective in her work, which shows that every story suggesting final solutions, absolute happiness, the truth, etc., is a negative myth, because it avoids the duality and complexity of life. It is always shown to be a destructive illusion. Any idea of an absolute love defining one's identity and giving meaning to one's whole life, for instance, is an example of just such a myth, against which Atwood repeatedly addresses warnings like this: "*The desire to be loved is the last illusion: / Give it up and you will be free*" ("A Sunday Drive" in *Interlunar*, 52).

Atwood supports only those myths that claim no absolutes and no destructive power over others, especially the myths of human freedom and creativity, though both are necessarily connected with their dualistic opposites, necessity and the strong influence of the status quo. A myth for her is still predominantly a primal, unpremeditated story, laden with emotion, providing meaning and intelligibility for people.

As no absolute and final status of human life is regarded as ever being attainable, although people always strive to achieve it, one could even say that for Atwood as well as for Northrop Frye the quest-myth is central. But in Atwood the quest is far from being "a central unifying myth" (Frye 1971, 192). And whether she actually creates a new myth or simply reflects and criticizes old ones is a question discussed among critics.[18] Atwood uses mythic material reflectively and critically, but the only myths she corroborates are those of human freedom, creativity, and the endless diversity of human life. They constitute, in her work, a peculiar mixture of modern and postmodern mythology. In connection with their refusal of any absolute unity, Atwood's constructive myths in the end significantly combine "logos and mythos" (Fiedler 1971, 518), as they are able to include contradictions, dualistic opposites, or any number of diverse elements, and are meant to be made conscious. For their expression, they use ordinary language with specific images and meanings, and they are not really a language of their own, as they were for Cassirer (1955, 38).

Re-Constructions of Language

Myths depend on language, and a language consists not only of words and rules for connecting them with one another, but also of the stories preserved in it: "A language is not words only, / it is the stories / that are told in it, / the stories that are never told" ("Four Small Elegies" in *Two-Headed Poems*, 55). A language, in this sense, could best be described as a discourse, which for Foucault (1974) constructs reality. When "early / languages are obsolete," they have lost their "stories / or surprises," the possibility of expressing new experiences. This loss is always connected with people no longer believing in these stories or myths, as is shown very clearly in "Eventual Proteus" (*The Circle Game*, 40–41), where Proteus is "shrunk" by the lyrical "I"'s "disbelief" in him and can, therefore, no longer "resume / the legends of [his] disguises"; his shape thus becomes "final" (41). In the same way as myths

---

[18] For Lauter (1984, 215) Atwood creates a new myth, namely "one which does not require the triumph of one person over another." See also Wilson in the present volume. Ostriker (1986, 68) on the other hand calls Atwood's re-constructions "revisionist mythmaking" only correcting old mythology, and Vespermann (1995, 188) also thinks that there is myth criticism and de-mythification in Atwood, "openings for the imagination," but no new mythology or new belief structures.

and stories change and depend on people's belief in them, language, too, is subject to change and to human re-construction.

Atwood is aware of the two-sided process connected with language. Language predetermines people's perceptions of reality, often to the extent of reifying life, and it is at the same time subject to being changed by humans. In either case it is a human construction. Change can be brought about by adding words, or more significantly by changing contexts:

> [The] meaning of a word changes according to its context in its constellation. The word *woman* already has changed because of the different constellations that have been made around it. Language changes within our lifetime. As a writer you're part of that process — using an old language, but making new patterns with it. Your choices are numerous. (Atwood in Ingersoll, 112)

Language predetermining people's perceptions is very strong in the *Moodie* poems, where Moodie disembarking in Quebec says, "I'm a word / in a foreign language" (11). As the language appropriate for the new country is not known, "prediction is forever impossible" (15). Similarly, in "Migration: C.P.R." (*The Circle Game*), "language is the law" because it predetermines people's views on the country, even though these people actively try to escape "from allegories" (65). But on their way west they detect everywhere the allegories of their native language in the foreign countryside, and words are "again / these barriers" that prevent unpremeditated and immediate perception. When people are "speechless," they are at last "unbound" (67), "without meaning" (68). But in this situation they are shown as "needing new / houses, new / dishes, new / husks" (68), and they end up unpacking those things they thought they had left behind, especially the categories and allegories connected with their language. They are eventually caught in the same net of images and categories: "The fishermen / are casting their nets here / as well" (69).

The first thing that needs to be accepted is that language, too, is never one-sided and absolute. "Escaping from allegories" and "wanting / a place of absolute / unformed beginning" (65) is an impossible myth for human beings. Instead of such a destructive illusion, a language of duality is needed. Susanna Moodie, for instance, learns to accept "The Double Voice" that combines idealism ("manners" and "watercolours," "uplifting verse") with materialism or realism ("men sweat / always and drink often," "unborn babies / fester like wounds in the body") (*Moodie*, 42). One must refuse to write or hope for "the true story," because "The true story lies / among the other stories"

(*True Stories*, 11), i.e. it lies, whenever read on its own and accepted as absolute truth, and it is always connected with multiple, eternally changing contexts, which endlessly give new meanings to it.

Language is thus both "random and necessary" ("Some Objects of Wood and Stone" in *The Circle Game*, 73), "always / and merely . . . a disease / of the mouth," but also "the hospital that will cure us, / distasteful but necessary" ("Two-Headed Poems" in *Two-Headed Poems*, 73). The need for language in human life is obvious, and Atwood makes her readers aware of its dangers as well as of its creative possibilities. She shares the modern "distrust of language," but also claims that it is

> one of the few tools we *do* have. So we have to use it. We even have to trust it, though it's untrustworthy.... The question is, How do we know "reality"? How do you encounter the piece of granite? How do you know it directly? Is there such a thing as knowing it directly without language? (Atwood in Ingersoll 1990, 209)

Her answer is clearly, no, there is no other way of knowing and understanding reality but through language. Every human being lives in and through their own words and those of others. Language is a light that illumines people and their lives, if only for a time: "You will flicker in these words / and in the words of others / for a while and then go out" ("Five Poems For Grandmothers" in *Two-Headed Poems*, 41).

Without language there is only death. But language, too, can be deadening, if it is used to destroy human freedom and creativity. In the language Atwood favors, meaning is not at all totally fixed, it is rather shown to exist only in connection with "this confusion, this largeness / and dissolving," this chaotic complexity of ordinary life, where any absolute, final, and wordless "identity" is always "something too huge and simple / for us to see" ("A Place: Fragments" in *The Circle Game*, 91). Eventually, Atwood again calls for the invention and construction of a language of the third kind, containing the polarities and dualities of everyday life:

> I think the push is towards a third language, if you like, or another language. And, of course, this is one of our difficulties: both in Canada and in Australia we write in English. And the French write in French. And that means that the literary tradition that history has provided us with was created in another country. (Atwood in Ingersoll 1990, 92)

The language problem is intricately connected with the difficulty of translating experience from one culture to another: "There's something tricky about 'reality,' let alone language. Insofar as language relates to a cultural experience of reality, to what extent is that transmissible? To what extent can you translate that into another language and have it understood?" (Atwood in Ingersoll 1990, 211). The answer suggested by Atwood's work is that this can be achieved only with reference to similar experiences of the people in the other culture. Without such similarities, no understanding is possible.[19] But these similarities between human beings, which make communication and understanding possible, in spite of numerous difficulties, are basic assumptions in Atwood, constructionism, and postcolonialism.

Atwood, Constructionism, and Postcolonialism

Atwood has repeatedly described Canada as a colonial country and compared colonialism with the predicament of women, as in both cases the "power is held by people other than those having the realization. In the case of women, it's men; in the case of Canada, it's Americans" (in Ingersoll, 119). Feminism and postcolonial liberation are part of a common "large issue: human dignity" (Atwood in Ingersoll 1990, 102), because for Atwood colonialism is always connected with "the feelings of cultural self-deprecation and insignificance" (Atwood 1972, 239). Liberating people from such feelings involves rewriting their histories, which is not merely "an affective reanimation," but a "reconstruction . . . [and] a reshaping of present possibilities" (Nicholson 1994, 43) very much in the sense of the Empire striking back "with a vengeance."[20]

With *Survival*, Atwood (1972) was engaged in rewriting the history of literature in Canada, which involved changing the Canadian mentality and providing it with an understanding of reality that included Canadian literature, where at that time only American and British

---

[19] Cf. the conclusion above that understanding others is only possible through oneself, and see Müller (1995) for modern precursors of this opinion.

[20] Rushdie (1982). It is in this liberating sense that Atwood is postcolonial, and it is in this context, too, that the word is written without a hyphen in this article, because when "we drop the hyphen, and effectively use 'postcolonialism' as an always present tendency in any literature of subjugation marked by a systematic process of cultural domination through the imposition of imperial structures of power, we can begin to see . . . [that this] form of 'postcolonialism' is not 'post-' something or other but is already implicit in the discourses of colonialism themselves" (Mishra and Hodge 1993, 284). This notion strongly conforms to Atwood's concept of duality.

literature was known.[21] This re-constructing of history is always connected in her work with a reclaiming of power, even if only small things are changed and everybody today in this postmodern intertextual world can only use words that have been used by millions of other people. Atwood's insistence on the importance of language and communication is pervasive: "A word after a word / after a word is power." Above all, the speaking of different words when other words have predominantly been used conveys a certain power, just as "spelling" implies the power "to make spells" ("Spelling" in *True Stories*, 63–64). And in this way it is even possible to express truth: "At the point where . . . the word / splits & doubles & speaks / the truth & the body / itself becomes a mouth" (64). Speaking the truth occurs by splitting and doubling, i.e. by revealing something other than the ordinary meanings and constructing new ones.

The new constructions in Atwood are always hybrids, or even a form of "pastiche" (*Robber Bride*, 402), where mimicry implies the opposite of simple adaptation and can become menacing for the dominant authority.[22] Atwood is involved in an intriguing counter-discourse that regards all identities derived from oppressive discourses, like the colonial identity, as a "'nervous condition' of fantasy and desire, a violent, neurotic relation" (Childs and Williams 1997, 123) between an imposing power and suppressed individuals. Resistance is, for Atwood (as for Foucault 1974), a condition produced by the dominant discourse itself, inherent in every discourse, as duality and multiplicity are inherent in human life. For her, the "subaltern" (Spivak 1993), who does not succumb to inertia, can always speak and has the "permission to narrate" (Said 1984), but will never write a completely authentic, true, essentialist, or homogeneous story. Identity for Atwood is a matter of "becoming" rather than of "being" and is connected with an endless process of transforming the past into the present and into a future which is different yet again.

---

[21] Cf. Atwood in Oates (1990, 85) and her PEN conference speech in Hamburg in 1986, where she said that "'for the Canadian writer, history is something that must be rediscovered, reclaimed, reinterpreted.'" The same needed to be done with space: "'Canadian writers have had to first name the ground'" (quoted in Staels 1995, 1).

[22] Mimicry is an important element especially in those of Atwood's characters who yearn for absolutes. For mimicry in postcolonialism, cf. Bhabha (1996) and McClintock (1995, 61–65). Hybridity or creolisation is regarded as a positive element in postcolonialism by Brathwaite (1971), Bhabha (1994), and Young (1995).

Atwood's insistence on transforming a reality that is already there rather than creating something completely new is a topical as well as old notion of metamorphosis, which is also reflected in the works of such contemporary writers as Caryl Churchill and Derek Walcott. In these works, people transform the fragments of reality they encounter. The awareness of fragmentation is a typical modern element that has been foregrounded in postmodernism and postcolonialism. There are interesting similarities between Atwood and Salman Rushdie in this respect. While Rushdie says that people know only fragments of reality, Atwood claims "Our fragments made us."[23] All of these writers maintain, like constructionists, that reality needs to be re-created and transformed out of real-life fragments.

Satisfaction with incompleteness and imperfection[24] is combined with its seeming opposite, a fear of inertia (*Handmaid's Tale*, 266), especially mental inertia, and a striving for improvement. Atwood is not concerned with "the poem that invents / nothing and excuses nothing, / because you invent and excuse yourself each day" ("Notes Towards A Poem That Can Never Be Written" in *True Stories*, 70). This poem and its title express significant elements of Atwood's poetics, namely, the inability to create a complete story and the endless involvement in constructing life against all odds. Atwood invites her readers to resist authoritarian power and to participate actively in re-constructing her texts.[25] And the readers' constructions go far beyond the ideas envisaged by the author, because, like Offred and Elaine, Atwood passes her works on to her readers and thus, like them, she "can no longer control [these works], or tell them what to mean" (*Cat's Eye*, 431). Their meanings now depend, at least in part, upon this dualistic process, on the contexts, the personal and cultural realities applied by every reader.

Constructionism asserts the processes of understanding oneself, others, and reality that are depicted in Atwood's work, and corroborates the fact, in connection with system theory, that human beings do

---

[23] Atwood in "Two-Headed Poems" (*Two-Headed Poems*, 59). Rushdie (1992, 10, 12).

[24] Cf. "The imperfect is our paradise" (*Alias Grace*, 502).

[25] Reading "allows for many more dimensions of experience than do movies or television. The writer suggests some things to you and helps you fill in, but really you're supplying all that sensory information yourself. . . . So the reader is actually participating in the creation of the book. Every time someone reads a book, a new book is being created in the reader's head. Reading is a creative activity" (Atwood in Ingersoll 1990, 169).

not really construct absolutely new things, but transform existing reality in an "autopoietic" process (Maturana and Varela 1980), which already includes the dualities and complexities described by Atwood. The terms "resistance" and "hybridity," which are heatedly discussed in postcolonial theory, become elements belonging to the system of "human life," and constructionism exposes, very much like postcolonialism, the "apparently monolithic European forms, ontologies, and epistemologies" (Ashcroft, Griffiths, and Tiffin 1989, 153) as one-sided and in urgent need of oppositional alternatives. Atwood points out this liberating need in contemporary everyday life, and she suggests alternatives that are never easily achieved but essential for a more humane existence.

Works Cited

Althusser, Louis. "Ideology and Ideological State Apparatuses." In Althusser, *Lenin and Philosophy and Other Essays*. London: NLB, 1971: 121–73.

Arbib, Michael A. and Mary B. Hesse. *The Construction of Reality*. Cambridge: Cambridge University Press, 1990.

Ashcroft, Bill, Gareth Griffiths, and Helen Tiffin. *The Empire Writes Back: Theory and Practice in Post-Colonial Literatures*. London: Routledge, 1989.

Atwood, Margaret. *Alias Grace*. London: Virago, 1997.

———. *Cat's Eye*. New York: Bantam, 1989.

———. *The Circle Game*. Toronto: Anansi, 1984.

———. *The Edible Woman*. Toronto: McClelland & Stewart, 1969.

———. *Good Bones*. Toronto: Coach House, 1993.

———. *The Handmaid's Tale*. London: Virago, 1987.

———. *Interlunar*. London: Cape, 1988.

———. *The Journals of Susanna Moodie*. Toronto: Oxford University Press, 1970.

———. *Lady Oracle*. Toronto: McClelland & Stewart, 1976.

———. *Morning in the Burned House*. London: Virago, 1995.

———. *Murder in the Dark: Short Fictions and Prose Poems*. London: Virago, 1994.

———. *Power Politics*. Toronto: Anansi, 1971.

———. *The Robber Bride*. Toronto: McClelland & Stewart, 1993.

———. *Second Words: Selected Critical Prose*. Toronto: Anansi, 1982. (1982a)

————. *Strange Things: The Malevolent North in Canadian Literature.* Oxford: Clarendon Press, 1995. (1995a)

————. *Surfacing.* London: Virago, 1985.

————. *Survival: A Thematic Guide to Canadian Literature.* Toronto: Anansi, 1972.

————. *True Stories.* London: Cape, 1982.

————. *Two-Headed Poems.* New York: Touchstone, 1980.

————. *Wilderness Tips.* London: Virago, 1992.

Barthes, Roland. *Mythologies.* Paris: Éditions du Seuil, 1957.

Bhabha, Homi K. *The Location of Culture.* London: Routledge, 1994.

————. "Of Mimicry and Men: The Ambivalence of Colonial Discourse." In *Modern Literary Theory: A Reader.* Ed. Philip Rice and Patricia Waugh. London: Arnold, 1996: 360–67.

Brathwaite, Edward Kamau. *The Development of Creole Society in Jamaica, 1770 – 1820.* Oxford: Oxford University Press, 1971.

Cassirer, Ernst. *The Philosophy of Symbolic Forms.* New Haven: Yale University Press, 1955.

Childs, Peter and Patrick Williams. *An Introduction to Post-Colonial Theory.* New York: Prentice Hall/Harvester-Wheatsheaf, 1997.

Delanty, Gerard. *Social Science: Beyond Constructivism and Realism.* Buckingham: Open University Press, 1997.

Dennett, Daniel C. "Why Everyone is a Novelist." *Times Literary Supplement,* 16–22 September 1988, 1016, 1028–9.

Eliade, Mircea. *Aspects du mythe.* Paris: Gallimard, 1963.

Fiedler, Leslie A. *The Collected Essays.* Vol 1. New York: Stein & Day, 1971.

Foucault, Michel. *The Archaeology of Knowledge.* London: Tavistock, 1974.

Fowler, Roger. *Linguistics and the Novel.* London: Methuen, 1977.

Frye, Northrop. *Anatomy of Criticism: Four Essays.* Princeton: Princeton University Press, 1971.

Goetsch, Paul. "Ökologische Aspekte der Werke von Margaret Atwood." In *Zur Literatur und Kultur Kanadas.* Ed. Dieter Meindl. Erlangen: Palm & Enke, 1984: 109–28.

Golinski, Jan. *Making Natural Knowledge: Constructivism and the History of Science.* Cambridge: Cambridge University Press, 1998.

Hall, Stuart. "Cultural Studies: Two Paradigms." In *What is Cultural Studies? A Reader.* Ed. John Storey. London: Arnold, 1996: 31–48.

Holstein, James A. and Gale Miller, ed. *Reconsidering Social Constructionism: Debates in Social Problems Theory.* New York: de Gruyter, 1993.

Howells, Coral Ann. *Margaret Atwood*. London: Macmillan, 1996.

Ingersoll, Earl G., ed. *Margaret Atwood: Conversations*. Princeton: Ontario Review Press, 1990.

Karrasch, Anke. *Die Darstellung Kanadas im literarischen Werk von Margaret Atwood*. Trier: Wissenschaftlicher Verlag, 1995.

Kitzinger, Celia. *The Social Construction of Lesbianism*. London: Sage, 1987.

Lauter, Estella. *Women as Mythmakers: Poetry and Visual Art by Twentieth-Century Women*. Bloomington: Indiana University Press, 1984.

Maturana, Humberto and Francisco J. Varela. *Autopoiesis and Cognition: The Realization of the Living*. Dordrecht: Reidel, 1980.

———. *The Tree of Knowledge: The Biological Roots of Human Understanding*. Boston: Shambala, 1984.

McClintock, Anne. *Imperial Leather: Race, Gender, and Sexuality in the Colonial Contest*. London: Routledge, 1995.

Michael, Mike. *Constructing Identities: The Social, the Nonhuman and Change*. London: Sage, 1996.

Mishra, Vijay and Bob Hodge. "What is Post(-)colonialism?" In *Colonial Discourse and Post-Colonial Theory: A Reader*. Ed. Patrick Williams and Laura Chrisman. New York: Prentice Hall/Harvester-Wheatsheaf, 1993: 276–90.

Müller, Klaus Peter. "'The Enactment or Bringing Forth of Meaning from a Background of Understanding' — Constructivism, Anthropology, and (Non-)Fictional Literature." In *The Anthropological Turn in Literary Studies*. Ed. Jürgen Schläger. Tübingen: Narr, 1996: 65–79.

———. "Transferring Culture in Translations — Modern and Postmodern Options." *Traduction, Terminologie, Rédaction: Études sur le texte et ses transformations* 8.1 (1995): 65–83

Nicholson, Colin. "Living on the Edges: Constructions of Post-Colonial Subjectivity in Atwood's Early Poetry." In *Margaret Atwood: Writing and Subjectivity: New Critical Essays*. Ed. Colin Nicholson. London: Macmillan, 1994: 11–50.

Nischik, Reingard M. *Mentalstilistik: Ein Beitrag zu Stiltheorie und Narrativik. Dargestellt am Erzählwerk Margaret Atwoods*. Tübingen: Narr, 1991.

Oates, Joyce Carol. "My Mother Would Rather Skate Than Scrub Floors." In Ingersoll 1990: 69–73.

Ostriker, Alicia Suskin. *Stealing the Language: The Emergence of Women's Poetry in America*. Boston: Beacon, 1986.

Potter, Jonathan. *Representing Reality: Discourse, Rhetoric and Social Construction*. London: Sage, 1996.

Riesman, David. *The Lonely Crowd: A Study of the Changing American Character*. 2nd ed. New Haven: Yale University Press, 1953.

Rushdie, Salman. "The Empire Strikes Back with a Vengeance." *The Times*, 3 July 1982, n.p.

———. "Imaginary Homelands." In Rushdie, *Imaginary Homelands: Essays and Criticism 1981–1991*. London: Granta, 1992: 9–21.

Said, Edward. "Permission to Narrate." *Journal of Palestine Studies* 13.3 (1984): 27–48.

Sartre, Jean-Paul. *L'être et le néant*. Paris: Gallimard, 1977.

———. *Qu'est-ce que la littérature?* Paris: Gallimard, 1972.

Shotter, John and Kenneth J. Gergen, ed. *Texts of Identity*. London: Sage, 1989.

Spivak, Gayatri Chakravorty. "Can the Subaltern Speak?" In *Colonial Discourse and Post-Colonial Theory: A Reader*. Ed. Patrick Williams and Laura Chrisman. New York: Prentice Hall/Harvester-Wheatsheaf 1993: 66–111.

Staels, Hilde. *Margaret Atwood's Novels: A Study of Narrative Discourse*. Tübingen: Francke, 1995.

Strauss, Claudia and Naomi Quinn. *A Cognitive Theory of Cultural Meaning*. Cambridge: Cambridge University Press, 1997.

Twigg, Alan. "Just Looking at Things That Are There." In Ingersoll 1990: 121–30.

Varela, Francisco J. *Kognitionswissenschaft — Kognitionstechnik: Eine Skizze aktueller Perspektiven*. 3rd ed. Frankfurt: Suhrkamp, 1993.

Varela, Francisco J., Evan Thompson, and Eleanor Rosch. *The Embodied Mind: Cognitive Science and Human Experience*. Cambridge: MIT, 1991.

Vespermann, Susanne. *Margaret Atwood: Eine mythokritische Analyse ihrer Werke*. Augsburg: Wißner, 1995.

Wise, Thomas J. and J. Alexander Symington, ed. *The Poems of Emily Jane Brontë and Anne Brontë*. Oxford: Shakespeare Head, 1989.

Wittgenstein, Ludwig. *Philosophical Investigations*. New York: Macmillan, 1969.

Young, Robert J. C. *Colonial Desire: Hybridity in Theory, Culture and Race*. London: Routledge, 1995.

IV.
Creativity — Transmission — Reception

Challenging the Reader:
An Analysis of Margaret Atwood's Creative Technique in Her First Published Novel

Helmut Reichenbächer (Toronto)

> Quand mon roman sera fini, dans un an, je t'apporterai mon manuscrit complet, par curiosité. Tu verras par quelle mécanique compliquée j'arrive à faire une phrase.
>
> — Gustave Flaubert

MARGARET ATWOOD'S NOVELS are read and disseminated throughout the world. Among the languages into which her work has been translated are Catalan, Estonian, Hebrew, Icelandic, Polish, Turkish, and Urdu, to name just a few of the twenty-two languages cited on Atwood's personal home page (http://www.web.net/ owtoad). Most readers and critics are able to consider her work only as a finished product, for, as a rule, the vast majority of readers study her work as a stable text, authoritatively fixed in print. In contrast, examining Atwood's texts in manuscript form — employing the methodology of genetic criticism — reveals a process in flux and a text which is continuously reshaped.[1]

Applying the methodology of genetic criticism to the analysis of the pre-publication material of *The Edible Woman* reveals Atwood's early techniques of composition and revision and provides critical insight into hidden layers central to the novel's interpretation. With a current total of 286 boxes or 44.5 meters of material, the collection of Margaret Atwood's manuscripts at the Thomas Fisher Library, University of Toronto, provides exceptional access to "the writer's study."[2] The At-

---

[1] Falconer defines genetic criticism as "any act of interpretation or commentary, any critical question or answer that is based directly on preparatory material or variant states of all or part of a given text, whether in manuscript or in print" (3).

[2] This figure is accurate as of June 2000. However, material is periodically accessioned to the collection.

wood collection permits the curious to peek into the work room and witness the physical evidence of the imaginative processes which produced the published text.

Genetic criticism extends the study of texts by an additional, temporal dimension in order to study the text in its process of formation (Biasi, 5). This widening of perspective leads Laurent Jenny and other critics to call the poetics of genetic criticism a "three-dimensional poetics" (15). Rather than working with the published, "closed text," which exists only in a "finished shape," the genetic critic constructs the relationship among drafts and published versions and "proceed[s] to a *literal* opening of the text onto the textual nebula that is its genesis. It would be this structural indeterminacy that would characterize open 'writing' in opposition to the [printed] text" (13). The geneticist draws on an open *avant-texte*,[3] a form which "exists only in the dynamic of its transformations" (15).

Unlike the various schools of textual criticism, genetic criticism has no teleological aim. Genetic criticism rather delights in the multitude of alternative readings without the necessity to unify them into a single, definitive interpretation. Genetic criticism sees variants as additional grist for the mills of literary interpretation. While critical editions produce a clear, stable text with the list of variant readings relegated to the apparatus,[4] genetic editions attempt to document the creative process as fully as possible, representing pre-publication documents in their near original state.[5] Such genetic editions are necessarily voluminous and expensive. New media such as CD ROM — a medium that Roland Reuß's and Peter Staengle's Kafka edition exploits — are ideal for making large amounts of pre-publication material accessible and linking interconnected documents. While classical philology eliminates variant readings in order to establish the best possible or "definitive" text, ge-

---

[3] At least since Jean Bellemin-Noël's *Le texte et l'avant-texte* (1972), the term has been current in genetic criticism.

[4] Typical examples for critical editions in the Anglo-American tradition are those approved by the Center for Editions of American Authors or those produced by the Centre for Editing Early Canadian Texts. The C.E.A.A. was established by the Modern Language Association in 1963. The C.E.E.C.T. was founded in 1979 and is based at Carleton University in Ottawa.

[5] For examples of genetic editions, see Marshall Waingrow's edition of *James Boswell's Life of Johnson: An Edition of the Original Manuscript in Four Volumes*, or the Heinrich Heine edition jointly published by the Centre National de la Recherche Scientifique, Paris, and the Akademie Verlag, Stiftung Weimarer Klassik.

netic criticism requires the simultaneous presence of all multiple readings in order to allow the full reconstruction of the author's creative process.

More recently, however, postmodernist editorial theories acknowledge a preference for "a textuality based on dispersal, fragmentation, and pastiche" (Greetham, 1998, 528).[6] These theories reject the concept of modernist editions which separate the notes and variant readings from the "clear text" and sometimes publish the apparatus in separate volumes. These postmodernist concepts reveal an increasing affinity with the goals and sensibilities of genetic criticism.[7]

In the field of Canadian literature, Margaret Atwood's first published novel yields a particularly interesting case study for a genetic analysis. *The Edible Woman* was composed in five distinct stages. Each stage is documented in the material held in manuscript collection MS 200 at the Thomas Fisher Rare Book Library, University of Toronto. The development of this work runs parallel to Atwood's first attempt at the genre of the novel, an unpublished manuscript called "Up in the Air So Blue."[8] The first stage of creating *The Edible Woman* comprises isolated pieces of writing which explore themes developed in the novel.

---

[6] Greetham especially refers to the scholarship of Peter Cohen, Peter Shillingsburg, and other "textuists" represented in *Devils and Angels: Textual Editing and Literary Theory.*

[7] The origins of genetic criticism as a rigorous discipline are closely connected with a particular set of manuscripts — the acquisition of Heinrich Heine's manuscripts in 1966 by the Bibliothèque Nationale in Paris — and the institutional history of what is today the "Institut des textes et manuscrits modernes" (ITEM) — now at the Centre National de la Recherche Scientifique (CNRS), where a team of researchers first came together in 1968 (Grésillon, 4). For the 1960s scholarly interest in creative processes, witness the series "Les Sentiers de la création" (Grésillon, 3), which produced volumes on writers, painters, critics, and intellectuals. While earlier manuscript studies exist, such as those by W. H. Auden (1948), these studies lacked the systematic approach of a more fully developed discipline. In the field of American literature, notable examples of manuscript studies and textual evolution include Victor Doyno's study of Mark Twain's writing of *The Adventures of Huckleberry Finn*. An especially wide range of studies may be found on the process of revision in Hemingway, including Balassi, Beegel, and Oldsey. However, as in other types of manuscript studies, the methodology of manuscript analysis is not developed into a full discipline.

[8] The unpublished manuscript of the novel "Up in the Air so Blue" was written in the winter of 1963–64 (McCombs, "Up in the Air") and may be found in the Atwood Papers, MS 200, Box 16.

This period of development is documented in preliminary texts which I indicate here by small letters, MS.a (MS = manuscript) through TS.h (TS = typescript), which can be dated to 1963 or 1964. While the first stage consists of isolated fragments, the second stage comprises the first attempt at elaborating these previously explored motives in a different genre, that of the novel. This kernel consists of a thirteen-page typescript, TS.aa, entitled "The Edible Woman" and dated fall 1964 and spring 1965.[9]

The third stage encompasses Atwood's first full draft in holograph, MS.A, and in typescript, TS.B, from May 1965 to August 1965. In Atwood's life, these dates correspond to the period after she completed her first year of teaching at the University of British Columbia. The revisions of this third stage resulted in a first submission of the novel's manuscript to the Canadian publishing house McClelland and Stewart in October 1965.[10] For almost two years, McClelland and Stewart did not respond to the submitted manuscript. In the spring of 1967, Atwood received a Governor General's Award for her collection of poetry *The Circle Game*, and the centennial issue of the *Toronto Star* contained a feature article on her (Reguly). When Atwood inquired about her manuscript again, in mid-July 1967, the publisher finally voiced an interest in publishing the novel. Atwood's introduction to the novel's Virago edition explains the incident:

> I finished *The Edible Woman* in November of 1965 and sent it to a publisher who'd displayed some interest in my previous book ["Up in the Air So Blue"]. After an initial positive letter, I heard nothing . . . After a year and a half I began probing and discovered that the pub-

[9] McCombs, "Narrator, Dark Self, and Dolls," 1. In "An Introduction to *The Edible Woman*," Atwood writes "the title scene dates from a year earlier" [i.e. 1964?] (369).

[10] See the publisher's form letter, acknowledging receipt of the manuscript (92.1.3), dated 28 October 1965. (The bracketed numbers indicate box, folder, and folio for the passage's location in the Atwood Papers, MS 200, Thomas Fisher Rare Book Library, University of Toronto.) From internal evidence of the three readers' reports from McClelland and Stewart, dated 1966, it may be deduced that the first version of *The Edible Woman* submitted to the publisher was a clean copy of TS.B. The third reader, who generally praises the novel, objects to Atwood's disguising real names: "Why 'Gorunto' and 'Rosevale' etc. The city of Toronto is no longer a village and the need for disguise is no more real than in the case of writing of London or New York" (95.1.4). Consequently, TS.B is the last draft which still uses these thinly veiled names.

lisher had lost the manuscript. By this time I was marginally visible, having won an award for poetry [the Governor General's Award], so the publisher took me out to lunch. "We'll publish your book," he said, not looking me in the eye. "Have you read it?" I said. "No, but I'm going to," he said.[11]

This renewed interest led to the fourth stage, a complete reworking of the novel while Atwood was teaching at the then Sir George Williams University in Montreal for the academic year 1967/68. TS.D and TS.E date from that period. Her university colleague and fellow writer, Clark Blaise, gave Atwood's novel a critical reading, which led to a significant reshaping of the text.[12] Blaise's comments, which are extant among the Atwood Papers (19.38.1r-4v), refer to what is now fragment TS.F and the passages which have been pulled from that version for use in later versions.[13] By March 1968, the fifth and final stage already included the revisions worked out with McClelland and Stewart's editor, Pamela Fry.[14]

A systematic analysis of Margaret Atwood's revisions to her first published novel, *The Edible Woman*, reveals a gradual elimination of

---

[11] In Atwood 1982, 370. For background to this incident, see also Atwood's letter to Earle Toppings, 6 March [1967], Atwood papers 92.2.14, and, for greater detail, Atwood's letter to her London agent, Hope Leresche, undated [1967], 95.6.1–3. The incident of the lost manuscript is also documented in Sam Solecki's edition of Jack McClelland's letters (153–59).

[12] In Clark Blaise's letter to Judith McCombs, 18 January 1986 (McCombs, "Narrator" n. 5), he recalls this revision as having taken place in 1966. However, after twenty years, he must have erred in the year, for Atwood actually taught in Montreal during 1967/68. In fact, in his autobiographical *I Had a Father*, Blaise describes his contact with Atwood as he was teaching creative writing at Sir George Williams University: "Over lunch one day she admitted that she'd also committed some fiction and asked if I would read the manuscript of a novel called *The Edible Woman*." In his autobiography he dates this incident as 1967 and refers to his written comments as "lunch-hour doodles, unkind queries, useless advice, question marks and exclamation points on the margins" (122).

[13] The version which Blaise read can be reconstructed from TS.F and from the pages pulled from that version which have been integrated into the last draft, TS.H. For details, see Reichenbächer, 264–68, Appendix 9, stemma of all drafts of *The Edible Woman*.

[14] Atwood letter to Pamela Fry, editor at McClelland and Stewart, 3 March 1968, Atwood Papers, 92.1.16. For a schematic overview of this time frame, see Reichenbächer 252–54, Appendix 1.

material from the six extant drafts. This process results in gaps which the reader is expected to fill while interpreting the text. The consequence of this strategy is what Wolfgang Iser calls "an interaction between text and reader" (Iser, 168). This technique appears to have been quite conscious. In a lecture on Susanna Moodie, Atwood explicitly refers to her interest in gaps: "What kept bringing me back to the subject [of Susanna Moodie] — and to Susanna Moodie's own work — were the hints, the gaps between what was said and what hoevered [sic], just unsaid, between the lines" (91.4.2–3) ("Susanna Moodie"). Gaps incite the reader to construct meaning; Iser even posits: "whenever the reader bridges the gaps, communication begins" (169). Gaps necessarily encourage the reader's more active participation.

In order to illustrate the methodology of genetic criticism, this article focuses on how Atwood rewrote key scenes and discusses her systematic elimination of interpretative labels in *The Edible Woman*. These scenes portray Marian's engagement, her discussion with her roommate and with her friend Clara, the moments of self-reflection on the Labor Day Monday, and in particular Marian's walk in the ravine with Duncan.

The first instance of Atwood's use of gaps technique appears when she removes explicit labels from her text while revising the moment of Marian's engagement. This key scene in draft and published novel shifts the relationship between Marian and Peter from a summer flirtation to a serious commitment. In the second draft, a Jane-Eyre-like thunderstorm clearly indicates the emotional impact of Peter's proposal of marriage. While a flash of lightning illuminates the couple, the second draft reads: "As we stared at each other in that brief light I could see my own fear mirrored in his eyes" (18.22.23).[15] Atwood here labels the engagement a fearful experience, to which Marian responds with an increasingly evident eating disorder. Yet while the first two drafts place fear at the center of this relationship, the next revision eliminates any

---

[15] Note how Charlotte Brontë's *Jane Eyre* functions as an intertext. Like Marian, Jane Eyre becomes engaged during an approaching thunderstorm with a lightning bolt, interrupting the bride-to-be's reply to the proposal (vol. II, chapter iii, 259). The element of pathetic fallacy in Brontë is strengthened through the author's earlier emphasis on the nature of presentiments (vol. I, chapter vi, 222). In Atwood, the fallacy takes on an ironic tone which underlines her tongue-in-cheek parody of the Victorian model. The lightning-struck chestnut tree in Brontë is paralleled with the damaged hedge in Atwood. Both function as symbols for the ill-starred nature of these relationships.

reference to Marian's fear. It is instead replaced with a more elusive recognition of her own mirror image.

A similar technique of revision can be recognized in the novel's next scene, occurring the following day, when Marian shares the news of her engagement with her roommate. The first draft again specifies Marian's emotional response through the key motif of fear: "'It scares,' I said faithfully, 'the plasm [sic] out of me'" (18.9.14). Significantly, Marian's feelings symbolically intertwine with her consumption of food. Sitting down to breakfast, she clumsily handles an egg so that she gets her thumb stuck into it. The egg "drooled glutinously; it wasn't done after all," underlining the premature nature of her decision to marry. While this early version stresses the parallel between Marian's metaphor for expressing fear — "It scares the plasm [sic] out of me" — and the egg's equivalent, "[it] drooled glutinously," the relationship of fear to food also signals the origins of Marian's anorexia.

Atwood's second draft muddies Marian's clear insight into her own admission of fear. While the statement itself remains, the revision turns the direct admission of fear into a subjective and tenuous expression: "I said, smiling, and wondered, as soon as I'd said it whether or not it was true" (18.23.3). Marian's emotional response — a moment of clear self-discovery — is submerged again; her fear disappears under a layer of cheerful optimism. In the final revision, Marian fears her roommate's disapproval more than the engagement itself (*EW*, 84). Marian appeals to the roommate's understanding, by claiming it was her subconscious wish to get engaged all along, thereby ending the discussion: the explicit reference to fear has disappeared. The clear label for Marian's emotional state has been removed.

Atwood's suppression of Marian's vague insights into her own emotions continues to take shape throughout the novel's six drafts. Even the protagonist's inability and unwillingness to consider rationally the effects of her engagement are deliberately suppressed. For example, Marian's dilemma is originally expressed in an extended nautical image. In the first two drafts, this description specifies the impact of her roommate's advice:

> The word 'think' fell into {the sluggish pond of} my consciousness like a waterlogged life buoy. I clutched at it, and it sank. I didn't want to think it over. ... I didn't want to think about it at all (18.23.2).[16]

---

[16] Text enclosed in brackets indicates Atwood's addition of text at a later stage of revision.

Rational analysis, "think," is seen as a life-saving instrument. However, Marian's psychological state renders her unable to clutch at rationality. While metaphorically drowning, Marian switches from acknowledging this inability to considering it a question of volition. The addition "sluggish pond" even reinforces Marian's waning self-analytic skill, diagnosing her own passivity. The extended metaphor also provides an early example of her expressing the psychological states of her protagonists through the use of water imagery, a recurrent technique in Atwood's later work. Here, the expression's precision awkwardly contrasts with Marian's characterization as an emotionally disturbed person. In the next revision, this self-reflective expression of Marian's character simply disappears. Readers are left on their own to construct a psychological motivation for Marian's irrational behavior.

Another moment of self-reflection takes place when Marian remembers the events leading up to her engagement on Labor Day Monday, while sitting in her bedroom. The revision removes Marian's definitive, rational processing of events — "Now that I thought it all through I feel a lot better" (19.21.20) — which implies analysis and reaching a conclusion. Instead, the revised version describes Marian's thought processes as "I've gone over it all in my mind," a linear activity — "to consider seriatim" (OED) — with implications of "examining something in detail" (OED) but not with any connotation of result. Drawing a much vaguer picture, the revision focuses on Marian's thought processes rather than on a conclusive analysis.

Still verbalized in the last preserved draft (19.45.26), even the protagonist's realization of her loss of judgment disappears from the final version:

> Little scraps and shreds of the weekend kept floating up to the surface of my mind, demanding to be examined, but eluding me when I tried to hang on to them long enough for a thorough look (18.24.2).

Explicit knowledge of Marian's loss of judgment and her inability to think critically is removed from the text. The change is particularly important at this late stage, the last chapter before Marian's first-person account shifts into a third-person narration, a shift symbolizing the alienation from her own self.

The revisions of Marian's visit to her friend Clara in the maternity ward provide particularly clear examples of Atwood's elimination of material. From the two early versions, Atwood's revisions remove the clear insight into the nature of Marian's attraction to Peter as revealed in her conversation with Clara. In the first two drafts, there is a far more extensive and pointed discussion of the protagonist's relationship, clarified by the use of Clara's relationship as a foil.

The first drafts provide a strong juxtaposition between Marian's practical and rational decision and Clara's idealistic and emotional motivation for a relationship. This contrast helps to characterize clearly the nature of Marian's attachment to her fiancé:

> "Well, I've never thought of Peter as Jesus Christ," Marion said. ~~Clara widened her eyes~~ '{You don't?} But you *ought* to,' Clara ~~she~~ said earnestly. 'Why are you marrying him then? You really ought to.'
>
> 'Now don't go all women's magazine on me,' Marion said, ~~acidly~~ {~~drawing down~~ feeling the corners of her mouth drawn down, she disliked sentimentality.}

While the first draft underlines Clara's position of unconditional adoration, Clara's insistence forces the resisting Marian to define the nature of her attraction to Peter, a far more reasoned approach than the final novel will allow. In the first draft, Marian replies: "Don't you think it's better to go into it without any illusions? I think we are being very sensible about it. Of course he ~~has some~~ {does have lots} of good qualities ~~too~~,' she added, {not wanting to sound too ~~unenchanted~~ coldly practical}." The lengthy discussion of their relationships has Marian argue with purely rational arguments, a strategy which the emotional Clara clearly dismisses: "'Sensible!' Clara ~~snorted~~ {said indignantly.} 'Anyone who's being just sensible should never get married at all. It's not a sensible thing to do. I mean, look at me.'" The argument is finally driven home with Marian's allusion to Clara and Joe's disorderly household which so clearly contrasts with Peter's obsession with disciplined neatness:

> "Well, it won't be chaos anyway," Marion said, seizing on this one word that summed up {so totally for her} the physical ~~side~~ {aspect} of Clara's household. "Peter is terribly neat."
>
> "~~A well~~ A good housebroken animal, eh? Won't muddy the carpets." Clara shook her pale head sadly. "~~Are you sure you aren't~~ {You sound as though you're} thinking of marriage as something you get in a card board box? Different brands for different tastes but all standardized? And Peter just because he's got the approximate good qualities? ~~You've got to marry a person~~. God, if I had to start trying to sort out Joe's good qualities from the rest of him I don't know what I'd do. {[insert from 3v:] He was such a mixed lot.} He just doesn't come apart in neat {detachable} little pieces like that" (18.11.4).

The debate clearly contrasts Clara's and Marian's differing needs in a relationship. This version allows Marian to formulate a vision of herself as organized and efficient, presenting her relationship as a rational choice. However, the seriousness with which Clara queries the emotional basis for Marian's attachment to Peter brings out the shortcomings of Marian's and Peter's relationship in a manner which the final novel no longer allows.[17]

In the first two drafts, the discussion of Marian's relationship with Peter culminates in Clara's direct question about Marian's feeling for Peter:

> "I mean don't you *love* him?" Clara was asking.
> "Of course I love him." {[insert from f4v:] more sharply, almost in the indignant tone she would ~~if~~ use in reply to someone who questioned the fact that she took baths. 'I am going to marry him, you know'} (18.11.5).

Here, Atwood directly confronts both Marian and the reader with the question of motive. Marian's brusque response in the first full draft clearly implies denial, refusing to further analyze their partnership. Far from questioning and examining the true nature of her feelings for Peter, she blocks the discussion. It is rhetorically significant that Marian takes her love of Peter for granted as much as her personal hygiene. Atwood developed the motif of the girl who didn't wash early in the writing process, initially as a short story draft called "Are You the Woman Who Washes" (79.11.1–12), part of the material preliminary to the novel. The rhetoric of her assertion evokes the office virgin's tale of "The Girl Who Didn't Wash" later in the novel, in which a woman's neurosis causes her to neglect her personal hygiene completely. Marian's sharp and certain response to Clara's question whether she loves Peter is thus undermined. The rhetorical figure which specifies the quality of her response — "the indignant tone she would use in reply to someone who questioned the fact that she took baths" — connotes less certainty than Marian believes. The connotation implies a psychological defect, a pathology which later Marian also finds threatening.[18] This parallel is lost through revision and Marian's discussion with Clara loses its pointed edge. While the final version still displays Clara's views on her own relationship, there is no longer a debate.

---

[17] Marian's emphasis on the rational combined with her neglect of the emotional parallels a recurring motif developed in the first two drafts, the motif of the "Snow Queen" who traps her victims in her ice-cold palace of rationality in which emotional warmth can never thrive, an intertextual reference to Hans Christian Andersen.

[18] Compare also the recurrence of the body hygiene motif in Marian's childhood fascination with a rubber-skinned washable doll, a typical example for Atwood's poetic style in the creation of networks of literary motifs.

Marian simply acquiesces to Clara and it is left to the reader to construct the difference between Clara's marriage with Joe and Marian's relationship with Peter.

In the first and second drafts, the problems with her relationship are misleadingly attributed to her confusion over the meaning of love and her failure to master conventional language. In the second draft, talking with Clara, Marian attributes her problems to a question of the semiotics of love rather than to the relationship itself: "'We probably mean something quite different.' Simple words like that seemed to be growing more and more opaque for her these days." To Marian, meaning becomes relative and increasingly escapes definition. Marian also admits to this loss of verbal skills at her workplace, an indication of her alienation from the job: "Even when she was working on a questionnaire, she would catch herself staring with sudden lack of comprehension at the words on the page."

The passage in the maternity ward expresses Marian's attempt to separate her own views from those of Clara: "It was like trying to straighten out a hopelessly knotted skein of wool that wasn't even wool but spaghetti: slipping too." At the end of this passage, Marian loses altogether her ability to resolve the dilemma:

> She made another stab at it, missed again, and substituted with, "Of course the word is very overworked these days. We hardly know what we mean by it anymore {exactly}" (18.25.14).

In this draft version of the maternity ward scene, Marian starts off with an awareness of two clearly opposing views, Clara's versus her own. Simultaneously, she is aware of her increasing inability to judge clearly. Words for Marian grow "more and more opaque." Dissolving meaning and denotation first appear in the context of the protagonist's relationship. "Love" loses its previously assumed clear definition. The dissolving language next affects Marian's workplace, an expression of her alienation from the consumer questionnaires. Food imagery is a third context in which this motif is explored. Atwood's choice of an extended food metaphor — the difficulty of eating spaghetti — describes Marian's inability to grasp and isolate meaning. The semiotics of love are thus initially coupled with a metaphorical expression of Marian's anorexia. Atwood's revision rejects the clear isolation of meaning, just as the protagonist's body rejects food.

The most drastic changes concern Marian's and Duncan's last two encounters, their walk in the snow and the final meeting in Marian's apartment. Atwood removes substantial passages of dialogue which function as a catalyst for Marian's insight into her own dilemma, a pat-

tern which we have already observed in the conversation between
Marian and her friend Clara. Marian and Duncan's walk in the snow
undergoes a particularly substantial revision. In the first two drafts,
Marian finds herself in the hands of an earnest and compassionate partner, a man who is willing to participate in an analytic discussion of her
affairs. In the first drafts, Duncan's repeated questioning actually leads
Marian to overcome her initial hesitation and to talk about herself.

> "I suppose I should say I want to be married, or I want to have a ca-
> reer or I want to be independent or have children or something, [. . .]
> but that isn't it. I want to be safe, I think I'm afraid that no matter
> what I do, I'll find out I really have nothing" (18.18.10v-11).

In this passage, Marian rationally diagnoses her problem as a set of binary choices between marriage or a professional career on the one hand
and financial security or financial risk on the other — a choice which
the final novel never can state in such direct terms. Atwood eliminates
these overt interpretative labels, and the neat solution in binary choices,
leaving her protagonist as well as her reader to construct their own
meaning.

The passages in which Marian achieves a significant level of self-
knowledge also reiterate the explicit references to the motif of fear:

> "I start feeling smothered by things and then I'm afraid of dissolving,
> but then at other times I seem to be afraid of something opposite,
> getting stuck, not being able to move. But most of all it's this food
> thing . . . I'm afraid of eating . . . , but I'm afraid of not eating too."
> Funny, she thought, how detached I'm being (18.32.7–8).

Particularly acute are Marian's observations about her threatened identity, which she expresses in three different metaphors: fear of suffoca-
tion, of dissolving, and of freezing, all of which Atwood connects to
Marian's eating disorder.[19]

---

[19] The metaphors of dissolving and freezing resonate with other passages in
the drafts. Marian's fear of dissolving occurs while taking a bath before the
engagement party and in the first draft after Peter's camera flash during the
party: "She sensed her face as vastly {spreading,} & thin + papery and slightly
dilapidated a huge ~~peeling~~ bill board smile, {peeling away in flabs and
patches,} the metal surface beneath showing through (18.17.5v)." In the second draft, the image of frozen memory occurs in a dream about her childhood: "The schools and the houses and the ponds and fields where she had
once learned the names of things were {all} frozen over, and she was walking
on the other side of the ice. She did not want to go back (18.28.3)."

Atwood manipulates this motif of fear in a way which disguises its overt psychological effect on the protagonist. Because of Atwood's revisions, neither the protagonist nor the reader knows exactly what causes Marian's anorexic behavior. Reader and protagonist therefore work much harder in order to close the gap and to understand her situation. This shift is particularly significant for developing the protagonist's character; her ignorance of the exact nature of her fears makes her behavior seem irrational to herself and the reader. This example shows how the reader is spurred into greater activity, turning reading into a more active process and encouraging readers to close the gaps which the author has created through her revisions.

In the drafts, the nonverbal, symbolic character of Marian's eventual solution is hinted at twice during Marian's conversation with Duncan. The first hint regarding Marian's solution occurs during her breakfast with Duncan. The previous night's sexual encounter had produced a moment of enlightenment. Although the meaning of the epiphany is lost, Marian is aware of the solution's nonverbal character:

> Finally last night it had all seemed cleared, resolved, the irrelevancies absorbed into *some wordless totality* that was able to include them all, . . . but it had been submerged in sleep (19.48.11).

In Atwood's revision, Marian's insight into the nature of a possible resolution as "some wordless totality" disappears. The final draft no longer specifies its nature and instead only offers the protagonist's vague awareness of her situation.

In the first two drafts, another clue exists for the novel's resolution. Marian and Duncan's discussion results in his offer of sympathetic advice. In order to remedy her situation, Duncan recommends that she make her own choices and that she "should *do* something, even if just as a token gesture" (18.18.11v). Duncan invokes the key elements to the novel's resolution. The protagonist is encouraged to be active and to discard her victim-like passivity: she must take charge of her life. Both passages prepare the reader for the novel's nonverbal, symbolic solution: Marian's famous cake.

Analyzing the key scenes with the methodology of genetic criticism demonstrates how Atwood manipulates gaps as a technique of revision. While the reader's reconstruction of gaps may not duplicate the material eliminated in the process of authorial excision, the underlying principle of gaps is crucial to both. Atwood herself refers to the "active participatory work of the reader." She confirms the reader's active role by stating that reading is "less passive than TV or movies." Reading is "to join in the actual creation, the re-creation, of the experience of the book. In other words you are asking the reader to put in some work."[20] Atwood's rhetorical strategy of delegating responsibility to the reader is therefore envisaged as an emancipatory process. Her use of this technique offers us an insight into the creation of *The Edible Woman* and provides new depths to the novel's interpretation.

Genetic criticism guides the researcher through Atwood's pre-publication materials or *avant-textes* and provides the literary critic with invaluable insights. Rather than having to rely on a single textual version, as most literary critics do, those studying manuscript materials can acquire greater understanding by reading through the several layers of texts behind the published text's surface. Access to this third dimension of the text also reinforces and illuminates the notion of writing as process. The published text is no longer an easily consumed, finished product. Rather it becomes a palimpsest of layered documentation, requiring rigorous discipline to recover each manuscript's place and meaning in that sequence of events which comprise the arduous process of literary creation.[21]

[20] "A Trip Through the Inferno" (90.40.5r).

[21] An earlier version of this paper was presented at "I Simposio Internacional de Estudios Canadienses" Universidad Autónoma de Madrid, November 1997. I would like to thank the Department of English, University of Toronto, for the assistance which they provided for me to attend the conference. Elements of this paper derive from the author's doctoral dissertation, Reichenbächer 1998.

Works Cited

Atwood, Margaret. Drafts for *The Edible Woman*. Atwood Papers, Thomas Fisher Rare Book Library, University of Toronto, Toronto. Boxes 18 and 19.

―――. "Introduction" to *The Edible Woman*. London: Virago, 1980: 7–8. Reprinted in *Second Words: Selected Critical Prose*. Toronto: Anansi, 1982: 369–70.

―――. "Susanna Moodie." Atwood Papers, Thomas Fisher Rare Book Library, University of Toronto, Toronto. Box 91, folder 3.

―――. "A Trip through the Inferno: The Act of Writing." Craft Lecture, Port Townsend, 1984. Atwood Papers, Thomas Fisher Rare Book Library, University of Toronto, Toronto. Box 90, folder 40.

Auden, W. H. "Squares and Oblongs." *Poets at Work: Essays Based on the Modern Poetry Collection at the Lockwood Memorial Library, University of Buffalo*. Ed. and Introd. Charles D. Abbot. New York: Harcourt, Brace, 1948.

Balassi, William. "The Writing of the Manuscript of *The Sun Also Rises*, with a Chart of Its Session-by-Session Development." *The Hemingway Review* 6.1 (1986): 65–78.

Beegel, Susan F. *Hemingway's Craft of Omission: Four Manuscript Examples*. Ann Arbor: University Microfilms International Research Press, 1988.

Bellemin-Noël, Jean. *Le texte et l'avant texte*. Paris: Larousse, 1972.

Biasi, Pierre-Marc. "La critique génétique." *Introduction aux méthodes critiques pour l'analyse littéraire*. Ed. Daniel Bergez, et al. Paris: Bordas, 1990: 5–40.

Blaise, Clark. *I Had a Father: A Post-Modern Autobiography*. Toronto: Harper Collins, 1993.

Boswell, James. *Life of Johnson: An Edition of the Original Manuscript*. Ed. Marshall Waingrow. 4 vols. The Yale Editions of the Private Papers of James Boswell. Edinburgh: Edinburgh University Press; New Haven: Yale University Press, 1994–97.

Cohen, Philip, ed. *Devils and Angels: Textual Editing and Literary Theory*. Charlottesville: University of Virginia Press, 1991.

Doyno, Victor. *Writing Huck Finn: Mark Twain's Creative Process*. Philadelphia: University of Pennsylvania Press, 1991.

Falconer, Graham. "Genetic Criticism." *Comparative Literature* 45.1 (1993): 1–21.

Flaubert, Gustave. *Carnets de travail: edition critique et génétique.* Ed. Marc-Pierre Biasi. Paris: Balland, 1988.

Greetham, David C. *Textual Scholarship: An Introduction.* New York: Garland, 1994.

———. *Textual Transgressions: Essays Toward the Construction of a Biobibliography.* New York: Garland, 1998.

Grésillon, Almuth. *Élements de critique génétique: lire les manuscripts modernes.* Paris: Presses universitaires de France, 1994.

Iser, Wolfgang. *The Act of Reading: A Theory of Aesthetic Response.* Baltimore and London: Johns Hopkins University Press, 1978.

Jenny, Laurent. "Genetic Criticism and its Myths." Trans. Richard Watts. *Yale French Studies.* "Special Issue on Drafts" 89 (1996): 9–25.

McCombs, Judith. "Early *Cat's Eye* Stories: Atwood's 1964–65 'Cut-Out,' 'Scribblers,' 'Suffer the Little Children,' and 'The Ravine.'" Unpublished paper presented in Margaret Atwood I: "Up to The Robber Bride"; ACSUS Convention, Seattle 1995.

———. "Narrator, Dark Self, and Dolls: From an Early Version to Atwood's *The Edible Woman.*" Unpublished essay, 1993.

———. "'Up in the Air So Blue': Vampires and Victims, Great Mother Myth and Gothic Allegory in Margaret Atwood's First, Unpublished Novel." *The Centennial Review* 33.3 (1989): 251–57.

Mendelson, Edward. "Revision and Power: The Example of W. H. Auden." *Yale French Studies.* "Special Issue on Drafts" 89 (1996): 103–12.

Oldsey, Bernard, ed. *Ernest Hemingway: The Papers of a Writer.* New York: Garland, 1981.

Reguly, Robert. "Impatient Poet — She wants us to buy Canada back." *Toronto Daily Star* (July 1, 1967): 70.

Reichenbächer, Helmut. "Reading Hidden Layers: A Genetic Analysis of the Drafts of Margaret Atwood's Novels *The Edible Woman* and *Bodily Harm.*" Diss. University of Toronto, 1998.

Reuß, Roland et al. *Franz Kafka Ausgabe.* Frankfurt: Stroemfeld/Roter Stern, 1995ff.

Solecki, Sam, ed. *Imagining Canadian Literature: The Selected Letters of Jack McClelland.* Toronto: Key Porter, 1998.

Creativity:
An Interview with Margaret Atwood[*]

Gabriele Metzler (University of Education, Freiburg)

*A*T THE END OF *MARCH 1994, Margaret Atwood visited Germany for a few days, stopping over at Frankfurt, Hamburg, and Berlin. One early Sunday afternoon, she let herself be led away from Frankfurt to the scenic "Bergstraße," which, somewhat unfortunately, was about one week short of breaking out in blossoms all over. Being an imaginative person, Margaret Atwood imagined the coming bloom and then soon focused, amongst other things, on advertisements for a concert by the German rock group "Die Toten Hosen," a name she found hilarious (cf. interview below).*

The following quickly improvised interview took place very early the next morning, during breakfast in Atwood's hotel in Frankfurt. We thank Margaret Atwood for very spontaneously fitting yet another date into her truly breathtaking schedule during her short stay in Germany. We sincerely hope that it did not spoil her breakfast!

GM: First a question about your novel *The Handmaid's Tale*. You once said, "There is nothing in the book that hasn't already happened. All things described in the book people have already done to each other" — so singular phenomena, that is well-known or known facts, do not make up a work of art, but rather a combination of them? And the next question: Does the process of creativity then resemble the devising of a mosaic?

MA: Only up to a point. No, I don't think so. What I said about *The Handmaid's Tale* applied only to the plot and the events, but then there is a whole other part to the book which is the interior monologue. That has to do with the experiencing of the events rather than the fact itself. It's how the fact feels to a human being. So that part is not like a mosaic.

[*] This is a slightly shortened version of an interview first published in the *Zeitschrift für Kanada-Studien* 15.1 (1995), 143–50.

GM: But then you have to have the feeling first so that you can give your characters that feeling, so that you know how they feel.

MA: I think a lot of novel writing comes from the childhood playing of games and the assumption of roles, and if we watch children playing you will hear them say: "You'll be the mother" or "You'll be the maid" or "I will be the leader" and then they change the roles, they take turns playing out these roles, and you can see that they indulge in a lot of imitation and mimicry. What they are doing is they are acting how they think the mother would act or how they think the leader would behave, and then the other people have to act out the other role: how they think the follower would behave, or how they think the bandit would behave or whatever it is. Children do this all the time, they do it unconsciously. So it's really telling a story. You do the same thing, you enter into the story. There is nothing very mysterious about it.

GM: So do you think artists *during their lifetime* feel and behave in a comparable manner to children, or they don't lose ...

MA: They don't lose the ability to imagine. And a lot of what people do in their later lives is also role-playing. They act in a way that they think a doctor should act or they act in a way that they think a businessman should act. They are playing out the role of the businessman or the role of the doctor. And part of what you are probably trying to do is to get them to expand their role definition so that they can act with more flexibility; that a businessman does not just put on a suit and sit behind a desk, he also does these other things. What you're trying to do is to give these people permission to expand their roles and play them more imaginatively. But it's not just artists who role-play, everybody does. They behave in manners that they feel are appropriate and they've learned those manners. . . . In other words, rather than confining themselves to one role, they — certain kinds of artists — have the ability to take on more than one role or to imagine what it is like to be another person. But everybody needs this ability. I have a book on negotiations which is called *Getting to Yes Without Backing Down*. It's published by Penguin and it's by a group of people who work on nothing but negotiations. They're called "The Harvard Negotiating Team," and one of the first things they tell you is "Try to imagine what it is like to be the other person." In other words, the United States should try to imagine what it is like to be Saddam Hussein. Because if you can see the problem from the point of view of the other person, you have a much better chance of resolving it. And that is the use of your imagination, to be somebody else.

GM: So, you think that the origins of creativity are not inheritance or socialization or lack of something else?

MA: All children are creative. Some to a greater degree, but they all have this and it's how they learn. If you watch a child, all children sing, all children experiment with language, all children draw, all children role-play, all children tell stories. It seems to be a part of child development and if you remove this from the child, the child's growth will be stunted. So, let us just take it as a given that all children are creative and then ask: What causes some people to continue to be creative and what stops other people? Probably we'll find in everybody's life a little corner where they keep their creativity; maybe it's gardening. . . .

GM: Regarding *The Handmaid's Tale*, did you have that idea of writing a negative utopia first, and did you then collect the facts systematically?

MA: No.

GM: Or were there all these facts which led you to the idea of creating the Gilead system?

MA: Neither one. I think that when you have ideas they come out of a lot of work or experience that you may have done earlier without thinking it was going to lead to that. For instance, at one point in my life, I studied very intensively the American Puritans of the seventeenth century and in another period of my life I read quite intensively a very large number of utopias and dystopias. But I did that many years before. I first read George Orwell's *1984* when I was fourteen — without thinking, "Now I am going to write a negative utopia." So, what happens, I think, with the creative idea is that a lot of work that you may have done before comes together at a certain point, and any scientist will tell you this as well. Archimedes would not have had his eureka experience in the bathtub if he had not been thinking about physical principles. Newton would not have had his intuition about gravity when the apple fell on his head if he hadn't been thinking about it. In other words, you don't have creative ideas about things that you never think about.

GM: So it's not like a flash of lightning, it's a gradual process?

MA: No, it could be a flash of lightning, but it's a flash of lightning connected with what you've already been doing. I'm never going to have a brilliant mathematical intuition because I don't deal with mathematics. On the other hand, Einstein wasn't a very good poet. In fact, he probably wasn't a poet at all.

GM: Do you design your plot elaborately before you start to write?

MA: No.

GM: Not like a diagram?

MA: No.

GM: Do you see your characters visually?

MA: Yes.

GM: Do you draw them?

MA: Do I draw them? Not much. You can tell I can see them visually because I describe them visually. But any novelist will do this; you always hear what the people look like.

GM: You develop the plot during the process of writing?

MA: Yes. If I were a writer of murder mysteries I'd have to know what the plot was before I begin because — as Edgar Allan Poe said — all mysteries are written backwards. You have to know who done it before you begin. Then you can plant the clues as to who the murderer is. You have to know in advance who is the murderer. So when you begin a novel you know some things about the characters, but I don't like to know too much because then it gets boring to write it. So I don't write murder mysteries. The end would be too predictable, because I already know it.

GM: When you are writing a novel, do you start from the beginning?

MA: No, usually not. Sometimes I do, sometimes I don't. I'll often write a part that then migrates somewhere else in the book. With *The Handmaid's Tale* it began with the hanging scene, which is now quite towards the back of the book. If you watch two-year-olds playing in a sand table, it's much the same thing. They arrange something, they dig it out, they rearrange it, they take elements that they have and make something out of it. People mystify creativity a lot. They make it into a very mysterious process. Partly it is mysterious. We don't know where we got our ideas, they just come to us, etc. But it's not some very rare esoteric thing that only a few people have.

GM: Are there different phases during the process of writing? For instance, a high concentration phase combined with a withdrawal from human relations, from life in general?

MA: That's a very romantic thought. Occasionally you find that in the biographies of men. They are able to do this because they have somebody else who is doing the dishes for them and the laundry and preparing the meals. Sometimes I go off by myself for short periods of time. I wrote part of *The Robber Bride* spending a week in a log cabin with no electricity. And I go to other countries to write, but withdrawal from human relations — no, you can't do that if you have a family.

GM: But sometimes men say that they wrote a book in one stormy night. For instance, Rilke. He said that he wrote a book [*Die Weise von Liebe und Tod des Cornets Christoph Rilke*] in one stormy night, which is not true because there are three really different versions.

MA: Well, he may have written the first draft in one stormy night. Like Rider Haggard said, he wrote *She* in six weeks, etc., etc. Obviously you have periods when you are working more quickly than in other periods. But so it is with any kind of human endeavor.

GM: Do you sometimes suffer when you're writing?

MA: This is another romantic idea. Everybody suffers anyway. It's not just artists who suffer. Artists articulate suffering, but that doesn't mean that other people don't suffer. The reason that people turn to certain kinds of music and poetry is that those kinds of music and poetry articulate what they themselves are feeling. I once had a young writer say to me: "In order to be a writer, do I have to go out and suffer?" And I said, "Don't worry about it. You get the suffering anyway. You don't have to go out looking for it."

GM: Goethe once said, "Mir gab ein Gott zu sagen, was ich leide." God gave me the gift to say how I suffer.

MA: Yes, but notice that it was the gift of saying, not the gift of suffering.

GM: So you wouldn't say that there are clear-cut phases in the process of writing?

MA: The thing about people who do this a lot is that they don't usually think much about how they do it. It's other people who are interested in analyzing creativity, not creative people. So I suppose you could discover this from looking at the journals of some artists. But I don't think that you can necessarily say — in a way that applies to all creative artists — first you do this, then you do this, and after that you do this. Obviously, first I write a first draft, then I revise it. In other words, you can't revise it before you have written it. So there are some things that logically follow. Then you think about the cover design, etc. I think one generalization you can make is that in order for a new idea to come you need a certain amount of empty space in your life. Someone who is continuously occupied with many small details is unlikely to have the space for a new idea to come into their life, and often the work ethic interferes with creative ideas because the work ethic says that every minute of our time has to be filled with work that we do. Well, for a creative person, some of the work is doing nothing. It drives other people crazy. But unless you have that moment of listening, unless you're able to listen . . . You need silence within yourself in order to listen. When you're talking all the time you're not listening. Unless you can listen, you won't hear anything.

GM: Do you think if people have lost creativity they could go, say, to the desert and live there for some days or weeks because there is silence?

MA: It's an old shamanistic technique. Well known to the prophets. Yes, of course. And it doesn't have to be the desert. The sea-shore will do or any place where they are not pursuing their ordinary round of chores. That's why people take vacations. They take vacations to have what they call "time to themselves." But what does that mean, time to yourself? It means time when you are not occupied with the small, usual concerns of your world. Some people use that time just to rest. If you want to go and renew your creativity you probably need longer than two weeks. So what you're going to be writing about is executive burn-out. People who feel that their energy has all been used up.

GM: Are you sometimes afraid to lose your creativity?

MA: No.

GM: Are you afraid of the burn-out syndrome?

MA: No. That doesn't mean that I think that it can't happen. If it does happen I will do something else.

GM: You once said: "My life is full of unfinished stories. It always has been."

MA: That's right. Yeah, but I might lose interest in finishing them.

GM: So there are thousands of ideas. What leads you then to this particular idea which you then develop in your writing?

MA: It becomes the most interesting.

GM: Do you write a daily diary?

MA: No. No, I'm very unsatisfactory in that respect. I know that everybody is constantly telling people to do this. I don't do it and I never have. I might write in a journal once a month and once every two months. That's pretty sporadic.

GM: What disturbs you most when you're working on a text?

MA: People phoning me.

GM: You already said that yesterday, thousands of phone calls.

MA: Yes. I have an assistant and she gets most of the phone calls. Before the invention of the telephone, it used to be people knocking on the door that would interrupt people.

GM: Are artists somewhat like vampires?

MA: Well, that's another romantic idea. It was much promoted in the nineteenth century. I don't think so. I mean you can be very interested in Gothic horror, you can write stories like that, you can make that equation. But I think it's only one way of looking at things. With "vampires" do you mean that they take real life and use it for their own ends? I think that might be true if nobody else ever read what they wrote. But in fact whose ends are they really using it for? If you postulate an art which has no readers or if you postulate a painting that has no viewers or a musical composition that has no listeners, then you could say that the artist was selfishly taking this material and using it only for his or her gratification, but what the artist really does is take the material, make it into something and then give it back. Vampires are not noted for giving things back.

GM: Do you believe in the concept of creative writing? Do you think that you can teach writing literature?

MA: You can do workshops that are helpful to people, but you cannot tell another person how or what to write, especially what. You can't turn a person who is really not very gifted into a person who is a genius. You can take someone who is not a very good writer and turn them into a competent writer. That's about it.

GM: What do you think could be literature's contribution to the economic world? Flexibility, for instance?

MA: The economic world makes a lot of money out of literature. Think of all the printers, designers, booksellers, etc. that it actually supports in a very simple-minded way. Papermaking, printing. But apart from that, well, every single human being has a "story of my life." Everyone has his or her own narrative, which he or she is constantly revising. By which I mean that the story you tell about yourself now is quite different from the story you told about yourself ten years ago, though it might contain the same events. Your point of view about those events has shifted and the story that you will tell about yourself ten years from now is going to be different again. Certain things are very important to you at one age that practically fade out of existence later on. Certain fears that you may have when younger disappear when you are older because the thing that you were afraid of has already happened. So, everybody is involved in narrative and to that extent, everybody is involved in fiction. Because people fictionalize themselves. They turn themselves into characters in their own dramas and they turn other people into characters in their own drama, so they fictionalize other people constantly. They project onto other people roles that they carry around inside their heads, probably left over from their childhoods and families, and they see other people in their lives as those roles. Often quite unjustly. So that by studying real fiction they might gain an insight into how they themselves are fictionalizing and they might gain more insight into what is really fiction, that is, what they've made up about other people, and what is really real, that is, what is really there. So they might gain some insight into the process that they themselves are constantly doing.

GM: So does literature serve to problematize reality as well?

MA: No, to deproblematize it. If you look at how fiction writers problematize it, you can see that it's partly an invention. Then you can see to what extent you yourself are inventing, so you can demythologize the way you're connecting your life and divest yourself of dangerous illusions which you have invented yourself. Some psychoanalysts describe what they are doing with their patient is they are "working on the patient's narrative." They are working on the patient's fiction. It is not that it's safe to become a fiction entirely because we can't do that, we will continue to fictionalize. That's what human beings do. But they can revise the fiction, so that it's a more optimistic fiction and less prone to disaster. In other words, if the scenario that you have written for yourself is a tragedy, you will constantly arrange your life so that the outcomes to your adventures will be tragic, because that is what fits your narrative. Whereas if your fiction is comic, then your episodes will probably have happier outcomes for you because you will not arrange to have these psychic disasters occur.

GM: Would you say you look at life in a rather optimistic way?

MA: I don't really — I try to avoid saying anything like that. That's what critics do. They are welcome to it. It keeps them busy. I hope they enjoy themselves, but I'm not going to do it for them.

GM: Is there anything else you want to say about creativity that I haven't asked?

MA: I think everybody should go out and get themselves a set of colored pencils and play with them, they will have fun. I think one thing about being an adult is that the role definition that we have made up for adults is that they have to be very serious and boring all the time. So I think that if we expanded the role definition of adults to include more play — and I don't mean just golf — probably people would be happier and would enjoy their stay on earth more than they do.

GM: You are tremendously encouraging ...

MA: Well, I'm just old. You get that way after a while. Especially men, they think they have to be really serious all the time. Poor things. Think of how difficult it is for them. I think women have more latitude for play, if only in the clothing department.

GM: That's a beginning.

MA: Yeah, well. People often say women are frivolous for being so interested in clothes, but I think dressing up is a form of play. Clothing yourself in different ways is again a continuation of what children do when they play dress-up.

GM: Yesterday I read in the newspaper that bikers use masks now.

MA: While they are on their bikes? Doesn't that interfere with their vision? I mean if you're wearing a mask you can't see very well. I hope these are masks that are not going to cause them to crash into things.

GM: They are masks which protect the face of the people if they maybe get into accidents. But now these masks are colorfully decorated.

MA: Well, they always have been very interested in decorating their bikes and in creative leather work. Yes, so it's costume and outing, a lot of it. And that's what rock music is, too. I mean you can't say it's the music. Most of the music is pretty horrible and repetitive, but what people are drawn to is the theater. What do the "Dead Trousers" wear?

GM: Who?

MA: The "Dead Trousers." Remember we saw "Die Toten Hosen?"

GM: Oh . . . Black leather clothes.

MA: Black leather, yes.

GM: And very crazy hairdos ...

MA: A lot of gel.

GM: Yes.

MA: Yes, well, a theatrical dress like that is assumed to differentiate those people from the suit and tie worker role and therefore to say, we're expressing things that you aren't allowed to express during the work day.

GM: I think men are very creative in the military.

MA: You mean in the costumes?

GM: Yes.

MA: Well, they used to be. Yes, and they still are, although their battle dress of course is utilitarian, it's camouflage. What amazes me is that the military uniforms of the eighteenth century were very counterproductive. If you dress in red and light blue, you are a very visible target. So, I think, the other reason for a uniform is so that you can tell who is on your side and who isn't. So that even the rock music thing is a uniform that allows us to say, these people belong to this tribe and they are different from those people over there who are wearing those suits. The suit people also think, we belong to this tribe, we are the proper people, we have on our ties and those other people are not proper.

...

MA: This is my workbook that I carry around and I will show you a manuscript. This is a manuscript. There's another one. There is more of it. Sometimes I start at the back. This is the beginning of an essay that I'm doing. There are some notes to it. You can see how messy it is. Not very orderly. On the other hand, that's how people work.

Working with Margaret Atwood

Ellen Seligman (Toronto)

Ellen Seligman is Editorial Director of Fiction at McClelland & Stewart, Toronto.

THE DISTINCTION BETWEEN Margaret Atwood the writer and the public persona, who has given so generously of her time in Canada and elsewhere on behalf of writers and national cultural issues, is particularly meaningful. It is not the recognition that there is a distinction between the artist and the celebrity writer, which is hardly a surprise to anyone. Rather, it is the nature of this distinction, how it comments on the power and calling of Margaret Atwood's own deeply private creative realm, as well as on the degree of discipline and savvy she must possess. Her skill at maintaining a workable balance, while giving so much through her art and her deeds, should never be underestimated.

With a degree of delicious secrecy unusual to most writers, Margaret Atwood does not discuss her work in progress with her publishers, perhaps with anyone. She will give no hints as to the shape or nature of her current manuscript other than to talk about its progress in general, and then, timed it seems perfectly with the publishers' own scheduling considerations for future lists, she will alert us to her delivery date — a date she has never missed.

When, and on the day we've been told to expect it, a new manuscript is put into our hands — into mine, Nan Talese's, and Liz Calder's simultaneously and in Toronto (where we eagerly hole up in our respective hotel rooms, or, in my case, at home, to read and then discuss together with the author and her agent, Phoebe Larmore) — we literally have no idea what awaits us in the manuscript, other than the very good likelihood that we will once again be taken aback, in all the right ways, by Margaret Atwood's consummate artistry, by her ability to weave anew a rich and multilayered narrative, whatever her subject and chosen time frame.

To journey through the intricate labyrinth of language, theme, character, and story an author constructs, exploring it from the inside out, not only as a reader but as nitpicker and linguistic psychoanalyst, and later to move through the text with the author, is an experience like no other. It can be wonderfully dynamic, intensely focused, often very rewarding. The first time I edited a book by Margaret Atwood (this was *Cat's Eye*, 1988) I admit to having initially felt somewhat daunted. But, when I sat down with Atwood to discuss my comments, it seemed that the dialogue we had was a good one, that I seemed to be talking about her book in terms that she recognized (not always the case in an author-editor dialogue, and a clear kiss-of-death scenario when this particular connection does not exist). It was a great relief to me, needless to say, that we could communicate well, and no doubt to her. I had not known Margaret Atwood before, except perfunctorily, and I was struck then, when I first began working with her, as I continue to be, by her quicksilver intelligence, her playfully wicked humor and sense of fun, her extreme perfectionism and professionalism.

Over the years, with each subsequent book, and during our sometimes day-long editorial sessions reviewing the manuscript together page by page, at her home or in McClelland & Stewart's offices, we have discussed all manner of things, from the psychological motivation of a particular character to the signposting of the passage of time to the name of a particular piece in a game of Monopoly, down to the pros and cons of the serial comma. At times when I have just begun to sidle up to a specific point in the text and raise a question or comment, she quickly anticipates what I intend, and, even in instances where we might not agree, she is never less than totally responsive to points I've raised.

Margaret Atwood has a good eye for type and design and likes to be involved at all stages of the book's production. For example, she envisioned and then supplied the intricate quilt patterns, carefully transcribed, which appear on the section titles for *Alias Grace*, and it was she who led us to the haunting portrait by Dante Gabriel Rossetti, which bears an uncanny resemblance to the character of Grace Marks as we imagine her through Atwood's prose, and which came to be used on the covers of numerous editions of *Alias Grace*.

There is a building sense of excitement and anticipation as we look forward to the next manuscript from Margaret Atwood. Based on what's gone before, we have good reason to count on her to dazzle us with a book that, in its very particular way, turns us around — to a way of looking back at ourselves and the world through which we navigate, to something which has probably been there all along if only we'd known where to find it.

Charted and Uncharted Courses

Nan A. Talese (New York)

Nan A. Talese is Publisher and Editorial Director of Nan A. Talese / Doubleday, New York.

IN THE 24 YEARS I HAVE BEEN Margaret Atwood's editor in the United States, I have enjoyed a relationship with her and her work that is not like that with any other writer. I have before me an enigmatic chart of her progress on a new book. There will be 11 "sections" and most of the boxes which follow each "section" have been x'd through. As of July, there are seven almost empty boxes. Seven chapters to be completed; five seem not yet to have been started, but the last three chapters — the whole of the 11th "section" — are done. The subject of the book is unknown to me — it has not even been hinted at — nor will it be known until the manuscript is before me. I get bulletins from the author from time to time informing me what page she has completed, but that is the extent of the updates. On July 5th, she was on page 478.

But what I do know is that when the manuscript arrives I will be surprised, delighted, enriched — and it will probably make me both laugh and cry. For Atwood is a writer with a wicked sense of humor and an insight into human behavior which goes laser-deep. While she has been taken up by feminists, the truth is that she is equally observant of men and women, and is remarkably unjudgmental. She also relishes ambiguity, not to obscure, but to bring the reader's mind to bear upon the scene.

Our exchanges, once I have read the manuscript, inevitably take an uncharted course. Atwood is interested in my reaction to the novel; we talk about the characters, the story, and the underlying nuances. I tell her what delights me, what I find confusing or not logical to my mind. And then she listens, rarely attempting to explain. I remember how with one particular novel, after I began to read, I got up and pulled a soft white blanket out of the cupboard in the Toronto hotel room in which I was staying, and settled onto the sofa, knowing I was in for a delicious treat. The pleasure of marvelous storytelling with a cast of fascinating characters who simply pull you into their world was evident from the outset. It was a long book and it took me a few days to read, because I like to think about a book during the day, to explore the ideas, not just take it in one gulp. We had spoken several times about the novel before I was finished, but I felt that Atwood had spent less time on the last section than on the previous ones. I telephoned her just before going to the airport.

"What was it that bothered you?" she asked.

I explained, and told her I had made some notes and would send them to her.

"No," she said. "Keep them. I am going to be in France for two months and will be working on the book."

When she returned, I read the final draft and found that she had addressed each "problem" I had had. There was still one scene that I was not sure was supposed to be real or hallucinatory, and I suggested the readers might not understand. She paused for a while and then said, "I don't care."

Quintessential Atwood, the consummate artist, sure of her own vision, willing to test and not let things be too easy, somewhat mischievous with that enigmatic smile starting at the corners of her mouth. In two and a half months, I expect to begin another adventure from the mind of Margaret Atwood.

(New York, August 1999)

On Loyalty and Love

Liz Calder (London)

Liz Calder is Publisher of Bloomsbury Publishing, London.

My GREATEST DEBTS TO MARGARET ATWOOD are in the rarefied realms of loyalty and love. I first published her work in 1980 just after I had joined Jonathan Cape as Editorial Director. *Life Before Man* was one of my first acquisitions at that house and marked the beginning of a relationship that has lasted twenty years. At that time Margaret Atwood's critical stock in the UK was high but she was not widely known to the reading public. This, of course, all changed with the publication of her superb body of work during the 1980s and 1990s and with the Virago publication of her books in paperback. Her audience now is enormous and each new book is eagerly awaited and avidly devoured. Not long ago I watched hundreds of people being turned away from the Royal Festival Hall as she spoke and read to a thousand spellbound seat-holders.

But it was with the publication of her poetry collection, *True Stories*, in 1982, that she shot the fatal dart in my direction. Admittedly, I was that year in that dicey state known as "in love" and there are poems in that collection which cut to the quick like no others I know. For instance, in a poem called "Nothing" we read:

> Nothing like love to put blood
> back in the language,

or again in "Variation on the Word *Sleep*":

> I would like to be the air
> that inhabits you for a moment
> only. I would like to be that unnoticed
> & that necessary.

The question of loyalty comes to the fore at every publication. I can think of few other authors who have remained so faithful to their editors and agents. These relationships are cemented by mutual trust and

292 ON LOYALTY AND LOVE

are in marked contrast to much of what happens in pursuit of fame and fortune in the book business. In 1986, when I left Cape and joined three others to found Bloomsbury Publishing, the question of "my" authors and what they would do inevitably arose. I cannot remember a moment of greater joy in my professional life than when someone handed me a scrap of paper at the Booksellers' Conference in Eastbourne in 1988 on which was written "We've got the Atwood." I still have the scrap of paper. *Cat's Eye* was the novel and remains the one I am likely to take on any desert island.

It has been a source of wonder to me to have worked with a writer whose books and characters so vividly reflect her incisive, wise, and witty mind and her generous heart.

Representing Margaret Atwood

Phoebe Larmore (Venice, California)

Phoebe Larmore has been Atwood's literary agent for some 30 years.

I HAVE BEEN MARGARET ATWOOD'S LITERARY AGENT for almost 30 years. Our relationship started shortly after the publication of her first novel *The Edible Woman* and for me it had an auspicious beginning. It began when on a weekend holiday in Montreal in 1969 I purchased a copy of the novel and read it as I traveled back to New York City. Captivated by it, on Monday morning, I undertook to find out whether its author had an agent. So I telephoned the US publisher, Atlantic-Little Brown, and learned the book's editor was Peter Davison. His phone line was busy, so I left a message. As I was putting down the phone receiver, a call came in on my second line. Incredibly, it was Mr. Davison, calling to ask if I would consider becoming the agent for a talented young writer he was publishing named Margaret Atwood.

As I reflect now on the past three decades of my representation of this extraordinary novelist, poet, and essayist, I am flooded by rich memories, for it has been quite a journey we have been on together, a journey which has been a central one in my life. *Surfacing* was the first novel I represented, and it was after I read it as a manuscript that I fully realized the enormous talent of Margaret Atwood. I vividly remember that day in New York in 1971, for it was shortly after I had turned 30 and had opened my own agency. The impact of this poignant and powerful novel was so immense that I could not contain my reactions within the walls of my apartment/office. So I went outside to the city streets where I walked many miles to fully grasp that what I had read was a brilliant novel destined to be a classic and that being Margaret Atwood's agent was an immense responsibility as well as a rare gift.

Through the years, I have continued to consider it an immense privilege and challenge to be the agent for Margaret, or Peggy as she is known to me and the others who comprise her inner circle of family, friends, and colleagues. Year by year, title by title, I have dedicated myself to shepherding and championing her work within the publishing community, to laboring to expand her reading audience throughout the world, and to obtaining for her as much financial recompense as possible, so that she could be not only financially secure but also well rewarded for her creations. Thus, it has been with great pride and enormous pleasure that I have watched as her books have become increasingly widely read and critically acclaimed. So that now on this the 60th anniversary of her birth, it is as it should be — Margaret Atwood is internationally acknowledged as one of the most important writers of our times.

Once not so very long ago, she wrote me a valentine verse thanking me for being her agent. It is one of my most prized possessions and as I conclude this brief reflection on our extraordinary relationship, it is a poetic valentine I wish I had the ability to write—to thank her for being my client and such an author supreme. She has not only chronicled all our lives and times with her magnificent stories, poems, and essays, she has also personally etched herself deeply within our hearts. For Margaret Atwood is not only a great writer, she is also a great woman, and thus I have been greatly blessed that it has been my fate to be her literary agent and her friend these many years.

Assisting Margaret Atwood

Sarah Cooper (Toronto)

Sarah Cooper is Assistant to Margaret Atwood.

Basically, it is my job to simplify Margaret's life so that she has time to write. Under that general category comes a whole range of activity, from research and correspondence to banking and book-keeping. It is a full-time job: just to give you a glimpse of the tip of the iceberg, consider the fact that we get between 20 and 50 pieces of mail a day. Somehow, I have to whittle that stack down to a reasonable amount that will leave Margaret time to do other things, like write books, and read them, and to visit her mother.

Being assistant to Margaret Atwood has made it really clear to me that one of the problems with being famous is that you get asked to do way more than any one person could ever actually accomplish. Even though Margaret is very willing to spend a lot of her time helping out with various causes and interests, from charities to research projects, she cannot do everything. My job is to help her keep a balance between all of the various demands on her time.

It is not only a privilege but a pleasure to do so. I believe very strongly in the value of what she does, in the value of stories, particularly those as well-wrought as hers. That belief is very satisfyingly reinforced by the people who write to her thanking her for the difference she has made in their lives. And Margaret herself is a pleasure to work with: she is generous, considerate, and, perhaps most important, fun!

Reminiscing

Helmut Frielinghaus (New York)

Helmut Frielinghaus was editor for Atwood's first publisher in Germany, Claassen Verlag in Düsseldorf (1979–1988).

IN 1985 THE GERMAN EDITION of Atwood's first novel *The Edible Woman* (1969) was published in German as *Die eßbare Frau*. We know from Margaret Atwood herself that she had written *The Edible Woman* some twenty years earlier at the age of twenty-four, before the new women's movement was even in sight in North America and Europe. Those who remember the early sixties, or know how much they at first resembled the fifties, will have an idea of how much Margaret Atwood risked in striking out on her own with her first novel. What she had written was something new; it was extremely intelligent and witty, but that did not distract from the fact that it was also aggressive and challenging. In the preface she wrote in 1979 in Edinburgh for the English edition, and which I included in the German edition, she comments on the novel in one of her typical, seemingly funny and yet serious statements: "Its more self-indulgent grotesqueries are perhaps attributable to the youth of the author, though I would prefer to think that they derive instead from the society by which she found herself surrounded."

In this preface Atwood also recalls how hesitantly and almost accidentally her Canadian publisher decided to publish the novel after putting it on hold for four years. He felt pushed because in the meantime the author had gained a reputation for herself as a poet in the English-speaking world. The impact and significance of *The Edible Woman* became apparent much later, only after the novel — in the Virago paperback edition — had turned into a big, lasting success in the second half of the seventies. In the English women's movement, *The Edible Woman* was considered for a while one of the cult texts.

In the Federal Republic of Germany, Margaret Atwood was published by Claassen Verlag, then in Düsseldorf, from 1979 onwards. The publisher and editor-in-chief, Arnulf Conradi, had recognized the significance of the author and bought the German rights for all the novels and short story collections by Atwood that had been published up to that point. *Surfacing* was published by Claassen in 1979 as *Der lange Traum*, *Life Before Man* in 1980 as *Die Unmöglichkeit der Nähe*, and in 1982 *Bodily Harm* followed as *Verletzungen*. When Conradi left Claassen to go to S. Fischer in Frankfurt, he persuaded the author to remain with Claassen and me, his successor — a generous act of friendship, supported by the agents and friends of the author, Ruth Liepman, Ruth Weibel, and Eva Koralnik of Liepman AG Zurich, who have played the role of fairy godmothers. They had been among the first to recognize "Peggy's" talent, the high literary quality coupled with her ability to amuse and entertain, which was already apparent in her early novels.

With the assistance of the Zurich Agency and generous financial aid from the Canada Council of Ottawa as well as friendly support from the Culture Department of the Canadian Embassy, I moved in two directions over the next few years: back to the author's beginnings and ahead. In other words, I published her early novels and short stories — one after the other — in German, and at the same time I brought out her new books in German as soon as possible after their publication in English. Of those, *The Handmaid's Tale*, the German title being *Der Report der Magd* (1987), became a huge success in Germany. When I had to leave Claassen in 1988, Margaret Atwood went to S. Fischer where she rejoined Arnulf Conradi, whom she followed once again when Conradi founded his Berlin Verlag in Berlin, Germany.

I recall with great pleasure *Lady Oracle*, published in German in 1984 as *Lady Orakel*, and I have to confess that I asked myself at the time whether the book was based on the experience of the author or, to be more precise (for the book is, of course, full of the author's experiences), whether Margaret Atwood — like her protagonist Joan Foster, or like Doris Lessing and Joyce Carol Oates — had published books, possibly even trashy novels for the mass market, under a nom-de-plume. I should have realized that she had done precisely that with *Lady Oracle*, right in front of her readers, under her own name *and* under the nom-de-plume of Joan Foster — a more intelligent and attractive variant of the game of being oneself and somebody else at the same time, which authors find so seductive. *Lady Oracle* is an entertaining novel and at the same time a clever "essay" translated into a novel-plot, full of irony and addressing questions of identity and the imagination, of the invention of characters and fates, of the act of writing.

In celebration of the fiftieth anniversary of the Claassen Verlag, a volume of Atwood's poems was published in German under the title of *Wahre Geschichten* (*True Stories*). In order to demonstrate the wealth of her austere lyrical coloring, I had the poems translated by five German poets and translators. I realized in the process, and later when I edited her extremely funny very short texts, *Murder in the Dark*, published in Germany as *Die Giftmischer*, how dense, concentrated, and sarcastic Margaret Atwood's use of language could be. Right from the beginning, as early as *The Edible Woman*, another quality becomes apparent, which is characteristic of her narrative prose and essays as well as her poetry — the quick changes in the language, sometimes only for an instant, to irony, anger, maliciousness, and sarcasm, or, the other way round, from serenity to the humor of a quite unchallengeable statement.

I met Margaret Atwood in the mid-eighties, in Hamburg and Berlin. In Hamburg she was attending an international PEN Congress. In the evening, after a reading, I accompanied her to a writers' reception hosted by Fritz J. Raddatz. With great charm, he honored her by going down on his knees in front of her, but after casting her eye over the assembled guests, Margaret Atwood declared that she was too tired for such a party. Later on, in the bar of the Hotel Atlantic, she told ghost stories from her English or Scottish family.

Only recently, in 1998, I saw Margaret Atwood again, this time in New York, at the 92nd Street Y, where she was to read from her latest novel, *Alias Grace*. She came onto the stage, beautiful and radiant, looking the way Isolde Ohlbaum had photographed her in the early eighties — as if the imaginary veil had been lifted for a brief moment, for this one evening. She read only briefly, she was more inclined towards telling stories, and she told them, amusingly and wittily, the way she writes, and her audience loved it.

(New York, July 1999; translated by Susanne Höbel)

On Translating Margaret Atwood

Brigitte Walitzek (Berlin)

Brigitte Walitzek has translated several of Margaret Atwood's books into German.

I HAVE TRANSLATED SOME OF Margaret Atwood's books and will, hopefully, have the opportunity to work on her newest one, which I am really looking forward to. Nevertheless, I cannot say much about translation problems. Of course, there are Canadianisms which do pose problems, for example in a text Atwood wrote on "The North." Talking to US-American students, I found that she uses a whole list of words they are not familiar with. *Mackinaw* is the first one. I looked it up. A heavy, double-sided material for coats; a thick, short, double-breasted plaid coat. There is no word in German for the thing. Do I explain, sounding like the dictionary I consulted, or do I just leave the expression? On the other hand there is *moose*. I do not know why these American students have problems with that, it seems like an ordinary enough word, and the German word for it is "Elch," which everybody knows. The (fairly far-fetched) alternative would be "Karibu," which is perhaps not as well known, but the snag is that a moose is not a caribou. *Loon*, a very Canadian bird, would be another example. In German I can take my pick and translate it either as "Seetaucher" or as "Eistaucher" (which other Atwood-translators before me decided on, which is why I choose it too). But the feelings that Canadians obviously connect with these loons are not conveyed by "Eistaucher." As Margaret Atwood herself puts it: "How do you tell that to people who don't know it because they've never had any to begin with?" Yes, how?

Apart from these localisms there are the general problems that every translation poses for every translator, namely, how do you put whatever is written down into a form that does justice to the original? And I cannot analytically explain why I do things a certain way in order to achieve that end. I do them because I have the *feeling* that that is the best way. Of course I go over a book three, four times, of course I go to the library again and again because I cannot find certain expressions, sayings, quotes (oh, those quotes!), of course I write and rewrite and rewrite again before I finally get that *feeling* of rightness, if I get it at all; but I am not aware of any real reason why a particular version and not the one before (or after) is the one that finally gets sent off to the publisher.

The difference with Margaret Atwood novels is that that *feeling* comes more easily to me than with most other books (at least that is what I think, although it may sound a bit conceited). Or, to put it another way, if there are problems, I do not mind them, because I love her books so much.

The J-Stroke

Arnulf Conradi (Berlin)

Arnulf Conradi is the Publisher of Berlin and Siedler Verlag and has been Atwood's German editor and publisher for many years.

IN THE SUMMER OF 1990 I spent two weeks with my sons Lenni and Malte, then thirteen and ten, in a lodge in Ontario Provincial Park. The place, called Killarney Lodge, consisted of two or three main buildings and about twenty cottages, all log structures, strung along the shoreline of the Lake of Two Rivers. Those two rivers feeding into the lake were important, because they ensured that you could paddle your canoe out of the lake and into others of equal beauty and interest, and on into others and others, if you had the stamina and were not afraid to miss the excellent five-course-dinner in the evening.

My sons loved the canoes and the daily trips and, of course, swimming in water that was so clear you could drink it. But most of all we wanted to watch birds, and a canoe is an ideal vehicle for birdwatching. If you stop paddling you can approach the bird — let's say an American Bittern — noiselessly, just gliding through the calm water, very slowly, driven gently by the last strokes. We were all equipped with binoculars, we had a book on the birds of Eastern America, and we were totally happy. The American Bittern in question was a strange bird. This species has an interesting method of camouflage: it tries to melt into the surrounding bushes and reeds and arundinaceous plants by stretching head and neck straight up and standing totally still. In other words, the bird tries to look like the reeds and usually succeeds in doing so. A bittern is hard to detect. This one, however — it might have been a young bird — did not have a reliable footing. Both feet rested on a wet, blackish stump of wood, but one of them kept slipping off. It was a very noticeable movement, which it tried to correct several times: it drew back the foot that had slipped and reverted to its inertness, neck, head, and beak pointing to the sky. Then the foot slipped again. This happened three times, then the bittern gave up, looked at us for a moment, and flew off.

I write this down with a smile. The whole thing was enormously funny. There was an expression of deep embarrassment in the desperate look it cast at us before taking to the air. I swear there was, and the boys immediately agreed. The bittern was plainly disgusted at its own poor performance. This was a cause of great hilarity whenever we mentioned it in later years. You will say that ascribing human feelings to animals is called "anthropomorphism" and constitutes a grave offense in the world of serious ornithology, but I cannot help myself. That bittern definitely was embarrassed.

To my comfort I found a rather reassuring example of the sin of anthropomorphism in a great, probably the greatest, German ornithologist, Naumann, who lived in the second half of the nineteenth century in Sachsen-Anhalt, and wrote and illustrated the famous twelve-volume *Birds of Europe*, which even a millionaire could not buy any more. It was the essay on the European cuckoo. This cuckoo smuggles its egg into the nests of smaller birds, warblers for instance. Nobody should believe, Naumann writes, that the birds who raise a cuckoo instead of their own offspring do not know that this big young bird, often twice or thrice their size, is not theirs. They know very well it is not a young warbler. But now that they have adopted it, what can they do, let it starve? Naumann was serious about this. Isn't that deeply amusing as well?

Everybody knows that Margaret Atwood and her husband Graeme Gibson are passionate birdwatchers, so you all know that I have been talking about and to them all along. They suggested that I go to Killarney Lodge with my boys, and they came to visit us there and spent a night with us, and Margaret tried to instruct me in the art of the J-stroke. Even before that she had sent two warm sweaters for the boys to the Lodge. She did not trust me at all, not even to keep them warm. And she warned me: "The Canadian wilderness is unforgiving!" I was European; I did not know the first thing about nature.

The J-stroke is designed to propel the canoe and to keep it on course at the same time. It is one of those wonderfully intelligent and simple inventions that have never failed to earn my total admiration. When you paddle a canoe you have to sit on one side of the boat in the back, and if you simply paddle you drive the light craft to the left if you sit on the right side, and to the right if you choose the left side. To correct this slight deviation at every stroke, which adds up to create a curve you do not want, you press the blade of the paddle inwards, towards the canoe, steering it for just a fraction at the end of your stroke, working against its tendency to veer off course, away from the paddle-side. If you do this correctly, and it is not as easy as it sounds, you can propel yourself in a straight line wherever you want to go — towards an island or back to the Lodge or into the reeds to embarrass a bittern.

It is a simple maneuver but a subtle one at the same time, and in a speech in Frankfurt during the book fair I once compared it cautiously to Margaret's art of storytelling — always driving energetically forward, but with a twist to keep the story in line. I added back then that I knew Margaret was tired of traveling, but that there was one trip she would have to make one day: the one to Stockholm. And I hope we will all be there with her.

Margaret Atwood in Statements by Fellow Writers

[The first five statements are reprinted here from other sources. The subsequent statements were written for this volume.]

Superlative. — Angela Carter

Margaret Atwood is the quiet Mata Hari, the mysterious, violent figure . . . who pits herself against the ordered, too-clean world like an arsonist.
— Michael Ondaatje

In a century shaken by gender politics, these seminal poems [Power Politics] *remind us of the deepest kind of change. Love is the real power, demanding — and offering — no less than the transformation of self. Atwood dares to imagine realpolitik at the heart of love's mystery. It is a measure of her achievement that, over decades, these masterful poems continue to speak with undiminished accuracy.*
— Anne Michaels

Power Politics *changed the definition of the love poem, the long poem, and, I believe, the course of Canadian poetry. It cuts like a laser beam. It goes beyond sexual politics into the dark heart of a tottering global village.*
— Phyllis Webb

Symons, and a lot of others, simply can't stand the fact that Atwood is unapologetically — and successfully — who she is and what she knows. And they can't stand the fact that she writes the best sentences currently being written in this country, and that she is a world-class writer who remains world class no matter what she thinks, speaks, or writes about.

I trust Atwood's skills and her motives because she's earned that trust, just as I've come to trust and follow her lead in the arena of cultural and sexual politics. Rather than pick her apart or view her achievements with envy, we ought to be trying to talk her into running for prime minister — providing it would allow her enough time to go on writing.
—Brian Fawcett

Margaret Atwood is first and foremost the English-Canadian literary genius of my generation. Her novels, stories, poems, and social criticisms have defined English Canada in a way that moved us culturally to a new stage of literary development. Atwood, along with a few others, made the world aware that a Canadian place is a specific somewhere that is profound, banal, interesting, tragic — in a word, as human as any other town or city around the globe. The day her work is dismissed will likely be a bad omen for the writing of women and a sign that cultural envy and literary backstabbing have become more important than talent and intelligence.
— Susan Swan

If Margaret Atwood had never used the word "survival," we would read her engagements with the geographies of Canada and community and self in quite different ways. She has the uncanny vision of a prospector. She looks at the Canadian Shield (the Canadian psyche?) that we have all looked at — and she guesses the site of the vein of ore that no one guessed before. With daring accuracy she reads geologic configurations and metallic tastes and the colors of mosses and lichens. Then she dazzles us with refinements of language and story.
— Robert Kroetsch

It's hard to know where to start when trying to say something about Margaret Atwood. I'm talking about the poet here, although the fiction writer has become more famous. I guess I'd start with her wit. In many ways, it's that, the sly, intelligent way her language leads us on, then pulls the rug out from under us in many of her poems. This is not to deny the often stark emotional power of many poems, the way they deal with the pain of living, but it is to suggest that in even the most apparently personal and lyric poems, a reader always feels the sharp stab of intelligence, the sense of a very aware mind at work.

When Stephen Scobie and I were editing The Maple Laugh Forever: An Anthology of Canadian Comic Poetry, *we had one section titled "Brevity Is the Soul of Wit." Fully aware that we would get some flack for doing so, we opened the section with the epigrammatic opening quatrain to* Power Politics. *Margaret Atwood didn't question our choice, although many reviewers did. We stand by our sense then that it is a superb example of black humor. Well, we laughed, anyway.*

Atwood has been "there" for close to four decades now. As I'm sure is the case with many of my colleagues, wherever in the world I travel to talk about Canadian literature, there are many fine writers I might discuss whom my audiences do not know. But they all know Margaret Atwood and her work.

In many cases, she is what they know as Canadian literature — an honor, and a heavy burden, both of which she bears with her usual wit and grace.
— Douglas Barbour

The number of times we needed something and there she was with something I cannot tell you. She used to iron her famous hair before it was all that famous, this was in Toronto where the rivers are gone. Hardly anyone knows about the famous pajamas so I am not about to break the news here but they were sometimes red. She always knows someone who can do just the thing you need so badly that if life were to go on without her, how could it. Peggy, she is not exactly leggy, but she can move faster than you can, even when she seems to be sitting still, in a rocking chair, with a caftan, and a kitten. Can you think of anything she has not written, neither can I, and I have been around longer than you have, and it seems as if she just got here. Someone said you cannot put a comma after a first person singular, does that have anything to do with anything? She said that in French her name would be du Bois, but no one I know ever thought of calling her Whitey. If there is a heaven, I am hoping to see her there, but with my luck she will be sitting at the gate with a fountain pen and a big book. Ah, the world of literature pokes its nose in everywhere, preventing some people from being the immortal home economics teachers they could have been. Poet, that's easier to say. Novelist. Voice on the phone. Really good friend.
—George Bowering

These days, it is difficult to treat Margaret Atwood as anything other than an icon, such are her achievements in the cultural field both in Canada and abroad. But I would like to avoid terms like "icons" and "fields," with their tendency to enshrine and inter, and speak instead of the intensely lively and acutely responsive Margaret Atwood whose life as a writer we are celebrating here. The Margaret Atwood who, when she was writer-in-residence at Massey College more than a quarter century ago, gave patient, honest and encouraging advice to young, would-be writers, myself included. The Margaret Atwood who did not leave Canada to establish a literary life elsewhere, and who, in so doing, expanded and deepened the possibilities for Canadian writers everywhere. The Margaret Atwood who has so many times and with such heartening effect spoken out and acted on issues of urgent cultural, social, and political significance. And finally the Margaret Atwood who, in works from Surfacing *and* The Circle Game *to* Alias Grace *and* Morning in the Burned House, *has*

given her readers what they most require — a way of seeing and speaking that does justice to the exigencies and mysteries that make us fully human.
— Janice Kulyk Keefer

Recently, Greg Gatenby wrote me asking what my name was in the early seventies, when I lived in Toronto. He needed to look up my address in the telephone book for 1972, for his book on the homes of Toronto writers. His question took me back to those early years. It was a quiet time, an invisible time, a time before everything began. One moment stands in my memory from then. I opened the morning paper, The Globe and Mail, *and there was a big picture of Margaret Atwood with an article about how sudden fame had changed her life. That was somehow a pivotal moment for me; the kind of moment that can't exactly be described to others. My words for it now are: encouraging, inspiring. Here was a woman who made Canadian literature interesting to Canadians. Who made it possible to be a woman and a poet. Who made poetry itself newsworthy. Since then, I have been a loyal reader of Atwood, and her work has continued to encourage and inspire me. I studied her poetry in university, I read her books at home. My first publisher was The House of Anansi, which she helped found. My editor then was James Polk, her first husband. Everywhere I went, I was in the footsteps of her presence. When I became a professor, I started teaching her books. The short story, in particular, where I could show how it is possible to write from the underside of a character, and show the light of a person from within. How the cruelty of modern life can be beautiful. How the ugly insides of a person can be brought into the open and redeemed. I liked the hard edges of her writing. The cool realism and the calculated cynicism. The presence of awe in simple things like vegetables. And Margaret Atwood's career itself has the qualities of a great story. Her presence has rippled through the writing world for three decades, and she has paved the way for many poets and writers who came after. In an interview for CBC, Ann-Marie MacDonald said it for so many of us: she said "I'm lucky, I don't have to do all the groundbreaking, pathmaking work. Margaret Atwood did it for us." To that observation of MacDonald's, I can add that she has done it with grace, dignity, courage, and a special genius for the tenor of the times.*
— Kristjana Gunnars

Two moments with Margaret Atwood:
The first happened in the autumn of 1967, when Atwood was already known in Canada, but not widely in the rest of the world, as a superb poet. She and I went to a lunch-hour poetry reading at the University of Alberta in Edmonton. At one point she tilted her startling hair towards me

and whispered in my ear, "To eat an apple while someone is reading a poem aloud is utterly improper."

The second took place twenty years later, in Vancouver. We had been conversing for some time in all the general noise and dancing of a Writers' Union party, when she decided that, if I was to be the chairperson of the Union — I had been elected that afternoon — then it was essential that I know how to dance. And she would teach me. On the dance floor, after some moments of more or less inept motionlessness on my part, she abruptly stood stock-still and looked me in the eye.

"Rudy," she said, in that steady voice which so often reminds me of a distant tundra horizon, "you don't want to dance."

She was, as always, right; both times. A person of awesome intelligence and energy, of warmth and immense understanding and, above all, as it seems, limitlessly imaginative in word and image: even the memory of knowing her is an aesthetic pleasure.

— Rudy Wiebe

It's easy to appreciate the grand array of Margaret Atwood's work — the novels, the stories, the poems, in all their power and grace and variety. This work in itself has opened the gates for a recognition of Canadian writing all over the world. That's enough to be grateful for, enough for a writer to do. In fact you could pick out a favorite poem, a favorite novel, and say, that's enough, that justifies a lifetime given to writing, in a way it justifies us all.

But her life has not been given up entirely to writing, or to her own writing. She has never worked in isolation. She has read, it would seem, practically everybody who has ever published in Canada and she has never let up in her efforts to promote and sustain other writers. Some of this work is done publicly and some of it is done in ways that go unnoticed and may never be noticed, even by the people who benefit directly from it. Her generosity is not showy, but constant and practical, and I have to say that when I think of it, and put it together with her writerly gifts and achievements, it takes my breath away.

— Alice Munro

For almost thirty years, I have depended on Margaret Atwood for books that treat women as full human beings. It is still rare for writers, female or male, to depict women as intelligent, active beings with the capacity for moral choice and moral error: they are still often depicted as people whose single choice concerns the disposal of their genital organs. I count on Atwood to be brilliant, perceptive, profound, and searching, someone who does not avoid the "darker" sides of female being, the weak or wavering or

foolish. She has a great range — from poetry to a visionary fable like The Handmaid's Tale *to profound meditations like* Life Before Man. *She is a great writer, whose work will live.*
— Marilyn French

Margaret is important to me as a friend and as a fellow writer. I much admire her for her literary work, which is always so politically committed, so serious and pure, so full of audacity. I admire her as well for her generous personality, her sensibility to the human problems of the day. Her work is full of dedication, a dedication which she also shows in her personal life, where her humanity manifests itself with such strength and compassion.
— Marie-Claire Blais

Atwood (noun, verb, adjective and adverb atypical): au fond an atwood, atomic despite size, astronomical, astute, assiduous; an arrondisement of ardent images, with glimpsed aperatures of azure or antimony. Meaning can apportion alignment, alarm, alabaster, even alcove, azalea, and alligator, but more likely to arouse alleviate, averring, argentine, arabesque, or apocryphal. Definitely beyond axiomatic or aphoristic. Has been declared to possess acidulous accuracy; has been accused of upsetting apple carts. Never awry. Audible through the mutters of time. Asparagus, green and slender in sentence. Always awake, an avatar, an autograph alight with austerity and augury. Known to be a delicious arsenic, an articulate arpeggio. Contains sufficient apothegm to apocalypse. Occasionally ammonal. An adhesive acrobat; antidote to both anteriors and anthologies; anaesthetist of angels; anaphoric without repetition; astringent amputate. Ambidextrous ambassador, altruistic and allusive; affricative as air and its ahems; advocate of admeasurement; abbess of abbreviation.

Above all, an alias: for Atwood, Margaret.
— Aritha van Herk

Cartoons by and on Margaret Atwood

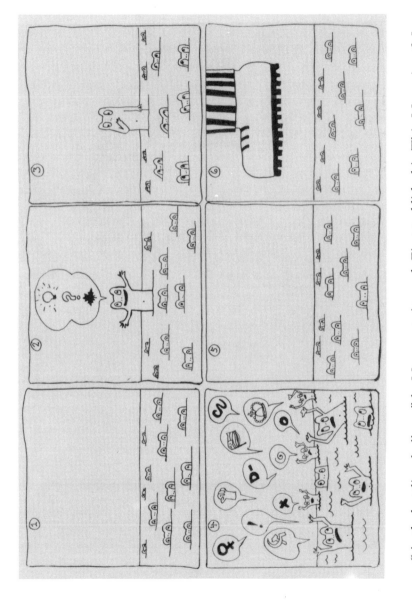

"As the battling bulb . . ." by Margaret Atwood. First published in This Magazine 9.1 (March-April 1975): 35. (Courtesy of Margaret Atwood.)

"Meanwhile the entire . . ." by Bart Gerrard (Margaret Atwood).
First published in This Magazine 9.2 (May–June 1975): 35.

"It's the confrontation . . ." by Bart Gerrard (Margaret Atwood). First published in This Magazine 10.1 (February–March 1976): 35.

"Portrait of the Artist ..." First published in The Graduate
5.1 (Fall 1977): 8–9.

Cartoon of Atwood by Charles Altman.

Cartoon of Atwood by Isaac Bickerstaff.
From the Isaac Bickerstaff fonds, Special Collections,
MacKimmie Library, University of Calgary, Calgary, Alberta.

Bibliography

Books by Margaret Atwood

Poetry

Double Persephone. Toronto: Hawkshead Press, 1961.

The Circle Game. Toronto: Anansi, 1966.

The Animals in That Country. Toronto: Oxford University Press, 1968.

The Journals of Susanna Moodie. Toronto: Oxford University Press, 1970.

Procedures for Underground. Toronto: Oxford University Press, 1970.

Power Politics. Toronto: Anansi, 1971.

You Are Happy. Toronto: Oxford University Press, 1974.

Selected Poems 1: 1965–1975. Toronto: Oxford University Press, 1976.

Two-Headed Poems. Toronto: Oxford University Press, 1978.

True Stories. Toronto: Oxford University Press, 1981.

Interlunar. Toronto: Oxford University Press, 1984.

Selected Poems 2: Poems Selected and New 1976–1986. Toronto: Oxford University Press, 1986.

Selected Poems: 1966–1984. Toronto: Oxford University Press, 1990.

Morning in the Burned House. Toronto: McClelland & Stewart, 1995.

Eating Fire: Selected Poetry, 1965–1995. London: Virago, 1998.

Novels

The Edible Woman. Toronto: McClelland & Stewart, 1969.

Surfacing. Toronto: McClelland & Stewart, 1972.

Lady Oracle. Toronto: McClelland & Stewart, 1976.

Life Before Man. Toronto: McClelland & Stewart, 1979.

Bodily Harm. Toronto: McClelland & Stewart, 1981.

The Handmaid's Tale. Toronto: McClelland & Stewart, 1985.

Cat's Eye. Toronto: McClelland & Stewart, 1988.

The Robber Bride. Toronto: McClelland & Stewart, 1993.

Alias Grace. Toronto: McClelland & Stewart, 1996.

The Blind Assassin. Toronto: McClelland & Stewart, 2000.

Short Stories

Dancing Girls and Other Stories. Toronto: McClelland & Stewart, 1977.

Bluebeard's Egg. Toronto: McClelland & Stewart, 1983.

Wilderness Tips. Toronto: McClelland & Stewart, 1991.

The Labrador Fiasco. London: Bloomsbury, 1996.

Short Prose/Prose Poetry

Murder in the Dark: Short Fictions and Prose Poems. Toronto: Coach House Press, 1983.

Good Bones. Toronto: Coach House Press, 1992.

Children's Fiction

Up In The Tree. Toronto: McClelland & Stewart, 1978.

Anna's Pet. Co-written with Joyce Barkhouse. Illustrated by Ann Blades. Toronto: James Lorimer, 1980.

For the Birds. Toronto: Douglas & McIntyre, 1990.

Princess Prunella and the Purple Peanut. Illustrations by Maryann Kovalski. Ontario: Key Porter Kids, 1995.

Criticism & Theory

Survival: A Thematic Guide to Canadian Literature. Toronto: Anansi, 1972.

Second Words: Selected Critical Prose. Toronto: Anansi, 1982.

Strange Things: The Malevolent North in Canadian Literature. Oxford: Clarendon Press, 1995.

In Search of Alias Grace: On Writing Canadian Historical Fiction. Ottawa: University of Ottawa Press, 1997.

Further Works

Days of the Rebels: 1815–1840. Toronto: Natural Science of Canada, 1977.

The New Oxford Book of Canadian Verse in English. Ed. Margaret Atwood. Toronto: Oxford University Press, 1982.

The Oxford Book of Canadian Short Stories in English. Ed. Margaret Atwood and Robert Weaver. Toronto: Oxford University Press, 1982.

The CanLit Foodbook: From Pen to Palate — *a Collection of Tasty Literary Fare*. Toronto: Totem Books, 1987.

Best American Short Stories, 1989. Ed. Margaret Atwood and Shannon Revel. Boston: Houghton Mifflin, 1989.

Barbed Lyres: Canadian Venemous Verse. Toronto: Key Porter Books, 1990.

The Poetry of Gwendolyn MacEwen. Vols. I & II. Ed. Margaret Atwood and Barry Callaghan. Toronto: Exile Ed, 1993.

A Quiet Game and Other Early Works. Ed. and annotated by Kathy Chung and Sherrill Grace, with an introduction by S. Grace and illustrations by K. Chung. Edmonton, Alberta: Juvenilia Press, 1997.

Two Solicitudes: Conversations. By Margaret Atwood and Victor-Levy Beaulieu. Toronto: McClelland & Stewart, 1998.

Books on Margaret Atwood

Beran, Carol. *Living over the Abyss: Margaret Atwood's* Life Before Man. Canadian Fiction Studies 23. Toronto: ECW Press, 1993.

Bouson, J. Brooks. *Brutal Choreographies: Oppositional Strategies and Narrative Design in the Novels of Margaret Atwood*. Amherst: University of Massachusetts Press, 1993.

Cooke, Nathalie. *Margaret Atwood: A Biography*. Toronto: ECW Press, 1998.

Davey, Frank. *Margaret Atwood: A Feminist Poetics*. Vancouver: Talonbooks, 1984.

Davidson, Arnold E. and Cathy N. Davidson, ed. *The Art of Margaret Atwood: Essays in Criticism*. Toronto: Anansi, 1981.

Davidson, Arnold E. *Seeing in the Dark: Margaret Atwood's* Cat's Eye. Toronto: ECW Press, 1997.

Dvorak, M., ed. The Handmaid's Tale: *Margaret Atwood*. Paris: Ellipses, 1998.

———, ed. *Lire Margaret Atwood:* The Handmaid's Tale. Rennes: Presses Universitaire de Rennes, 1999.

Fee, Margery. *The Fat Lady Dances: Margaret Atwood's* Lady Oracle. Canadian Fiction Studies 15. Toronto: ECW Press, 1993.

Grace, Sherrill E. *Violent Duality: A Study of Margaret Atwood*. Montreal: Véhicule, 1980.

Grace, Sherrill E. and Lorraine Weir, ed. *Margaret Atwood: Language, Text, and System*. Vancouver: University of British Columbia Press, 1983.

Hengen, Shannon. *Margaret Atwood's Power: Mirrors, Reflections, and Images in Select Fiction and Poetry.* Toronto: Second Story Press, 1993.

Howells, Coral Ann. *Margaret Atwood.* Basingstoke: Macmillan, 1996.

———. *York Notes on Margaret Atwood's* The Handmaid's Tale. London: Longman York, 1993.

Ingersoll, Earl G., ed. *Margaret Atwood: Conversations.* Willowdale, Ont.: Firefly/ Princeton, N.J.: Ontario Review Press, 1990.

Irvine, Lorna. *Collecting Clues: Margaret Atwood's* Bodily Harm. Canadian Fiction Studies 28. Toronto: ECW Press, 1993.

Karrasch, Anke. *Die Darstellung Kanadas im literarischen Werk von Margaret Atwood.* Trier: WVT, 1995.

Keith, W. J. *Introducing Margaret Atwood's* The Edible Woman. Canadian Fiction Studies 3. Toronto: ECW Press, 1989.

Lacroix, J.-M. and J. Leclaire, ed. The Handmaid's Tale/Le Conte de la Servante: *The Power Game.* Paris: Presses de la Sorbonne Nouvelle, 1998.

Lacroix, J.-M., J. Leclaire, and J. Warwick, ed. The Handmaid's Tale: *Roman Proteen.* Rouen: Université de Rouen, 1999.

Ljungberg, Christina. *To Join, to Fit, and to Make: The Creative Craft of Margaret Atwood's Fiction.* Bern: Lang, 1999.

Mallinson, Jean. *Margaret Atwood and Her Works.* Toronto: ECW Press, 1984.

McCombs, Judith, ed. *Critical Essays on Margaret Atwood.* Boston, Mass.: Hall, 1988.

McCombs, Judith and Carole L. Palmer, ed. *Margaret Atwood: A Reference Guide.* Boston, Mass.: Hall, 1991.

Mendez-Egle, Beatrice, ed. *Margaret Atwood: Reflection and Reality.* Edinburg, Tex.: Pan American University, 1987.

Mycak, Sonia. *In Search of the Split Subject: Psychoanalysis, Phenomenology, and the Novels of Margaret Atwood.* Toronto: ECW Press, 1996.

Nicholson, Colin, ed. *Margaret Atwood: Writing and Subjectivity: New Critical Essays.* London: Macmillan, 1994.

Nischik, Reingard M., ed. *Margaret Atwood: Polarities: Selected Stories.* Stuttgart: Reclam, 1994 [with an introduction, story analyses, and annotations].

———, ed. *Margaret Atwood: Works and Impact.* Rochester, N.Y.: Camden House, 2000.

———. *Mentalstilistik: Ein Beitrag zu Stiltheorie und Narrativik. Dargestellt am Erzählwerk Margaret Atwoods.* Tübingen: Narr, 1991.

Rao, Eleonora. *Strategies for Identity: The Fiction of Margaret Atwood.* New York: Lang, 1993.

Rigney, Barbara Hill. *Margaret Atwood*. London: Macmillan, 1987.

Rosenberg, Jerome H. *Margaret Atwood*. Boston, Mass.: Twayne, 1984.

Roth, Verena Bühler. *Wilderness and the Natural Environment: Margaret Atwood's Recycling of a Canadian Theme*. Tübingen/Basel: Francke, 1998.

Schall, Birgitta. *Von der Melancholie zur Trauer: Postmoderne Text- und Blickökonomien bei Margaret Atwood*. Trier: WVT, 1995.

Staels, Hilde. *Margaret Atwood's Novels: A Study of Narrative Discourse*. Tübingen/Basel: Francke, 1995.

Stein, Karen F. *Margaret Atwood Revisited*. Boston, Mass: Twayne, 1999.

Sullivan, Rosemary. *The Red Shoes: Margaret Atwood Starting Out*. Toronto: Harper Flamingo, 1998.

Thompson, Lee Briscoe. *Scarlet Letters: Margaret Atwood's* The Handmaid's Tale. Toronto: ECW Press, 1997.

VanSpanckeren, Kathryn and Jan Garden Castro, ed. *Margaret Atwood: Vision and Forms*. Carbondale/Edwardsville: Southern Illinois University Press, 1988.

Vespermann, Susanne. *Margaret Atwood: Eine mythokritische Analyse ihrer Werke*. Augsburg: Wißner, 1995.

Vevaina, Coomi S., and Coral Ann Howells, ed. *Margaret Atwood: The Shape-Shifter*. New Delhi: Creative Books, 1998.

Wilson, Sharon R. *Margaret Atwood's Fairy Tale Sexual Politics*. Jackson/Toronto: University of Mississippi Press/ECW Press, 1994.

Wilson, Sharon R., Thomas B. Friedman, and Shannon Hengen, ed. *Approaches to Teaching Atwood's* The Handmaid's Tale *and Other Works*. New York: MLA, 1996.

Woodcock, George. *Introducing Margaret Atwood's* Surfacing. Canadian Fiction Studies 4. Toronto: ECW Press, 1990.

York, Lorraine M., ed. *Various Atwoods: Essays on the Later Poems, Short Fiction, and Novels*. Toronto: Anansi, 1995.

Zimmermann, Hannelore. *Erscheinungsformen der Macht in den Romanen Margaret Atwoods*. Frankfurt: Lang, 1998.

Notes on the Contributors

CHARLES ALTMAN is a writing coach for adults with learning disabilities at Concordia University in Montreal. He is also the author of instructional materials for business school students to improve the quality of case study analyses and collaborative writing projects. His drawings have appeared in various Montreal newspapers. He holds a Bachelor of Commerce degree and plans to do graduate work in educational psychology and continue his work with student writers.

SUSANNE BECKER. Dr. phil. University of Mainz. Editor in the Culture Department of German TV (ZDF) in Mainz. She has written essays on American, Canadian, and English literature and contemporary culture. Her book *Gothic Forms of Feminine Fictions* (Manchester: Manchester University Press, 1999) includes a major chapter on Atwood's work. Susanne Becker has taught various courses on Atwood's work at the University of Mainz (between 1990 and 1998), as well as at Columbia University, New York (1991/92). She has interviewed Margaret Atwood for German TV, notably for the cultural magazines *Aspekte* (ZDF), *KultUhr* (3sat), and METROPOLIS (arte).

ISAAC BICKERSTAFF is the nom de plume of Don Evans. A resident of Orillia, Ontario, Bickerstaff is widely regarded as Canada's pre-eminent literary caricaturist. An archive of his work is housed at the University of Calgary Library.

LIZ CALDER. Publisher of Bloomsbury Publishing, London. She began her publishing career at Victor Gollancz in the early 1970s. She moved to Jonathan Cape in the early 1980s where she published two Booker Prize winners: *Midnight's Children* by Salman Rushdie and *Hotel du Lac* by Anita Brookner. She became one of the founding directors of Bloomsbury Publishing in 1986. She has been Margaret Atwood's British publisher since 1980.

ARNULF CONRADI. Dr. phil. Publisher of Berlin and Siedler Verlag. He studied German Literature, English, and Philosophy at the University of Kiel and at the Free University in Berlin, earning an M.A. in American Studies. His Ph.D. thesis was on the Modern American Novel. After two years as an assistant at the University of Kiel, Arnulf Conradi moved to Düsseldorf in 1977 to start working as a literary editor for Claassen Verlag. Five years later he was offered the position of editor-in-chief of S. Fischer and Wolfgang Krüger. He was literary director of Fischer from 1987–1993. In 1993 he left Frankfurt and went to Berlin to found Berlin Verlag. In 1998 he sold the majority of Berlin Verlag to Bertelsmann and is now publisher of Berlin and Siedler Verlag.

NATHALIE COOKE. Ph.D. University of Toronto. Associate Professor of Canadian Literature at McGill University, Montreal, Canada. Published works: articles on Canadian literature, contemporary poetry, and women's domestic narratives, and various books, including: *Margaret Atwood: A Biography* (Toronto: ECW, 1998); *Lorna Crozier* (Toronto: ECW, 1995); (co-ed.) *An Anthology of Canadian Literature in English*, revised and abridged edition (Toronto: Oxford University Press, 1990). Senior Editor of the Hugh MacLennan Poetry Series (McGill-Queen's University Press). Cooke first taught Atwood's work at the University of Toronto in 1987. Since then she has given courses on Atwood at McGill University, and presented papers on her work in Canada, the United States, and Brazil. Between 1992 and 1995, Nathalie Cooke was President of the Margaret Atwood Society, an Allied Organization of the MLA.

SARAH COOPER worked in the publishing industry in Toronto before becoming Margaret Atwood's assistant in 1993. She graduated summa cum laude from York University in 1988 with a Honours Bachelor of Arts in English and Political Science.

HELMUT FRIELINGHAUS. Editor, translator, journalist, born 1931 in Braunschweig, Germany. From 1952 to 1957 he was a bookseller and translator in Madrid; from 1958 to 1994 editor and editor-in-chief at various German publishing houses: Claassen, Hamburg (1962–1967), Rowohlt, Reinbek near Hamburg (1967–1982), Claassen, Düsseldorf (1982–1988). Since 1994 he has been a freelance editor and journalist in New York.

PAUL GOETSCH. Dr. phil. Professor of English and American Literature at the University of Freiburg, Germany. Books on the short story, English and American drama of the 20th century, Dickens, Hardy, Hugh MacLennan as a literary nationalist, and the British novel at the turn of the century. Articles on these and other fields, including essays on Canadian literature and Margaret Atwood. Paul Goetsch has taught a course on Margaret Atwood and included some of her novels in other courses.

RONALD B. HATCH. Ph.D. Associate Professor, Department of English, University of British Columbia, Canada. Published works: articles on 18th- and 19th-century English Literature and 20th-century Canadian literature, and various books, including, *Crabbe's Arabesque: Social Drama in the Poetry of George Crabbe* (Montreal/Toronto: McGill-Queen's University Press, 1971); (ed.) *Clayoquot & Dissent* (Vancouver: Ronsdale, 1994); (ed.) *Modern Korean Verse* (Vancouver: Ronsdale, 1997); Transl. with J. Kim, *Fugitive Dreams: Selected Poems of Sowol Kim* (Vancouver: Ronsdale, 1998); Transl. with J. Kim, *Love's Silence by Jong-un Han* (Vancouver: Ronsdale, 1999).

LOTHAR HÖNNIGHAUSEN. Dr. phil. Professor of British, American, and Canadian Literature at the Rheinische Friedrich-Wilhelms-Universität Bonn, Germany. He is editor of the book series Transatlantic Perspectives. He is also director of the interdisciplinary North America Program and the Transatlantic Summer Academy at the University of Bonn. Among his more recent books: (ed.) *Regional Images and Regional Realities* (Tübingen: Stauffenburg, 1999); (ed. and intro.) *William Faulkner: German Responses 1997*, special issue of *Amerikastudien/American Studies*, 42.4 (1997); *Masks and Metaphors* (Jackson: Mississippi University Press, 1997); (ed., with Valeria G. Lerda) *Rewriting the South: History and Fiction* (Tübingen/Basel: Francke, 1993); *The Symbolist Tradition in English Literature: A Study of Pre-Raphaelitism and Fin-de-Siècle* (Cambridge: Cambridge University Press, 1988); *William Faulkner: The Art of Stylization in his Early Graphic and Literary Work* (Cambridge: Cambridge University Press, 1987). Lothar Hönnighausen has taught several courses on North American literature in which Atwood's work has played a major role. He has also taught a seminar on Atwood's fiction and poetry.

CORAL ANN HOWELLS. Ph.D. University of London. Professor of English and Canadian Literature at the University of Reading, England. Published works: articles on Commonwealth women's writing, especially contemporary Canadian women writers and Gothic fiction, and various books, including: *Private and Fictional Words: Canadian Women Novelists of the 1970s and 80s* (London/New York: Methuen, 1987); *Jean Rhys* (Hemel Hempstead: Harvester-Wheatsheaf, 1991); (ed., with Lynette Hunter) *Narrative Strategies in Recent Canadian Literature: Feminism and Postcolonialism* (Milton Keynes: Open University Press, 1991); *York Notes on* The Handmaid's Tale (London: Longman York Press, 1993), revised as *York Notes Advanced on* The Handmaid's Tale (London: York Press, 1998); *Margaret Atwood* (London: Macmillan, 1996), which won the Atwood Society Best Book Award 1997; (ed., with Coomi S. Vevaina) *Margaret Atwood: The Shape-Shifter* (New Delhi: Creative Books, 1998); *Alice Munro* (Manchester: Manchester University Press, 1998). Professor Howells is associate editor of *The International Journal of Canadian Studies,* and has been teaching Canadian literature at the University of Reading since 1982. She has lectured extensively on Atwood's writing in Britain, Europe, Australia, Canada, the United States, and India.

LORNA IRVINE. Professor of English and Women's Studies and Senior Fellow in the Office of the Provost, George Mason University, Fairfax, Virginia, USA. Published works: articles on Canadian and British writers such as Sylvia Fraser, Michael Ondaatje, Gail Scott, Pierre Berton, Margaret Drabble, Mavis Gallant, Richard Rohmer, and Audrey Thomas. Books: *Collecting Clues: Margaret Atwood's* Bodily Harm (Toronto: ECW Press, 1993); *Critical Spaces: Margaret Laurence and Janet Frame* (Columbia, S.C.: Camden House, 1995); *Sub/Version: Canadian Fictions by Women* (Toronto: ECW Press, 1986). She has served on Executive Committees for Canadian Literature for the MLA, ACSUS, and the American Popular Culture Association, and is on the editorial board of Quebec Studies. She has received a number of grants to pursue work in Canadian Studies. Currently, she is preparing a study of the work of Carol Shields. Irvine teaches Atwood's work in undergraduate classes on second-world fiction and on literature by women, in graduate classes on feminist theory and on postcolonial fiction and, recently, to a large group of people involved in George Mason's Learning in Retirement Institute.

PHOEBE LARMORE began her career as a literary agent in New York City in January of 1964 in the employ of the Paul R. Reynolds Agency, the oldest established literary firm in the United States. In 1968 she joined the John Cushman Agency, then the US branch of Curtis Brown London. Three years later, in 1971, she opened the Larmore Literary Agency in New York City and in the late 1970s, she moved her agency to its present locale in Los Angeles, California.

GABRIELE METZLER. Dr. rer. pol. University of Tübingen. Senior Lecturer at the University of Education in Freiburg, Germany. Published works: articles on International Relations, Canadian politics, gender studies, creativity, and didactic aspects of political science; published literary works: short fiction and poetry, parts of which were set to music by the German-American composer, pianist, and professor Konrad Wolff, and were first performed in New York; various journalistic works for radio and newspapers; books: *Frauen, die es geschafft haben: Portraits erfolgreicher Karrieren* (2nd ed., Düsseldorf/Wien/New York: Econ, 1986) and *Umwelt retten — wie fangen wir es an?* (ed., Wiesbaden, 1995). Working at the intersection of the social sciences, teaching, and literature, Gabriele Metzler is an admirer of Margaret Atwood's creativity.

KLAUS PETER MÜLLER. Dr. phil. University of Bonn. Postdoctoral degree in English philology from the University of Düsseldorf. Senior Lecturer in English at the University of Stuttgart, Germany. Published works include articles on English and Canadian literature, literary theory, and the relationships between literature and epistemology, anthropology, and culture; and various books, including: *Epiphanie: Begriff und Gestaltungsprinzip im Frühwerk von James Joyce* (Frankfurt: Lang, 1984); (ed.) *Contemporary Canadian Short Stories* (Stuttgart: Reclam, 1990); (ed.) *Englisches Theater der Gegenwart: Geschichte(n) und Strukturen* (Tübingen: Narr, 1993); (with Barbara Korte and Josef Schmied) *Einführung in die Anglistik* (Stuttgart/Weimar: Metzler, 1997); (ed., with Barbara Korte) *Unity in Diversity Revisited? British Literature and Culture in the 1990s* (Tübingen: Narr, 1998). Klaus Peter Müller has taught courses on Atwood since 1985, looking at her work in the contexts of contemporary novel writing, literature written by (Canadian) women, contemporary poetry, the development of new literatures in English, and postcolonial literature.

REINGARD M. NISCHIK. Dr. phil. University of Cologne. Professor of American Literature at the University of Constance, Germany. Published works: articles on American, Canadian, and English literature and culture, on literary theory, and various books, including: *Mentalstilistik: Ein Beitrag zu Stiltheorie und Narrativik. Dargestellt am Erzählwerk Margaret Atwoods* (Tübingen: Narr, 1991); (ed. & intro.) *Margaret Atwood, Polarities: Selected Stories* (Stuttgart: Reclam, 1994); (ed. & intro., with Robert Kroetsch) *Gaining Ground: European Critics on Canadian Literature* (Edmonton: NeWest, 1985); *Short Short Stories Universal* (Stuttgart: Reclam, 1993); (ed. & intro.) *Leidenschaften literarisch* (Konstanz: UVK Universitätsverlag Konstanz, 1998). Editor of the book series European Studies in American Literature and Culture (ESALC) for Camden House Publishers, Rochester, N.Y., and co-editor of the interdisciplinary journal *Zeitschrift für Kanada-Studien*. Reingard M. Nischik taught her first course on Atwood as an Assistant Professor at the University of Cologne, Germany, in 1982, after having returned from a year at the University of British Columbia as a Canada Council scholar. Since then, she has taught courses on Atwood at the Universities of Mainz, Freiburg, and Constance.

WALTER PACHE (†). Dr. phil. University of Cologne. Former Professor of English Literature at the University of Augsburg, Germany. Published works: articles on British, Canadian, and Comparative Literature; books include: *Profit and Delight: Didaktik und Fiktion als Problem des Erzählens, dargestellt am Beispiel des Romanwerks von Daniel Defoe* (Heidelberg: Winter, 1980); *Einführung in die Kanadistik* (Darmstadt: Wissenschaftliche Buchgesellschaft, 1981); *Degeneration / Regeneration: Beiträge zur Literatur- und Kulturgeschichte zwischen Dekadenz und Moderne* (Würzburg: Königshausen & Neumann, 1999); translations and bilingual editions of William Shakespeare's *Measure for Measure* (1990) and *The Comedy of Errors* (1998). After 1973 Walter Pache taught courses on Canadian literature (including Margaret Atwood) at the Universities of Cologne, Trier, and Augsburg, having returned from a year at the University of Toronto as a Canada Council scholar. He was a founding member of the Gesellschaft für Kanada-Studien. In 1985 he received the Five Continents Award in Canadian Studies. He died suddenly in January 2000.

ALICE M. PALUMBO. Ph.D. University of Toronto. Instructor in the Canadian Studies Program at University College, University of Toronto, Toronto, Canada. Alice Palumbo received her doctorate for a thesis on Margaret Atwood's novels, *The Recasting of the Female Gothic in the Novels of Margaret Atwood*. Since 1995 she has been secretary of the Margaret Atwood Society. Published works: articles on Canadian literature and the Gothic.

HELMUT REICHENBÄCHER. Ph.D. University of Toronto, Staatsexamen University and College of Music, Cologne. Editor of Publications of the Canadian Opera Company, Toronto, Canada. Publications include: "Von 'The Robber Bridegroom' zu *Bodily Harm*: Eine Analyse unveröffentlichter Entwürfe Margaret Atwoods," *Zeitschrift für Anglistik und Amerikanistik*; "Wagner's Adaptation of Gottfried von Straßburg's *Tristan*," *University of Toronto Quarterly*; "Butterfly Flaps Her Wings: Cultural Appropriation: Alexina Louie and David Henry Hwang's work in progress for the Canadian Opera Company," *The*

Globe & Mail (Toronto); book reviews for *University of Toronto Quarterly* and *Canadian Literature*. Helmut Reichenbächer received his doctorate for a thesis on the drafts of Atwood's *The Edible Woman* and *Bodily Harm*.

BARBARA HILL RIGNEY. Ph.D. Ohio State University. Professor of 20th Century British and American Literature. Published books on Atwood are *Margaret Atwood* (London: Macmillan, 1987), *Madness and Sexual Politics in the Feminist Novel: Studies in Bronte, Woolf, Lessing, and Atwood* (Madison, Wis.: University of Wisconsin Press, 1978), and *Lillith's Daughters: Women and Religion in Contemporary Fiction* (Madison, Wis.: University of Wisconsin Press, 1980). More recent works include *The Voices of Toni Morrison* (Columbus: Ohio State University Press, 1997), and *Exile: A Memoir of 1939*, introduction and ed. with Erika Bourguignon (Columbus: Ohio State University Press, 1998). Professor Rigney has taught 20th century British and American literature and courses on women writers, all of them categories in which Atwood's works are relevant.

CAROLINE ROSENTHAL. Studied English and German at the University of Freiburg. Lecturer in American Literature at the University of Constance, Germany. Presently working on her dissertation on contemporary Canadian and US women writers. She has so far published articles on the construction of gender and identity in works of Daphne Marlatt, Audrey Thomas, and Maxine Hong Kingston. Caroline Rosenthal has been teaching American and Canadian literature at the University of Constance since 1995. Atwood's works have been included in courses on Historiographic Metafiction, introductions to Canadian Studies, short story and literary theory courses.

ELLEN SELIGMAN. Born and raised in New York City, Ellen Seligman received her Bachelor of Arts degree at the University of Wisconsin. She began her publishing career in New York, and later worked as an editor at a publishing house in London, England. She moved to Toronto, Canada, in 1976, and shortly thereafter joined the prestigious Canadian publishing house McClelland & Stewart. In the late 1980s, she became their Editorial Director of Fiction. Ellen Seligman has been the editor for many currently celebrated Canadian authors, including Margaret Atwood, Michael Ondaatje, Anne Michaels, Rohinton Mistry, André Alexis, and Jane Urquhart. As well, she is known for her development of new writers, having worked with some from the beginning of their careers. In 1996, Ellen Seligman was given a Toronto Arts Award for her contribution in the field of writing and publishing.

CHARLOTTE STURGESS. Ph.D. Queen Mary and Westfield College, London University. Lecturer in American and Canadian Literature at Marc Bloch University, Strasbourg, France. Published works: articles on Canadian literature for journals and collections in France, Canada, and England. These include work on English, French, and Caribbean Canadian women's writing. Charlotte Sturgess has taught at several French universities, and as head of the Canadian Studies Center in Strasbourg, teaches a Master's seminar largely devoted to Margaret Atwood's work.

NAN A. TALESE is a Senior Vice President of Doubleday and the Publisher and Editorial Director of Nan A. Talese/Doubleday, a trade book publishing imprint. Nan Talese entered book publishing at Random House in 1959 as a copyeditor, rising to the positions of assistant editor, associate editor, and, finally, editor eight years later. Joining Simon & Schuster in 1974, Nan Talese began her long editorial relationships with such authors as Margaret Atwood and Ian McEwan, Barry Unsworth, and Thomas Keneally, the latter three Booker Prize winners. At Houghton Mifflin, which she joined in 1981 as Executive Editor, eventually becoming Editor-in-Chief and Publisher, she edited books such as *August* by Judith Rossner and *The Handmaid's Tale* by Margaret Atwood. Nan Talese came to Doubleday as a Senior Vice President in 1988, and two years later introduced her author-oriented imprint dedicated to the publication of a select list of quality fiction and nonfiction. Nan A. Talese/Doubleday debuted with books by Brian Moore, Alice Miller, and Gordon Parks. The critically acclaimed and best-selling titles she has published this decade include *Alias Grace* by Margaret Atwood as well as works of Ian McEwan, Pat Conroy, Antonia Fraser, Peter Ackroyd, and Alison Lurie, among others.

BRIGITTE WALITZEK. Studied English and French at the Institute for Applied Linguistics in Heidelberg, Germany. Freelance translator since 1980. Translated *The Robber Bride, Good Bones, Alias Grace,* and *The Blind Assassin* by Margaret Atwood into German as well as *Orlando, The Years* (not yet published in German) and two volumes of *Letters* (also awaiting publication) by Virginia Woolf.

SHARON R. WILSON. Ph.D. University of Wisconsin, Madison. Professor of English and Women's Studies at the University of Northern Colorado, Greeley, Colo., USA. Published works: articles on Margaret Atwood, Doris Lessing, Samuel Beckett, E. R. Eddison, the film *Citizen Kane*, and a book: *Margaret Atwood's Fairy-Tale Sexual Politics* (Jackson and Toronto: University of Mississippi Press and ECW Press, 1993). Co-editor, with Thomas B. Friedman and Shannon Hengen, of *Approaches to Teaching Atwood's* The Handmaid's Tale *and Other Works* (New York: MLA, 1996). She is currently working on Contemporary Women's Metafiction and a collection of Atwood criticism. Sharon Wilson began writing about Atwood in 1980, was Founding Co-President, with Arnold Davidson, of the Margaret Atwood Society in 1983, and has taught both graduate and undergraduate courses on Atwood and Canadian, US, British, and postcolonial literature.

Index